B. [1]School officials complain about vandalism that leaves classrooms wrecked and damages expensive equipment. [2]Teachers complain about the low salaries they get for their difficult and important jobs. [3]And parents complain that their children's test scores are dropping, that their children can't read or do math. [4]The problems within our school systems are diverse and affect almost everyone involved.

Topic sentence(s): _____

C. [1]Every thirty-seven seconds, a car is stolen somewhere in the United States. [2]Although this statistic is frightening, it is possible for drivers to prevent car theft if they take a few simple precautions. [3]When they leave their cars, they should lock all valuables in the trunk or glove compartment to avoid tempting a thief to break in. [4]Parking in the middle of the block on a busy, well-lighted street will deter thieves with tow trucks. [5]The most obvious precaution, of course, is always to lock the car and take the keys—even if the driver is stopping for just a minute. [6]One out of every five stolen cars was left unlocked with the keys in the ignition.

Topic sentence(s): _____

D. [1]One of the most significant factors in selling a product is how it is packaged. [2]When Stuart Hall Company, which manufactured notebooks and paper products for students, realized its sales were declining because fewer children were being born, it decided to change its products' appearance. [3]So, beginning in 1968, the company replaced its plain tablets with colored paper and decorated the covers of its notebooks with the Pink Panther and other cartoon characters. [4]Students loved the new designs, and sales soared. [5]Packaging, therefore, can be a method of solving marketing problems.

Topic sentence(s): _____

Topic Sentences That Cover More Than One Paragrap

At times you will find that a topic sentence does double duty—it provides the main idea for more than one paragraph. This occurs when an author considers the development of the main idea to be too lengthy for one paragraph. He or she then breaks up the material into one or more added paragraphs, making it visually easier for the reader to absorb.

See if you can find and write down the number of the topic sentence for the paragraphs below. They are taken from an essay on factors involved in highway accidents. Then read the explanation that follows.

Topic sentence: _____

[1]In addition to poor highway and automobile design, people's attitudes about driving also contribute to the high rate of traffic accidents. [2]Some people persist in believing that they can drink and be alert drivers. [3]Yet alcohol is estimated to be a factor in at least half of all fatal highway accidents. [4]Refusing or forgetting to wear safety belts also increases fatalities. [5]A negative attitude about wearing seat belts is inconsistent with statistics showing that the chances of being seriously hurt or dying in a car accident are greater when a seat belt is not worn.

[6]Another potentially deadly attitude is the point of view that the best driving is fast driving. [7]Again, statistics contradict this attitude— fast driving is more likely to be deadly driving. [8]Since the speed limit was lowered in 1973 to fifty-five miles per hour, traffic fatalities fell significantly. [9]Evidence on speed limits in other countries is just as telling. [10]Where high-speed driving is permitted, a higher rate of accidents occurs.

After you read the first paragraph, it becomes clear that sentence 1 includes the main idea: "people's attitudes about driving also contribute to the high rate of traffic accidents." Sentences 2 and 3 deal with the attitude of those who feel that drinking does not interfere with driving. Sentences 4 and 5 deal with the feeling that using seat belts is not important.

By beginning with the words "another potentially deadly attitude," the first sentence of the next paragraph tells us that it will continue to develop the topic sentence of the previous paragraph. The author has simply chosen to break the subject down into two smaller paragraphs rather than include all the information in one long paragraph. This relationship between the two paragraphs can be seen clearly in the following outline:

Main Idea: Some attitudes about driving contribute to traffic accidents.

1. Drinking does not interfere with driving.
2. Seat belts are not important.
3. Good driving is fast driving.

Main Ideas That Are Unstated

Sometimes a selection lacks a topic sentence or a thesis statement, but that does not mean it lacks a main idea. The author has simply decided to let the details of the selection suggest the main idea. You must figure out what that main idea is by deciding upon the point of all the details. For example, read the following paragraph.

In ancient times, irrational behavior was considered the result of demons and evil spirits taking possession of a person. Later, the Greeks looked upon irrational behavior as a physical problem—caused by an imbalance of body fluids called "humors"—or by displacement of an organ. In the highly superstitious Middle Ages, the theory of possession by demons was revived. It reached a high point again in the witch-hunts of eighteenth-century Europe and America. Only in the last one hundred years did true medical explanations gain wide acceptance and were categories of illnesses changed.

You can see that no sentence in the paragraph is a good "umbrella" statement that covers all the others. We must decide on the main idea by considering all the details and asking, "What is the main point the author is trying to make with these details?" Once we think we know the main point, we can test it out by asking, "Does all or most of the material in the paragraph support this idea?" In this case, the details show that *people have explained mental illness in many different ways over the years.* Although this idea is not stated, you can see that it is a broad enough summary to include all the other material in the paragraph—it is the main idea.

Now read the paragraph below and see if you can pick out which of the four statements that follow it expresses the main idea. Circle the letter of the statement you choose, and then read the explanation that follows.

More and more commuters are deciding to form carpools. One reason is that commuters save money in gas, tolls, and wear and tear on their cars. Also, the special (and often faster) lanes many expressways provide for cars with three or more passengers during the rush hours can make the commute shorter and more hassle-free. Finally, carpooling can reduce the boredom of the daily drive back and forth to work. Members who are not driving can talk, eat breakfast, read the paper, or get a head start on the day's work.

a. Carpools are becoming more popular.
b. Carpooling saves commuters money.
c. Everyone should join a carpool.
d. There are several reasons that more commuters are forming carpools.

As we begin to read this paragraph, we might think that the first sentence is the topic sentence: "More and more commuters are deciding to form carpools." If that was the main idea, however, then the details in the paragraph would have to be about the increasing numbers of people in carpools. Such a paragraph might include statistics on the growth of carpooling. But as we continue to read, we find that the paragraph is instead telling *why* more and more commuters are carpooling, and so answer *a* is incorrect. The rest of the paragraph is devoted to giving the reasons that carpooling is growing in popularity. Thus, the correct answer is *d* Answer *b* is too narrow to be the main idea—it is simply one of the details that support the main idea. Answer *c* is incorrect because it goes beyond the details of the paragraph, which do not include any judgment about what people *should* do.

▷ *Practice 6*

All of the following paragraphs have unstated main ideas, and each is followed by four sentences. In each case, circle the letter of the sentence that best expresses the implied main idea. Remember to consider carefully all of the details and ask yourself, "What is the main point the author is trying to make with these details?" Then test your answer by asking, "Does all or most of the material in the paragraph support this idea?"

1. One misconception about exercise is that if women lift weights, they will develop large muscles. Without male hormones, women cannot increase their muscle bulk as much as a man's. Another exercise myth is that it increases the appetite. Actually, regular exercise stabilizes the blood sugar level and keeps hunger pains from forming. Some people also think that a few minutes of exercise a day or one session a week is enough, but at least three solid workouts a week are needed for muscular and cardiovascular fitness.
   a. Women who lift weights cannot become as muscular as men.
   b. Many people have the wrong idea about exercise.
   c. Exercise is beneficial to everyone.
   d. People use many different excuses to avoid exercising.

2. One way to prevent fireworks-related injuries on the Fourth of July is to store the fireworks in a cool, dry place and avoid handling them roughly. Careless handling can damage the fuses, causing a malfunction. Also, be sure to light firecrackers only outside and well away from buildings, dry brush, or anything else that could be set on fire. Defective firecrackers should be soaked thoroughly in water to prevent future attempts at using them. Of course, parents should be sure to keep fireworks out of the hands of young children, who might think of them as pretty toys without realizing how dangerous they are.
   a. With the proper precautions, fireworks can be used safely.
   b. Firecrackers should be kept far away from buildings and children.
   c. Fireworks are an important part of any Fourth of July celebration.
   d. Certain procedures must be followed for a successful fireworks show.

3. The work housewives do is essential to the economy. The estimated value of the cleaning, cooking, nursing, shopping, child care, home maintenance, money management, errands, entertaining, and other services housewives perform has been estimated at equal to roughly one-fourth of the gross national product. . . . In fact, the Commerce De-

partment's Bureau of Economic Analysis has proposed a revision of the gross national product that would take into account the value of the housewife's services. But housewifery is not formal employment that brings money or prestige. No financial compensation is associated with this position, and the *Dictionary of Occupational Titles* places mothering and homemaking skills in the lowest category of skills, lower than the occupation of "dog trainer."

a. We no longer value the work done by housewives.

b. Housewives should receive salaries for their work.

c. Because housewifery is unpaid labor, its true value is often ignored.

d. The *Dictionary of Occupational Titles* is incorrect in its judgment of housewives' skills.

► *Review Test 1*

Each of the following groups of statements includes one topic, one main idea (topic sentence), and two supporting ideas. Identify each item in the space provided as either the topic (**T**), the main idea (**MI**), or a supporting detail (**SD**).

Group 1

_____ a. The need for stretching exercises.

_____ b. Limbering up after strenuous exertion reduces the risk of stiffness, soreness, and injury.

_____ c. Slow, simple stretching before exercising make muscles more pliable so that vigorous activity becomes easier.

_____ d. Stretching is important both before and after strenuous exercise.

Group 2

_____ a. Beethoven composed his greatest masterpieces after he became completely deaf.

_____ b. Sometimes he tried out passages at the piano to make sure they could be played, but his playing was agonizing to hear.

_____ c. Every day at dawn Beethoven began working at his desk, writing down the music he heard in his head.

_____ d. Beethoven's composing when deaf.

Group 3

_____ a. Rubbing one's nose and eyes transfers viruses to the hands, which then contaminate whatever they touch, such as a table top or telephone.

_____ b. Because the dried cold virus can live as long as three hours, you can pick it up long after the person with a cold is gone.

_____ c. One way that colds spread.

_____ d. The most likely way to catch a cold is by touching an object that someone suffering from a cold has handled.

Group 4

_____ a. Books signed by their authors or containing illustrations are likely to be worth more than other books.

_____ b. What makes a book valuable.

_____ c. Look through old books before you discard them because some old books are valuable.

_____ d. Rare first editions by respected authors bring high prices, especially if they are in excellent condition.

Group 5

_____ a. The failure of love at first sight.

_____ b. Couples who knew each other only slightly but fell instantly in love found that their feelings for each other grew weaker instead of stronger.

_____ c. Instant sexual attraction was a poor basis for a happy marriage, according to a study of one thousand married and divorced couples.

_____ d. The couples who considered themselves happily married reported that they were not powerfully attracted to their partners when they first met, but that they gradually found each other more attractive as they grew to know and understand each other.

► Review Test 2

The following paragraphs have main ideas (topic sentences) that may appear at any place within the paragraph. In one case, the main idea appears at both the beginning and the end of the paragraph. Identify the topic sentence of each paragraph by filling in the correct sentence number in the space provided. Fill in two numbers where the main idea appears twice.

1. ^{1}People who are interested in physical fitness need not spend hundreds of dollars on fancy exercise equipment or health club memberships. ^{2}Instead, they can get into good shape simply by climbing stairs. ^{3}Stair-climbing helps in weight loss; just walking up and down two flights of stairs a day instead of riding an elevator will take off six pounds a year.

[4]Climbing stairs is also good for the heart and can prevent heart attacks. [5]And frequent stair-climbing strengthens the muscles of the legs and buttocks.

Topic sentence(s): _____

2. [1]A town in New York has begun an unusual community-service sentencing program for nonviolent offenders. [2]For example, a man found guilty of drunken driving was ordered to clean the elephant cages at the zoo. [3]A shoplifter who was also a singer was required to give four concerts for senior citizens. [4]And a man who had been caught growing marijuana in his attic was sentenced to grow fifty houseplants for a nursing home.

Topic sentence(s): _____

3. [1]For many couples, the first vacation they take together can either make or break their relationship. [2]If they both have careers, the daily pressures of work and home responsibilities may have covered up sources of disagreement. [3]However, without these distractions, the disagreements can surface. [4]In addition, if one wants to splurge and the other prefers a no-frills camping trip, or if one is a neat packer and the other is disorganized, conflicts will certainly result. [5]Unless both partners communicate, are willing to compromise, and remain flexible during the vacation, their first trip together may be their last.

Topic sentence(s): _____

4. [1]The scene is the lunchroom of an elementary school. [2]It is noon; the room is filled with fourth graders chattering as they nibble on hot dogs or trade the sandwiches from their lunchboxes. [3]As they get louder, a traffic light mounted high on the wall turns yellow, then red. [4]All talking suddenly stops. [5] The traffic light is connected to a sound meter, and the students know that anyone caught talking when the light is red will get an official warning. [6]In this ingenious way, a Tennessee school principal has dealt with the recurring problem of too much noise in the lunchroom.

Topic sentence(s): _____

5. [1]A series of crises punctuated the decade of the 1960's. [2]At the beginning of the 1960's, the Cuban missile crisis brought America and the Soviet Union to the brink of nuclear war. [3]Only after a nerve-racking week of uncertainty, when the Soviets backed down and agreed to remove their missiles from a base in Cuba, was the crisis resolved. [4] The assassinations of political leaders also rocked the country; President Kennedy, Robert F. Kennedy, and Martin Luther King were all murdered

within a few short years. [5]Other crises that simmered and eventually boiled over in this decade were the civil-rights movement and the protest against the Vietnam War. [6]The Watts riots, the underground terrorism of groups such as the Weathermen, and violent demonstrations at the 1968 political conventions were a few of the examples of the general sense of unrest.

Topic sentence(s): _____

3

Identifying Key Supporting Details

What if you were setting off on a long car trip and your next-door neighbor said to you, "Don't forget to eat a good meal on the way"? If you thought at all about this advice, it might just be to wonder, "What does eating a good meal have to do with a long car trip, anyway?" Without additional information, the statement would not make sense. The additional information needed to back up and explain this or any idea is called *supporting details*.

MAJOR AND MINOR DETAILS

There are two kinds of supporting details—major and minor. Taken together, the main idea and its major supporting details form the basic framework of paragraphs. The major details are the primary points that support the main idea. Paragraphs often contain minor details as well. While the major details explain and develop the main idea, they, in turn, are expanded upon by the minor supporting details. An important reading skill is the ability to find these major details and to distinguish them from the minor ones.

To get a better idea of how major and minor supporting details function, consider the following:

Main Idea

Stopping to eat a good meal during a long ride helps drivers keep their reactions sharp.

This sentence immediately brings to mind some questions: How do we know this statement is true? And what is meant by a "long ride"? This is where supporting details come in: they clarify and explain. Here, for example, is that same main idea with a major supporting detail:

Main Idea and Major Detail

Stopping to eat a good meal during a long ride helps drivers keep their reactions sharp. In one test in which drivers spent eight hours on the freeway with one stop after four hours, those drivers who ate a hearty meal during the stop performed better than those who didn't.

Now we have a better idea of what the main idea really means and are more convinced of its truth. Often, however, the major details themselves can be further explained, and that's where the minor support comes in. Major details introduce new points, and minor details elaborate on those points. Here is the same paragraph with a minor detail added:

Main Idea and Major and Minor Detail

Stopping to eat a good meal during a long ride helps drivers keep their reactions sharp. In one test in which drivers spent eight hours on the freeway with one stop after four hours, those drivers who ate a hearty meal during the stop performed better than those who didn't. Whether they stopped for an hour or for fifteen minutes didn't matter, as long as they ate a solid meal.

Try your hand at separating major from minor support in the following paragraph. It begins with the main idea and continues with several major and minor details. (To round off the paragraph, the main idea is restated at the end.) See if you can locate and put a check in front of the *three* details that give major supporting information about the main idea.

As you read, keep an eye out for transition words that can help you locate the major details. Transition words that are often used to signal new points include such words as "first," "next," "in addition," and "finally."

Service Stations No More

Gas stations still provide gas, but often they no longer provide service. For one thing, attendants at many stations no longer pump gas. Motorists pull up to a combination convenience store and gas island where the attendant with clean hands is comfortably enclosed in a glass booth with a trap for taking money. Drivers must get out of their cars to pay for and pump their own gas, which has the bonus of perfuming their hands and clothes with a hint of gas. In addition, even at stations with "pump jockeys," workers have completely forgotten other services that once went hand in hand with pumping gas. They no longer know how to ask, "Check your oil or water?" Drivers must plead with attendants to wash windshields. And the last attendant who checked tire pressure must have died at least ten years ago. Finally, many gas stations no longer have mechanics on the premises. Limping down the highway in a backfiring car for emergency help at the friendly service station is a thing of the past. Car owners cannot even assume that their neighborhood station offers simple maintenance services. The skillful mechanic who can replace a belt or fix a tire in a few minutes has been replaced by a bored teenager in a jumpsuit who doesn't know a carburetor from a charge card. Today's gas stations are fuel stops, but too often that is all they are.

Now see if you correctly checked the three major supporting details. You'll find them after the main idea in the following outline of the paragraph:

Main idea: Many gas stations no longer provide service.

1. At many stations, attendants no longer pump gas.
2. Even at stations with "pump jockeys," workers have forgotten other services.
3. Many gas stations no longer have mechanics on the premises.

A more complete outline, showing minor details as well, would be as follows:

Main idea: Many gas stations no longer provide service.

1. At many stations, attendants no longer pump gas.
    a. Stations are often combined with convenience stores, at which attendants only take money.
    b. Drivers must get out of their cars to pay for and pump gas.
2. Even at stations with "pump jockeys," workers have forgotten other services.
    a. Attendants do not ask to check oil and water.
    b. Attendants do not wash windshields.
    c. Attendants do not check tire pressure.
3. Many gas stations no longer have mechanics on the premises.
    a. The neighborhood station can no longer be counted on to help in emergencies.
    b. Stations may not even offer simple maintenance services.
    c. Skillful mechanics have been replaced by attendants who are ignorant about cars.

Notice how the above outline goes from the general to the specific. The more general statements are clarified and developed by the points beneath them. At a glance, you can see that the major supporting details introduce new points and that the minor details elaborate on those points. The outline, by its very nature, divides the paragraph into main idea, major supporting details, and minor supporting details.

One excellent way, then, to gain experience in identifying major supporting details is to outline a selection. In doing so, you make clear the relationships between the parts of a piece. Seeing such relationships is a critical skill for effective study. Less successful students often concentrate on the individual details and miss their meaning as a group.

HOW TO LOCATE MAJOR DETAILS

To locate major details, you must (1) find the main idea and (2) decide on the points that are *primary support* for that main idea. Practice these steps by reading the paragraph below. Identify the main idea or topic sentence; then ask yourself, "What are the chief points the author uses to back up the main idea?"

> [1]Two influences in particular help create adolescent underachievers—those who test well in intelligence and ability tests but do poorly in school. [2]Many such underachievers have experienced poor relationships with their parents. [3]For example, parents may be poor role models, may reject their children, interact inconsistently with them, or neglect to urge them to be independent. [4]Not surprisingly, the parents of underachievers often are anxious and unhappy with themselves as parents. [5]Another important influence on underachieving adolescents is the school itself, which may simply be too boring to these students. [6]The fault may lie with teachers, curriculum, or both.

By the time you finished the paragraph, you probably realized that the first sentence presents the main idea. The rest of the paragraph then develops that idea. The two types of influences are introduced in sentences 2 (poor relationships with parents) and 5 (the school). These two sentences, then, are the major supporting details—both essential to the author's explanation. The other sentences (3, 4, and 6) go on to develop those major points—they are the minor supporting details. Minor supporting details may be important to a thorough understanding, but they can be eliminated without removing the author's primary points. Note how the following version of the paragraph—*without* the minor details—still makes sense.

> [1]Two influences in particular help create adolescent underachievers, those who test well in intelligence and ability tests but do poorly in school. [2]Many such underachievers have experienced poor relationships with their parents. [5]Another important influence on underachieving ad-

olescents is the school itself, which may simply be too boring to these students.

▷ *Practice 1*

Major and minor supporting details are mixed together in the three lists that follow. The details of each list support a given main idea. Separate the major, more general details from the minor ones by filling in the outlines. Some details have been filled in for you.

List 1

Main idea: There are several reasons for the failure of the neighborhood clothing store.

- Relied on word of mouth
- Poor advertising
- Unexpected rise in wholesale prices
- No display ad in Yellow Pages
- Bad location
- High salaries for workers

1. _____
    a.   Two competitors within two blocks
    b.   Faced a side street

2. _____
    a.   _____
    b.   _____

3. High expenses
    a.   _____
    b.   _____

List 2

Main Idea: People can be classified by how they eat pizza.

- The Clean-up Crew
- Order large, deluxe supreme pizzas
- Eat leftover crusts
- Fold and swallow slices whole
- Nibble at the edges
- The Wolfers
- Eyeball other people's pizza after theirs is gone

- Order slivers of pizza
- The Sparrows

1. _____

    a. _____

    b. _____

2. _____

    a. _____

    b. _____

3. _____

    a. _____

    b. _____

List 3

Main idea: Not all addictions are to drugs and alcohol.

- Cannot function without a boyfriend or girlfriend
- Always turn television on when home
- Spend weekends during football season in front of the television or at games
- Love addicts
- Make their summers revolve around baseball
- Television addicts
- Arrange their schedules around favorite shows
- Are unable to break off a damaging personal relationship
- Sports addicts

1. _____

    a. _____

    b. _____
    c.   Become depressed if a relationship does end

2. _____

    a. _____

    b. _____
    c.   Can't stand to miss their daily soap opera

3. _____

    a. _____

b. _____

c. Need daily fix of newspaper sports statistics each morning

▷ *Practice 2*

Here is another exercise that will give you practice in distinguishing major from minor details. Each passage below is followed by a list of five of its supporting details. Read each passage and then circle the letters of the *three* sentences that give the *major* supporting details. Note that each main idea appears in the first sentence of the passage.

1. A growing concern about the quality of student writing has led to new approaches to teaching writing. Attention to teaching students how to write is no longer always limited to English classes. Even math students are being asked to write essays which are being judged not only on *what* is being said but *how* it is said. At some colleges, freshmen are required to come to school early for special lessons in writing. In addition, on the assumption that teachers must know how to write well in order to teach writing, there are steps being taken to help them as well. One university project which began with twenty-five teachers in 1973 now trains thousands of teachers each year at well over one hundred locations.

    a. Attention to student writing is no longer always limited to regular English classes.

    b. Even math students are being asked to write essays which are being judged on the basis not only of *what* is being said but *how* it is said.

    c. Some freshmen are required to come to college early for special lessons in writing.

    d. In addition, on the assumption that teachers must know how to write well in order to teach writing, there are steps being taken to help them as well.

    e. One university project which began with twenty-five teachers in 1973 now trains thousands of teachers each year at well over one hundred locations.

2. Symbols, common to all societies, take many forms. What people wear, for one thing, often has symbolic meaning. Queens, priests, the police, and medicine men wear costumes that are symbols of their occupations. A wedding band signifies that one is married, and special buttons, ribbons, and tattoos can represent various group memberships. In fact, objects of any kind may be symbols. A brass ring has come to mean a prize or great opportunity in our culture. Flags are symbols of countries, states, ships, and organizations. And on our streets, red and green lights have specific meanings. However, the most common symbols of all in

human society are words, which have their meanings only because people agree on what they stand for.

   a.   What people wear often has symbolic meaning.
   b.   Queens, priests, the police, and medicine men wear costumes that are symbols of their occupations.
   c.   In fact, objects of any kind may be symbols.
   d.   Flags are symbols of countries, states, ships, and organizations.
   e.   The most common symbols of all in human society are words, which have their meanings only because people agree on what they stand for.

3.   While there are thousands of self-help groups, they all fall into three basic classifications. First, there are groups for people with various types of physical or mental illnesses. These provide emotional support and help in caring for the ill. One example of this type is Make Today Count, a group for cancer victims and their families. Another category of self-help group includes those designed to reform people with addictive behavior. Perhaps the best known of these are Alcoholics Anonymous and Gamblers Anonymous. Finally, there are the advocacy groups for various minorities, including older people and gays. Lobbying for legislation and social change are their main activities, but they also sponsor self-care and support programs. The Gray Panthers are one of the better known of this type of self-help group.

   a.   First, there are groups for people with various types of physical or mental illnesses.
   b.   These provide emotional support and help in caring for the ill.
   c.   Another category of self-help group includes those designed to reform people with addictive behavior.
   d.   Finally, there are the advocacy groups for various minorities, including older people and gays.
   e.   Lobbying for legislation and social change are their main activities, but they also sponsor self-care and support programs.

Asking Questions

We have seen that one way to identify major details is to find the main idea and ask, "What are the chief points the author uses to back up the main idea?" Another way to locate major details is to turn the main idea into a question that begins with such words as *who, what, when, why,* or *how.* For example, with the passage considered earlier on underachievers, we could have asked, "What are the two influences that help create adolescent underachievers?" See if you can turn the main idea of the paragraph below into a basic question about the passage. Then read the comments that follow.

Question formed out of the main idea:

Sexual abuse of the young—a tragedy that victimizes one in every four girls and one in every ten boys under age 18—can often be prevented. When children are very young, they should be taught that they have a right to the privacy of their own bodies. In addition, parents should teach children to recognize potential abusers and how to say "no" to adults. Having been trained to be obedient, children often hesitate to expose people who tell them to "keep our special secret," especially if those persons are friends or relatives. (As many as 85 percent of sexually abused children are victims of someone they know and trust.) Similarly, parents should encourage children to trust their instincts to run away from elders that make them feel uneasy.

The first sentence of this passage states that sexual abuse of the young can often be prevented. That probably made you think of the question: "How can sexual abuse of the young be prevented?" As you read on, you see that the passage describes three ways that sexual abuse can be prevented. By converting the main idea into a question, you have made yourself alert to the major supporting details of a passage.

▷ *Practice 3*

The main idea of each of the three following passages has been converted into a question beginning with a word like *who, what, why*, or *how*. Answer each question in the space provided. Your answers should be the major supporting details of each passage.

1. Hepatitis, an inflammation of the liver caused by a virus, is found in two forms. One is Hepatitis A, also commonly called infectious hepatitis. It is usually transmitted by fecal contamination of water or food. The second is Hepatitis B, also referred to as serum hepatitis. This form of the infection is transmitted through the blood. It can be passed on through blood transfusions, needles shared by drug users, or tattoo needles that have become contaminated.

   What are the two types and sources of hepatitis?

   a. _____

   b. _____

2. Parents and children often view each other in distorted ways because of their own needs. Parents frequently misjudge their children by seeing them as a means of satisfying their own unfulfilled dreams. The father,

for example, who never made it to law school may see a son whose talents are artistic as a future criminal lawyer. Children make the same sort of mistake about their parents. Being very dependent, children need to feel their parents are unquestionably dependable. That is why they tend to view parents as all-knowing, immensely wise, and capable.

What needs cause (a) parents and (b) children to view each other in distorted ways??

a. _____

b. _____

3. When we call someone "pig" or "swine," we do not mean it as a compliment. But pigs do not deserve to be used as a symbol for an insult. They are probably not as dirty as they are made out to be. According to one pig keeper, swine are very clean when allowed to live in a clean environment. He feels pigs are usually dirty simply because their keepers don't clean their pens. In any case, no one has proven that the pig that wallows in mud prefers that to a cool bath. Furthermore, pigs are smarter than most people think. Many farmers, for example, have observed that pigs frequently undo complicated bolts on gates in search of greener pastures or romance. So the next time you call someone a pig, perhaps it ought to be someone you wish to praise.

Why doesn't the pig deserve to be the symbol for an insult?

a. _____

b. _____

➤ *Review Test 1*

Major and minor supporting details are mixed together in the four lists below. The details of each list support a given main idea. Complete the outlines that follow each list by filling in *only the major supporting details*.

List 1

Main idea: Recent research suggests certain diet habits should be encouraged.

- Unrefined cereals
- Eat foods high in vitamin A
- Eat low-fat foods
- Unrefined breads
- Skim-milk products
- Leaner meats
- Green leafy vegetables

- Orange vegetables
- Eat more whole grains

1. _____

2. _____

3. _____

List 2

Main idea: There are advantages to owning a dog.

- Owner must bathe and groom the dog regularly.
- Dog accompanies owner on walks and rides.
- Dog barks to warn of intruders.
- Dog provides protection.
- Owner must walk and feed dog.
- Dog provides companionship.
- Dog always greets owner enthusiastically.
- Dog deters prowlers while owner is absent.
- Dog requires care, which develops owner's sense of responsibility.

1. _____

2. _____

3. _____

List 3

Main idea: My freshman English course is demanding.

- Weekly essay
- Extensive reading load
- Three major tests
- Frequent test situations
- Term paper
- Five novels
- Assignments from short-story anthology
- Comprehensive final exam
- Frequent in-class writing assignments
- A few written summaries of articles assigned
- Surprise quizzes
- A great deal of writing

1. _____

2. _____

3. _____

List 4

Main idea: The risk of suicide is greatest at those stages in life when depression is more likely.

- Academic stress
- Middle age
- Loss of lifelong friends and loved ones
- Men's career goals may now seem unattainable
- College years
- Financial hardships on Social Security
- Parental disapproval
- Old age
- Children leave home

1. _____

2. _____

3. _____

► Review Test 2

A.   Major and minor supporting details are mixed together in the list below. The details of the list support the main idea shown. Complete the outline that follows, filling in *both major and minor supporting details*.

Main idea: In general, I have had two types of college teachers.

- Has strict attendance policy
- Gives long and challenging exams
- Gives little homework
- Demanding teacher
- Assigns long term paper
- Never takes roll
- Gives easy exams
- Doesn't assign term paper
- Excuses class before period is over
- Undemanding teacher
- Assigns a lot of homework
- Sometimes keeps class after period is up

1. _____

     a. _____

     b. _____

     c. _____

d. _____

e. _____

2. _____

   a. _____

   b. _____

   c. _____

   d. _____

   e. _____

B. Below each of the following passages is a question raised by the main idea of the passage. After reading each passage, answer the question by stating the major supporting details.

1. If your wooden porch is dry and splintery, it's time to recondition it. Begin by correcting any structural problems. Hammer down loose nails, and nail down loose boards. If you run across boards that are weakened beyond repair, replace them. Then apply a wood preservative with a brush or paint roller. Wood naturally tends to dry out, and being out-doors at the mercy of the seasons hastens the process. Use a thick preservative, which is more protective than a more diluted one. After allowing at least twenty-four hours for the preservative to dry, apply a coat of outdoor paint. You can do a neater job by using a straight-edged applicator on any edges that are next to your house.

    What are the steps to reconditioning a porch?
    (Note that the main idea here—there are several steps to reconditioning a porch—is implied.)

    a. _____

    b. _____

    c. _____

2. Dr. Elisabeth Kubler-Ross has identified five stages in the reactions of dying patients. The first stage, she says, is denial. Patients will at first deny the seriousness of their illness, claiming that some error has been made. Then patients become angry. They ask, "Why me?" Their anger may be directed against God, fate, or even their doctors. Next comes depression. During this stage, patients feel hopeless and lose interest in life. After depression comes bargaining—patients try to bargain for their lives. They may promise God or their doctors that they'll be good, stop smoking, give up alcohol or do whatever is necessary if they can only

survive. The fifth stage is that of acceptance. Patients finally resign themselves to the inevitable. They are not joyful, but they gain a sense of inner peace. While there has been some criticism of Kubler-Ross's stages, her work has contributed much to making death a more comfortable and better understood subject.

What are Kubler-Ross's five stages of dying?

a. _____

b. _____

c. _____

d. _____

e. _____

4

Understanding Relationships I: Transitions

"I dislike my job. The pay is good," said Burt.

Lena enjoys working in her yard. She likes growing vegetables.

"Open your books to page 22," the teacher said. "Hand in your papers."

Does Burt dislike his job because the pay is good? Is growing vegetables all Lena does in her yard? And does the teacher expect students to open their books and hand in their papers at the same time? We're not sure because the above sentences are unclear. To clarify them, transitions are needed. *Transitions* are words and phrases that show the relationships between ideas. They are like signposts that direct travelers. To show how they guide us between ideas, here are those same sentences, but this time with transitions:

"I dislike my job, *even though* the pay is good," said Burt.

Lena enjoys working in her yard. *For example*, she likes growing vegetables.

"Open your books to page 22," the teacher said, "*after* you hand in your papers."

Now we know that Burt dislikes his job despite the good pay and that cultivating vegetables is just one of the yard projects Lena enjoys. We also now know that the teacher wants the papers handed in before books are opened. Transitions have smoothed the way from one idea to the other. In Latin, *trans* means "across," so transitions live up to their name—they carry the reader "across" from one thought to another.

There are a number of ways in which transitions connect ideas and show relationships. Here is a list of the major types of transitions.

1   Words that show addition

2   Words that show time

3   Words that show contrast

4   Words that show comparison

5   Words that show illustration

6   Words that show location

7   Words that show cause and effect

8   Words that summarize or conclude

9   Words that emphasize or clarify

Each of these kinds of transitions will be explained in the pages that follow.

1 WORDS THAT SHOW ADDITION

These transitions tell you that the writer is presenting two or more ideas that continue along the same line of thought. They introduce ideas that *add to* a thought already mentioned. Here are common addition words:

and	in addition	first of all	furthermore
also	moreover	second	last of all
another	next	third	finally

Examples:

My friend Ellen is so safety-conscious that she had her wooden front door replaced with a steel one. *Also*, she had iron bars inserted on all her apartment windows.

By recycling, our township has saved thousands of dollars in landfill expenses. *Furthermore*, we have made money by selling recycled glass, paper, and metal.

There are several places you can enjoy with your family on weekends without spending much money. *First*, the hands-on science museum downtown asks only for a donation. *Next* there is the zoo, which is free on Sundays.

▷ *Practice 1*

Insert an appropriate addition word or phrase from the list above into each of the following sentences. Try to use a variety of transitions.

1. As soon as the weather turned warm, ants invaded our kitchen. A few

   _____ visited the bathrooms.

2. There are several ways to use old jeans. _____ , you can use them for patching other jeans.

3. One million stray dogs live in the New York City metropolitan area.

   _____ , there are more than 500,000 stray cats in the same area.

4. One reason why people are renting more videotaped movies is that they

   cost less than ever before; _____ reason for their popularity is that they are easily available in supermarkets, gas stations, and drug-stores.

5. " _____ , and most important," said my adviser, "you've got to complete that term paper or you won't graduate on time."

2 WORDS THAT SHOW TIME

These transitions indicate a time relationship. They tell us *when* something happened in relation to something else. Here are some common time words:

first	next	as	while
then	before	now	during
often	after	until	immediately
since	soon	previously	frequently
		following	

Examples:

First I skim the pages of the television guide to see what movies will be on. *Then* I circle the ones I want to record on the VCR.

As I got ready to go home, my boss asked me to sweep the stock-room floor.

During World War II, meat was rationed.

Helpful Points About Transitions

There are several helpful points to keep in mind about transitions. Certain words within a group mean very much the same thing. For example, "also," "moreover," and "furthermore" all mean "in addition." Authors typically change transitions from one idea to the next for the sake of variety. Another point is that in some cases the same word can function as two different types of transition, depending on how it is used. For example, the word "first" may be used to signal that the author is continuing a train of thought, as in the following sentence:

My mother has some strange kitchen habits. *First*, she loves to cook with the radio on full blast. Moreover, ...

"First" also may be used to signal a time sequence, as in this sentence:

Our English class turned into a shambles this morning. *First*, the radiator began squeaking. Then, ...

Finally, two ideas may be connected with more than one type of transition. The first sentence above, for instance, might also be written with a transition that signals illustration instead of addition, as follows:

My mother has some strange kitchen habits. *For example*, she loves to cook with the radio on full blast.

▷ *Practice 2*

Insert an appropriate time word from the list above into each of the following sentences. Try to use a variety of transitions.

1. _____ I took a long shower, there was no hot water left.

2. Current technology makes it possible to treat babies _____ they are born.

3. _____ the tour boat headed back toward shore, several finback whales cavorted nearby.

4. I _____ stay late at school to study at the library.

5. To make chicken stock, begin by boiling a pot of water. _____ drop in a chicken and some cut-up celery and onions.

3 WORDS THAT SHOW CONTRAST

These transitions signal a change in the direction of the writer's thought. They tell us that a new idea will be *different* in a significant way from the previous one. Here are some common contrast words:

but	in contrast	conversely	on the other hand
however	instead	nevertheless	on the contrary
yet	still	even though	
although	in spite of	despite	

Examples:

Some people think they have to exercise every day to stay in shape. *However,* three workouts a week are all they need to do.

There are those who look upon eating as something to be done quickly, so they can get on to better things. *On the other hand,* there are people who think eating *is* one of the better things.

Professional writers don't wait for inspiration. *On the contrary,* they stick to a strict schedule of writing.

▷ *Practice 3*

Insert an appropriate contrast word from the list above into each of the following sentences. Try to use a variety of transitions.

1. You use seventeen muscles when you smile; _____ , you use forty-three muscles to frown.

2. _____ the diner was a pleasant place to eat, it still went out of business.

3. At first we were planning on spending our vacation at a campgrounds, _____ now we've decided just to relax at home.

4. Paula was not satisfied with her paper _____ the fact that she had already written five drafts.

5. Keeping his independence is important to Michael; _____ , he likes to consult his parents before he makes certain decisions.

4 WORDS THAT SHOW COMPARISON

These transitions signal that the author is pointing out a similarity between two subjects. They tell us that the second idea is *like* the first one in some way. Here are some common comparison words:

like	likewise	similarly
as	in like manner	in a similar fashion
just like	equally	in the same way
just as		

Examples:

Outdoor floodlights make a home safer and more attractive; *similarly*, landscaping can be planned to increase both a home's security and its appeal.

When movie makers have a big hit, they tend to repeat the winning idea in their next movie instead of trying something new, *just like* certain authors who keep writing the same type of story over and over.

When individuals communicate, they are more likely to solve their problems. *In like manner*, countries can best solve their problems through communication.

▷ *Practice 4*

Insert an appropriate comparison word or phrase from the list above into each of the following sentences. Try to use a variety of transitions.

1. When my mother buys milk, she always takes a bottle from the back of

   the shelf. _____ , when my husband buys a newspaper, he usually grabs one from the middle of the pile.

2. Simple, inexpensive tests can detect breast cancer; _____ , routine tests can be given for osteoporosis.

3. The sound of a faucet dripping makes me cringe. June bugs bumping

   into our screens affect my wife _____ .

4. Japanese women once blackened their teeth to improve their appearance.

   _____ , some Indian women stained their teeth red.

5. _____ rats become hostile when they are made to live in a crowded enclosure, humans become more aggressive in crowded conditions.

5 WORDS THAT SHOW ILLUSTRATION

These transitions indicate that an author will provide one or more examples to develop and clarify a given idea. They tell us that the second idea is *an example of* the first. Here are some common illustration words:

for example	to illustrate	once
for instance	such as	specifically
as an illustration	to be specific	including

Examples:

My grandmother doesn't hear well anymore. *For instance*, whenever I say, "Hi, Granny," she answers, "Fine, just fine."

There are various ways you can save money, *such as* bringing lunch to work and automatically putting aside a small portion of your check each week.

My cousin Dave will do anything on a dare. *Once* he showed up for a family dinner wearing only swimming trunks and a snorkeling mask.

▷ *Practice 5*

Insert an appropriate illustration word or phrase from the list above into each of the following sentences. Try to use a variety of transitions.

1. People have chosen to end their lives in a variety of ways. _____, in ancient China people committed suicide by eating a pound of salt.

2. I've become very absentminded lately. Last week, _____ , I went to work on my day off.

3. Ladies and gentlemen, I can spell any word in the dictionary backwards. _____ , I will now write the Pledge of Allegiance backwards on this chalkboard.

4. Moving is increasingly common; _____ , one in five families moves every year.

5. Animals were once tried for crimes. _____ , in 1740 a cow convicted of sorcery was hanged by the neck until dead.

6 WORDS THAT SHOW LOCATION

Location transitions show relationships in space. They tell us *where* something is in relation to something else. Here are some common location words:

next to	inside	across	over
in front of	outside	beneath	under
in back of	opposite	in the middle of	behind
above	on top of	on the other side of	beyond
below	nearby	at the end of	near
between	within	ahead of	far

Examples:

On the wall *in back of* my daughter's bed are twelve pictures of Luther Vandross.

"*At the end of* the maze," said the genie, "is a basket of pearls."

You have to go quite a bit *beyond* the city limits to see a crystal clear sky with all its stars.

▷ *Practice 6*

Insert an appropriate location word or phrase from the list above into each of the following sentences. Try to use a variety of transitions.

1. _____ the housetops was an unattractive forest of television antennas.

2. Because my closet is so crowded, I keep my shoes _____ my bed.

3. The next person who throws a wad of paper _____ this room will also be thrown—out of class.

4. Felicia hung mistletoe _____ every doorway in the house.

5. The magician's assistant was hiding _____ the empty box.

7 WORDS THAT SHOW CAUSE AND EFFECT

Cause and effect transitions signal that the author is going to describe results or effects. They tell us what happened or will happen *because* something else happened. Here are some common cause and effect words:

thus	as a result	therefore
because	consequently	since
if . . . then	accordingly	so

in response

Examples:

My sister became a vegetarian *because* she doesn't want to eat anything that had a mother.

If you leave your seatbelts in the middle of the car seat, *then* you'll be reminded to use them when you sit down.

My boss's correspondence had built up while he was on vacation. *As a result*, I've been typing letters for the last two days.

▷ *Practice 7*

Insert an appropriate cause and effect word or phrase from the list above into each of the following sentences. Try to use a variety of transitions.

1. _____ property taxes in the city have gone sky high, many corporations are moving to the suburbs.

2. Lisa's resume is impressive; _____ , she has already had several job interviews.

3. _____ the varnish wore off our wooden patio table, fungus has begun to grow on it.

4. Some zoo animals have not learned how to be good parents. _____ , baby animals are sometimes brought up in zoo nurseries and even in private homes.

5. Car dealers like to score a lot of sales in any given month. They are _____ more likely to hold sales near the end of a month.

8 WORDS THAT SUMMARIZE OR CONCLUDE

These transitions signal that the author is about to summarize or come to a conclusion. They tell us that the idea that follows *sums up* what has gone before it. Here are some common summary words:

in summary	all in all	to sum up	to conclude
in conclusion	in brief	on the whole	
in short	in other words	ultimately	

Examples:

At the banquet, the candidate for state senator spoke for an hour and a half without interruption. He finally concluded by saying, "*In brief*, ladies and gentlemen, vote for me."

The governor, ending his speech on an optimistic note, said, "*All in all*, we have laid the groundwork for a stronger economy in the coming year."

After a twenty-minute analysis of my financial situation, my accountant told me, "*To sum up*, Mr. Mills, you're broke."

▷ *Practice 8*

Insert an appropriate summary word or phrase from the list above into each of the following sentences. Try to use a variety of transitions.

1. After explaining the vastness of the oceans, the teacher said,

   " _____ , if the earth were equally flat everywhere, ocean water two feet deep would cover the whole world."

2. "The Age of Enlightenment, _____ , is well named," said the professor as the bell rang.

3. _____, despite the cash rebates, Beverly could not afford a new car.

4. That, ladies and gentlemen, is the story of union-management relations at this company in recent years. _____ , I believe our very existence depends on a fundamental reform of those relations.

5. The movie critic ended his brutal review by writing, "_____,

if you had a free pass, this film still would not be worth the price of admission."

9 WORDS THAT EMPHASIZE OR CLARIFY

These words signal that the author is about to clarify or interpret a certain point. They tell us that the second statement is *an expansion of* a previous one. Here are some common emphasis and clarification words:

clearly	evidently	in fact	in other words
obviously	certainly	to be sure	truly
of course	as a matter of fact	undoubtedly	

Examples:

I hate sardines. *In fact*, if sardines were being served for dinner, I'd be at McDonald's.

Research has shown that students do better when their teachers expect them to do well. *Clearly*, a lot of teachers have low expectations.

Before the '88 presidential election, journalists didn't report on politicians' sex lives. *Evidently*, journalistic standards have changed.

▷ *Practice 9*

Insert an appropriate emphasis or clarification word or phrase from the list above into each of the following sentences. Try to use a variety of transitions.

1. There's no point in rushing to get to the restaurant on time. The Currans,

    _____ , will be late as usual.

2. _____ , not every smoker will be harmed by cigarettes, but the only way to discover who can safely smoke is to see who becomes ill.

3. _____ you may bring your dog along, as long as he stays in the car.

4. Nero did not fiddle while Rome burned; _____ , the fiddle had not yet been invented.

5. Because of man, the world's rain forests are being destroyed, and several

    species of animals are on the verge of extinction. _____ ,
    we've been greedy and shortsighted.

➤ *Review Test 1*

Complete each sentence with the appropriate transition word or phrase.
Then circle the kind of transition you have used.

1. a. My car keeps breaking down; _____ , I am often late
        for class.

                          nevertheless   also   therefore

    b. The transition indicates

                    addition   cause and effect   illustration

2. a. Brushing your teeth is important, _____ it's not
        enough for good dental care.

                            thus   but   so

    b. The transition indicates

                    cause and effect   time   contrast

3. a. Our instructor told us to answer the questions _____
        the chapter.

                    then   in summary   at the end of

    b. The transition indicates

                    time   location   summary

4. a. _____ the cashier forgot to give me my receipt, I
        didn't have to pay for my order.

                In the same way   Because   Even though

    b. The transition indicates

                contrast   comparison   cause and effect

5. a. My dog can catch a Frisbee in midair; _____ , he can
        throw it back to me.

                    in the same way   because   moreover

    b. The transition indicates

                    comparison   addition   clarification

6. a. _____ going into the pool, please rinse off your feet.

                    Because   Before   In spite of

    b. The transition indicates

                    addition   contrast   time

7. a. My cousin did very poorly in high school; _____ , she
        has done very well in college.

                    similarly   as a result   on the other hand

   b. The transition indicates

      contrast   cause and effect   comparison

8. a. This year our fund-raising campaign has yielded the highest collection ever; _____, we surpassed our goal by 10 percent.

      however   similarly   as a matter of fact

   b. The transition indicates

      location   comparison   clarification

9. a. On the last day of school, the teacher said, "_____, class, you have made a great deal of progress this semester."

      instead   all in all   for instance

   b. The transition indicates

      contrast   summary   illustration

10. a. Fast-food places have gradually increased their menus over the last few years; _____, many of them now have salad bars.

      in addition   in brief   for example

   b. The transition indicates

      summary   illustration   addition

► Review Test 2

Complete each sentence with the appropriate transition word or phrase. Then circle the kind of transition you have used.

1. a. The cat decided to have her babies _____ the clothes dryer.

      instead of   inside   despite

   b. The transition indicates

      contrast   illustration   location

2. a. Television often replaces socializing and reading. _____, it frequently interferes with family communication.

      On the other hand   In other words   Furthermore

   b. The transition indicates

      contrast   addition   illustration

3. a. I can always count on meditation to relieve any stress I've built up. Jogging _____ relaxes me after a tough day.

      on the contrary   likewise   for example

   b. The transition indicates

      comparison   contrast   clarification

4. a. There are several things that can be done to reduce exposure to pesticides, _____ peeling fruits and vegetables.

    such as   also   until

    b. The transition indicates

    addition   contrast   illustration

5. a. Fewer people are buying homes these days; _____, high mortgage rates are discouraging people.

    however   obviously   to illustrate

    b. The transition indicates

    illustration   clarification   contrast

6. a. An open parachute floats down slowly because of air pressure; _____, flying squirrels "fly" by opening wing-like folds of skin.

    as a result   similarly   in contrast

    b. The transition indicates

    comparison   cause and effect   contrast

7. a. Frozen pizza is inexpensive, nutritious, and easy to prepare. _____, it is one of the largest selling frozen foods.

    Consequently   Next   Conversely

    b. The transition indicates

    contrast   time   cause and effect

8. a. Many people do not know how to respond when someone they know is dying. Hospice workers, _____, are experienced in giving comfort to dying people.

    first   on the other hand   in the same way

    b. The transition indicates

    contrast   time   comparison

9. a. We refinished our cabinets in several steps. _____, we stripped off the old stain.

    To conclude   In like manner   First

    b. The transition indicates

    time   comparison   summary

10. a. "Sales are up, profits have increased, and employee turnover is low," said the manager. "_____, it's been a good year."

    In like manner   On the whole   Frequently

    b. The transition indicates

    time   summary   cause and effect

5

Understanding Relationships II: Patterns of Organization

To help readers understand their main points, authors try to present supporting details in a clearly organized way. They might use any of several common patterns to arrange their details. Sometimes authors may build a paragraph or longer passage exclusively on one pattern; often, the patterns are mixed. By recognizing them, you will be better able to understand and remember what you read.

Here are some common basic patterns of organization:

1 Time order

2 List of Items

3 Comparison and/or Contrast

4 Cause and Effect

5 Definition and Example

All five of the patterns are based on relationships you learned about in the last chapter. All five, then, involve transition words that you should now recognize. The time order pattern, for example, is marked by transitions that show time (*then, next, after,* and so on). Here are the kinds of transitions used with the other four patterns:

Pattern	*Transitions Used*
List of Items	Words that show addition (*also, another, moreover* . . .)
Comparison/Contrast	Words that show comparison or contrast (*like, just as, however, in contrast* . . .)
Cause and Effect	Words that show cause and effect (*because, as a result, since* . . .)
Definition and Example	Words that show illustration (*for example, to illustrate* . . .)

Explanations and illustrations of each pattern follow. To help you recognize them, a list of transitional words is given for each.

1   TIME ORDER

When a series of events or steps in a process are being presented, the order in which items are organized is crucial. In such cases, material is arranged in a *time order*. It would make very little sense, for example, to discuss the incidents of World War II or the steps in a psychology experiment in just any order—the information would not be logical or clear. Dates, events, and steps must be presented in a meaningful sequence with those that come before and after them.

As a student, you will see time order used frequently. Textbooks in all fields describe various events and processes, for instance: the events leading to the Boston Tea Party, the important incidents in Abraham Lincoln's life, how a bill travels through Congress, or the working of photosynthesis.

The following transitions often signal that a time pattern of organization is being used:

first	next	as	while
second	before	now	during
then	after	until	when
since	soon	later	finally

To get a better sense of the time-order pattern, do the two exercises below, and then read the answers that follow. Note that the first passage presents a series of events, and the second presents steps in a process.

Following is an example of a paragraph in which events are organized according to time order. Using the spaces provided, complete the outline of the paragraph by listing the events in the order in which they happened. One point has already been done for you.

It was the history-making afternoon of July 20, 1969, when the lunar module, the *Eagle*, landed on the moon. Inside it were astronauts Neil Armstrong and Edwin Aldrin. Six and a half hours after landing, the hatch of the *Eagle* was opened and Armstrong began to descend a ladder to the surface of the moon. On the way, he let down a television camera that would record for viewers on Earth the first human foot on the moon. Then Armstrong stood on the moon and said the line for which he is famous: "That's one small step for a man, one giant leap for mankind."

Main idea: *The history-making hours on the moon, afternoon of July 20, 1969*

1. *Armstrong and Aldrin landed in the Eagle.*

2. _____

3. _____

4. _____

Below is an example of a paragraph in which steps in a process are organized according to time order. Using the spaces provided, complete the outline of the paragraph that follows by listing the steps in the correct sequence. The first step has been done for you.

To stop a nosebleed, you must first sit down and lean forward slightly. Your head should be above the level of your heart. For five minutes, pinch the soft parts of your nose firmly together. Next, to constrict blood vessels, apply ice wrapped in a washcloth to your nose and cheeks.

Main Idea: *Steps to stopping a nose bleed*

1. *Sit down and lean forward slightly.*

2. _____

3. _____

For the first outline, you should have had this sequence: (1) Armstrong and Aldrin landed in the *Eagle*. (2) Armstrong left the *Eagle* and began going down the ladder. (3) He lowered a TV camera to broadcast his first step. (4) Then he stood on the moon and said his famous line.

For the second outline, you should have had this sequence: (1) Sit down and lean forward slightly. (2) Pinch soft parts of nose together. (3) Apply ice to nose and cheeks.

▷ Practice 1

The following three passages describe either a sequence of events or steps in a process. Complete the outlines that follow each passage.

A.   Here is a way to relax that is easy and can even be done in just a few minutes. First, lie down with your arms at your sides and your fingers open. When you are comfortable, close your eyes and put all distracting thoughts out of your mind. Next, tighten all the muscles of your body at once. Push your toes together, tighten your buttocks and abdomen, clench your fists, and squeeze your eyes shut. Hold this position for about seven seconds. Then, let everything relax, and feel the tension flow out of your body. After that, take a deep breath through your mouth and hold it for twenty seconds; then let it out slowly, and breathe slowly and easily, as you do when you are sleeping. Finally, think of a pleasant scene. Concentrate on this scene as you feel your whole body becoming calm and relaxed.

Main idea: *Steps in a relaxation technique*

1. _____

2. _____

3. *Tighten all muscles, and then relax* _____

4. _____

5. _____

B.   After resting for fifteen hundred years, Italy's Mount Vesuvius erupted in the early afternoon on August 24, 79 A.D. The residents of Pompeii, four miles away, could see and hear the explosion, which sent a black cloud into the sky. However, it wasn't until a second and greater explosion soon followed that the city directly suffered the effects of the volcanic eruption. Within a day, Pompeii and its inhabitants were buried under thirty to fifty feet of stones and ash. Soon after, a river of mud and ash buried the nearby city of Herculaneum.

Main idea: *Eruption of Mount Vesuvius in 79 A.D.*

1. _____

2. *Second explosion*
   a. *Pompeii is buried under stone and ash*
   b. _____

C. There are several steps to remembering your dreams. First of all, you must make up your mind to do so, for consciously deciding that you want to remember increases the likelihood that it will happen. Then put a pen and a notebook near your bed, so that you can write down what you remember as soon as you wake up. When possible, turn off your alarm before you go to sleep so that you can wake up gradually, which will increase the likelihood of remembering your dreams. Finally, when you wake up in the morning and remember a dream, write it down immediately, even before getting out of bed.

Main idea: _____
1. *Make up your mind to remember your dreams.*

2. _____

3. _____

4. _____

2 LIST OF ITEMS

A *list of items* refers to a simple series of details or reasons that support a point. The items are not presented in a time order but are listed in a way the author feels is important. The transitions used in organizing lists of items tell us that another item is being added to one or more items already mentioned. The following are some of the transitions that often signal a listing pattern of organization:

and	in addition	first of all	furthermore
also	moreover	first	last of all
another	next	second	finally

In the passage below, the main point has been italicized. See if you can count the number of items in the author's list and also identify the type of item being listed. Note that transitions will help you find two of the items. After doing this exercise, read the explanation that follows.

In September, 1666, a great fire blazed out of control in London, England, reducing nearly five-sixths of the city to ashes. Before it was over, more than 13,000 houses had been burned to the ground. In addition, eighty-nine churches were left in ruins, including St. Paul's Cathedral, the grandest building in England at that time. Hundreds of warehouses containing valuable merchandise were also lost, bankrupting many of the country's richest merchants.

Number of items listed: _____

What type of item is listed? _____

_____

This paragraph consists of a main point, stated in the topic sentence (the first one), followed by a list of three items, each in a sentence of its own and all supporting the main point. The type of item listed is the *parts of London destroyed by the fire* (houses, churches, and warehouses). Notice that the items might have been listed in any order without affecting the point of the paragraph.

▷ *Practice 2*

The following three passages use a listing pattern. Underline the main idea in each, and then count the number of items used to support each main idea. Notice that in some cases, more than one sentence is devoted to a single item. Finally, indicate what type of item is being listed in each passage.

A.   Parents should seriously consider their children's requests for a pet, for there are several advantages to owning a pet. First, if parents set down rules and stick to them, a child can learn responsibility by taking charge of feeding and, in the case of dogs, walking a pet. Also, while caring for any pets, such as tropical fish or hamsters, children learn about the animals' characteristics and habits. And finally, the unconditional love most pets express for their owners is another advantage; children benefit from the warmth and love their pets provide.

Number of items listed: _____

What type of item is listed? _____

_____

B.   There are several ways to be an active listener. A common way to show that you are listening and interested is to ask questions about what the other person is saying. You can also rephrase what the other person has said to be sure you have understood. For example, you might say something like, "So what you're saying is . . . ." Yet another way to show your interest is to watch for clues to feelings in the other person's tone of voice or posture. That allows you to comment on or ask about the emotional reactions you notice, which shows that you care about that person's feelings.

Number of items listed: _____

What type of item is listed? _____

_____

C. When your children are untruthful, you can react in a number of ways. If you feel children deserve a reprimand, a reasonable explanation should be enough to help them understand what is unacceptable behavior. A second reaction in some cases can be to simply acknowledge the fact that your children are fantasizing or exaggerating, rather than accusing them of being liars. In response to a tall tale, for instance, you might say something like, "Wouldn't it be nice if that were true?" Finally, you can respond to your children's storytelling by looking for the underlying reason behind it. Once that reason is dealt with, your child will no longer have the same need to continue lying.

Number of items listed: _____

What type of item is listed? _____

_____

3 COMPARISON AND/OR CONTRAST

The *comparison-contrast* pattern shows how two things are alike or how they are different, or both. When things are *compared,* their similarities are pointed out; when they are *contrasted,* their differences are discussed. In our daily lives we compare and contrast things all the time, whether we are aware of it or not.

For example, a simple decision such as whether to make a hamburger or a Swiss-cheese sandwich for lunch requires us to compare and contrast the two choices. We may consider them both because of their similarities—they both taste good and are filling. We may, however, choose one over the other because of how they differ—a hamburger requires cooking while a cheese sandwich can be slapped together in about thirty seconds. If we are in a rush, we will probably choose the sandwich. If not, we may decide to have a hot meal and cook a hamburger instead.

Here are some common transitions showing comparison and contrast:

Comparison Signals

like	likewise	similarly
just like	equally	similarities
just as	resembles	same
alike	also	similar

Contrast Signals

however	on the other hand	different
in contrast	as opposed to	differently
instead	unlike	differs from

In the following sample exercise, the main idea is stated in the first and second sentences. As is often the case, the main idea indicates that a comparison-contrast pattern will be used. Read the paragraph and answer the questions below. Then look at the explanation that follows.

In middle age, men and women often view life very differently. This is especially true for couples who have led traditional lives in which the wife has stayed home to rear the children and the husband has devoted most of his energy to his career. By middle age, the husband is often comfortable in his position at work and has given up any dreams of advancing further. He may then become more family oriented. In contrast, once the children are grown, the wife may find herself free to explore interests and develop abilities she has had no time for in the previous fifteen or twenty years. Unlike her husband, she may be more interested in non-family activities than ever.

1. Is this paragraph comparing, contrasting, or both?

    _____

2. What two things are being compared and/or contrasted?

    _____

3. Which three comparison or contrast signal words or phrases are used in the paragraph?

    _____

This paragraph is only contrasting, not comparing—it discusses only differences, not similarities. The two things being contrasted here are the views on life held by middle-aged men and by middle-aged women who have led traditional lives. The signal words used to indicate contrast are "differently," "in contrast," and "unlike."

▷ Practice 3

Read the following passages and indicate whether the author is comparing items or contrasting items by checking the appropriate space below each one. If a passage both compares *and* contrasts, check both spaces. In addition, write down the two things that are being compared or contrasted in each passage.

A. Although mysteries and science fiction may seem like very different kinds of writing, the two forms share some basic similarities. First of all, both are action-oriented, emphasizing plot at the expense of character development. Possibly for this reason, both types of literature have been scorned by critics as being "mere entertainment" rather than "literature." But this attack is unjustified, for both mysteries and science fiction share a concern with moral issues. Science fiction often raises the question of whether or not scientific advances are beneficial to humanity. And a mystery story rarely ends without the guilty person being brought to justice.

Comparison _____   Contrast _____

What two things are being compared and/or contrasted?

_____

B. People are different from other primates, but not as different as they would like to think. It's true that that there are significant contrasts in size and proportion between humans and other primates. And, of course, humans are by far the more intelligent. Nevertheless, the similarities among primates are notable. To use chimpanzees as an example, both they and humans have the same muscles and bones, located in almost the same places and working in nearly the same ways. The internal organs of both animals are also very much alike, as are their blood and other body fluids. Seen under a microscope, even their genes are strikingly similar.

Comparison _____   Contrast _____

What two things are being compared and/or contrasted?

_____

C. The conflict over secrecy between the federal government and journalists arises from the different roles they play in society. The government has the job of conducting foreign policy. To do so effectively, government officials sometimes prefer to distort or withhold information. Journalists, however, see their role as digging up and giving information to the public. If they always sought government permission before publishing information, they would be able to print or broadcast only what the government wanted to appear in the media.

Comparison _____   Contrast _____

What two things are being compared and/or contrasted?

_____

4 CAUSE AND EFFECT

Information that falls into a *cause-effect* pattern addresses itself to the questions "Why did, or why would, an event happen?" and "What are, or what would be, the results of an event?" In other words, "What are the *causes* of an event?" and "What are the *effects* of an event?"

Authors usually explore events using a cause-and-effect approach. In other words, they don't just tell what happened; they try to tell about events in a way that explains both *what* happened and *why*. A textbook section on the sinking of the ship the *Titanic*, for example, would be incomplete if it did not include the cause of the disaster—going at a high speed, the ship collided with an iceberg. Or if the banks of the Mississippi River are flooded, a newspaper will not simply report about the flooding. An article on this event would also tell why the flooding happened—heavy rains caused the river to overflow. An important part of any effort to understand events and processes includes learning about cause-effect relationships.

Explanations of causes and effects very often use transitions such as the following:

thus	as a result	therefore
because	result in	since
because of	result	leads to
causes	effects	brings about

Read the paragraph below and see if you can answer the questions about cause and effect. Then read the explanation to see how you did.

Drinking alcohol can lead to different states of consciousness. Although the changes vary from person to person, some broad generalizations are possible. One or two drinks usually result in feelings of warmth, relaxation, and decreased inhibitions. Slightly heavier drinking often causes people to believe they can do things better than they really can. For example, after a few drinks a person may believe he is speaking eloquently when, in fact, his speech is slurred or even unintelligible. Or someone may believe she can drive perfectly well when her reactions and judgment have actually been weakened by alcohol.

1. What are the two *causes* described in this paragraph?

    a. _____

    b. _____

2. What are the two kinds of *effects*?

    a. _____

    b. _____

3. What three cause-effect signal words or phrases are used?

    _____

While this paragraph discusses drinking alcohol as a cause in general, it divides drinking into two categories—"one or two drinks" and "slightly heavier drinking." The first cause, then, is "one or two drinks"; its effect can be "feelings of warmth, relaxation, and decreased inhibitions." The second cause is "slightly heavier drinking"; its effect can be to make drinkers "believe they can do things better than they really can." The cause-effect signals here are *lead to*, *result in*, and *causes*.

▷ *Practice 4*

The three activities that follow (A, B, and C) will give you a sharper sense of cause-and-effect relationships.

A. The following sentences all describe a cause-and-effect relationship. For each of them, identify both the cause and the effect.
    1. Since unemployment has fallen 5 percent in the last year, many more people can now afford to buy expensive consumer goods, such as cars and television sets.

        Cause: _____

        Effect: _____

2. Last winter I twisted my ankle by slipping and falling on a patch of ice.

   Cause: _____

   Effect: _____

3. Mr. Coleman's bankruptcy was the result of his compulsive gambling.

   Cause: _____

   Effect: _____

4. When Melba saw that her new boss did not appreciate her excellent work habits, she began to do her work carelessly.

   Cause: _____

   Effect: _____

5. The orange crop in Florida is poor this year because of a late spring freeze.

   Cause: _____

   Effect: _____

B. The following sentences all list either two causes leading to the same effect or two effects resulting from a single cause. Identify causes and effects in each sentence. Here is an example of how to do this activity.

Example

High winds and hailstones as big as golf balls resulted in $10,000 worth of property damage.

High winds: *cause*
Hailstones: *cause*
Property damage: *effect*

6. Uncontrolled high blood pressure can lead to a stroke or a heart attack.

   Uncontrolled high blood pressure: _____

   Stroke: _____

   Heart attack: _____

7. Because the defense lawyer's objection was valid, the judge threw out the evidence and dismissed the case.

   Valid objection: _____

   Thrown-out evidence: _____

   Dismissed case: _____

8. After ammunition and food supplies had run low, the general surrendered.

   Ammunition was low: _____

   Food supplies were low: _____

   The general surrendered: _____

9. When the company needed more office space, the boss rented an additional floor in the building and moved the shipping room to the basement.

   The company needed more space: _____

   The boss rented an additional floor: _____

   The boss moved the shipping room to the basement: _____

10. Since baseball season started today, many people called in sick to work and played hooky from school.

    The start of the baseball season: _____

    People called in sick to work: _____

    People played hooky: _____

C. The following passages all list either several causes leading to the same effect or several effects resulting from a single cause. In the spaces provided, identify the causes and effects in each sentence.

1. Even the best listeners cannot possibly listen carefully to everything that they hear. Among the reasons for this is the overload of messages most of us encounter each day. Besides the numerous hours we spend hearing other people speak, we may spend several more hours listening to the radio or television. It isn't possible to avoid having our attention wander at least part of all this time. Preoccupation with our personal concerns is another reason we don't always listen carefully. A romance gone sour or a good grade on a test may take prominence in our mind even as someone is speaking to us. In addition, the simple fact that we are at times surrounded by noise interferes with listening. For example, many voices at a noisy party or the sound of traffic may simply make it difficult for us to hear everything that is being said.

   Inability to listen carefully all the time: _____

   Message overload: _____

   Preoccupation with personal concerns: _____

   Surrounding noise: _____

2. Research over the last decade or so has shown meditation can have positive effects on drug users and people with certain health problems. Studies have demonstrated that when people who take drugs become meditators, they either cut back on drug use or stop using drugs altogether. In one study of a group that practiced transcendental meditation, for example, the number of marijuana users fell from 78 percent to 12 percent after twenty-one months of meditation. Meditation has also been shown to lower blood pressure and regulate the heart beat, both of which may be of considerable help to those with cardiovascular problems. And because meditation is a highly effective relaxation technique, it can also prove useful to those with stress-related diseases.

Meditation: _____

Decrease or elimination of drug use: _____

Cardiovascular improvements: _____

Stress relief: _____

3. Children's names can have far-reaching effects on them, according to scientists. Some researchers have found that there is a tendency for children with popular names, such as Jennifer or Robert, to do better in school and be better liked than children with names that are considered undesirable. Also, children's self-images may be influenced by the stereotypes that are associated with their names. Thus a child named Gertrude may feel ugly, and a Percy may think of himself as weak. And children with strange names, like Throckmorton, tend to have more frequent behavior problems.

Children's names: _____

Popularity: _____

Self-image: _____

Behavior: _____

5   DEFINITIONS AND EXAMPLES

To communicate successfully, an author must help readers understand the words and ideas that are being expressed. If a word is likely to be new to readers, the author may take time to include a *definition* before going on. Then, to clarify the definition, which might be too general to be easily understood, the author may present explanatory details, including one or more *examples*. Examples help readers better understand what is meant and strengthen support for the ideas they illustrate.

Textbooks often contain definitions and examples. They introduce students to new words and provide examples of how those words are used to make them clearer and more familiar. Of course, definitions may be given without examples, and examples are frequently used to illustrate general statements other than definitions.

Examples are often introduced by transitions like the following:

for example	to illustrate	one
for instance	such as	specifically
as an illustration	to be specific	including

The following paragraph defines a word, explains it a bit, and then gives an example of it. After reading the paragraph, see if you can answer the questions that follow.

¹Acrophobia is an intense, unreasonable fear of high places. ²People with acrophobia exhibit physical symptoms in response to being at great heights. ³One sufferer from extreme acrophobia, Sally Maxell, is unable to go above the third floor of any building without feeling enormous anxiety. ⁴Her acrophobia began one evening when she was working alone in her office on the eighth floor of a large building. ⁵Suddenly she was struck with terror by the idea that she might jump or fall out the open window. ⁶She crouched behind a steel filing cabinet, trembling, unable to move. ⁷When she finally gathered her belongings and left the building, she was sweating, her breathing was rapid, and her heart was pounding. ⁸Yet she had no rational explanation for her fears.

What word is being defined? _____

What is the definition? _____

_____

Which sentence explains more about the word? _____

In which sentence does the example begin? _____

The word "acrophobia" is defined in the first sentence—"an intense, unreasonable fear of high places." The second sentence explains a bit more about acrophobia. The story about Sally Maxell, which begins in the third sentence, provides an example of how acrophobia affects one sufferer; by including it, the author makes the new term more clear by helping readers better visualize what it means.

▷ *Practice 5*

The following three passages include a definition and one or more examples. The passages may also include sentences that explain more about the term being defined. In the spaces provided, write the number of the definition sentence and the number of the sentence where each example begins.

A.   [1]A boycott is an organized refusal by a group of people to deal with another person or group to achieve a specific goal. [2]An illustration is the famous boycott that began in 1955 when Mrs. Rosa Parks of Montgomery, Alabama, refused to obey a local ordinance requiring black people to sit at the back of city busses. [3]Mrs. Parks was arrested, and that sparked off a boycott of the Montgomery bus system by blacks. [4]The boycott was organized and led by Dr. Martin Luther King, Jr. [5]Rather than continue to lose revenue needed to run the bus system, the city repealed the ordinance.

Definition _____   Example _____

B.   [1]Eidetic imagery is the technical term for what most people know as photographic memory. [2]A person with eidetic imagery can recall every detail of a memory as clearly as if he or she were looking at a photograph. [3]People often wish they had this ability, but it can lead to trouble. [4]For example, a law student with eidetic imagery was accused of cheating on an examination because his test paper contained exactly the words in his textbook. [5]To prove his innocence, he studied an unfamiliar passage for five minutes and then wrote down more than four hundred words from it without making a mistake.

Definition _____   Example _____

C.   [1]A common type of psychological defense mechanism is rationalization. [2]Rationalization is a seemingly reasonable explanation that distorts the truth in order to maintain self-esteem. [3]It explains a situation that threatens the ego in a less truthful but more acceptable way. [4]A person who excuses himself for doing poorly on a test because he wasn't feeling well or the test was unfair is probably rationalizing in order to make his grade more acceptable. [5]One Aesop fable provides a classical example of rationalization. [6]In this fable, a fox wants some tempting grapes that grow in a hard-to-reach spot. [7]When he can't reach them, he tells himself that the grapes must have been sour anyway.

Definition _____   Example 1 _____

Example 2 _____

➤ *Review Test 1*

Identify the patterns used in each of the groups of sentences below by writing in the spaces provided one of the letters of the following:

a. Time order
b. Items in a list
c. Comparison and/or contrast
d. Cause and effect
e. Definition and example

_____ 1. The construction of federally subsidized highways and the shortage of housing in central cities led to the movement to the suburbs.

_____ 2. While some birds meet only to mate, others stay together and share in the child-rearing.

_____ 3. Propaganda is information of any type, whether true or false, that is designed deliberately to persuade an audience to adopt a particular point of view. Advertising is an obvious form of propaganda.

_____ 4. A good study space is well lighted and well supplied with paper, pens, and study aids. In addition, it is quiet and free from distractions such as television or stereo.

_____ 5. To begin word processing, first turn on the computer. Next, insert the master editing diskette into Drive A. Then put a blank, formatted diskette into Drive B and get ready to write.

_____ 6. Today's telephones offer various convenient features. Computerized dialing is one popular feature; another is automatic redialing of a telephone which is busy or unanswered.

_____ 7. Television news stories resemble newspaper articles in being timely and appealing to a wide audience. However, television news coverage tends to be more superficial, emphasizing the visual aspects of a story rather than important background issues.

_____ 8. Many drivers take to the roads in July and August, when families traditionally go on vacation. As a result, oil companies raise the price of gasoline during the summer months.

_____ 9. Even before he meets the three witches, Macbeth has dreamed of becoming king of Scotland. Then the witches predict he will be king; finally, his wife convinces him to murder King Duncan and take over the country.

_____ 10. In a mystery story, the term "red herring" refers to a false or misleading clue inserted into the story to deceive the reader. One famous red herring is Sherlock Holmes' farewell note to Dr. Watson in "The Final Problem," which leads the reader to believe Holmes has fallen to his death.

➤ *Review Test 2*

Circle the letter that correctly identifies the pattern of organization in each of the following passages.

1. Successful garage sales are planned well in advance. About a month before the sale, find out whether your municipality requires you to get a permit to hold your sale. Then ask your friends whether they want to participate. Gather the items you want to sell, and spruce them up whenever possible by washing or repairing them. Decide how much to charge for each item. Then print and post notices of your sale. Finally, arrange your merchandise on card or picnic tables and get ready to collect your well-earned profits.

   a. time order   b. comparison/contrast   c. cause and effect

2. Middle-aged adults are returning to school in increasing numbers. Some of them want to keep up with new developments in their fields or improve their skills in order to do their jobs better. Others return to school because they hope to equip themselves to win promotions or raises. Also, dissatisfaction with their current jobs or interest in new fields, such as telecommunication and computer programming, motivates some adults to return to the classroom. Finally, others want to study subjects they did not have time for earlier, such as foreign languages, history, or literature. These classes help them spend their time in more productive and interesting ways and deepen their understanding of themselves and their world.

   a. time order   b. definition and example   c. cause and effect

3. Is your child gifted? If your child does things better, quicker, and earlier than other children, you may have a gifted child. The term "gifted" was once applied only to children with IQ scores of about 130 (100 is an average score). Today, the term has been expanded to include a variety of special talents, such as unusual ability in art, music, or dance. Gifted children tend to have a variety of interests, and because their attention spans are long, they enjoy pursuing their interests independently. Their memories are unusually good, and they are surprisingly imaginative. Contrary to popular belief, gifted children usually have many friends and are often natural leaders. One young man who spends hours each week practicing the piano is also an avid baseball player and class officer at his school.

   a. list of items   b. cause and effect   c. definition and example

4. Throughout history, people middle-aged and older have gotten married, just as they do today. In the past, however, the most common reason for losing a spouse and thus being available to remarry was death. Today, life spans are longer, and both members of a newly formed couple may well have been divorced. Because families were larger in the past, the remarried couple was likely to have more children than they do today. As a result, couples living together without children were rare. Today, most couples can look forward to twenty years together after the last child has grown up and left home.

   a. comparison/contrast   b. list of items   c. definition and example

5. The psychological process by which children learn their sex roles contains three main elements. One is conditioning through rewards and punishments. For example, boys who play with model airplanes and girls who play with dolls will usually be encouraged by their parents. On the other hand, boys who prefer dolls and girls who prefer airplanes will often be criticized or even punished. Another element is imitation. Young children will usually imitate adults who they think are like themselves. This means that boys will usually imitate their fathers and girls their mothers. The third and perhaps the most important element is self-definition. Children quickly learn that all people are either male or female and define themselves as belonging to one sex rather than the other. They then use this self-definition to choose their future interests and to develop their personalities and social roles.

   a. time order   b. list of items   c. definition and example

6

Distinguishing Facts from Opinions

To be a skilled reader, you must be able to distinguish *fact* from *opinion*. Sorting out facts from opinions is something you do already, perhaps without even realizing it. For example, a friend might say to you, "I saw a science-fiction movie last night about aliens invading Earth. The special effects were great; the aliens looked like reptiles—they had green skin and forked tongues. The acting was terrible, though." Hearing this description, you would probably realize that your friend's comments are a mixture of fact and opinion.

FACTS

A *fact* is a statement that can be checked and proven through objective evidence. This evidence may be in the form of the testimony of witnesses, agreed-upon observations, or the written records of such testimony and observations. The statements of fact among your friend's comments are that he went to a science-fiction movie last night, that the movie was about aliens invading Earth, and that the aliens had green skin and forked tongues. If you wanted to, you could check the truth of all these statements by questioning witnesses or watching the movie yourself.

Following are some other statements that are facts—they can be checked for accuracy and proven to be true.

FACT: The Quad Tower is the tallest building in this city. (A researcher could go out and, through inspection, confirm that the building is the tallest.)

FACT: Albert Einstein willed his violin to his grandson. (This statement can be checked in historical publications or with Einstein's estate.)

FACT: The 1986 New York Mets won the World Series in seven games. (Anyone can check sports records to confirm this.)

OPINIONS

An *opinion* is a statement that cannot be objectively proven true or false. Opinions usually express the beliefs, feelings, or judgments that a person has about a subject. Your friend, for instance, said that the movie's special effects were great and that the acting was terrible. These statements may be based on certain reasonable factors, but they cannot be proven. They are opinions. You might see the movie and reach very different conclusions.

Here are some other statements that are opinions:

OPINION: The Quad Tower is the ugliest building in the city.
(There's no way to prove this statement because two people can look at the same building and come to different conclusions about its beauty. "Ugly" is a *value word*, a word we use to express a value judgment. Value words are signals that an opinion is being expressed. By their very nature, these words represent opinions, not facts.)

OPINION: Einstein should have willed his violin to a museum.
(Who says? Not his grandson. This is an opinion.)

OPINION: The 1986 New York Mets were the best team in the history of baseball.
(Whether something is "best" is always debatable. "Best" is another value word.)

▷ *Practice 1*

Now read the following statements and decide whether each is fact or opinion. Put an **F** (for "fact") or an **O** (for "opinion") beside each statement. Then read the explanations that follow.

_____ 1. My brother Gary is very handsome.

_____ 2. Last night, a tree outside our house was struck by lightning.

_____ 3. Installing a new sink is an easy job for the do-it-yourselfer.

——————— 4. Richard M. Nixon was the worst president our country ever had.

——————— 5. Certain birds bury their eggs on the slopes of a dying volcano, where heat from volcanic steam incubates the eggs.

——————— 6. Margie believes in astrology.

——————— 7. Ostriches do not hide their heads in the sand.

——————— 8. The economy, in fact, is in the worst shape it's been in for years.

——————— 9. The Grimm brothers collected their fairy tales from other collections and from storytellers.

——————— 10. Harold is a bad influence on my son.

Explanations:

1. This is an opinion. You may like the way your brother looks (maybe because he looks so much like you), but other people might not find him so attractive. The word "handsome" is another value word.

2. This is a statement of fact. You and your family might have seen or heard the lightning strike, or you could go outside later and see the type of damage done to the tree.

3. This is an opinion. The word "easy" suggests a judgment is being made and can mean quite different things to different people.

4. This is an opinion. Not everyone would evaluate Nixon's performance in this way. Here the value word "worst" shows us that a judgment is being expressed.

5. This is a statement of fact. People have observed and recorded this aspect of the life of these birds; it's not a matter of opinion.

6. This is a fact. Margie's belief is an opinion, but the fact that she has that belief can be confirmed—we can ask her.

7. This is a fact (contrary to popular opinion) which can be checked through observation and reports of observations.

8. This is an opinion. Just because someone says something is a fact doesn't make it so. Different people will judge economic factors differently.

9. This is a fact. It can be confirmed through the Grimms' writings and research on the background of their stories.

10. This is an opinion—it all depends on what someone considers "bad."

Other Points About Fact and Opinion

There are several added points to keep in mind when distinguishing fact from opinion.

1 Statements of fact may be found to be untrue.

Suppose you went to the science fiction movie your friend spoke of and discovered the aliens actually had blue rather than green skin. (Perhaps your friend is color-blind.) You would then call his statement an error, not a fact. Sometimes, then, in the process of checking out whether a statement of fact is true, you will learn that it is not true, that it is not a fact at all. It was once considered to be a fact that the world was flat, but that "fact" also turned out to be an error.

2 Opinions may be masked as facts.

People sometimes present their opinions as facts, as shown in statement 8 in the above practice. Here are two more examples:

In point of fact, neither candidate for the mayor's office is qualified.

The truth of the matter is that frozen foods are just as good-tasting as fresh foods are.

Despite the words to the contrary, the above are not statements of fact but statements of opinion.

3 Remember that value words by nature represent opinions. Here are examples of value words:

best	great	beautiful
worst	terrible	bad
better	lovely	good
worse	disgusting	wonderful

These and other value words express personal judgments about the world. They are subjective rather than objective. While factual statements report on observed reality, subjective statements interpret reality. For example, the observation that it is raining outside is an objective one. The statement that the weather is bad, however, is a subjective one, an interpretation of the facts. (If there were a severe water shortage, rain would be welcome.)

4 Finally, remember that much of what we read and hear is a mixture of fact and opinion.

Being able to separate fact from opinion is important because much information that at first sounds factual turns out to be opinion. A political candidate, for example, may say, "My record is an outstanding one." Voters would be wise to wonder what the value word "outstanding" means to this candidate. Or an advertising copywriter might write that a particular automobile model is "the most economical car on the road today," a statement that at first glance seems factual. But what is meant by the word "economical"? If the car offers the most miles per gallon but the worst record for expensive repairs, you might not agree that it's economical.

▷ Practice 2

Here are some fact and opinion statements. Remember that the facts can be proven objectively but the opinions give personal views. Identify the statements of fact with an **F** and the statements of opinion with an **O**.

_____ 1. Too many drugs are prescribed for people suffering from depression.

_____ 2. Depression is most common among those between the ages of twenty-five and forty-four.

_____ 3. Henry Ford was wrong when he claimed that laziness and idleness cause most of the world's troubles.

_____ 4. A Colorado farmer wrote Henry Ford asking to exchange six mounted moose heads for a new car.

_____ 5. Letting a faucet drip continually is the best way to prevent frozen water pipes.

_____ 6. Permanent precautions against frozen pipes include wrapping them in fiberglass insulation or heat tape.

_____ 7. In Timeo, a language based on numbers, "1-80-17" means "I love you."

_____ 8. If everyone in the world spoke the same language, there would be fewer wars.

_____ 9. Japanese knotweed was introduced in America as a garden plant, but now grows wild in vacant lots, along roadsides, and on stream banks.

_____ 10. Today, only gardeners with poor taste would allow Japanese knotweed in their gardens.

▷ Practice 3

Some of the sentences below state facts, some express opinions; in addition, three include both facts and opinions. Identify statements of fact with an **F**, statements of opinion with an **O**, and statements of fact *and* opinion with an **F + O**.

_____ 1. German shepherds are the scariest dogs alive.

_____ 2. The dog that bites people the most often, according to one twenty-seven-year study, is the German shepherd.

_____ 3. German shepherds, which always make poor pets, are used in police work and as guide dogs for the blind.

_____ 4. Because many studies have concluded that smoking is a health hazard, cigarettes should be banned.

_____ 5. Smokers have no regard for other people's health.

_____ 6. Smoking is a major cause of lung cancer.

_____ 7. Executives of corporations that pollute the environment should be jailed.

_____ 8. Waste chemicals from some companies have gotten into community water supplies.

_____ 9. Canada is negotiating with the United States on acid rain, the biggest pollution problem of all.

_____ 10. In point of fact, pollution is the greatest danger humankind faces today.

► *Review Test 1*

A. Some of the sentences below state facts, and some express opinions. Identify statements of fact with an **F** and statements of opinion with an **O**.

_____ 1. A bouquet of red roses is an ideal Mother's Day gift.

_____ 2. Roses have been found in dry bouquets in ancient Egyptian tombs.

_____ 3. The voting age in America is eighteen.

_____ 4. If eighteen-year-olds are old enough to be drafted, they're old enough to vote.

_____ 5. For a good cup of coffee, add some chicory to the coffee grounds.

_____ 6. Professional coffee tasters use the words "harsh," "musty," and "acidy" to describe the flavors of coffee.

_____ 7. Charlie Chaplin never won an Oscar.

_____ 8. Charlie Chaplin should have won an Oscar.

_____ 9. Business management is more interesting than computer programming.

_____ 10. The fact is that *M*A*S*H* is one of the funniest television series ever made.

B. Some of the sentences below state facts and some express opinions; in addition, three include both facts and opinions. Identify statements of fact with an **F**, statements of opinion with an **O**, and statements of fact *and* opinion with an **F + O**.

_____ 1. My son once left half a sandwich under his bed for over a week.

_____ 2. My son is a delightful companion to everyone who knows him.

_____ 3. My son got a B in history this semester, but he deserved an A.

_____ 4. New York City is not the capital of New York State.

_____ 5. New York City, where visitors can see Broadway plays, museums, and the Statue of Liberty, is the perfect place for a summer vacation.

_____ 6. The Empire State Building is easily the most memorable of all the sights in New York.

_____ 7. Elephants are the largest of all land animals.

_____ 8. Researchers have found that elephants react nervously to rabbits and dachshunds, but not to mice.

_____ 9. Maybe the lively scampering of the rabbits and dachshunds is what makes elephants nervous.

_____ 10. Because they use their trunks both to clean themselves and to eat, elephants are the most fascinating animals in the zoo.

➤ *Review Test 2*

Each of the passages below contains five sentences. Two of those sentences are facts, two are opinions, and one combines both facts and opinions. Identify statements of fact with an **F**, statements of opinion with an **O**, and statements of fact *and* opinion with an **F + O**.

A. [1]There are few more annoying problems than hiccups, which can last for hours or even days. [2]According to one doctor who has studied them, hiccups are usually caused by eating or drinking too quickly. [3]People do some pretty strange things to remedy this ridiculous problem. [4]Some common remedies include holding your breath, eating a teaspoon of sugar, and putting a paper bag over your head. [5]Undoubtedly, that last one is the strangest one of all.

1. _____   2. _____   3. _____

4. _____   5. _____

B. [1]The Lincoln Memorial is America's best loved public monument. [2]Designed by Henry Beacon, it was dedicated on Memorial Day, 1922, more than fifty years after a memorial to Lincoln was first proposed. [3]Built to resemble a Greek temple, it contains a seated figure of Lincoln by sculptor Daniel Chester French. [4]Many people learn to admire the monument long before they visit it in person through seeing its picture, which is on the penny and the five-dollar bill. [5]All Americans feel pride mingled with sorrow when they come to Washington in person and look up at the kindly, mournful face of Abraham Lincoln.

1. _____   2. _____   3. _____

4. _____   5. _____

C. [1]A California student conducted a six-day experiment that involved hitchhiking back and forth over the same one hundred miles. [2]His idea, a very clever and worthwhile one, was to see how drivers would react to his clothing, which was old and casual on half of the days and more neat and formal on the other days. [3]On the days he was casually dressed, he got picked up only by drivers of old Volkswagen busses and a pickup truck; on the days he dressed in an ironed shirt and permanent-press pants, he got rides in Cadillacs and Oldsmobiles. [4]Apparently, people who drive fancy cars have no desire to associate with those they think dress more poorly than they do. [5]This experiment proves that people will always be more drawn to those they think are most like themselves.

1. _____   2. _____   3. _____

4. _____   5. _____

D. [1]There's no doubt that this world is getting crazier by the minute. [2]Now there's a dentist who offers a limousine ride to his office and a catered lunch there. [3]While he says he offers these services to help patients get a lot of dental work done in a short time, it's clear that nobody in his right mind would want to pay extra for such benefits. [4]One of the dentist's own comments on the cost was: "We're not cheap." [5]He should have added to that: "We're not sane."

1. _____   2. _____   3. _____

4. _____   5. _____

E.   [1]Many food products are promoted as being "natural," which is more a result of corporate greed than concern for good food. [2]In point of fact, all the products that are called "natural" should be called "unnatural." [3]Manufacturers are allowed to call anything "natural" because the federal government has no regulation governing that word's use. [4]It's not rare for foods advertised as "natural" to contain artificial ingredients such as preservatives and artificial coloring. [5]If consumers would complain more about such deceptions, the government would respond quickly.

1. _____   2. _____   3. _____

4. _____   5. _____

7

Drawing Inferences

You have probably heard the expression "to read between the lines." When you "read between the lines," you pick up ideas that are not directly stated in what you are reading. These implied ideas are usually important for a full understanding of what an author means. Discovering the ideas in writing that are not stated directly is called *drawing inferences*.

INFERENCES IN EVERYDAY LIFE

Consider first how often you make inferences in everyday life. For example, suppose you are sitting in a coffee shop at lunchtime. A woman sits down at the next table. Here is what you observe:

- She is wearing an expensive-looking suit, a silk blouse, gold jewelry, and a gold band on the third finger of her left hand.
- The woman opens a brief case and takes out some manila folders; she begins to study them.
- You notice that she also has a child's crayon drawing in the briefcase.

As you sit in the coffee shop, you may make several inferences about this woman:

- She's on her lunch break.
- She works in an office, perhaps as a lawyer or an executive.
- She is married and has a young child.

How did you arrive at these inferences? First of all, you used your experience and general knowledge of people. Secondly, you made informed guesses based on the facts you observed. Of course, not all your inferences might prove true. For example, the woman could own her own business, or she could be an heiress about to discuss her financial holdings over a business lunch with her attorney or stockbroker. The child's drawing might have been done by her nephew or niece or younger sibling. You cannot prove or disprove your guesses without asking the woman directly, but your inferences may well be correct.

Take a moment now and jot down what you might infer if you saw each of the following:

1. A high school has uniformed security guards patrolling the halls.

    Your inference: _____

2. A dog cringes when someone tries to pet him.

    Your inference: _____

The inferences you probably made are that, in the first situation, the high school has had some very disturbing discipline problems and, in the second situation, the dog has previously been mishandled.

INFERENCES IN READING

In reading, too, we make logical leaps from the information given in a straightforward way to ideas that are not stated directly. As the scholar S. I. Hayakawa has said, inferences are "statements about the unknown made on the basis of the known." To draw inferences, we use all the clues provided by the writer, our own experience, and logic.

In this book, you have already practiced making inferences in the chapter on context clues. There you had to use clues within sentences to infer the meanings of words. The intent of this chapter is to broaden your ability to make inferences about what you read.

Now read the following passage and then circle the letters of the three inferences that can logically be drawn from it.

A famous psychology experiment conducted by Dr. John B. Watson demonstrates that people, like animals, can be conditioned—trained to respond in a particular way to certain stimulations. Watson gave an eleven-month-old baby named Albert a soft, furry white rat. Each time Albert tried to stroke the rat, Dr. Watson hit a metal bar with a hammer. Before long, Albert was not only afraid of white rats but also of white rabbits, white dogs, and white fur coats. He even screamed at the sight of a Santa Claus mask.

a.   Dr. Watson did not like small children.

b. Before the experiment, Albert was not afraid of white rats.
c. Albert had been familiar with rats before the experiment.
d. If he had seen a black fur coat, Albert would have screamed.
e. Albert connected the loud noise of the hammer striking the metal bar with the white rat.
f. Albert was afraid of loud noises from the beginning.

Here is an explanation of each item:

a. This is not a logical inference. While the passage may make us wonder about Watson's attitude toward babies, it doesn't give enough information for us logically to infer that he did not like small children.

b. This is a logical inference. Because Albert tried to pet the rat, it is fair to assume that he wasn't frightened of the animal.

c. This is not a logical inference. The passage gives no clues about Albert having previous experience with rats.

d. This is not a logical inference. The passage makes no mention of Albert's response to any color but white.

e. This is a logical inference. Because the loud noise appears to have changed Albert's attitude toward the rat, we can assume he associated the noise with the rat.

f. This is a logical inference. Since the noise is what made Albert afraid of the rat, we have to infer that he was afraid of the noise. In addition, experience tells us that babies are likely to be frightened of unexpected loud noises.

The following activities will improve your ability to make inferences as you read.

▷ *Practice 1*

Circle the letter of the inference *most logically based* on the information in each of the following. The first one is explained for you.

1. A student always sits in the back of the classroom.
   a. The student dislikes the course.
   b. The student is unprepared for class.
   c. The student feels uncomfortable in the front of the room.
   d. The student is farsighted.

The correct answer is *c*. Based on the information we are given, we can conclude only that the student—for some reason—does not like sitting in the front. We are not given enough information to know *why* the student feels this way.

2. A store owner has held six "Going Out of Business" sales in two years.
   a. The store owner is crazy.

    b. The store is not really going out of business.

    c. The store owner borrowed enough cash each time to stay in business.

    d. The store owner can't make up his mind.

3. A woman, holding a canvas money bag and several rolls of coins, leaves a mall bank.

    a. The woman is taking the money to a business she owns in the mall.

    b. The woman has robbed the bank.

    c. The woman has withdrawn money from the bank.

    d. The woman is a coin collector.

4. A pencil has teethmarks on it.

    a. The person who used the pencil was nervous.

    b. The pencil was chewed up by a toddler or pet.

    c. Someone or something chewed the pencil.

    d. The pencil belongs to someone who is trying to quit smoking.

5. A man buys a six-pack of beer at a bar at 7:30 A.M.

    a. The man has been an alcoholic since his teens.

    b. The man is going to drink beer on the way to work.

    c. The man wanted beer and found time to buy it then.

    d. The man is returning to an all-night party that is still going on.

6. A person is in a wheelchair.

    a. The person is paralyzed.

    b. The person would like someone to push him or her.

    c. The person is disabled in some way.

    d. The person has just been discharged from the hospital.

7. A car has bumper stickers that read, "I Brake for Animals," "Save the Whales," and "Have You Thanked a Green Plant Today?"

    a. A driver of the car supports environmental issues.

    b. A driver of the car is an environmental scientist.

    c. A driver of the car has pets.

    d. The owner of the car is a college student.

8. A girl wearing a school uniform is walking down the street at 3:30 P.M. on a weekday.

    a. The girl goes to a parochial school.

    b. The girl doesn't go to a public school.

    c. The girl prefers jeans.

    d. The girl prefers a uniform.

9. The street is wet, but the sidewalks are dry.

    a. An unusual rain fell only on the street.

b. It rained everywhere, but someone dried the sidewalks.

c. A street-cleaning vehicle sprayed the street.

d. Children with waterguns must have played on the street.

10. Inside of a car with an out-of-town license are several maps, suitcases, and bags of snacks.

a. The driver of the car is on vacation.

b. The driver of the car is on a business trip.

c. The driver of the car has children.

d. The driver of the car is on a trip of some kind.

▷ *Practice 2*

Read the following passage. Then circle the letter of the *most logical* answer to each question, based on the facts given in the passage.

A corporate president recently made a visit to a nearby Indian reservation as part of his firm's public relations program. "We realize that we have not hired any Indians in the five years our company has been located in this area," he told the assembled tribesmen, "but we are looking into the matter very carefully." "Hora, hora," said some of the Indians. "We would like to eventually hire 5 percent of our total work force from this reservation," he said. "Hora, hora," shouted more of the Indians. Encouraged by their enthusiasm, the president closed his short address by telling them that he hoped his firm would be able to take some hiring action within the next couple of years. "Hora, hora, hora," cried the total group. With a feeling of satisfaction the president left the hall and was taken on a tour of the reservation. Stopping in a field to admire some of the horses grazing there, the president asked if he could walk up closer to the animals. "Certainly," said his Indian driver, "but be careful not to step in the hora."

1. To get the main point of this passage, the reader must infer

a. the location of the reservation.

b. what kind of company the president headed.

c. the meaning of the word "hora."

2. From the president's speech, we can infer that

a. his firm had a great interest in hiring the Indians.

b. his firm had little interest in hiring the Indians.

c. his firm had a stated policy never to hire Indians.

3. From the passage, we can infer that

a. the Indians believed the president's speech.

b. the Indians did not believe the president's speech.

c. the Indians were confused by the president's speech.

4. From the passage, we can infer that the president
   a. thought the Indians deserved to be hired.
   b. thought his company should not hire the Indians.
   c. misinterpreted the Indians' reaction to his speech.

5. From the passage, we can infer that the main reason the president spoke to the Indians about jobs was that
   a. they needed the jobs.
   b. he thought promising jobs to the Indians would make his company look good.
   c. he thought hiring the Indians would be good for his company.

▷ *Practice 3*

Read the following passage and circle the numbers of the three statements that can be logically inferred from the given facts.

> The Chicago Tribune once called Henry Ford an ignoramus in print. Ford sued, challenging the paper to "prove it." During the trial, Ford was asked dozens of simple, general information questions: "When was the Civil War?" "Name the presidents of the United States." And so on. Ford, who had little formal education, could answer very few. Finally, exasperated, he said, "I don't know the answers to those questions, but I could find a man in five minutes who does. I use my brain to *think*, not store up a lot of useless facts."

1. Henry Ford was probably angered by the article in the *Chicago Tribune*.

2. Ford frequently sued people.

3. Ford won the case in court.

4. The *Tribune* won the case in court.

5. Ford would have been more successful had he had a formal education.

6. Ford believed that knowing where to find a fact is at least as good as knowing the fact.

7. Ford regretted not having a more formal education.

8. Ford believed that knowing how to think is more important than knowing facts.

► *Review Test 1*

After reading each passage, put a check by the two inferences that are most firmly based on the given facts.

1. Pulling the collar of his ragged jacket up against the rain, the unshaven man headed for the shelter of a store doorway. He bit his lip as he thought about how wet everything would be tonight and wondered if he would need to pay for a dry bed.

    _____ a.   The man is homeless.

    _____ b.   He's thinking of stealing some money.

    _____ c.   He sometimes sleeps outside at night.

2. The young woman, wearing a business suit and high heels, grabbed a pack of disposable diapers and several cans of infant formula off the shelves. Then she rushed to the express check-out line, hoping to get home before it was dark.

    _____ a.   The woman is buying something for a baby.

    _____ b.   She works.

    _____ c.   She is rushing home to relieve the babysitter.

3. The man handed me the keys and reminded me that only the first hundred miles were free. I hoped the garage would be able to fix my car soon.

    _____ a.   The speaker is renting a car.

    _____ b.   The speaker's own car is in the garage.

    _____ c.   The speaker's own car had been in an accident.

4. The freak weather transformed the outdoors into a rigid fairyland. Young leaves hung stiffly, and the daffodils seemed buried alive under a glass-like coating.

    _____ a.   The daffodils were encased in ice.

    _____ b.   Such weather had never happened before.

    _____ c.   Rain had turned to ice in spring.

5. The man lifted the girl onto his lap again and told her this would be the last story before bedtime. Then he pushed some hair out of her eyes as he tried to think of a good story.

    _____ a.   The man is the girl's father.

    _____ b.   He had already told her a story.

    _____ c.   The girl is young.

6. Henry decided it was better to be late for English 101 than to get soaked. He should have brought an umbrella, but now he'd just wait at the bookstore until the worst was over.

    _____ a.   Henry is a college student.

    _____ b.   He dislikes English 101.

    _____ c.   It is raining outside.

7. Two women and a man sat in the food court conversing in sign language. There was a paper cup in front of each one.

    _____ a.   They are all deaf.

    _____ b.   At least one of the group is deaf.

    _____ c.   They stopped to relax with a beverage.

8. "My feet are killing me," Ella said as she plopped on a chair and put her feet up on the coffee table. "Remind me never to shop for Christmas presents at the last minute."

    _____ a.   Ella is tired after shopping for Christmas gifts.

    _____ b.   She has been doing last-minute shopping.

    _____ c.   She will never again shop for Christmas presents at the last minute.

9. Carrying his music book, six-year-old Donnie hummed as he approached his teacher's house. Then spotting a large daddy longlegs crawling in the middle of the sidewalk, he turned pale and ran crying all the way back home.

    _____ a.   Donnie was on his way to a music lesson.

    _____ b.   Donnie is afraid of all insects.

    _____ c.   Donnie is afraid of daddy longlegs.

10. Shortly after the young woman sat down in the bus, she lit a cigarette. The man next to her waved some smoke away, nudged her, and pointed to the sign at the front of the bus.

    _____ a.   The man had never smoked.

    _____ b.   The smoke was bothering the man.

    _____ c.   The man pointed to a no-smoking sign.

► Review Test 2

Each passage below is followed by five statements. Two statements are inferences that can definitely be made on the basis of the information in the selections. The three other statements are questionable—they are not logically supported in full by the facts given. Put a **D** beside inferences that DEFINITELY CAN BE MADE and a **Q** beside inferences that are QUESTIONABLE.

1. A restaurant by the name of Broiler Inn was very successful. There was another restaurant by the same name in a town a hundred miles away. One day, the second Broiler Inn was temporarily shut down by the health department because several customers had suffered food poisoning. The case received a lot of publicity in the newspapers. Before long, that Broiler Inn went out of business, and the first one suffered a great loss of customers. Within a few months, it too had to close.

_____ a. Both restaurants were run by the same people.

_____ b. The customers with food poisoning sued the restaurant.

_____ c. The health department must have tried to find the cause of the food poisoning.

_____ d. The publicity about the second Broiler Inn affected the first one.

_____ e. There was an excellent chance of getting food poisoning at the first Broiler Inn.

2. "I would suggest you concentrate your studying on the last chapter of the text," said Professor Howard. "And it would be a good idea to review the grammar rules we've discussed because errors will count against your grade. Finally, I'm going to pass out copies of a short story by Edgar Allan Poe, which will be the basis of an essay question. Study it well. Good luck to you all, and have a nice summer."

_____ a. Professor Moore is teaching an English class.

_____ b. He is a tough grader.

_____ c. The test will be all essay questions.

_____ d. The class has read other short stories by Poe.

_____ e. The test marks the end of the spring session.

3. In the middle of the intersection were an old Chevy Nova and a Cadillac that looked permanently joined, the Nova's front end intruding into the

trunk of the Caddie. Soon, a wail announced the arrival of an ambulance, which pulled up right beside the two cars.

——————— a.   The driver of the Cadillac had stopped suddenly to let an unexpected car pass by.

——————— b.   The Nova had been driving behind the Cadillac.

——————— c.   The driver of the Nova was at fault.

——————— d.   Someone had been hurt in the accident.

——————— e.   Someone riding in the Nova had been hurt.

4. The pleasant heat of the sun made Hector feel sleepy. He felt like shutting his eyes, but he was afraid she might pass by when he wasn't looking. He had seen her here yesterday but hadn't the courage to introduce himself. Maybe today he could remedy that. In the meanwhile, he dug his toes into the sand and watched the children playing at the water's edge.

——————— a.   Hector is at the beach.

——————— b.   He is interested in meeting a particular woman.

——————— c.   He came to the beach especially to meet a woman.

——————— d.   He is afraid of women.

——————— e.   He adores children.

5. Michelle opened the mailbox at the curb and pulled out a white envelope addressed to her and her husband. She opened it before she even reached her front door. She had barely gotten past "Dear Mom and Dad" when tears began streaming down her face. She would have to call Roger and tell him the news.

——————— a.   Michelle lived in that home.

——————— b.   The letter was from her son.

——————— c.   The letter brought sad news.

——————— d.   Michelle felt deeply about the message in the letter.

——————— e.   Roger was Michelle's husband.

8

Understanding Purpose and Tone

An important part of reading critically is realizing that behind everything you read is an author. This author is a person who has a certain reason for writing any particular piece, who works from a personal point of view, and who may reveal more or less of that view in writing. To fully understand and evaluate what you read, you must recognize *purpose*—the reason why the author writes. You must also distinguish *tone*—the manner in which an author's attitude is expressed. Both purpose and tone will be discussed on the pages that follow.

PURPOSE

Authors write with a reason in mind, and you can better evaluate what is being said by determining what that reason is. The author's reason for writing is also called the *purpose* of a selection. Three common purposes are:

To inform—to give you factual information about a subject

To entertain—to amuse you; to appeal to your senses or your imagination

To persuade—to get you to change your mind about a subject

Read each of the three paragraphs below and decide whether the author's purpose is to inform, to entertain, or to persuade. Write your answer in the space provided, and then read the explanations that follow.

1. Using the present measurement system is as inefficient and old-fash-

ioned as using Roman numerals. If more Americans realized how easy it is to convert milliliters to liters as opposed to converting tablespoons to quarts, the metric system would be adopted immediately.

Purpose: _____

2. About 113 billion people have lived and died in the history of our planet, according to scientific estimates. Of all these people, the names of about seven billion, or approximately 6 percent, are recorded in some way—on monuments or in books, manuscripts, and public records. The other 106 billion people are gone without a trace.

Purpose: _____

3. Because of the contrast between his medium-size wardrobe and his extra-large-size body, my brother has made a commitment to only three meals a day. His definition of a meal, however, is as broad as his belly. If we spot a pretzel salesman or a hot-dog stand on our way to an Italian restaurant, for example, he is not beyond suggesting that we stop. "It'll make a good appetizer," he says.

Purpose: _____

In the first paragraph, the writer's purpose is *to persuade* the audience that Americans should change over to the metric system. That is clear because the author claims that our present system is "inefficient and old-fashioned," that conversions in the metric system are "easy," and that people would prefer the metric system. These are statements that are used to convince us rather than to inform us. The purpose of the second paragraph is *to inform*. The author is simply providing readers with information about the number of people who have lived and died on Earth. In paragraph three, the playful and exaggerated details tell us the author's main goal is *to entertain* with humor.

At times, writing may seem to blend two purposes. An informative article on losing weight, for example, may include comic touches, or a persuasive letter to the editor may contain factual information. Remember in such cases to focus on the author's primary purpose. Keep asking yourself, "What is the author's main idea?" That will help you determine his or her principal intention.

▷ Practice

In the space provided, indicate whether the purpose of each statement is primarily to inform (**I**), to persuade (**P**), or to entertain (**E**).

_____ 1. In the 1886 baseball World Series, sixty-three errors were committed.

_____ 2. Nurses assigned to intensive care units should be given shorter shifts and higher pay because the work is unusually demanding and stressful.

_____ 3. It's easy to quit smoking; I've done it hundreds of times.

_____ 4. Shoparama has low, low prices, an outstanding selection of health and beauty products, and a convenient location near you.

_____ 5. I like everything about adulthood except the paperwork.

_____ 6. Alice was easy to trail; she was so preoccupied with her secret anxieties that she never noticed the small space ship that followed her for days.

_____ 7. An artificial odor is added to natural gas so that people can tell whether or not gas is leaking.

_____ 8. The best approach to take when you feel the urge to exercise is to lie down quickly in a darkened room until the feeling goes away.

_____ 9. More women should get involved in local politics and support the growing number of female candidates for public office.

_____ 10. In ancient Egypt priests plucked all the hair from their bodies, including their eyebrows and eyelashes.

TONE

A writer's tone reveals the attitude he or she has toward a subject. Tone is expressed through the words and details the writer selects. Like tone of voice, tone in writing is a clue to the author's feelings and purpose. Any attitude that can be expressed through a tone of voice can be expressed in writing as well. An author can show dislike, respect, admiration, or sympathy—or even choose to laugh at his or her subject.

The box on the next page gives a list of words that are commonly used to describe tone.

To appreciate the differences in tone that writers can employ, read the following versions of a murder confession:

"I have just shot my husband five time in the chest with this .357 Magnum." (Tone: matter-of-fact, objective.)

"How could I ever have killed him? I just can't believe I did that! (Tone: incredulous, surprised.)

"Oh, my God. I've murdered my husband. How can I ever be forgiven for this dreadful deed?" (Tone: remorseful.)

"That dirty rat. He's had it coming for years. I'm glad I finally had the nerve to do it." (Tone: vindictive, revengeful.)

straightforward	sorrowful	cheerful
serious	pessimistic	informal
matter-of-fact	distressed	mocking
objective	regretful	irreverent
formal	remorseful	ironic
bitter	depressed	cynical
cruel	outraged	sarcastic
malicious	angry	joyous
vindictive	indignant	excited
revengeful	critical	chatty
grim	outspoken	sentimental
solemn	arrogant	self-pitying
tragic	comic	impassioned
tolerant	amused	forceful
forgiving	humorous	surprised
sympathetic	playful	disbelieving
compassionate	light-hearted	ambivalent
loving	optimistic	evasive

Practice 1

Below are five statements expressing different attitudes about a shabby apartment. Five different tones are used: *optimistic, tolerant, humorous, bitter,* and *self-pitying.* In the space provided, label each statement according to which of these five tones you think is present. Then read the explanation that follows.

_____ This place is too grim, dingy, and threadbare for anyone to live in.

_____ This isn't the greatest apartment in the world, but it's not really that bad.

_____ If only there were some decent jobs out there, I wouldn't be reduced to living in this miserable dump.

_____ This place does need some repairs, but I expect the landlord to get around to them any day now.

_____ When we move away, we're planning to release three hundred cockroaches and two mice so we can leave the place exactly as we found it.

Item 1 is bitter. The words "grim, dingy, and threadbare" are clues to the writer's angry feelings. In item 2 "not really that bad" shows that the writer is tolerant, accepting the situation while recognizing that it could be better. Self-pitying describes the tone in item 3. The writer blames himself or herself for dropping out of school and refers to being "reduced" to living in a "miserable dump." Item 4 is more optimistic since the writer is expecting repairs to be completed soon. Item 5 is humorous. Its writer claims to be planning a comic revenge on the landlord by returning the apartment to the intolerable condition it was in when the tenants moved in.

A Note on Irony

One commonly used tone is that of irony. When writing has an ironic tone, it says one thing but means the opposite. We frequently use an ironic tone in everyday conversation in the same way writers do. Following are a few examples; notice that the quotation in each says the opposite of what is meant.

If at the beginning of a semester you discover that one of your teachers is particularly demanding, you might comment, "This class is sure going to be a barrel of laughs!"

After seeing a terrible performance in a movie, someone might say about the actor involved, "Now there's a person with a great chance for an Oscar."

If someone is a klutz, we might remark, "There goes an Olympic champion."

Irony also refers to situations in which what happens is the opposite of what we might expect. We could call it ironic, for example, if a man bites a dog. So another way for a writer to be ironic is to describe such situations. Here are a few more examples of this type of irony:

Helen won a lifetime supply of Marlboros a week after she quit smoking.

To get some quick extra cash, Elliot sold his stereo. For his birthday the next day, his girlfriend bought him the new Prince album.

Lenny, who adored basketball, was five feet five inches tall. His brother Frank, who planned on being a meteorologist and had no interest at all in sports, was six feet three.

Practice 2

A.   Below are five statements expressing different attitudes about an upcoming marriage. Five different tones are used: *delighted, cautious, objective, disbelieving*, and *hostile*. In the space provided, label each statement according to which of these five tones you think is present in it.

_____ 1. Al's getting married? Impossible! He's the last guy I expected to see at the altar.

_____ 2. Congratulations, Al! I couldn't be more happy and proud.

_____ 3. If Al marries that snob Bernita, he'll regret it for the rest of his life.

_____ 4. The engagement of Bernita Kaplan and Albert Moore was announced on June 27 at a candlelight dinner party at the home of the bride's parents, Bernice and David Kaplan.

_____ 5. Long engagements are a good idea, Al. Take my advice and don't rush into anything.

B. Below are five statements expressing different attitudes about a manager. Five different tones are used: *admiring, sympathetic, objective, ironic,* and *critical.* In the space provided, label each statement according to which of these five tones you think is present in it.

_____ 6. Tony is an excellent manager—the best one I've ever had.

_____ 7. Under Tony Robertson's leadership, sales in the appliance division have increased thirty per cent in the last six months.

_____ 8. Tony's too ambitious for his own good; if he doesn't change, that ambition will destroy him.

_____ 9. I know Tony's boy has been sick. Naturally it's hard for him to concentrate on work right now.

_____ 10. Tony's wonderful, all right. He's gotten as far as he has without the slightest idea of how to manage a division.

▷ *Practice 3*

The following passages illustrate five different tones, each of which is identified in the box below. In the space provided, put the letter of the tone that applies to each passage.

a.	matter-of-fact	d.	concerned
b.	affectionate	e.	sad
c.	scornful		

_____ 1. Spam—that slimy canned pork product—is surprisingly still around after more than fifty years. Despite its high fat content (more than three and a half teaspoons per two-ounce serving) and high calorie count (171 calories per serving), more than four billion cans have been sold since 1937. Spam's greasy, rubbery consistency and salty flavor have made it the butt of many jokes—such as David Letterman's suggestion of Spam-on-a-rope for people who want to eat and shower at the same time. Shareholders in George Hormel and Company must be laughing all the way to the bank. More than three cans of Spam are consumed every second, despite its high cost—pound for pound it costs about the same as strip steak.

_____ 2. My grandfather lived with my family as I grew up, and some of my warmest early memories revolve around him. He was a sweet man with simple tastes. He liked Western movies, and when I was a preschooler, he often took me along to see them. After the movies, we would go to a nearby Bridgeman's ice-cream shop. He would order a hot chocolate. It always came with a couple of sugar cookies, which he would give to me to eat with my scoop of ice cream. Once I began school, he would go to the Westerns alone. But it wasn't unusual for me to come home from school and find those same sugar cookies waiting for me in a Bridgeman's napkin.

_____ 3. By the year 2000 there will be nearly ten million Americans over the age of eighty. Can we expect these people to be cared for by their relatives, who are themselves in their sixties? If the caregivers are retired, they may have more time to take care of older family members, but the costs of such care (especially in terms of retirement income) are high. As the retirees grow older, the task of caring for older people becomes harder. This is made more difficult by the fact that old age can be distressing because it is a time of continual loss. Too often adults take in ailing, elderly relatives without being aware that they are taking on an immense full-time job. Such caregivers should have somewhere to turn for help.

_____ 4. The bearded chameleon is a lizard native to the cool highlands of Kenya. It often sits in one spot on a branch for days, waiting for an insect or spider to come within range of its sticky tongue, which can extend to a length equal to that of the chameleon's body plus its tail. Thus, a six-inch-long chameleon can have a tongue six inches long. The bearded chameleon is able to hunt when it is only an hour old. At this age it can already grip its perch with its hind feet and tail while it captures its lunch with its long tongue.

_____ 5. My mother died a week after I had given birth to my first child. Mother and I had both wanted desperately for her to see little Emily. And Mom had managed to hang on for months, despite the cancer that was ravaging her body. I had just spoken to her the night before, and my plans were to bring Emily the fifty miles to see Mom that weekend. "I'm going to do it," Mom had said. "I'm going to hold my granddaughter before I die." But it was not to be.

► *Review Test 1: Purpose*

In the space provided, indicate whether the primary purpose of each passage is to inform (I), to persuade (P), or to entertain (E).

_____ 1. The phone rang six times, then seven. Jim hated to answer it, but finally he did. Holding the receiver away from his ear so that it did not touch him, he could hear the tones of his mother's voice as it rose and fell, but he could not understand what she was saying. He felt a certain satisfaction as he looked at his kitchen. Every dish he owned was dirty. Last night he had eaten his take-out pizza on the flowered cake platter, and tonight he was planning to eat it straight out of the box.

_____ 2. Americans love parks and wildlife refuges, but the crowding they find there is a national disgrace. Parking lots are packed, and roadways through parks and refuges are often so jammed that they might as well be the parking lots. Playing fields and barbecue grills are claimed early in the day, and even on remote trails voices can be heard from every direction. Americans badly need more land devoted to open space where nature walks, picnics, and camping can take place in uncrowded tranquility. Communities across the nation should establish parks and trails that provide free access to open space for everyone.

_____ 3. Sediment will sometimes accumulate in shower heads, causing the water to flow unevenly or completely clogging the shower head. Sometimes briskly opening and closing the adjustment mechanism a few times is enough to solve the problem. If this does not work, remove the shower head from the wall, holding onto the pipe while you unscrew the shower head so that you do not loosen the pipe inside the wall. Once you have removed the shower head, try cleaning it with a toothpick or wire. If necessary, take the shower head apart and soak it in water overnight to soften the mineral deposits.

_____ 4. One afternoon a man entered a bar with his dog and ordered two martinis. He drank one martini, and his dog drank the other. The same thing happened for the next three days. On the fifth afternoon, the dog came in alone, and the bartender served him a drink without even asking. The next day the man came in carrying a box. "You were so nice to my dog yesterday that I brought you a present," he said. "It's a king crab." "Oh, thanks," said the bartender. "I'll take him home for dinner." "Oh no," said the man. "He's already had dinner. Why not take him out to a movie instead?"

_____ 5. Students should consider taking life-skills courses in addition to their usual classes. While the ordinary curriculum focuses on skills such as reading, writing, and mathematics, training in life skills teaches people what they need to know in order to live. Training is provided in four basic areas: identity, relationships, decision making, and health. Thus, life skills courses can help people find purpose in their lives, get along with others, solve problems, and lead healthy lives.

_____ 6. Wallace had intended to go through with his wedding, just as his older brothers and his friends had gone through with theirs. But somehow, when Reverend Tindall asked him if he would take Bonnie as his wedded wife, he said, "No, not really" in a loud, clear voice. He was just as surprised as everyone else was. People milled around, some of them crying and some of them raising their voices in angry or excited tones. Eventually he decided that he might as well go to Bermuda since he had the plane tickets. He was in his hotel room overlooking the beach before he started to cry about what had happened and then after a while started to laugh.

_____ 7. During the fifties and sixties, researchers discovered that monosodium glutamate (MSG), commonly used to flavor foods, caused brain damage in baby rats, mice, and monkeys. In 1970, a National Academy of Sciences committee concluded that MSG in food is unlikely to harm human infants, but the committee nevertheless recommended that MSG not be used in baby food. By then, however, the baby-food industry had already stopped using MSG because of public pressure.

_____ 8. If you want to encourage your children to be open with you, you must give them respect and make time for their needs. When they want to talk, stop watching television or doing household chores—just as you would do if an adult friend wished to talk. Concentrate on hearing and understanding their viewpoints rather than constantly interrupting with opinions and advice. When they see you really care about what they are thinking and feeling, they won't feel it is useless to tell you what is on their minds.

►*Review Test 2: Tone*

A. Each passage illustrates one of the four different tones in the box below. In the space provided, put the letter of the tone that applies in each case.

---

a.	objective	c.	sentimental
b.	self-pitying	d.	indignant

_____ 1. Emperor penguins are among the most adorable animals in the world. Like all penguins, they look like cute little people dressed in tuxedos. They flap their wings and waddle into the water in an utterly charming way. The most enchanting thing they do is care for their sweet little babies. The newborn chick squats on its father's feet, where it is warmed by his body and cared for affectionately until its mother returns from a hunting trip to find food. Emperor penguins love their babies so much that they have been known to try to hatch blocks of ice if their own little ones die. This is a delightful testimony to the power of parental affection.

_____ 2. When I agreed in September to put out the newsletter, I wanted to create something that would unite the residents in our community. Now, due to lack of support from you, I must discontinue. I had assumed that residents would welcome and support the newsletter. Only one resident, Cindy Sherwood, answered my pleas for help with distributing the newsletter. I have been willing to volunteer a great deal of time to working on this project, yet no one has come to the meetings I have planned to discuss it. There has been a total lack of response when I asked for ideas and input. It seems that I'm the only person in this community who really cares.

_____ 3. The first radio advertisement was broadcast on August 28, 1922, on New York station WEAF. A real estate firm, Queensboro Corporation, bought a ten-minute segment for one hundred dollars in order to advertise its apartments. According to the advertisement, the apartment complex, Hawthorne Court, was named after the American author Nathaniel Hawthorne. The apartments were described as conveniently near the subway but also "right at the boundaries of God's great outdoors" near golf and tennis courts and other "pleasure-giving, health-giving activities." As a result of the advertisements, two apartments were sold, and commercial radio was born.

_____ 4. Relentless greed and appalling dishonesty characterized the treatment of Indians in the 1860's and 1870's, when massacres of native Americans were commonplace. The massacre at Sand Creek in Colorado in 1864 was sadly typical. The territorial governor had persuaded the Indians to gather there and had promised them protection. Despite this pledge, Colonel J. M. Chivington's militia attacked the defenseless Indian camp. They disregarded that sacred symbol, the American flag, and the white flag of truce that the Indians were flying at Sand Creek. Four hundred fifty peaceful Indians—men, women, and children—were slaughtered in what has been called "the foulest and most unjustified crime in the annals of America." This was only one of the heartless massacres that history records.

B. Each passage illustrates one of the four different tones identified in the box below. In the space provided, put the letter of the tone that applies in each case.

a.	objective	c.	indignant
b.	pleading	d.	complimentary

_____ 5. Recently I shared a book with a little girl from a home where no one reads. When I finished the book, the girl urged, "Read it again." I was reading one of my own books, *Barbie and the Bandits*, so her request was one of the most satisfying I could receive. Yet what I felt was not pleasure, but dismay. This little girl's family, like many families, is indifferent to books. What will happen to children from homes like these? Will they ever learn to love books? It is unlikely, unless you do something. I know you believe in the joy and power of reading. Don't let the burdens you face—cataloguing books, preparing budgets, and meeting with the library board—keep you from a more important purpose: bringing the joy of reading to children who might otherwise never know it.

_____ 6. All animals that move have home ranges, the areas they use to find food, to mate, and to care for their young. Some animals are also territorial. This means individuals, pairs, or groups maintain exclusive use of specific areas. Controlling territories singly or in pairs is the most efficient way to use an abundant and predictable food supply. Some birds and bottom-dwelling fish have this type of territory. On the other hand, group control of territories works best when the food supply is unpredictable or unevenly distributed. Baboons, wolves, hyenas, and lions have group territories.

_____ 7. *Stepping Out* provides a wealth of valuable advice on where to go and what to do for a perfect day or evening on the town. In this practical, readable book, Mary Beth Cho provides a superb account of the area's attractions. She has an insider's eye for events and places where you will be sure to enjoy yourself immensely. With *Stepping Out* as your guide, you will find yourself doing things you never even dreamed of before— and having the time of your life.

_____ 8. When I hired Atlas Carpets to install a new wall-to-wall carpet in my living room, I relied on your firm's excellent reputation for quality work. However, as I have told you repeatedly on the telephone, I am deeply dissatisfied with the job you did in my home. In one corner near the fireplace the carpeting is poorly fitted, and some of the flooring shows through. Some of the tacks are already coming loose, and I have had to hammer them in again myself even though I have a bad back. Moreover, one of your workmen put a hot cup down on my coffee table, leaving a stain for which I hold you responsible. If we cannot agree to a reasonable adjustment promptly, I will turn the whole matter over to my lawyer, as well as tell all my friends about my exasperating experience with Atlas.

9

Detecting Bias and Propaganda

On the television police drama *Dragnet*, whenever a witness would begin to speak emotionally, the hero, Sgt. Joe Friday, would ask for "just the facts." He wanted neutral, unbiased information—the kind that can be proven true or false—rather than the witness's interpretation of what happened.

The kind of information Sgt. Friday preferred, however, isn't easy to come by. Most speakers and writers include their point of view in what they communicate. What they say is therefore *biased*. It is based, at least partly, on their own particular view of a subject.

While a certain amount of bias is unavoidable, many writers do try to remain as objective as possible. News articles, encyclopedia entries, and scientific reports are examples of writing in which the authors try to be unbiased. Other writers, however, make no effort to conceal their point of view. Their goal is to try to convince readers who have different viewpoints to change their minds. Examples of this kind of writing are editorials, political speeches, and advertisements.

Writing intended to convert readers to a particular point of view is sometimes called *propaganda*. Propaganda can be used to sell products, to elect political candidates, or to change people's minds about social or religious issues. The point of view may be good or bad, and the arguments used may be valid or invalid.

Both neutral and biased writing can be valuable. As a reader, however, you must be able to tell one kind from the other. Just as some people end up agreeing with everyone they talk to, some readers believe that if something is in print, it's probably true. Do not make this mistake. Your goal should be to think for yourself, and a knowledge of bias and propaganda should protect you from being too easily persuaded.

BIASED LANGUAGE

Look at the following sentences:

1.   Frank spends very little money.

2.   Frank is thrifty.

3.   Frank is a cheapskate.

Each of these three sentences describes the same person and behavior. The first one is entirely *neutral*. It simply tells what Frank does without making a judgment about it. The second one, by using the word "thrifty," hints that Frank should be praised for his careful money management. By using the word "cheapskate," the third sentence strongly suggests that Frank's behavior is undesirable.

Just by choosing one word rather than another, an author expresses a viewpoint. In choosing the phrase "spends very little money," the writer of the first sentence remained objective—neither for Frank nor against him. The writer of the second sentence expressed a bias in Frank's favor, and the writer of the third sentence expressed a bias against him. Word choices like the positive word "thrifty" and the negative word "cheapskate" are sometimes called "emotionally loaded" or simply "loaded" words. In addition to their dictionary meaning or *denotation*, they also carry an extra "load" of emotional meaning or *connotation*. This emotional loading allows the writer to express a positive or negative attitude towards a subject.

Suppose you were writing the following sentence and had to choose between the two words in parentheses. Which word choice suggests a bias?

Cynthia performed her work so (a. slowly; b. dreamily) that everyone else was finished before she was half done.

The biased word is *b*. The first word, "slowly," describes Cynthia's pace without interpreting it. She may daydream; on the other hand, she may be an especially careful person or merely someone who does not think as quickly as her coworkers. The second word, "dreamily," interprets her slow pace. It suggests she should work faster and could speed up if she would only keep her mind on what she was doing.

▷ *Practice 1*

Each sentence below can be completed in two ways, one neutral and the other biased. Choose the letter that identifies the biased word, and write it on the line next to each sentence.

_____ 1. An old (a. tramp; b. man) asked us for a dollar.

_____ 2. The personnel manager spoke to us (a. briefly; b. abruptly).

_____ 3. The company will introduce its (a. improved; b. new) detergent next week.

_____ 4. Mr. Meyers told the (a. teenagers; b. rowdies) to get off his lawn.

_____ 5. The speaker (a. lectured; b. babbled) about fashion design for an hour.

Longer passages may contain a whole series of words that work together to suggest a bias. These words are meant to cause emotional reactions in readers. The following passage describes creation science (the belief that the account of creation in the Bible can be proven scientifically) from the viewpoint of someone who does not believe in it. Select the group of words from the three groups below that reveal the author's bias, and write its letter on the line provided. Then read the explanation that follows.

Biased words: _____

> "Creation science" is not often taught in schools for the simple reason that it is false. Good teachers understand how false it is and how it undermines the very nature of science. What could destroy good teaching faster than a law compelling honorable teachers to betray their sacred trust by giving equal time to ideas they know to be not only false but also intellectually dishonest?

a. simple, understand, teaching, law

b. undermines, honorable, sacred, dishonest

c. creation, science, ideas, intellectually

The words "undermines" (which suggests the action of enemy agents destroying something secretly from within), "honorable," "sacred," and "dishonest" are all loaded words that indicate the writer's bias against creation science. The correct answer, then, is _b_. In the remainder of the essay from which this passage is taken, the writer may give excellent reasons for believing that creation science is wrong and dangerous. Here, though, he or she is simply expressing a bias in strong terms.

▷ *Practice 2*

Read the passages below to see if you can detect the words that reveal the authors' bias. Write the letter of the biased language in the space provided.

_____ 1. Food additives are far better for people than irresponsible activists would have us believe. Public prejudice against additives has led to the elimination of propionates from bread. Because these valuable additives have been eliminated, large amounts of bread have been wasted.

    a.   irresponsible, activists, prejudice, valuable

    b.   food, people, believe, led

    c.   additives, public, propionates, bread

_____ 2.   Some genetic disorders are untreatable cripplers and killers. Pioneers in the prevention of these disorders advocate the use of amniocentesis. In this painless procedure, a thin needle is inserted in the pregnant woman's abdomen to retrieve a small amount of fluid to be tested. If the test shows that a fetus has an untreatable disease, the pregnancy can be aborted.

    a.   genetic, advocate, procedure, abdomen

    b.   amniocentesis, needle, fluid, fetus

    c.   cripplers, killers, pioneers, painless

_____ 3.   Some parents are dressing their two-year-olds in outrageously expensive designer clothing and adorable little two-hundred-dollar running shoes. Upscale dogs are even being fed gourmet chow at two dollars a pound. When so many people are unemployed or underemployed in this country, the wealthy should hesitate to waste their money on such pretensions.

    a.   dressing, chow, country, money

    b.   outrageously, waste, pretensions

    c.   designer, dollars, unemployed, wealthy

Half-Truths

Half-truths are another way to express biases. A *half-truth* combines a fact and an interpretation. Once readers accept the factual part of the statement, they are often willing to accept the rest of it without checking very closely. But the interpretive part really needs additional evidence to support it, which the writer does not include. Take the following statement, for example:

> Medical malpractice suits are more common than ever before because everyone distrusts doctors nowadays.

The first part of this statement, "Medical malpractice suits are more common than ever," is a fact, as statistics on the number and kinds of lawsuits filed in American courts clearly show. Many television shows and newspaper articles have been devoted to this subject, so most readers are prepared to accept it as true even if they don't recall the details.

The second half of the statement, however, is an unjustified conclusion. The increase in medical malpractice might arise from exactly the opposite reason: most people nowadays have so much faith in doctors in general that when a cure fails to work, they assume that their own doctor was negligent. Or the increase might have been caused because more and more patients know about their right to sue (perhaps because lawyers have recently been permitted to advertise). An accurate explanation may be a combination of these reasons or of others.

The following statement is another half-truth. Cross out the part that is an unjustified interpretation:

> You kids must be watching too much MTV because you're getting C's and D's in school.

If you crossed out the first part ("You kids must be watching too much MTV"), you are correct. Sometimes people who are biased against something think it is the cause of many problems. Perhaps some students do watch a lot of music videos. However, the problem here may not be too much MTV but simply too little studying. It might be possible for the students to continue watching as much MTV as they do and still improve their grades.

▷ *Practice 3*

The following items are half true—half fact and half interpretation. In each item, cross out the part that is an unjustified interpretation or a conclusion.

1. Sharon Hogan is a genius; her most recent movie has been very successful.

2. President Chun Doo Hwan announced that South Korea will hold elections next month, proving that modern democracy is a far stronger force than Communism.

3. An excellent day-care program is guaranteed because parents serve as volunteers.

4. The Brewers lost three games in a row, proving that they will never be a successful team.

5. Very few people ran for campus offices this year, which shows that students today are more cynical and apathetic than they were in the past.

Stereotypes

A comedian once came up with the following definition: "Hell is the place where the British do the cooking, the Germans tell the jokes, and the French direct the traffic." This bit of humor, if taken literally, suggests some startling "facts": that British people cannot prepare a tasty meal, that German people have no sense of humor, and that French people cannot drive.

These statements cannot possibly be true. Countless English eat well, Germans laugh, and French reach their destinations by automobile every day. The comedian who first told the joke was basing it on a kind of bias known as *stereotyping*. A stereotype is a combination of two kinds of biased thinking. First, the speaker *assumes* that members of a particular group of people have a certain way of thinking or acting. Then, the speaker *generalizes*: if *some* members of the group are like this, then they *all* are. The resulting unfair generalization is the stereotype of that particular group of people. And if the speaker then decides, on the basis of this stereotype, that he or she would rather not be with these people, the speaker is guilty of something even more serious: prejudice.

To some degree, we all tend to think stereotypically. Close your eyes for a moment and try to visualize each of the following people:

- a police officer
- a fashion model
- a star basketball player
- a librarian

If you saw the police officer as a burly male, the model and the librarian as either a very attractive or very unattractive female, and the basketball star as black, you are assuming that *all* police or librarians or models or basketball players have the same gender, race, or physical description. In other words, you are using stereotypes.

See if you can detect the stereotyped thinking in the example below. After you read it, answer these two questions: a. What group of people is being stereotyped? b. What is the speaker assuming about all of these people? Write your answers on the lines. Then read the explanation that follows.

"I don't want to live in that dorm. It's full of athletes. I'll never get any studying done if I live there."

Group being stereotyped: _____

Assumption: _____

The group being stereotyped is college athletes, and the assumption being made about them is that they are too busy practicing (or partying) to spend much time with their books. They would therefore be a bad influence on the speaker, who would rather study than play (in either sense). Actually, many college athletes are on scholarships and must keep their grades above a certain average to remain in school. And just as many know how to give equal time to sports and studies. Unfortunately, some biased speakers or writers don't recognize these things. They have made up their minds in advance.

▷ *Practice 4*

Each of the items below contains stereotyped thinking. On the lines below the item, identify (a) the group of people that is being stereotyped and (b) the assumption that is being made about them.

1. I don't want Terry and Mac in our house any more. I hear they're members of a motorcycle gang.

   Group being stereotyped: _____

   Assumption: _____

2. No wonder Rita is always getting into fights with her husband. She's a redhead, isn't she?

   Group being stereotyped: _____

   Assumption: _____

3. Girls have no business trying to play Little League baseball. Baseball is too rough a sport for them, even at that age.

   Group being stereotyped: _____

   Assumption: _____

4. No matter when I call Dr. Putter, his answering service says he's not in his office. He must really enjoy his golf game.

   Group being stereotyped: _____

   Assumption: _____

5. It's no use offering anyone in that family a job. They've been on welfare for as long as I can remember.

   Group being stereotyped: _____

   Assumption: _____

Omitted Details

Part of every writer's job is to choose what information to include and what to omit. This right to choose also carries a responsibility. When making a case, writers are occasionally tempted to omit facts that disprove their arguments. Writers should face those facts and either explain why they do not apply, or, if that proves impossible, modify their original arguments. But the temptation to take a short cut and ignore unpleasant facts is sometimes too strong to resist.

In legal language, deliberately leaving out inconvenient facts is called "suppressing evidence." In advertising, such evidence is sometimes suppressed in the interests of selling a product. For example, advertisements for the drug Tylenol call it "the pain reliever hospitals use most," and this statement is perfectly true. What these advertisements fail to mention is that the manufacturer of Tylenol offers hospitals large discounts. Since other drug companies do not offer similar discounts, most hospital administrators choose to buy Tylenol. They probably would not do so if Tylenol did not work as well as other similar drugs, but the advertising campaign depends on people jumping to the conclusion, "Hospitals use more Tylenol than any other pain reliever. They must consider it the best drug of its kind available."

Read the following passage and then the list of omitted details below it. Then decide which of the missing details you think Credit Information Services deliberately left out of its ad.

> For only forty dollars, Credit Information Services will provide a copy of your credit report. Haven't you been wondering what information a potential lender gets when you apply for a loan? Now you will have all the information you need for a single low yearly fee.

Missing details:

a.   Each additional use of this service will cost only thirty-five dollars.

b.   Credit Information Services already has 300,000 customers nationwide.

c.   Federal law gives you the right to find out what is in your credit report—free.

Answer: _____

If you chose *c*, you are right. If you know this detail, you are not likely to send forty dollars to Credit Information Services.

▷ Practice 5

Which of the details missing from the paragraphs below does the reader need to know in order to avoid being tricked? Choose the detail that the advertiser has intentionally omitted and write its number in the answer space provided.

_____ 1.   Congratulations! You have just won an all-expenses-paid three-night vacation to Atlantic City, New Jersey. You will dine at glamorous restaurants, enjoy stage shows, and swim in the beautiful Atlantic Ocean—all free. This free trip has been awarded to only a handful of selected winners in your area.
     a.   The voucher for your free trip will arrive by registered mail within two weeks of your acceptance of this offer.

    b.   You may stay at your choice of two casino hotels: Trump's Castle or Resorts International.

    c.   You must pay $399 to join a travel club before you become eligible for your free trip.

_____ 2.   For a set fee you can make as many long-distance calls as you wish at special times. This is your chance to get back in touch with all the family members and friends you've been meaning to call. Now you can afford the pleasure of talking regularly with the people who mean the most to you. Talk as long as you wish to anyone in the continental United States for only one hundred dollars a month.

    a.   Merely dial the number you want. You need not dial extra access numbers.

    b.   The service is available now in your area.

    c.   Calls can be made only between 10 P.M. and 6 A.M.

_____ 3.   Sunnyside College offers a wide choice of majors, ranging from liberal studies to high technology. On its beautiful campus students can take advantage of up-to-date laboratory equipment, an Olympic-sized swimming pool, and a new four-story library. The faculty are well known for their contributions to scholarly and scientific research, but more importantly, for their commitment to students.

    a.   More than eighty percent of the students are from the northeastern part of the country.

    b.   Fewer than one third of the entering students graduate.

    c.   More people major in high technology than in liberal studies.

Sources

Another important question about anything you read is "Who wrote it?" Sometimes you will recognize the name of an author because you have read something by him or her before. Your recollection of the author's bias in works you have already read might serve as a guide to the work you are now reading.

Similarly, certain publishers or other organizations are more likely to produce works with particular biases. For example, the magazine *Consumer Reports*, published by Consumers Union, a consumer protection group, is far more likely to contain an article critical of big business than is a pamphlet published by the Better Business Bureau, an organization of business people. Religious organizations and political groups of all sorts have a right to express their opinions. However, you should be alert to their biases. If a publication is distributed free of charge, it is more likely to express a biased point of view than if it is for sale. People who distribute free literature usually have a strong—and probably selfish—motive for doing so.

Read the following passage, for example, and decide which of the three publications listed below it might have been its source:

> You have the right to know the purposes of any tests your doctor gives you. Insist on being told why a test is being given and what your doctor hopes to find out from the results. The doctor is obligated to tell you of any risks involved in taking the test. He or she should also inform you how much the test will cost and how long it will take. Once the results of the test are available, you have the right to a clear explanation of what the results mean.

The source of this passage is most likely to be:

a. a textbook for medical students

b. a pamphlet published by a consumer group

c. a press release publicizing a new kind of blood test

The most likely source for this passage is *b*, a pamphlet published by a consumer group. For one thing, it is plainly addressed to patients rather than doctors. But more important, by telling patients how to protect themselves against unnecessary and costly tests, it reveals a bias toward the consumer's point of view.

▷ *Practice 6*

Look for the bias in each passage below. Then identify the likely source in each case.

1. Few people die in hotel fires. Most of those that do are not burned to death but die as a result of panic, which usually results because people have not stopped to think about what they would do in case of a fire. When you check into your room, take a moment to locate the exits and the nearest fire alarm. This simple precaution will help to ensure that you have a safe and enjoyable stay.

    What is the most likely source of this passage? _____

    a. a brochure provided by the owners of the hotel
    b. a letter to a newspaper from a woman whose husband was killed in a hotel fire
    c. a novel set in a large hotel

2. The people of North Brookfield are completely forgotten until something goes wrong. We feel the pain of having been shut out too long. Too many of us are unemployed. Too often we face discrimination. In three years the streets in this neighborhood have never been swept, and

our repeated complaints about the need for sewer repairs have been ignored. The county never forgets to collect taxes from us, but when it comes to doing what needs to be done, we are forgotten.

What is the most likely source of this passage? _____

a. a report from the tax collector of Brookfield County
b. a scholarly article by a sociology professor at Brookfield College
c. a letter to a newspaper from a resident of North Brookfield

3. Why should cable television customers be trapped into choosing between one cable company and no service at all? Just as people choose cars and clothing, they should be able to choose among competing cable companies. This kind of free choice is the basis of our free enterprise system. And this competition will have direct benefits for you: lower prices, better programming, and improved service.

What is the most likely source of this passage? _____

a. a letter to city residents from a cable company that wants to begin offering service
b. a textbook for a college course in the mass media
c. an article in a local newspaper

A Final Word about Bias

Knowing that a publication is biased does not necessarily mean that you should not read it. Some articles and books are so biased that they are almost worthless, but the vast majority are simply trying to express a particular viewpoint as effectively as possible. A good strategy is to read the article or book as if you have been assigned to write an essay disagreeing with it. This method will help you to spot the weak points in the opposing argument and at the same time learn why the author feels as he or she does. And you might find the reading experience informative—or even convincing. Sometimes, after trying our hardest to disprove a particular argument, we wind up agreeing with it.

PROPAGANDA TECHNIQUES

Clear thinking is hard work. To construct a valid argument, you must organize your thoughts, make certain all your evidence leads logically to your conclusion, and then check again to make sure your conclusion follows logically from the evidence. Evaluating other people's arguments is almost equally difficult. You must check to see if they have organized their thoughts and conclusions in the same logical way. No wonder it is said, "You can fool some of the people all of the time and all of the people some of the time."

It is much easier to accept arguments at their face value than to evaluate them properly.

Many people who use propaganda, however, care more about the cause they are trying to promote than about making sound arguments. They rely on the fact that most people cannot or will not evaluate arguments intelligently. As a result, propagandists are able to use many unsound forms of argument about important issues to make up people's minds for them. Here are some of the most popular.

1   Bandwagon

Old-fashioned parades usually began with a large wagon carrying a brass band. To "jump on the bandwagon," therefore, means to join a parade. For example, we are often told to buy a product or vote for a political candidate because, in effect, "everybody else is doing it." An ad for a cereal may claim that "Taste-O's is Everybody's Favorite Breakfast." A political commercial may show people from all walks of life all saying they will vote for Candidate Harry Hogwash. The ads imply that if you don't jump on the bandwagon, the parade will pass you by.

Here are two examples of real TV ads that have used the bandwagon appeal:

> To a background of appealing music, shots of many people wearing the sponsor's jeans appear on the screen.

> On a beautiful day, almost everyone on the beach leaves in a hurry in order to attend the sponsor's sale.

2   Testimonial

Famous athletes often appear on television as spokespersons for all sorts of products, from soft drinks to automobiles. Movie stars make commercials endorsing products and political issues. The idea behind this approach is that the testimony of famous people influences viewers that admire these people.

What viewers must remember is that famous people get paid to endorse products. In addition, these people are not necessarily experts about the products or political issues they promote. This does not in itself mean that what they say is untrue. But realizing that celebrities receive money to recommend products that they may know little about may help consumers think twice about such messages.

Here are two examples of real ads that have used the appeal of testimonials:

> A famous comedienne, now a senior citizen, promotes a cleaner for false teeth.

A popular singer with a wholesome image is spokesperson for a breakfast cereal.

3 Transfer

Just as advertisers try to improve the images of their products by paying celebrities to endorse them, they also try to associate the products with symbols that people respect or revere. Calling an automobile "The All-American Car" appeals to prospective buyers' patriotism. So does using an eagle as a symbol, as the United States Post Office knows, judging by its "Express Mail" service.

Consider some other examples as well. Political candidates often take care to speak with an American flag in the background or have themselves photographed at a Fourth of July picnic. Calling one's business the "American Widget Company" may attract some customers, even though the business is no more American than any other U. S. company that makes the same kind of product. There is also a good deal of transfer value in children, pets, or good-looking actors and actresses. Consumers transfer the positive feelings they have towards an appealing-looking person or animal to the product being advertised.

Finally, here are two examples of real ads that have used the transfer appeal:

A picture of a cuddly-looking child adorns packages of toilet paper.

An insurance company associates itself with a cliff made of rock, a symbol of a dependable presence for years to come.

4 Plain Folks

Some people distrust political candidates who are rich or well educated. They feel that these candidates, if elected, will not be able to understand the problems of the average working person. Therefore, candidates often try to show they are just "plain folks" by referring in their speeches to how poor they were when they were growing up or how they had to work their way through school. They also pose for photographs wearing overalls or buying a hot dog from a curbside vendor. Likewise, the presidents of some companies appear in their own ads, trying to show that their giant enterprises are just family businesses. If a corporation can convince potential customers that it is run by people just like them, the customers are more likely to buy the corporation's product than if they felt it was run by ruthless millionaire executives. In other words, people using the plain-folks approach tell their audience, "We are ordinary folks, just like you."

Here are two examples of real ads that have used the appeal of plain folks:

Characters representing friendly, down-to-earth men promote an alcoholic beverage.

Average-looking American kids are shown trying and enjoying a cereal.

5 Name Calling

Name calling is the use of emotionally loaded names, or labels, to turn people against a rival product, candidate, or movement. An example of name calling would be a political candidate's labeling an opponent "uncaring," "radical," or "a wimp." Or a manufacturer may say or imply that a competing product is "full of chemicals," though in reality everything is made up of chemicals of one kind or another. Or one group may call another group's beliefs "un-American" when all they mean is that they disapprove of them.

Here are two examples of name calling taken from real life:

In the early days of the "cold war" with the Soviet Union, in the 1950s, an exaggerated concern about communism in this country brought charges of un-Americanism against many.

A fast-food chain accuses a competitor of having small hamburgers, using the charge "Where's the beef?"

6 Glittering Generalities

In a sense, all propaganda techniques use generalities. A generality is a form of emotional language that sounds impressive but really says nothing important. A glittering generality is an important-sounding claim about some product, candidate, or cause that cannot be proved true or false because it really says little or nothing. One form of glittering generality, used in selling, is called *puffery*. "You won't find a better TV set on the market!" a salesperson might say. Later, if you think you have, it is just your opinion against the TV salesperson's. "Janet Jones has the Right Stuff! Vote Jones for Congress," a campaign slogan might claim. But what seems like "the right stuff" to her campaign manager might seem very wrong to you. The point is that the phrase sounds good but says nothing definite.

Here are two examples of glittering generalities that have been used:

A popular beverage is promoted as "The Real Thing."

A canned-food ad boasts of "nutrition that works."

▷ *Practice 7*

In each pair of sentences below, the first sentence does not illustrate a propaganda technique, but the second one does. On the line, write the letter of the propaganda technique used in the second sentence.

_____ 1. Many parents enroll infants in day-care centers.
Only a bad parent would enroll an infant in a day-care center.
a. bandwagon   c. testimonial
b. transfer   d. name calling

_____ 2. Sureguard sunglasses are dark enough to filter out harmful ultraviolet rays.
"I'm proud to wear Sureguard sunglasses," says actress Judy Winsor. "You'll love them too."
a. testimonial   c. plain folks
b. transfer   d. name calling

_____ 3. As a young man, Candidate Alan Wilson had a variety of jobs working in offices and on a farm.
As a young man, Candidate Alan Wilson learned what it means to work hard by spending long hours in the fields as a farm laborer.
a. name calling   c. plain folks
b. bandwagon   d. glittering generalities

_____ 4. Two recent polls suggest that Dick Levy may win next week's election.
Add your vote to the landslide victory Dick Levy will win in next week's election.
a. bandwagon   c. transfer
b. testimonial   d. name calling

_____ 5. Starn pianos are sold in every major city in the United States.
Starn pianos are used in the finest concert halls around the world.
a. plain folks   c. bandwagon
b. name calling   d. testimonial

_____ 6. Stamp collecting is a fascinating educational hobby.
Comedian Bill Groff says, "Stamp collecting is a fascinating educational hobby."
a. glittering generalities   c. testimonial
b. plain folks   d. name calling

_____ 7. Twin Oaks is a residential development near Des Moines, Iowa.
There's nothing else quite like Twin Oaks, an exclusive residential community where you will be proud to live.
a. bandwagon   c. transfer
b. testimonial   d. glittering generalities

_____ 8. People who do not shovel their walks immediately after storms are subject to a fine under Municipal Law 1364A.
People who do not shovel their walks immediately after storms are inconsiderate and selfish.
a. plain folks   c. glittering generalities
b. name calling   d. transfer

_____ 9. Country-Style Butter does not contain artificial coloring or preservatives.

Old-fashioned Country-Style Butter is just like the butter your mother used to serve.

a.	plain folks	c.	glittering generalities
b.	testimonial	d.	transfer

_____ 10. Linda Byrne will make an impressive mayor; her record as deputy mayor and state senator shows that she is an excellent speaker, a hard worker, and a capable administrator.

Linda Byrne will make an impressive mayor; she's a natural wonder.

a.	bandwagon	c.	glittering generalities
b.	testimonial	d.	transfer

► *Review Test 1: Bias*

A. Each passage below contains some examples of biased language. On the line next to the passage, write the letter of the group of words that reveals the author's bias.

_____ 1. In the last ten years, five hundred children have been born to surrogate mothers, women who were paid to bear children and then give them up. This situation raises some deeply troubling questions. How will the children of surrogate mothers feel when they are old enough to realize that their natural mothers sold them? Will they ever be able to give and receive love naturally after their unnatural births? Surrogate motherhood is an abominable experiment conducted at the expense of innocent children. Tragically, in this situation the sins of the parents will be visited upon their children.

a.	paid, sold, visited	c.	children, mothers, love
b.	questions, realize, situation	d.	unnatural, abominable, tragically

_____ 2. Unsuspecting readers of your magazine have some disappointments in store if they enjoy going to movies. My wife and I were looking forward to seeing *Wicked Werewolves* until we read your review, which completely spoiled the movie for us. Its author thoughtlessly revealed that both Terry and his brother would be transformed into gruesome creatures with the eerie ability to read the minds of their victims. Worse, the photograph next to the review clearly showed Terry being killed with a silver harpoon. Printing this review was irresponsible, and it ruined the movie's impact for everyone who read it. After this, leave the storytelling to the movie makers.

     a. thoughtlessly, irresponsible,   c. review, ability, photograph
       ruined   d. completely, revealed, impact
     b. enjoy, forward, clearly

_____ 3. Parents with children are increasingly finding themselves on the street with no place to go. When the homeless were mostly single men and women, the situation was bad enough. Today, almost a third of the homeless are families, and, sadly, the numbers are growing. Life on the street can be devastating for children. Facing the taunts of schoolmates is hard enough, but the frightening risks of sleeping on the street or in a shelter are worse.

     a. sadly, devastating, frightening   c. homeless, numbers, sleeping
     b. street, situation, single   d. place, schoolmates, shelter

_____ 4. The recent political campaign was more brutal than any in recent memory. The candidates guilty of the mudslinging offered extremely weak excuses for their excesses. Not surprisingly, each one blamed someone else for starting the negative campaigning, and they all claimed that rather than running dirty campaigns, they were merely alerting people to their opponents' faults. But nasty references to opponents' family life and education have no place in a campaign that should educate voters about candidates' policies.

     a. campaign, recent, alerting   c. mudslinging, dirty, nasty
     b. memory, starting, family   d. candidates, people, policies

   B. Each passage below has one sentence that contains biased language. On the line next to the passage, write the number of the sentence that contains biased language.

_____ 5. [1]Grilling hot dogs is a popular summer pastime, but any way you cook them, hot dogs are among America's favorite foods. [2]A typical hot dog is firm and moist, and most are mildly seasoned. [3]A few have a delicious smoky flavor, and innovative manufacturers have recently produced a clever new idea, hot dogs stuffed with cheese and even chili sauce, producing a marvelous blend of flavors. [4]And the newest poultry franks have less than ninety calories per hot dog.

_____ 6. [1]Do you feel obligated to read all the mail you get, regardless of its worth? [2]Probably as little as half the mail you receive is personal. [3]The rest is a combination of advertisements, catalogues, sweepstake offers, letters soliciting contributions, and other mail aimed at separating you from your money. [4]Are you still opening and reading all this unrequested and unwanted mail? [5]It's time to free yourself from this foolish habit and toss your obnoxious junk mail where it belongs—in the trash. [6]You didn't ask for it, and you don't have to read it.

_____ 7. [1]Would you like lovely, healthy-looking skin undamaged by the harshness of the sun's rays? [2]Sun can thicken your skin and eventually wrinkle and dry it. [3]But you can prevent such effects by choosing one of the many sun screens on the market today. [4]The higher the sun-protection factor of the sun screen you select, the longer you can stay in the sun without burning. [5]Apply the sun screen before you go out into the sun to give sun-blocking ingredients a chance to start to work, and reapply it throughout your stay in the sun, especially if you perspire.

_____ 8. [1]After Sarin Rom came to this country from Cambodia ten years ago, he went to work stocking shelves in a local grocery store. [2]Today, he manages Apex Grocery, which is located at the corner of Main Street and Fifth Avenue. [3]Business at Apex Grocery has increased during each year of Sarin's management. [4]He usually works twelve to eighteen hours a day, supervising employees and helping customers. [5]A typical immigrant to this country from the Far East, this hard-working man inspires respect and esteem in all who are privileged to know him.

▶ *Review Test 2: Propaganda*

Each of the passages below illustrates a particular propaganda technique. On the line next to the passage, write the letter of the technique being used.

_____ 1. The most beautiful hair this season has shape, style, and a luxuriant, natural feel. Leslie Langtree, the television actress whose lovely hair is her trademark, reveals that her secret is Flirt. "Flirt softens my hair and gives it great body," Leslie says. "Thanks to Flirt, my hair has never looked better."

    a. plain folks   c. name calling
    b. testimonial   d. bandwagon

_____ 2. Senator Bernita Walters does not know the most elementary facts about how to represent her state. To call her a legislator is laughable. She is dishonest, lazy, and stupid—the last person you should consider supporting in next fall's election.
    a. glittering generalities   c. testimonial
    b. transfer   d. name calling

_____ 3. Liberty Bell Airlines flies anywhere in this great land, from sea to shining sea. We proudly hail America's finest: Liberty Bell.
    a. plain folks   c. transfer
    b. testimonial   d. name calling

_____ 4. Monroe Archer is a millionaire and the president of a large corporation, yet he has never lost touch with his small-town roots. Despite his power and fame, he still likes returning to his hometown to enjoy a summer band concert and a simple supper at Charley's Diner.
   a. name calling   c. plain folks
   b. bandwagon   d. testimonial

_____ 5. Feel like a princess on your wedding day! Beth's Bridal Shop features exact replicas of the stunning dresses worn by Great Britain's royal brides, Lady Di and Fergie, whose weddings were televised all over the world. With a dress from Beth's Bridal Shop, you can have the same glamor and prestige on your own wedding day.
   a. transfer   c. plain folks
   b. glittering generalities   d. name calling

_____ 6. Come one! Come all! Everybody's going to Linwood Furniture for the big eighth annual sale, a sale so big we rented a tent to hold it all!
   a. name calling   c. transfer
   b. bandwagon   d. testimonial

_____ 7. Cast your vote next Tuesday for George Lewis. This fine man has much to offer his community and his nation. As your representative, he pledges to do his best to better conditions and to bring you closer to the fulfillment of your highest dreams.
   a. glittering generalities   c. bandwagon
   b. transfer   d. name calling

_____ 8. One of the hottest trends this season is shorter skirts. In the office, on the street, in restaurants—everywhere you look, increasing numbers of women are switching to this new look.
   a. name calling   c. transfer
   b. testimonial   d. bandwagon

_____ 9. "I love Miami," says Dolphins' star George Raymond. "The fans here are great, and I recommend Miami as a wonderful place to live."
   a. plain folks   c. name calling
   b. bandwagon   d. testimonial

_____ 10. Home Town Cheese Bits taste just like the snacks you loved as a kid. You don't need fancy snacks at fancy prices, just simple food with a goodness that doesn't quit.
   a. testimonial   c. name calling
   b. plain folks   d. bandwagon

10

Evaluating Arguments

What do you think of the following series of statements?

1. Many traffic accidents are alcohol-related.

2. If people drank less when they were away from home, there would be fewer traffic accidents.

3. But many bars offer late-afternoon "happy hours" during which drinks are sold at half price. This practice encourages people to drink more before they go home.

4. Consequently, happy hours should be outlawed.

This chapter is about the use of sound reasoning to reach a valid conclusion, and thus it concerns *arguments*. An argument, in this sense, is not a dispute between two people. Rather, it means the advancing of reasons to support a conclusion. With this definition in mind, you can see that the above discussion of happy hours is an argument. It offers reasons (the first three statements) to support the conclusion (in the last statement) that "happy hours should be outlawed."

An argument, as we are defining it, may involve a conclusion that very few would argue about:

Because the sun has always risen in the morning, it will surely rise tomorrow morning.

(Reason: the sun has always risen in the morning. Conclusion: it will surely rise tomorrow morning.)

But most arguments we encounter are not so clear-cut (those on abortion and legalization of drugs, for example), and we may or may not agree with their conclusions. It is therefore important to be able to evaluate the soundness of arguments. In this chapter, we will explore ways to recognize arguments and evaluate how well-grounded, or valid, they are.

RECOGNIZING ARGUMENTS

As we have seen, an argument consists of two parts: one or more *reasons* and a *conclusion*. The reasons are the evidence given to support the conclusion. The critical reader must be able to recognize when an argument is being advanced and to identify its reasons and conclusion. The reader can then evaluate the worth of the argument.

Transition words can be useful in recognizing arguments and in identifying their reasons and conclusions. In the following argument, for example, note the transition words, which are in italics.

"*First of all*, what people wear affects their attitude; jeans make people feel more casual than a suit.

"*Second*, the students in this school need to take their classes more seriously.

"*Consequently*, the school should institute a policy forbidding certain types of clothing."

Words and phrases that frequently signal reasons include:

first of all	in view of the fact
secondly	as indicated by
because	for the reason that
for example	since

Words and phrases that frequently signal conclusions include:

therefore	it follows that
so	as a result
thus	then
as a result	consequently

Arguments do not always include such transition, or signal, words, and the signal words do not always mean an argument is being made. But signal words can be useful in making you aware of an argument and in helping you identify its reasons and conclusion.

As you examine arguments, keep in mind that not all arguments are arranged in the same order. While a conclusion does follow logically from the reasons supporting it, it need not come at the end of the argument.

Examine, for instance, the following speech by an irate teacher. Though the teacher's argument does not include signal words, see if you can identify which statements are the reasons and which one is the conclusion.

Philip, I think you really aren't very interested in passing this course. You've been late to class five times now and absent twice. Moreover, your last quiz shows you aren't studying very hard, either. What have you got to say for yourself?

The teacher stated the conclusion first and then gave reasons to support it. The conclusion is that Philip is not very interested in passing the course. This conclusion is based on three reasons: (1) Philip has been late five times. (2) He has been absent twice. (3) He has failed his last quiz.

Signal words can help you even when the words are not used in an argument. If you are having trouble identifying the reasons and conclusion of an argument, restate it to yourself, using signal words; they will show you the relationship between the parts of the argument. For example, you could restate the teacher's argument in this way:

Because you've been late to class five times, have been absent twice, and have failed your last quiz, *it follows that* you really aren't very interested in passing this course.

In this way, you can separate a conclusion from its support.

▷ *Practice 1*

In each of the following groups of statements, one or more of them are reasons, and one is a conclusion. On the line before each statement, write **R** if it is a reason or **C** if it is a conclusion. (Hint: Try inserting signal words, such as *because* or *therefore*, in front of the sentences.)

1. _____ I can't keep my eyes open any longer.

    _____ I'd better take a nap.

2. _____ That traffic light has stayed red for at least five minutes.

    _____ That traffic light must be broken.

3. _____ My grades in all my courses have been steadily improving this semester.

    _____ I must be using better study techniques.

4. _____ A new experimental asthma drug should be made available to all patients.

    _____ This new drug has proved effective in 85% of all cases treated.

5. _____ Our hall closet really needs cleaning out.

_____ There isn't room in it for one more sweater.

_____ Something is always falling off the shelf and hitting me on the head when I open the door.

6. _____ The temperature is supposed to hit 90 degrees every day this week.

_____ I'd better water the lawn before the grass dies.

_____ It hasn't rained in a month.

7. _____ You're looking awfully tense these days.

_____ I see that you're smoking more than usual.

_____ Whenever I ask you how you are, you make a face and turn away.

_____ Something must really be bothering you.

8. _____ We've known each other for just a few weeks.

_____ You still have a year and a half of college ahead of you.

_____ We'd better break off our engagement.

_____ At last Saturday's party, I met someone new I'd really like to go out with.

9. _____ The library should be kept open on Sundays and holidays.

_____ Many students save their studying for days when they do not have classes.

_____ Library facilities are already overcrowded on weekdays.

_____ It's difficult to find research materials during the week; other students are often using the books.

10. _____ The dialogue sounded like junior high school jokes.

_____ The monsters belonged in a salad, not a laboratory.

_____ *Invasion of the Asparagus People* is the worst science fiction movie I've ever seen.

_____ The ending just didn't make sense. Who ever heard of bacteria that like to eat asparagus?

Valid Conclusions

A conclusion is *valid* if it follows logically from the reasons—the evidence—given to support it. We can say that the teacher's conclusion that Philip is not very interested in passing the course is valid; the teacher's reasons logically support this conclusion. If the teacher had said that Philip was not interested in graduating from school, however, he or she would have been making too general a statement for the evidence given. Perhaps Philip did very well in his other classes.

Now examine the following argument. Does the conclusion follow logically from the reasons?

> Reason 1: Congressman Hill omitted some of his income from his income tax form last year.

> Reason 2: Governor Moore exaggerated her charitable contributions on her income tax last year.

> Conclusion: Most politicans cheat on their income tax.

This argument is illogical, even though both reasons may be true. Two politicians are not enough evidence for such a sweeping conclusion. The speaker is making a *hasty generalization*, a general statement based on a small sample of cases. It is the same type of mistake in reasoning Philip's teacher would have made in claiming Philip was not interested in graduating from school. This type of error in logic is called a *fallacy*, an error in reasoning.

In the argument below, three reasons are given, followed by four possible conclusions. Three of the conclusions are hasty generalizations which cannot logically be drawn from the small amount of evidence given. The fourth is a valid conclusion. Choose the one conclusion you think is valid and put a check mark beside it. Then read the explanation that follows.

1. The first time I went to that beach, I got a bad case of sunburn.

2. The second time I went to that beach, I couldn't go in the water because of the pollution.

3. The third time I went to that beach, I stepped on a starfish and had to go to the emergency room to have the spikes removed from my foot.

Which of the following is a valid conclusion that can be drawn from the evidence above?

_____ a. That beach is unsafe and should be closed.

_____ b. I'm never going to that beach again.

_____ c. I should stay away from beaches—they're no good for me.

_____ d.   I've had a string of bad experiences at that beach.

The correct answer is *d*. Answer *a* is simply not supported by three isolated instances; we'd need many more reports of dangerous conditions before considering having the beach closed. Answers *b* and *c* also assume more than is stated in the evidence; perhaps the speaker is persistent and will give the beach another chance. Only answer *d* is fully supported by the three reasons given in the argument.

Other common fallacies will be discussed later in this chapter, but the following exercises will give you practice in recognizing and avoiding unsupported arguments.

▷ *Practice 2*

Circle the letter of the sentence that states a valid conclusion based on the evidence in each group below. Remember that the conclusion should follow logically from the evidence. Do not jump to a conclusion that is not supported.

Group 1

1. My grandmother's cottage is in the country.

2. The only sounds we hear are bird calls and the wind rustling in the pine trees.

3. On Grandmother's front porch, we often enjoy watching the sunset over the lake.

   Which of the following is a valid conclusion that can be drawn from the evidence above?
   a.   The speaker would rather be at his grandmother's cottage than anywhere else.
   b.   His grandmother often invites him to her cottage.
   c.   His grandmother's cottage is the most peaceful place he's ever been.
   d.   His grandmother's cottage at the lake is very peaceful.

Group 2

1. Scanning rather than reading every word when you look for information allows you to skip over repetitive or irrelevant material.

2. Skimming material before you start to read orients you to main ideas so that you can find key points more quickly.

3. Practicing and timing your reading also helps improve your reading rate.

Which of the following is a valid conclusion that can be drawn from the evidence above?
  a. Speed-reading courses are definitely worth the money.
  b. You can increase your reading speed by following some specific guidelines.
  c. Understanding the principles of speed reading will guarantee that you more than double your reading speed.
  d. Good readers are always speed readers.

Group 3

1. Some people put off writing a letter or visiting a friend because they feel they did not have time to do it right, but a quick note or whirlwind visit is often better than nothing.

2. Sometimes it makes sense to do a routine chore quickly rather than perfectly in order to save time for something more important.

3. Even a desk and office need not be perfectly neat; sometimes cleaning them up is just an excuse for putting off more important work.

Which of the following is a valid conclusion that can be drawn from the evidence above?
  a. Perfection is not always a worthwhile goal.
  b. People who aim for perfection never get around to important tasks.
  c. You can be better organized if you plan each day more carefully.
  d. Getting things done haphazardly is always better than not getting them done at all.

Supporting a Conclusion

As you have seen, in a valid argument the conclusion must follow logically from the evidence provided to support it. Moreover, the evidence itself should be *dependable*, *sufficient*, and *relevant*.

Dependable Evidence

Evidence is more *dependable* when it is based either on someone's first-hand experience or on expert sources. Let's say that it's 4 P.M. and you're getting ready to go to the library to study. The last time you were out, at noon, the sun was shining brightly. Which of the following would convince you that you needed to take an umbrella with you?

a. The weather forecast in last night's newspaper that predicted a thunderstorm for late this afternoon.

b. A student who says he looked out the window a few minutes ago and thinks that it's raining outside.

c. Another student who comes in from outside and reports that it's just started to rain heavily.

Similarly, which of the following people would be most likely to convince you that certain lizards are able to grow new tails?

a. Your seven-year-old brother.

b. A cab driver.

c. A well-known biologist.

In each case, the correct answer is *c*. There's simply no substitute for the first-hand account or the acknowledged expert in a field. Both can be depended on. And the more dependable the evidence is, the more accurate it is likely to be. (Further information about dependable evidence may be found in the section on "Sources" in Chapter 9, "Detecting Bias and Propaganda.")

Sufficient Evidence

An argument without *sufficient* evidence is thin and unconvincing. Suppose you are about to register for an English class and meet a friend who is a year ahead of you in school. You tell her you are trying to find a good instructor for English, and the conversation continues as follows:

"Whatever you do, don't take Mr. Smith," says your friend.

Mr. Smith teaches the section that best fits your schedule, so you ask, "Why not?"

"Just don't take him," your friend answers. "If you do, you'll be sorry. I certainly was."

"Is he unreasonable?" you ask. "Is he dull? Does he give low grades? Too many papers? Not enough papers? What's wrong with him?"

"Okay," your friend replies. "Take him if you insist. Just remember that he was the biggest disappointment of my college career."

You might wind up taking Mr. Smith's class just to find out what he is like. Your friend's weak argument may have made you suspect she did not know what she was talking about.

Whether in writing or in speaking, a critical thinker will be skeptical about any conclusion that is supported by insufficient reasons. If a writer wishes to argue against capital punishment, he or she will not be very persuasive with just one example or one statistic. After all, that one example or statistic could be an accident. And a poll taken among a thousand people will be more reliable than one taken among only a hundred. In other words, don't settle for just *some* evidence—demand *enough* evidence.

Relevant Evidence

Supporting evidence must also be *relevant*. Just as a conclusion must follow logically from the evidence, the evidence presented must lead logically towards the conclusion. A statement may be true but have nothing to do with the issue. Read the following paragraph and try to find the sentence that does not support the conclusion.

> Sigmund Freud was one of the most important scientists of the twentieth century. He was among the first to study mental disorders, such as hysteria and neurosis, in a systematic way. He developed the theory of the unconscious and showed how people's behavior is greatly affected by forgotten childhood events. His discoveries are the basis of psychoanalysis, a method of treating mental illness that is still important today. He was highly regarded by scientists of his time.

The conclusion of this argument is that Freud "was one of the most important scientists of the twentieth century." Any statement that doesn't help prove this conclusion is irrelevant. The manner in which the scientists of his day viewed Freud isn't a logical reason for his being one of the most important scientists of this century. Many scientists have been highly regarded in their time without being very important. Thus the last sentence is irrelevant to the argument. In including it, the author was (intentionally or not) changing the subject, another type of error in reasoning.

▷ *Practice 3*

A. *Dependable Evidence*

In each of the items below, circle the letter of the most convincing source of evidence for that statement.

1. To strengthen the economy, the President should propose an across-the-board tax cut of 20 percent.
    a. Your college roommate
    b. Your father
    c. An editorial in the local newspaper
    d. This year's winner of the Nobel Prize in Economics

2. Staying together "for the sake of the children" is a bad idea. The children always know when their parents aren't getting along, and constant marital bickering can hurt children more than it hurts their parents.

a. A child who grew up in a happy, stable home
b. The neighbor of parents who didn't stay together for their children
c. A recently divorced woman with no children
d. An experienced child psychologist

3. Bullfighting is a vicious and brutal sport. It should be outlawed.
a. A friend who has several pets
b. A recent visitor to Spain who witnessed several bullfights
c. A high-school English teacher
d. Your next-door neighbor

B. Sufficient Evidence

For each item below, write **S** on the line if the evidence given is sufficient to be convincing. Write **N** if there is not enough evidence given to support the conclusion.

_____ 1. The Miss America Pageant should be taken off the air. It's boring, and it blatantly discriminates against women.

_____ 2. Every child should be encouraged to get a summer job as soon as he or she is of working age. I got my first summer job when I was fourteen, and I really got a lot out of the experience as well as making some decent money.

_____ 3. That store must be going out of business. The last time I was there, the shelves were nearly empty, some of the display cases had "Sold" signs on them, and the floor was littered with signs reading "Final Days—Everything Must Go!"

C. Relevant Evidence.

One of the sentences in each paragraph below does not support the conclusion of the argument. Read the paragraph, and then decide which sentence is not relevant to the argument. To help you decide if a sentence is irrelevant or not, ask yourself, "Does this have anything to do with the point that is being proved?" (Remember that evidence may be relevant even if you don't agree with it.)

1. [1]Soon, the personal computer will be as necessary to every American home as the telephone is today. [2]Personal computers have many different uses, and each family member will enjoy several. [3]Parents will find a computer of value for keeping family information such as tax records and recipe collections. [4]Software programs now exist even for such annoying chores as balancing the family checkbook. [5]Of course, banks are already beginning to offer a computer service that balances customers' checkbooks for them. [6]In addition, children's grades will improve when they use a computer to master a subject or write an English paper. [7]And

everyone will enjoy taking a break with one of the popular computer games.

Which of the following statements does not contribute to the author's conclusion that soon every American home will have a personal computer?
a. Sentence 3
b. Sentence 4
c. Sentence 5
d. Sentence 6

2. [1]The proposed new highway linking Interstate 95 with the turnpike is a disaster. [2]The plans for this highway were drawn over thirty years ago, when the affected area was lightly settled. [3]Now, a generation later, the area has become developed, and hundreds of families would lose their homes if the highway were built. [4]There are already too many forces weakening the American family structure these days. [5]The environment will also be negatively affected by the construction of a new superhighway. [6]Hundreds of thousands of birds and small animals, including several endangered species, will lose their natural habitats and may die out.

Which of the following is not a sound argument in support of the author's conclusion that the proposed highway is a disaster?
a. Sentence 2
b. Sentence 3
c. Sentence 4
d. Sentence 6

3. [1]Sex education should take place in the home, not in school. [2]Parents have a right to have such a personal topic taught according to their own standards of sexual behavior, which may differ from what is taught in school. [3]After all, children are our country's most precious asset. [4]In addition, the fact that sex is included in the curriculum may give students the impression that schools are not against them having sex. [5]Clearly, many parents may prefer their children don't get such an impression.

Which of the following is not relevant to the author's point that sex education should take place in the home?
a. Sentence 2
b. Sentence 3
c. Sentence 4
d. Sentence 5

SOME LOGICAL FALLACIES

A *fallacy* is a flaw in reasoning that leads to an illogical argument. Like propaganda, fallacies often seem reasonable at first, but a closer look reveals how illogical they are. Learning to spot fallacies will help you in evaluating the *validity* (soundness) of arguments. A conclusion that is reached because of a fallacy may be a *good* one, but it will not be a *valid* one if it has not been proven by the evidence given.

Following are explanations of eight common types of fallacies. The first four have to do with ignoring the issue; the second four involve arguments that overgeneralize or oversimplify issues. Exercises follow each group of four.

Fallacies That Ignore the Issue

1. No Support: Circular Reasoning

Part of a conclusion cannot reasonably be used as evidence to support it. That type of argument is called *circular reasoning*, also known as *begging the question*. A simple and obvious example of such reasoning is: "Mr. Green is a great teacher because he is so wonderful at teaching." The reason given in this argument ("he is so wonderful at teaching") is really the same as the conclusion ("Mr. Green is a great teacher"). We still do not know why he is a great teacher. No real reasons have been given—the statement merely has repeated itself.

Can you spot the circular reasoning in the following arguments?

A. Vitamins are healthy, for they improve your well-being.

B. Abstract art is rubbish because it is not realistic.

C. The evil practice of abortion ought to be abolished because it is wrong.

Let's look more closely now at these arguments:

A. The word "healthy," which is used in the conclusion, conveys the same idea as "well-being."

B. To say that abstract art is not realistic is only repeating that it is abstract; no real reason is given for why it's rubbish.

C. The claim that abortion "is wrong" is simply a restatement of the idea that it is an "evil practice."

In all these cases, the reasons merely repeat an important part of the conclusion. The careful reader wants to say, "Tell me something new. You are reasoning in circles. Give me evidence, not a repetition."

2. Wrong Support: Personal Attack

This fallacy often occurs in political debate. Here's an example:

> Senator Snerd's opinions on public housing are worthless. He is the type of man who is soft on communism, having consistently voted against funding our democratic allies in Central America.

> Senator Snerd's position on Central America may or may not be wrong, but it has nothing to do with the value of his opinions on public housing. This kind of fallacy ignores the issue under discussion and concentrates instead on the character of the opponent.

3. Wrong Support: Straw Man

An opponent made of straw can be defeated very easily. Sometimes, if one's real opponent is putting up too good a fight, it can be tempting to build a scarecrow and battle it instead. For example, take the following passage from a debate on the death penalty.

> Ms. Collins opposes capital punishment. Letting murderers out on the street to kill again is a crazy idea. If we did that, no one would be safe.

> Ms. Collins, however, never advocated "letting murderers out on the street to kill again." In fact, she wants to keep them in jail for life rather than execute them. This fallacy suggests that the opponent favors an obviously unpopular cause—when the opponent really doesn't support anything of the kind.

4. Wrong Support: Changing the Subject

This method of arguing tries to divert the audience's attention from the true issue by presenting evidence that actually has nothing to do with the argument. You have already encountered this fallacy in the discussion and practice on relevant reasons. Here are other examples:

> I think you should buy a bird, not a dog; many dogs shed all over the house.
> (Saying that many dogs shed is beside the point; it is possible to buy a dog that does not shed.)

> The congressman is clearly an able leader; he has a warm family life and attends church every Sunday.
> (Mention of the congressman's family and church life sidesteps the issue of just how able a leader he is.)

This fallacy is also called a *red herring*. In a fox hunt, drawing a red herring across the dogs' path causes them to lose the scent and allows the fox to escape. Someone who changes the subject when arguing may hope the audience will lose track of the real point of the argument.

▷ *Practice 4*

In each case below, the conclusion does not follow from the evidence given. Circle the letter of the mistake in reasoning that is present.

1. Robert Major does not deserve a harsh punishment for stealing from his clients. After all, he has served many of his clients well.
   a. Statement repeats itself (circular reasoning)
   b. Shifts argument to irrelevant personal criticism (personal attack)
   c. Suggests that the opponent has a position not actually held (straw man)
   d. Evidence sounds good but has nothing to do with argument (changing the subject)

2. Horror movies are bad for children. Such movies scare them unnecessarily.
   a. Statement repeats itself (circular reasoning)
   b. Shifts argument to irrelevant personal criticism (personal attack)
   c. Suggests that the opponent has a position not actually held (straw man)
   d. Evidence sounds good but has nothing to do with argument (changing the subject)

3. The people who support raising the speed limit are immature showoffs and highway menaces.
   a. Statement repeats itself (circular reasoning)
   b. Shifts argument to irrelevant personal criticism (personal attack)
   c. Suggests that the opponent has a position not actually held (straw man)
   d. Evidence sounds good but has nothing to do with argument (changing the subject)

4. Ginger Beckman supports the proposal for changes in our county government. That is just what I would expect from an inexperienced housewife.
   a. Statement repeats itself (circular reasoning)
   b. Shifts argument to irrelevant personal criticism (personal attack)
   c. Suggests that the opponent has a position not actually held (straw man)
   d. Evidence sounds good but has nothing to do with argument (changing the subject)

5. The people who are in favor of gun control are obviously not concerned about criminals taking control of this fine country.
   a. Statement repeats itself (circular reasoning)
   b. Shifts argument to irrelevant personal criticism (personal attack)
   c. Suggests that the opponent has a position not actually held (straw man)
   d. Evidence sounds good but has nothing to do with argument (changing the subject)

Fallacies That Overgeneralize or Oversimplify

5. Hasty Generalization

To be valid, a conclusion must be based on an adequate amount of evidence. Someone who draws a conclusion on the basis of insufficient evidence is making a *hasty generalization*, a fallacy dealt with earlier in this chapter (page 136). This is a very common fallacy. It is not unusual, for instance, to hear an argument like this one:

> The Chinese people have an inherent talent for art. Two Chinese girls took an art course with me last semester, and they were the best students in the class.

> Forming a conclusion about the quarter of a billion Chinese people in the world based on two examples is an illogical jump.

6. False Cause

You have probably heard someone say as a joke, "I know it's going to rain today because I just washed the car." The idea that someone can make it rain by washing a car is funny because the two events obviously have nothing to do with each other. However, with more complicated issues, it is easy to make the mistake known as the fallacy of *false cause*. The mistake is to assume that because Event B follows Event A, Event A has *caused* Event B.

Cause-and-effect situations can be difficult to analyze, and people are often tempted to oversimplify them by ignoring other possible causes. To identify an argument using a false cause, look for alternative causes. Consider this argument:

> The Macklin Company was more prosperous before Ms. Williams became president. Clearly, she is the cause of the decline.
> (Event A: Ms. Williams became president.
> Event B: The Macklin Company's earnings declined.)

What other possible causes could have been responsible for the decline? Perhaps the policies of the previous president are just now affecting the company. Perhaps the market for the company's product has changed. In any case, it's easy but dangerous to assume that just because A *came before* B, A *caused* B.

7. False Comparison

When the poet Robert Burns wrote, "My love is like a red, red rose," he meant that both the woman he loved and a rose are beautiful. In other ways—such as having green leaves and thorns, for example—his love did not resemble a rose at all. Comparisons are often a good way to clarify a point. But because two things are not alike in all respects, comparisons (sometimes called *analogies*) often make poor evidence for arguments. In the error in reasoning known as *false comparison*, a comparison is made in which the differences between two things are more important than their similarities. For example, read the following argument.

It didn't hurt your grandfather in the old country to get to work without a car, and it won't hurt you either.

To judge whether or not this is a false comparison, consider how the two situations are alike and how they differ. They are similar in that both involve a young person's need to get to work. But the situations are different in that the grandfather didn't have to be at work an hour after his last class. In fact, he didn't go to school at all. In addition, his family didn't own a car he could use. The differences in this case are more important than the similarities, making it a false comparison.

8. Either-Or Fallacy

It is often wrong to assume that there are only two sides to a question. Offering only two choices when more actually exist is an *Either-Or Fallacy*. For example, the statement "Either you are with us or against us" assumes that there is no middle ground. Or consider the following:

People opposed to unrestricted free speech are really in favor of censorship.

This argument ignores the fact that a person could believe in free speech as well as in laws that prohibit slander or that punish someone for yelling "Fire!" in a crowded theater. Some issues have only two sides (Will you pass English, or won't you?), but most have several.

▷ *Practice 5*

In each case below, the conclusion is invalid because the speaker has over-generalized or oversimplified. Circle the letter of the mistake in reasoning that is present.

1.   When I was in New York City, every clerk I encountered was rude. New Yorkers are obviously very unfriendly people.
   a.   Generalization based on insufficient evidence (hasty generalization)
   b.   Assumption that order of events alone shows cause and effect (false cause)
   c.   Assumption that things being compared are more alike than different (false comparison)
   d.   Assumption that there are only two sides to a question (either-or fallacy)

2.   After visiting Hal today, I came home with a headache. I must be allergic to his dog.
   a.   Generalization based on insufficient evidence (hasty generalization)
   b.   Assumption that order of events alone shows cause and effect (false cause)
   c.   Assumption that things being compared are more alike than different (false comparison)
   d.   Assumption that there are only two sides to a question (either-or fallacy)

3.   You'll either have to get a good job soon or face the fact that you'll never be successful.
   a.   Generalization based on insufficient evidence (hasty generalization)
   b.   Assumption that order of events alone shows cause and effect (false cause)
   c.   Assumption that things being compared are more alike than different (false comparison)
   d.   Assumption that there are only two sides to a question (either-or fallacy)

4.   The current world situation is exactly like the crisis that preceded World War II. Unless we take decisive action immediately, the whole world will soon be at war.
   a.   Generalization based on insufficient evidence (hasty generalization)
   b.   Assumption that order of events alone shows cause and effect (false cause)
   c.   Assumption that things being compared are more alike than different (false comparison)
   d.   Assumption that there are only two sides to a question (either-or fallacy)

5. Both of my sisters' husbands left them for other women. There aren't any loyal men left in this world.
    a. Generalization based on insufficient evidence (hasty generalization)
    b. Assumption that order of events alone shows cause and effect (false cause)
    c. Assumption that things being compared are more alike than different (false comparison)
    d. Assumption that there are only two sides to a question (either-or fallacy)

➤ *Review Test 1: Evaluating Conclusions*

A. One or more statements in each cluster below are reasons. One statement is a conclusion. Label each as a reason (**R**) or a conclusion (**C**).

1. _____ I like home-grown tomatoes, but there's no room in our yard for a garden.

   _____ I'm going to grow tomatoes in some pots on our front steps.

2. _____ I think I'll look for another pre-school for my son.

   _____ He says he hates his pre-school teacher.

   _____ Yesterday he hid under his bed when it was time to go to pre-school.

3. _____ The math tutors at school have helped many students raise their math grades.

   _____ I'm having trouble with math this quarter.

   _____ I think I'll make an appointment to see a tutor.

4. _____ Scientists have proven that acid rain harms trees and bodies of water.

   _____ Laws should be passed to reduce acid rain.

   _____ The damage done by acid rain is hard or impossible to undo.

5. _____ The roaches seem to be taking over this apartment.

   _____ I'm going to look for another apartment.

   _____ The landlord refuses to fix the leaky faucet.

   _____ The people upstairs make a lot of noise.

B. Circle the letter of the conclusion that is most solidly based on the evidence in each of the following groups.

Group 1

- There's been a Shrimp Boat seafood restaurant on Thayer Street for about five years.
- Last week, two new Shrimp Boats opened in local shopping malls.
- A display ad in the classified section reads, "Shrimp Boat: Franchises Available in Top Money-Making Locations."

Which of the following is a valid conclusion that can be drawn from the evidence above?

a.   Shrimp Boat serves the best seafood in town.

b.   The Shrimp Boat chain is expanding.

c.   People who work for Shrimp Boat can expect to make a lot of money.

d.   Anyone who wants to can open a Shrimp Boat restaurant.

Group 2

- Last week, when I tried to take a copy of *Readings for Managers* out of the library, it wasn't on the shelf.
- Yesterday, I tried again, and it still wasn't there.
- Today, I asked the librarian, who said there was no record of anyone borrowing that book.

Which of the following is a valid conclusion that can be drawn from the evidence above?

a.   *Readings for Managers* has been stolen.

b.   The librarian is careless.

c.   The book has been misfiled.

d.   The book is not where it is supposed to be.

Group 3

- One shelf of Peg's bookcase is filled with little wooden and ceramic owls.
- When she works out, Peg wears a T-shirt with a silk-screened drawing of an owl on it.
- Peg always signs her name with a little cartoon of an owl under her signature.

Which of the following is a valid conclusion that can be drawn from the evidence above?

a.   Peg likes owls.

b.   Peg is a birdwatcher.

   c.   Lots of people give Peg little owls as gifts.

   d.   Peg has a pet owl.

Group 4

- Whenever it rains, the roof leaks in about three places.
- People are always tripping over a loose board on the front porch.
- The paint on the woodwork around the windows is cracked and peeling.

Which of the following is a valid conclusion that can be drawn from the evidence above?

   a.   The house is a "handyman's special" and needs a lot of work.

   b.   The people who live there don't know how to take care of a house.

   c.   The owner of the house is too poor to make the needed repairs.

   d.   The roof, porch, and woodwork in the house need fixing.

Group 5

- The Coyotes have lost eleven of their last twelve games.
- None of their pitchers has been able to finish a game.
- Their best hitter is batting .238.

Which of the following is a valid conclusion that can be drawn from the evidence above?

   a.   The Coyote players have lost interest in the game.

   b.   The Coyotes are in a slump.

   c.   The Coyotes' manager has not been strict enough with his players.

   d.   The Coyotes' manager should be fired.

▶ *Review Test 2: Analyzing Arguments*

A. Circle the letter of the most *dependable* source of evidence for each statement.

1. The Sebring XZ is the best car for the money. You can't go wrong with this model.
    a. Your neighbor, who's owned a Sebring XZ for six months
    b. The salesman at the Sebring agency
    c. The annual automobile issue of *Consumer Reports*, a publication that rates all the new cars
    d. An ad for the Sebring XZ in *Road and Track* magazine

2. The world will come to an end in 50,000 years.
   a. The author of a horoscope column appearing in over 150 daily newspapers
   b. A science-fiction author
   c. A politician
   d. A professor of astronomy at a major university

B. Write **S** on the line if the evidence given is *sufficient* to be convincing. Write **N** if there is not enough evidence given to support the conclusion.

_____ 1. You should not bother shopping at the Quick Pick. It doesn't have as many employees as regular markets. And it doesn't advertise in the paper as much.

_____ 2. Your little boy is getting cranky. A few minutes ago, he threw his toy out of his crib. Then he started whimpering, and just now, he bit me.

C. Circle the letter of the *irrelevant* sentence in each paragraph—the sentence that does not support the conclusion of the argument.

1. [1]If the township would put street lights along Dapple Drive, it would make life safer and easier for those of us who live along that street and our guests. [2]This township never seems to take the needs of the citizens into account. [3]It is so dark on Dapple Drive that people have trouble seeing where they are going. [4]A few months ago, an elderly woman visiting a neighbor's home couldn't see a step and fell, breaking her hip bone. [5]And people who visit my home frequently complain about not being able to see our address, even though we have a light outside our front door.

Which of the following is not relevant to the author's conclusion that it would be safer and more convenient if the township put in street lights?

a. Sentence 2   c. Sentence 4
b. Sentence 3   d. Sentence 5

2. [1]Children should be given an allowance as soon as they are old enough to want it. [2]Having to make decisions about what to do with their money is good training for the future. [3]They eventually learn to use their money on what they really want, instead of spending impulsively. [4]Furthermore, an allowance is one good way of telling a child that he or she is a responsible member of the family and that membership brings benefits as well as obligations. [5]That will make the expectation that they also have to do chores more reasonable. [6]Unfortunately, some people are reluctant to give young children an allowance.

Which of the following does not support the author's conclusion that children benefit from being given an allowance?

a. Sentence 2   c. Sentence 5
b. Sentence 3   d. Sentence 6

D. Each argument below contains a logical fallacy. Circle the letter of the statement which best expresses the type of fallacy contained in the argument.

1. Supporters of state lotteries apparently don't think that anyone should work hard for what he gets. They believe it's better to get something for nothing.
   a. Statement repeats itself (circular reasoning)
   b. Shifts argument to irrelevant personal criticism (personal attack)
   c. Suggests opponent holds a position not actually held (straw man)
   d. Evidence sounds good but has nothing to do with argument (changing the subject)

2. The company president could hardly be guilty of the charges of his opponents. In fact, he is a man who gives thousands of dollars to charity each year.
   a. Statement repeats itself (circular reasoning)
   b. Shifts argument to irrelevant personal criticism (personal attack)
   c. Suggests opponent holds a position not actually held (straw man)
   d. Evidence sounds good but has nothing to do with argument (changing the subject)

3. I knew I shouldn't have taken the baby to the park today. Now he's got a cold.
   a. Generalization based on insufficient evidence (hasty generalization)
   b. Assumption that order of events alone shows cause and effect (false cause)
   c. Assumption that things being compared are alike in all respects (false comparison)
   d. Assumption that there are only two sides to a question (either-or fallacy)

4. My sister gets great grades in everything except math. Women just aren't very good at math.
   a. Generalization based on insufficient evidence (hasty generalization)
   b. Assumption that order of events alone shows cause and effect (false cause)
   c. Assumption that things being compared are alike in all respects (false comparison)
   d. Assumption that there are only two sides to a question (either-or fallacy)

Part II

MASTERY TESTS

Try to figure out the meaning of the following ten words by studying how each is used in context. Then, complete the matching and fill-in sections of the test.

1. **IMPLAUSIBLE**
(ĭm plô′ zuh buhl)

The students who walked into class late told the instructor an *implausible* story about stopping to watch a UFO.

The movie's ending was *implausible*; the woman welder became a famous ballerina.

2. **SYNOPSIS**
(sĭ nŏp′ sĭs)

Our instructor assigned a one-paragraph *synopsis* of the story we had just read.

The newspaper listed a *synopsis* of the plot of each movie playing in the area.

3. **EMACIATED**
(ĭ mā′ shē āt′ ĕd)

The prisoners liberated from the Nazi death camp were so *emaciated* they resembled skeletons.

The *emaciated* girl was a victim of anorexia—she had tried to starve herself.

4. **SPURIOUS**
(spyŏŏr′ ĭ uhs)

The *spurious* evidence presented by the defendant's lawyer was thrown out of court.

The letter supposedly written by Abraham Lincoln was proved to be *spurious*.

5. **DESTITUTE**
(dĕs′ tuh tūt′)

The *destitute* woman wore the same clothes every day and slept on a subway steam vent.

During the Depression, the problems of the *destitute* forced President Roosevelt to act decisively.

6. **SUCCINCT**
(suhk sĭngkt′)

A good speech is one that is *succinct*, brief and to the point.

Many politicians do not give *succinct* answers to questions, but long, vague ones.

7. **SURFEIT**
(sûr′fĭt)

After being in the hospital for two weeks, I had a *surfeit* of daytime TV programming.

Americans seem to take the *surfeit* of food in this country for granted.

8. **PLACATE**
(plā′ kāt)

The angry customer in the car showroom could not be *placated*; he wanted his "lemon" replaced.

England tried to *placate* Hitler before the war by compromising with him, a strategy which made the dictator bolder than before.

157

9. IMPROMPTU
   (ĭm prŏmp' tū)

The candidate reads speeches well, but his *impromptu* remarks sound nervous and confused.

The aging star did an *impromptu* dance as he came on stage to accept his Oscar.

10. VERBATIM
    (vuhr bā' tĭm)

The preacher claims to be able to recite *verbatim* the exact words of the entire Bible.

The student had copied the report *verbatim* from an encyclopedia.

NOTE: Key to pronunciation is on page 453.

A. Match the word with the definition:

1. implausible
2. synopsis
3. emaciated
4. spurious
5. destitute
6. succinct
7. surfeit
8. placate
9. impromptu
10. verbatim

_____ made thin, as by hunger

_____ brief; concise

_____ calm; soothe

_____ a summary

_____ word for word

_____ having no money

_____ unplanned; unrehearsed

_____ fake; false

_____ excess; overindulgence

_____ unbelievable; improbable

B. Fill in each blank with a word from the above list; use each word only once.

1. His _____ of the lengthy novel was _____ ; he covered the book's plot in very few words.

2. The organizer of the lecture tried to _____ the impatient crowd (which had been waiting for the speaker for an hour) by giving an _____ talk on the speaker's accomplishments.

3. The man's claim that he was _____ proved to be a _____ one, for the social worker discovered that he had several bank accounts.

4. The instructor had heard a _____ of Elliot's _____ excuses for not doing the assignments, so she failed him for the course.

5. The mayor recited _____ several paragraphs of the heart-rending newspaper story about the plight of the _____ _____women who searched in garbage cans for food.

┌───┐
│   **SCORE**   │
│   **100 − 5 for each one wrong = _____%**   │
└───┘

Try to figure out the meanings of the following ten words by studying how each is used in context. Then, complete the matching and fill-in sections of the test.

1. **CRYPTIC**
   (krĭp′ tĭk)

   A *cryptic* message written in a strange language had been scrawled on the mirror by the murderer.

   The Soviets are skilled at sending *cryptic* messages, open to several interpretations; our State Department spends many hours puzzling over their meanings.

2. **REDUNDANT**
   (rĭ dŭn′ duhnt)

   Readers become bored with writing that is *redundant*, repeating the same ideas over and over.

   "A passing fad" is a *redundant* phrase; all fads, by definition, are passing.

3. **INCESSANT**
   (ĭn sĕs′ uhnt)

   The Great Flood in the Bible was caused by *incessant* rain that fell for forty days and nights.

   The man's *incessant* coughing ruined the movie for many people.

4. **ITINERANT**
   (ī tĭn′ uhr uhnt)

   In pioneer days, an *itinerant* preacher would arrive in town by mule and perform weddings, baptisms, and funerals all in the same day, before moving on to the next town.

   Itinerant peddlers, who traveled from door to door, have modern counterparts in Fuller Brush and Avon salespeople.

5. **INHERENT**
   (ĭn hĕr′ uhnt)

   A free press is an *inherent* part of the American concept of a democracy.

   Inherent in the patient's complaints was the assumption that he could do nothing to control his own addiction.

6. **DEROGATORY**
   (dĭ rŏg′ uh tôr′ē)

   The actress sued the newspaper for its *derogatory* comments about her personal appearance, especially her weight.

   After reading the *derogatory* review of the TV miniseries, Martin decided to watch basketball instead.

7. **JUXTAPOSE**
   (jŭks' tuh pōz')

Cardboard shanties were *juxtaposed* next to mansions on the outskirts of the South American city.

The documentary about the 60s *juxtaposed* images of protesters burning the flag and patriotic rallies held at the national political conventions.

8. **INDICT**
   (ĭn dīt')

On the basis of overwhelming evidence, the grand jury *indicted* the company president for violations of toxic-waste laws.

The troubles of the homeless in our cities are an *indictment* of our entire society.

9. **MANDATE**
   (măn' dāt)

After winning 80 percent of the popular vote, the mayor claimed to have a *mandate* from the people.

The President gave the special prosecutor a *mandate* to root out corruption within the White House.

10. **IMBIBE**
    (ĭm bīb')

Bars can now be held liable for auto accidents caused by customers who *imbibe* too much alcohol.

The cult members sat before their leader in awe, hoping to *imbibe* some of their hero's wisdom.

NOTE: Key to pronunciation is on page 453.

A. Match the word with the definition:

1. cryptic
2. incessant
3. redundant
4. itinerant
5. inherent
6. derogatory
7. juxtapose
8. indict
9. mandate
10. imbibe

_____ needlessly repetitive; wordy

_____ place side by side

_____ secret; mysterious; uncertain

_____ charge with an offense; accuse

_____ traveling from place to place; covering a circuit

_____ part of the essential character; belonging by nature

_____ drink; absorb

_____ continuous; unceasing

_____ authoritative command; clear authorization to act

_____ degrading; expressing a low opinion

B. Fill in each blank with a word from the above list; use each word only once.

1. The father's _____ nagging to do homework was not only _____ , it was counterproductive—it made the children more determined than ever to avoid their homework.

2. When the _____ message sent by the enemy was _____d against the key to the code, it was easy to translate the message into English.

3. Although Frances doesn't mean to hurt people, she seems to have an _____ tendency to make _____ remarks about them.

4. Whenever the _____ salesman stopped on his route, he would _____ a sip of whiskey from his pocket flask.

5. The attorney general had the governor's _____ to _____ as many organized crime figures as possible.

SCORE
100 − 5 for each one wrong = _____%

Try to figure out the meanings of the following ten words by studying how each is used in context. Then, complete the matching and fill-in portions of the test.

1. BENIGN
   (bĭ nīn´)

   The tumor was *benign*, not life-threatening, but the doctors operated to relieve the pressure on the spine.

   The *benign* ruler stood in sharp contrast to the old dictator, who had been ruthless.

2. DISCERN
   (dĭ zūrn´)

   The night watchman thought he *discerned* a slight movement in a dark corner of the warehouse.

   The new tellers were taught to *discern* the difference between genuine and counterfeit bills.

3. SOLICITOUS
   (suh lĭs´ uh tuhs)

   In a *solicitous* tone, the police officer asked the grieving family, "Is there anything I can do to help?"

   Patients often expect nurses to be extremely *solicitous*, but they are often too busy to be anything more than competent.

4. INSCRUTABLE
   (ĭn skroo´ tuh buhl)

   Sometimes Sherlock Holmes' actions seem *inscrutable*, but by the end of the story, his methods make perfect sense.

   The negotiators came out of the arms control talks with *inscrutable* expressions; reporters could not tell if progress was being made or not.

5. DUPLICITY
   (dū plĭs´ uh tē)

   When the promised Christmas bonus was not given, the workers accused the boss of *duplicity*.

   Since the informant was well known for his *duplicity*, the FBI checked his story thoroughly.

6. PRUDENT
   (proo´ duhnt)

   Phil decided to be *prudent* and call ahead for reservations instead of just showing up.

   Teenagers often ignore their parents' *prudent* advice because they wish to rebel against their parents' values.

7. SURMISE
   (suhr mīz´)

   The teacher *surmised* that the little boy's anxiety might stem from problems at home.

   The tenants *surmised* from the landlord's notice of sharp rent increases that he might be trying to force them out of the building.

8. UTOPIAN
   (ū tō′ pĭ uhn)

Brave New World is a book about a *utopian* society that turns out to be less perfect than it seems.

Many *utopian* communities have been started in America by people who wanted to create an ideal society, but they have usually failed.

9. AMBIGUITY
   (ăm buh gū′ uh tē)

The *ambiguity* of Tom's directions made it difficult to find his house.

The *ambiguity* of the movie's ending left many viewers frustrated and dissatisfied; no one could figure out if the hero had died or not.

10. COMPLICITY
    (kuhm plĭs′ uh tē)

The woman was accused of *complicity* in the murder, for she had bought the gun for the suspect.

Some people have accused the CIA, the Russians, or the Cubans of *complicity* in the assassination of President Kennedy.

NOTE: Key to pronunciation is on page 453.

A. Match the word with its definition:

1. benign
2. discern
3. solicitous
4. inscrutable
5. duplicity
6. prudent
7. surmise
8. utopian
9. ambiguity
10. complicity

_____ involvement in wrongdoing; being an accomplice

_____ mysterious; unable to be understood

_____ guess

_____ kindly; gentle; not harmful

_____ vagueness; uncertainty

_____ anxious; concerned; attentive

_____ wise; practical; careful

_____ deceit; hypocrisy

_____ detect; distinguish

_____ founded upon imaginary perfection; idealistic and often impractical

B. Fill in each blank with one word from the list above; use each word only once.

1. Since the pitcher had never faced the pinch hitter before, he

_____d that the most _____ strategy was to walk him.

2.   Sally asked in a _____ tone how Ron was feeling, but,

     knowing her capacity for _____, he did not believe she
     really cared.

3.   The serial murderer's motives were completely _____

     —no one could _____ the meaning of his senseless and
     horrifying attacks.

4.   The _____ of the evidence left in doubt the extent of

     the mayor's _____ in the fraudulent scheme.

5.   The motives for starting a _____ community are usually

     _____—to create a better society, for instance, but jeal-
     ousies and petty disagreements often break up the group.

SCORE
100 − 5 for each one wrong = _____%

Try to figure out the meaning of the following ten words by studying how each is used in context. Then, complete the matching and fill-in sections of the test.

1. **IRRESOLUTE**
   (ĭ rĕz′ uh lo͞ot′)

   Voters seem to prefer that candidates have strong opinions, even on issues they know little about, rather than appear *irresolute*.

   Although the weather on the mountain had cleared, the climbers were *irresolute* about climbing any further in their weakened state.

2. **VIRULENT**
   (vĭr′ yuh luhnt)

   This year's flu bug is especially *virulent*, so all elderly people should be vaccinated.

   The television show *60 Minutes* received many *virulent* letters protesting its report on abortion.

3. **RETROACTIVE**
   (rĕt′ rō ăk′ tĭv)

   The workers received their pay raise on March 15, but it was *retroactive* to January 1.

   Anyone who bought a used car before this year cannot sue a dealer under the "lemon law," which is not *retroactive*.

4. **NOMAD**
   (nō′ măd)

   Many desert dwellers are *nomads*, following their herds from one poor grazing area to another.

   Hoboes live a *nomadic* life, never staying in one place for too long at a time.

5. **IMPECCABLE**
   (ĭm pĕk′ uh buhl)

   The job candidate's background was *impeccable*— good references and a great deal of experience; but the company did not hire her.

   The woman with the *impeccable* suit and hair looked completely different after putting on an old sweat shirt and torn jeans.

6. **SUMPTUOUS**
   (sŭmp′ cho͞o uhs)

   The people resented the *sumptuous* lifestyle of the king and his court, who spent freely while common folk starved.

   The *sumptuous* penthouse was furnished with thick Oriental carpets, antique furniture, and silken drapes.

7. **COVERT**
   (kŭv′ uhrt)

   The *covert* spy activities of the CIA were called into question by Congress in the 1970s.

   A *covert* agreement between the two countries to aid each other in the event of war was unknown to the citizens.

8. DISTRAUGHT   A thoughtless reporter shoved a microphone into the
    (dĭs trôt')   faces of the *distraught* parents, who had just learned of
                        their son's death.

                        The man in the doctor's waiting room seemed *dis-
                        traught*; he kept rubbing his hands and staring at the
                        floor.

9. LETHARGIC   The tranquilized polar bear was *lethargic* enough for the
    (lĭ thär' jĭk)   scientists to safely examine his teeth and tattoo his ear.

                        The manager fined the player $500 for his *lethargic* play,
                        saying he wasn't moving quickly enough on the field.

10. GIST   Having just ten minutes for her sales presentation, Fran
    (jĭst)   gave only the *gist* of her prepared talk.

                        The *gist* of my employer's message is that I might soon
                        be out of a job.

NOTE: Key to pronunciation is on page 453.

A. Match the word with the definition:

    1. irresolute   _____ member of a group whose lifestyle in-
    2. virulent   volves wandering from place to place;
    3. retroactive   aimless wanderer
    4. nomad
    5. impeccable   _____ very disturbed; agitated; confused
    6. sumptuous   _____ the central idea; essence
    7. covert
    8. distraught   _____ lavish; luxurious; expensive
    9. lethargic   _____ filled with hatred; bitterly hostile
    10. gist
                         _____ effective as of an earlier date; applica-
                                   ble to past events

                         _____ slow-moving; sluggish

                         _____ wavering; undecided

                         _____ flawless

                         _____ hidden; secret

B. Fill in the blanks with two words from the list above.

    1. After reading the critic's _____ attack on her perfor-

        mance, the actress became _____ and took two tran-
        quilizers.

2. Standing in front of the _____ banquet table, I became

    _____ about sticking to my diet.

3. The _____ of the court's decision was that the drug

    company would have to pay the victims' medical costs, _____
    to January 1 of the previous year.

4. The anthropologist reported that she had discovered a tribe

    of _____s whose movements were so _____
    that they had not been noticed for centuries.

5. Matthew seemed tired and _____ while sitting on the

    bench, but he put on an _____ performance when the
    coach put him into the game.

SCORE
100 − 5 for each one wrong = _____%

Try to figure out the meanings of the following ten words by studying how each is used in context. Then, complete the matching and fill-in sections of the test.

1. **LUCID**
   (lōo′ sĭd)

   Although the subject of nuclear power is technical, the speaker's *lucid* presentation made it easy to understand.

   The old footage showed a sharp contrast between the boxer's previously *lucid* speech and his current slurred voice.

2. **REGRESS**
   (rē grĕs′)

   Alzheimer's disease attacks middle-aged and elderly people and makes them *regress* to a state of near-total helplessness.

   Under hypnosis, the patient *regressed* until she became, mentally, her six-year-old self.

3. **SKEPTICISM**
   (skĕp′ tuh sĭz′ uhm)

   Skepticism is an intelligent reaction to the claims of many self-help books, which present simplistic solutions to life's problems.

   Many people regard the justice system with *skepticism*, for criminals seem to go free and victims are punished.

4. **IMMINENT**
   (ĭm′ uh nuhnt)

   When a hurricane is *imminent*, an eerie calm often occurs; the birds are silent, and the wind drops.

   The birth was *imminent*, so the police officer pulled over to the side of the road and told the expectant mother he would deliver her baby himself.

5. **INCONGRUOUS**
   (ĭn kŏng′ grōo uhs)

   It seems *incongruous* that Americans spend excessive prices for faddish dolls while real children are starving in parts of the world.

   The nominee wore an *incongruous* outfit to the awards ceremony—a tuxedo and sneakers.

6. **ABERRATION**
   (ăb′ uh rā′ shuhn)

   The teacher's absence was an *aberration*, for she normally showed up every day regardless of the weather.

   An *aberration* in behavior may be a warning signal that an individual is suffering from stress or depression.

7. **SPORADICALLY**
(spō răd′ ik ŭhl ē)

Some insect populations boom *sporadically*, causing much damage to plants, but then the insects die off.

When a person is rewarded *sporadically* (by playing a slot machine that occasionally pays out, for instance), the desire to continue that behavior is strong.

8. **EXPUNGE**
(ĭk spŭnj′)

Some governments have tried to *expunge* historical records in order to create their own version of past events.

After several years, records of driving violations are *expunged* so that an individual's record is clean.

9. **CORROBORATE**
(kuh rŏb′ uh rāt′)

Several reliable witnesses *corroborated* the teenager's story of seeing a strange light in the sky.

The consumer advocate was asked to *corroborate* his claim that the car model was dangerous by presenting facts and statistics.

10. **INUNDATE**
(ĭn′ uhn dāt)

Many cultures and religions have similar legends about a great flood *inundating* the earth.

Modern life *inundates* us with information from dozens of sources every day.

NOTE: Key to pronunciation is on page 453.

A. Match the word with its definition:

1. lucid
2. regress
3. skepticism
4. imminent
5. incongruous
6. aberration
7. sporadically
8. corroborate
9. expunge
10. inundate

_____ doubt; questioning attitude

_____ lacking agreement; inappropriate

_____ happening occasionally in scattered incidences

_____ flood; overflow; overwhelm

_____ clear; easily understood; rational

_____ confirm; support

_____ abnormality

_____ erase; blot out

_____ go backward; backslide

_____ about to happen; threatening

B. Fill in the blanks with two words from the list above.

1. The first few cases of the disease appeared _____, but when more and more were reported, doctors warned that an epidemic was _____.

2. A tidal wave threatened to _____ the island and _____ every trace of its existence.

3. _____ behavior, like laughing at a funeral or crying for no reason, is an _____ that may indicate a need for psychological help.

4. The patient seemed to be making progress and had begun to speak in a _____ manner when she suddenly _____ed to a coma-like state.

5. Mr. Atkins reacted with _____ to Harold's request for sick leave, for he had not _____d his claim to be in need of an operation with a doctor's note.

SCORE
100 − 5 for each one wrong = _____%

MAIN IDEAS: Test 1

Each of the following groups of statements includes one topic, one main idea (topic sentence), and two supporting ideas. Identify each item in the space provided as either the topic (**T**), main idea (**MI**), or a supporting detail (**SD**).

Group 1

_____ a. Personal checking and automatic teller machines are offered for a small monthly charge.

_____ b. Full-service banks can offer services unavailable at smaller financial institutions.

_____ c. Features of a full-service bank.

_____ d. Depositors have several investment options besides the traditional savings account, such as renewable certificates and money-market accounts.

Group 2

_____ a. Owning a videocassette recorder.

_____ b. Recording programs for later viewing permits daytime soap-opera fans to see their favorites at night.

_____ c. There are distinct advantages to owning a videocassette recorder.

_____ d. Owning programs on videotape allows viewers to "rerun" their favorites whenever they wish.

Group 3

_____ a. During the Middle Ages, wearing garlic was thought to protect people against werewolves and vampires.

_____ b. The Romans believed that eating garlic gave strength and courage.

_____ c. Throughout the ages, people have believed that garlic has special powers.

_____ d. Special uses of garlic from ancient times on.

Group 4

_____ a. A comparison of two forms of aerobic exercise.

_____ b. Since powerwalkers always have one foot on the ground, they feel only half as much impact when they touch down.

_____ c. For the city dweller, powerwalking—or walking briskly—has several advantages over jogging.

_____ d. The hard surfaces in our cities are much better suited to walking than to running.

Group 5

_____ a. Driving at night is less safe than in the daytime.

_____ b. Driving after dark.

_____ c. In 1981, 62 percent of all traffic deaths took place at night.

_____ d. The chances of being in a fatal accident are nearly four times greater at night than during the day.

SCORE
100 − 5 for each one wrong = _____ %

The following selections have main ideas (topic sentences) that may appear at any place within the paragraph. Identify the topic sentence of each paragraph by filling in the correct sentence number in the space provided. Fill in two numbers in the one case where the main idea appears twice.

_____ 1. [1]Scientists believe that tropical rain forests contain large numbers of plant and animal species still unknown to science. [2]Nevertheless, the rain forests of the world are being recklessly destroyed. [3]In order to grow more food, farmers burn down the forests and plant crops. [4]The nutrients in rain-forest soil, however, are quickly exhausted by farming. [5]Also, trees are cut down for their timber faster than new trees can grow to replace them. [6]Every year, an area of tropical forest the size of Switzerland is destroyed.

_____ 2. [1]Fire extended humans' geographical boundaries by allowing them to travel into regions that were previously too cold to explore. [2]It also kept predators away, allowing early humans to sleep securely. [3]Fire, in fact, has been a significant factor in human development and progress in many ways. [4]Obvious benefits of fire are its uses in cooking and in hunting. [5]Probably even more important, however, is that learning to control fire allowed people to change the very rhythm of their lives. [6]Before fire, the human daily cycle coincided with the rising and setting of the sun. [7]With fire, though, man gained time to think and talk about the day's events and to prepare strategies for coping with tomorrow.

_____ 3. [1]Our legislators, judges, and voters face a bewildering array of ethical problems that demand resolution. [2]One such problem is the so-called "right to die," meaning that terminally ill patients should not receive heroic measures to keep them alive. [3]Another ethical dilemma, one which has not yet been completely resolved, is the abortion issue. [4]A large segment of the population opposes abortion, despite the Supreme Court decision making the procedure legal. [5]Capital punishment is still a volatile issue. [6]Perhaps the most pressing problem we must resolve is the stockpiling of nuclear weapons that inches us ever closer to the unthinkable—a nuclear holocaust.

_____ 4. [1]Several warning signs can indicate car problems. [2]One of these warning signals is a puddle of dark liquid under the car, indicating a leak in the oil or transmission fluid. [3]Another is uneven wear on tire treads. [4]If the outer edge of the tire tread wears out before the center, the tire is under-inflated. [5]The most significant early warning signal, however, is lower mileage readings every time the tank is filled. [6]Lower fuel economy is caused by a variety of problems ranging from a clogged filter to ignition or carburetor trouble. [7]Any of these symptoms tells the driver that there is a significant problem that should be investigated at once.

_____ 5. [1]What looks like a precious diamond, reflects fiery light from its facets like a diamond, can etch glass like a diamond, and costs only a fraction of what a diamond costs? [2]It's cubic zirconia (or C-Z), an artificial crystal developed by Russian space scientists. [3]C-Z duplicates almost all the properties of the precious gemstone, while retailing for much less money. [4]When compared to a real diamond, C-Z matches almost all standard diamond characteristics. [5]Gemologists rate C-Z at 8.5 on the hardness scale, compared to 10 for a diamond; its weight and reflective index are also close to a diamond's. [6]In other words, only a jeweler could tell the difference. [7]Yet a flawless one-carat C-Z stone costs only $55, while a flawless one-carat diamond will put you $30,000 in debt.

> **SCORE**
> 100 − 20 for each one wrong = _____%

A. The following selections have main ideas (topic sentences) that may appear at any place within the paragraph. Identify the topic sentence of each paragraph by filling in the correct sentence number in the space provided.

_____ 1. ¹Finding a good way to get rid of garbage is a problem that faces many municipalities today. ²It may be of some consolation for them to know, however, that getting rid of garbage has almost always involved problems. ³When settlements were very small, garbage was simply thrown outdoors, where it eventually decomposed. ⁴But as communities grew, pigs and other animals helped clear away garbage by eating it; of course, the animals, in turn, recycled that garbage and thus created an even less appealing garbage problem. ⁵The first municipal effort to deal with garbage was begun by Benjamin Franklin, whose solution was to have it dumped into the Delaware River. ⁶A century later, municipal incinerators, generally located in the most crowded part of town, burned garbage and produced the worst of odors as a by-product.

_____ 2. ¹After World War II, the United States sought to establish networks of agents throughout Communist Eastern Europe. ²The Soviet Union, however, penetrated the networks and all but eliminated them. ³In 1958, rebel troops supported by the CIA failed to overthrow President Sukarno of Indonesia; the CIA's denial of involvement collapsed when one of its American pilots was shot down. ⁴Throughout the 1970s, the CIA supplied estimates of Soviet military spending that it later realized were much too low. ⁵And despite a pervasive CIA presence in Iran, the overthrow of the Shah in 1979 caught the Agency by surprise. ⁶Clearly, American intelligence has had its share of failures.

_____ 3. ¹Have you ever noticed how the bulge on the east coast of South America seems to match the indentation on the west coast of Africa? ²In fact, rock layers and mountain ranges of the two areas seem to match up, too. ³Identical types of ancient plant fossils, preserved for thousands of years, are found in both areas. ⁴In addition, the same species of living snails and earthworms appear on both sides of the Atlantic. ⁵Even the continental shelves, the parts of the coastlines that are submerged beneath the sea, have been "fitted" together by computer and are a perfect match. ⁶These facts are not mere coincidences. [7]All this evidence seems to prove the theory of continental drift, the idea that all of Earth's continents were once a giant single land mass that broke apart and formed the familiar continents of today.

B. The following paragraphs have unstated main ideas. Each paragraph is followed by four sentences. After reading each paragraph, circle the letter of the sentence that best expresses the implied main idea.

4. A good way to encourage your family to exercise more often is to use a positive approach. Instead of scaring them with statistics about heart attacks, emphasize how good they'll feel and how much better they'll look if they do daily calisthenics. Another method that works is to set an example. If they see you walking to the convenience store instead of driving, they might be encouraged to do likewise the next time they have errands in the neighborhood. Finally, make exercise a family activity. Suggest that the whole family go swimming together, take up early morning jogging, or join the Y at the group rate.
    a. If you want your family to exercise, use a positive approach.
    b. Exercise is good for the whole family.
    c. There are several ways to get your family to exercise.
    d. Most American families are in poor physical condition.

5. Salespeople who want to increase volume may make promises which the company's production and accounting departments find difficult to support. Production, for example, may not be able to meet the sales department's schedule because purchasing didn't get raw materials in time. While salespeople might like to have large inventories available, production and finance are likely to resist building up stocks because of the high cost of storage and/or owning unsold goods. Also, if production is in the middle of union negotiations, it is likely to feel they are more important than anything else. At the same time, however, salespeople may feel that nothing is more urgent than increasing sales.
    a. The demands of the sales department should be given priority in an organization.
    b. Union demands can slow up production.
    c. Businesses tend to be disorganized due to lack of communication.
    d. Different parts of an organization may have competing needs.

SCORE
100 − 20 for each one wrong = _____%

The following paragraphs contain main ideas that are either stated or unstated. Each paragraph is followed by four sentences. Circle the letter of the sentence that best expresses the main idea of each paragraph.

1. People who want to reduce the amount of salt in their diets should follow a few simple steps. When shopping for food, they should read labels carefully, looking for telltale ingredients like "sodium" and "monosodium glutamate" (MSG). Also, they should avoid salt-coated snacks such as potato chips, pretzels, and corn chips. Canned fish should be drained to remove the salted liquid it is packed in. Finally, people should take the salt shaker off the table, substituting onion powder, garlic powder, herbs or lemon juice—none of which contains salt—to give their food added taste.
   a. Other forms of seasoning can be substituted for salt.
   b. It is possible to lower the amount of salt in our diet in several ways.
   c. Eating too much salt can lead to health problems.
   d. Americans consume too much salt on a daily basis.

2. Sociologist Lucile Duberman suggests that married people think of marriage as "natural" in order "to justify their own state." Anyone who does not conform to this point of view is "challenging the social values." Indeed, most Americans are raised to believe that getting married and having a family are natural parts of growing up. When people remain single, their friends and families often think of them as odd and wait impatiently for them to finally get married. Furthermore, unattached people are often considered threats to married couples: "Will she or he steal my spouse?" As a result, singles have been treated—and often have come to think of themselves—as "different."
   a. Single people have a difficult time meeting suitable partners.
   b. In reality, there is nothing wrong with being single.
   c. In our society, single people are made to feel there is something different about them.
   d. Single people pose a threat to their married friends, who feel they might lose their spouses to them.

3. One good method of dealing with children's fears is to help them understand what they fear. Rather than laughing at the child's genuine feeling or insisting there is nothing to be afraid of, the parent should explain the situation or object of fear to the child. If the child knows, for instance, how a vacuum cleaner works, the appliance will not be so frightening. Another way to handle children's fears is to set an example for the child by remaining calm. If the parent is unafraid, the child may realize there is nothing to fear. Most importantly, parents should listen

to their children talk about their fears but not overindulge them—say, by canceling plans for an evening out—or the fears will remain.

   a.   Childhood fears are a normal part of growing up.

   b.   Parents should not laugh at their children's fears.

   c.   If parents do not learn to deal with their children's fears, the children will become increasingly anxious and dependent.

   d.   Several strategies can help parents deal with their children's fears.

4.   If you want to improve productivity, improve quality. Think about it. If every person and machine did things right the first time, the same number of people could handle much larger volumes of work. High costs of inspection could be channeled into productive activities, and managers could take all the time they spend checking and devote it to productive tasks. Wasted materials would become a thing of the past. In fact, it's been estimated that attention to quality can reduce the total cost of operations anywhere from 10 to 50 percent. As Philip Crosby said: "Quality is free. What costs money are the unquality things—all the actions that involve not doing jobs right the first time."

   a.   Too many workers are satisfied with low quality products.

   b.   The secret of better production is more attention to quality .

   c.   Managers could be more productive.

   d.   Productivity could be improved if managers spent more time checking up on employees.

SCORE

100 − 25 for each one wrong = _____%

The following paragraphs contain main ideas that are either stated or unstated. Each paragraph is followed by four sentences. Circle the letter of the sentence that best expresses the main idea of each paragraph.

1. A hidden treasure on Oak Island, a small island off Nova Scotia, is one of the most intriguing of unsolved mysteries. In 1795, three young men found a spot on the island with live oak trees—which are not native to the region. One giant tree was carved with figures and had a branch cut off four feet from the trunk. Under this branch was a slight depression in the ground. The men began digging there. They uncovered an oak platform ten feet under the ground. Two more platforms were found at twenty and thirty feet. The three men gave up, but others came to explore "the money pit." In 1849, drilling began. More oak was found at ninety-eight feet. When the drill bit came up, gold dust glittered on it. Unfortunately, sea water rushed into the underground chamber, ending the drilling. No one has yet reached the treasure, although digging continues. We know that it lies 170 feet down, and that it is protected by a series of tunnels that allow the tide to rush in. Who built such a complex system? What is buried down there? These questions still await answers.
   a. Nobody knows who buried the Oak Island treasure, what it is, or how to dig it up.
   b. There is something buried 170 feet below the surface of a small island near Nova Scotia.
   c. One day we will solve the mystery of the Oak Island treasure.
   d. A series of discoveries led to the location of the Oak Island treasure.

2. Police estimate that only 1 to 2 percent of unpleasant incidents are reported, and so there are no accurate statistics on the dangers of hitchhiking. Horror stories, however, are common. There was the 19-year-old woman who accepted a lift from three young men in New Jersey, expecting a ride across the bridge to New York City. Instead they drove to a motel, where they repeatedly raped her. She was lucky; she escaped with her life. Less fortunate was the 18-year-old woman student who disappeared from campus after accepting a ride with a stranger and whose decomposed body was found in a suburban sewage plant two years later. Male hitchhikers are less open to assault, but a number of incidents show that they are far from immune. Hitchhikers also face the hazards of riding with an intoxicated or stoned driver, not the least of which is an accident. They also risk assault or robbery by other hitchhikers and being stranded in out-of-the-way places. Drivers, too, are subject to assault and robbery. And they risk accident by stopping on a busy highway, or arrest if their passengers happen to be carrying drugs. Some male drivers have picked up young girls who threatened to call the police and cry rape unless the men handed over all their money.
   a. Although "horror stories" are common, nobody really knows how many people have been victimized while hitchhiking.

b. Hitchhiking can be dangerous to both hitchhiker and driver.
c. Women hitchhikers are more likely than men to be assaulted.
d. Hitchhiking should be prohibited because of the risks involved.

3. A clinical psychologist normally holds a Ph.D. or M.A. degree, while a psychiatrist is an M.D. The Ph.D. clinical psychologist has taken four or five years of postgraduate work; the M.A. clinical psychologist has had about two years of postgraduate work and works under the supervision of a Ph.D. psychologist. The psychiatrist, on the other hand, has gone to medical school and has then completed three or four years of residency training in psychiatry. This difference in training means that the clinical psychologist, who has no medical training, cannot prescribe drugs. It also means that whenever there is a possibility of a medical disorder, a patient should be examined by a psychiatrist. Further, only a psychiatrist can commit a patient to a hospital for care and treatment.
a. Patients should be under the care of psychiatrists, not psychologists.
b. Psychologists and psychiatrists must undergo a great deal of training.
c. Psychologists and psychiatrists differ in training and capabilities.
d. Medical disorders should be treated by psychiatrists.

4. If we compressed the entire history of life on the planet into a single year, the first modern human would not appear until December 31 at about 11:53 P.M., and the first civilizations would emerge only about a minute before the end of the year. Yet mankind's achievements in its brief history on earth have been remarkable. Some 15,000 years ago our ancestors practiced religious rituals and painted superb pictures on the walls of their caves. Around 11,000 years ago, some human groups began to domesticate animals and plants, thereby freeing themselves from total dependence on hunting and gathering food. About 6000 years ago people began to live in cities, to specialize in different forms of labor, to divide into social classes, and to create distinct political and economic institutions. Within a few thousand years empires were created, linking isolated groups and bringing millions under centralized rule. Advanced agricultural practices improved farming, resulting in growing populations and the emergence of large nation-states. A mere 250 years ago the Industrial Revolution began, thrusting us into the modern world of factories and computers, jets and nuclear reactors, instantaneous global communications and terrifying military technologies.
a. Human civilization is a very recent development.
b. In its short time on earth, humanity has accomplished a great deal.
c. Humans are the highest form of life on earth.
d. Until only 250 years ago, human society was based on agriculture.

| **SCORE** |
| 100 − 25 for each one wrong = _____% |

Major and minor supporting details are mixed together in the four lists below. The details in each list support a given main idea. Complete the outlines that follow each list by filling in *only the major supporting details*. Two items have been done for you.

A. Main idea: There are some easy ways to make studying more successful.

- Calendar marked with important semester dates
- Keep track of class assignments and tests
- Brief breaks while studying
- Recreation time
- Place without distractions
- Calendar marked with weekly study needs
- Have proper study environment
- Sufficient lighting

1. _____

2. _____

3. *Pace schedule to avoid exhaustion* _____

B. Main idea: There are ways to stay motivated to exercise.

- Picture yourself looking better.
- Picture yourself feeling better.
- Examine and reject your excuses.
- Use visualization.
- Reward yourself for your successes.
- Prepare for times of weakness.
- Choose exercises you enjoy.
- Make plans with others so you won't back out.

1. _____

2. _____

3. *Make it fun.* _____

C. Main idea: Cinderella was treated badly by her stepmother.

- Denied social equality
- Had to clean the house
- Made to cook all the food
- Deprived of material benefits
- No new clothing
- Forbidden to go to ball
- Made to work hard
- No comfortable bed
- Excluded from family social life

1. _____

2. _____

3. _____

D. Main idea: Divorce has serious negative consequences.

- Social adjustment is troublesome.
- Feelings of guilt and resentment may persist between the former husband and wife.
- Starting to date again can be nerve-wracking.
- Standard of living usually declines.
- Emotional difficulties among the original family members are common.
- Married friends may exclude singles from social plans.
- Financial problems occur.
- Children may be confused and hurt.
- Alimony, child support, and property dispersal must be dealt with.

1. _____

2. _____

3. _____

SCORE
100 − 10 for each one wrong = _____%

A. Major and minor supporting details are mixed together in the list below. The details of the list support a given main idea. Complete the outline that follows by filling in *both the major and minor supporting details*. Some details have been filled in for you.

Main idea: Television ads appeal to emotions.

- Beautiful people associated with products
- Appeals to worries about being socially unacceptable
- Concerns about bad breath and body odor
- Embarrassment over such things as "ring around the collar"
- Appeals to concerns for healthy diet

1. *Appeals to desire to be attractive*

    a. _____

    b. *Sex appeal used even to promote such things as cars and food*

2. _____

    a. _____

    b. _____

3. _____

    a. *Numerous foods claimed to be "natural"*

    b. *Foods associated with athletic activities*

B. Below each of the following passages is a question raised by the main idea of the passage. After reading each passage, answer the questions by stating the major supporting details. You may use either the words of the passage or your own words.

1. Most teenagers who smoke are familiar with the health hazards of smoking, yet for various reasons they drift into the habit anyway. A teenager with one parent who smokes is twice as likely to smoke as one with nonsmoking parents. Also, young people are more likely to smoke if their friends do. The chances are nine out of ten that a teenager whose best friend smokes will also start to smoke. In addition, teens who mature late are more likely to smoke than others, apparently because they hope that smoking will make them look more adult.

What are three factors that increase the likelihood that teenagers will smoke?

a. _____

b. _____

c. _____

2. New technologies provide companies with more useful information about consumers and their preferences than has ever been available before. For example, recording the license numbers of the cars in a store's parking lot is the first step in finding out where current customers live. A computer program then matches the license numbers with home addresses and creates a map that can be used as a basis for an advertising campaign directed to potential new customers. Another new way to gather information is to follow customers' eye movements with cameras that reveal exactly what captures people's interest in store displays.

What two kinds of information about customers can new technologies gather?

a. _____

b. _____

SCORE

100 − 10 for each one wrong = _____%

A. Major and minor supporting details are mixed together in the list below. The details of the list support a given main idea. Complete the outline that follows by filling in *both the major and minor supporting details*. Some details have been filled in for you.

Main idea: Some of my ways of cleaning house are strange, but they work for me.

- I pretend it's not part of the house and thus doesn't need cleaning.
- Those I look out of a lot are cleaned often.
- I don't mind getting wet then.
- It's easier to rinse off the soap when the shower's on.
- Magazines my husband saves go down there.

I. *I wash windows according to importance and convenience.*

   a. _____

      1. *Thus the kitchen windows get washed frequently.*

      2. *The windows in the children's bedrooms never get washed.*

   b. *When I'm sprinkling the lawn, I also spray the outside of nearby windows.*

II. *I clean the shower while showering.*

   a. _____

   b. _____

III. *The basement has a special place in my cleaning scheme.*

   a. _____

   b. *I put messes from other parts of the house there.*

      1. *Whatever is under the children's beds goes down there.*

      2. _____

B. Below each of the following passages is a question raised by the main idea of the passage. After reading each passage, answer the questions by stating the major supporting details. You may use either the words of the passage or your own words.

1. A new puppy will be a member of the family for a long time, so you should choose one carefully. Many people, however, make their selections impulsively because puppies are so cute. You can best resist this temptation by doing some reading even before you begin shopping for your pet, so that you can know ahead of time which

breeds suit your family's lifestyle. For example, if no one has time to walk the dog, don't pick a breed that needs a lot of exercise. Also, look for a curious pup when shopping, since curiosity is a sign of intelligence. One way to find a pet with a healthy dose of curiosity is to clap your hands and see which puppies act most interested.

Which are two things about a puppy that shoppers should look for?

a. _____

b. _____

2. You are part of a network of family and friends that can always be available to give you advice, emotional support, and practical help. However, this network works most effectively when you use it well. First, be sure you are willing to help others at least as much as they help you. When you do need advice or help, try to ask for only one thing at a time rather than overwhelming someone with too many requests. Finally, you should be willing to accept the advice and offers of help you do get. There is little benefit to brushing them off and giving excuses for not doing anything about the problems in your life.

How can the network of people who can help and advise you best be used?

a. _____

b. _____

c. _____

| **SCORE** |
| 100 − 10 for each one wrong = _____% |

A. Major and minor supporting details are mixed together in the list be-
    low. The details of the list support a given main idea. Complete the
    outline that follows by filling in *both the major and minor supporting
    details*. Some details have been filled in for you.

    Main idea: Several factors have been found to influence the justice
                system's treatment of criminals.

    • Race of offenders affects their treatment
    • Nonwhites awarded parole and probation less often
    • Young offenders given special treatment
    • Sex of offenders influences severity of sentences
    • Blacks executed more often for capital crimes

    1. _____
        a. *Women less likely to receive death penalty than men*
        b. *More reluctance to send a mother to prison than a father*

    2. _____
        a. _____
        b. _____

    3. *Age of offenders is considered in sentencing*
        a. _____
        b. *More lenient sentences for the elderly*

B. Below each of the following passages is a question raised by the main
    idea of the passage. After reading each passage, answer the questions by
    stating the major supporting details. You may use either the words of
    the passage or your own words.

    1. The American musical is faced with pressures that endanger it. Ris-
        ing costs make producing a musical riskier in two ways. First, inves-
        tors are becoming more cautious about risking the great amounts
        of money needed to back a production. Also, the more it costs to
        put on a musical, the more tickets cost, and so fewer people can
        afford them. Changes in musical taste may also help to doom the
        musical. Although some rock musicals have been successful, the tra-
        ditional musical relies on gentler rhythms and less harsh tones. It
        remains to be seen if this distinctly American art form can continue
        to adapt to new financial and musical demands.

        What two factors are endangering the musical?

        a. _____
        b. _____

2. The climate becomes colder when the amount of dust at high altitudes in the atmosphere increases. There are several ways that dust gets into the atmosphere. Volcanic eruptions can add so much dust that sunlight is scattered back to outer space. Chimneys, especially industrial smokestacks, also throw large amounts of dust into the atmosphere. The burning of tropical forests to clear land for farming is another way the amount of airborne dust is increased. One reason a nuclear war is so ominous is that it might add so much dust to the atmosphere that it could cause a new ice age—a nuclear winter in which the climate becomes so cold that no new crops can be grown.

What are three ways that dust gets into the atmosphere?

a. _____

b. _____

c. _____

SCORE
100 − 10 for each one wrong = _____%

Below each of the following passages is a question raised by the main idea of the passage. After reading each passage, answer the questions by stating the major supporting details. You may use either the words of the passage or your own words.

1. Early human handiwork suggests that ancient peoples had values much like our own. A round architectural foundation in Africa that is two million years old reveals an appreciation like our own for balance and form. A flower arrangement found in an ancient burial site in Iraq suggests that flowers were a symbol of comfort. Ice Age sculptures emphasize human sexuality, showing the importance of fertility to early people. And cave paintings dating back to 20,000 B.C. prove that the artists were keen observers of nature.

    What values of early man are seen in each of the four examples of ancient art?

    a. _____

    b. _____

    c. _____

    d. _____

2. Many tons of matter from outer space fall on the earth every day. Much of what falls to earth are tiny fragments of comets so light that they do not burn up as they float through the air. Sometimes pieces of comets are large enough to survive their passage through the air as shooting stars. These large meteorites can weigh as much as several tons. Also, at least one rock seems to have fallen to earth from the moon. It is a greenish-brown stone the size of a golfball which was found in Antarctica in 1982. It is identical in makeup to rocks brought back from the moon by the Apollo 15 astronauts. Other rocks have been found that are probably from Mars, although no positive identification can be made until astronauts bring rock samples back from Mars.

    Where did the rocks that have fallen to earth from space seem to have come from?

    a. _____

    b. _____

    c. _____

3. Everyone is familiar with steam heat, gas heat, and solar heat. But how about corn heat? Inventor Carroll Buckner has devised a stove that runs on raw kernels of corn. According to Buckner, the stove has several advantages. First, it's economical. He claims his invention can heat a

house in the winter for about thirty dollars a month, assuming that corn is two dollars a bushel. The stove can produce enough heat to warm an area of 2000 square feet. Also, whereas the emissions from wood-burning stoves can harm the environment, a corn-burning stove, says Buckner, doesn't pollute the air. Finally, by creating a demand for corn, the stove would create a new market for America's troubled farmers.

What are the advantages of the corn-burning stove?

a. _____

b. _____

c. _____

SCORE
100 − 10 for each one wrong = _____%

TRANSITIONS: Test 1

Complete each sentence with the appropriate transition word or phrase. Then circle the kind of transition you have used.

1. a. Our teacher was absent, _____ the test was postponed.
                    so   while   but
    b. The transition indicates
                    time   contrast   cause and effect

2. a. "_____ you chop an onion," Carla said patiently to Harry, "you must peel it."
                    Since   Before   Although
    b. The transition indicates
                    time   location   contrast

3. a. Clothing styles can reflect other aspects of society. One man,

        _____, uses the length of skirts to predict stockmarket moves.
                    for instance   to sum up   similarly
    b. The transition indicates
                    comparison   illustration   summary

4. a. The local wildlife sanctuary has a different guided walk every Saturday morning. Self-guided nature tours are _____ available.
                    accordingly   truly   also
    b. The transition indicates
                    cause and effect   emphasis   addition

5. a. This morning I yelled at my daughter for using my fountain pen and not returning it, and then I found it at the _____ of my briefcase.
                    first   bottom   conclusion
    b. The transition indicates
                    location   cause and effect   clarification

6. a. Jackie dresses well on a low budget. _____, she shops carefully.
                    As an illustration   Evidently   Still
    b. The transition indicates
                    addition   clarification   contrast

7. a. _____ humans keep cows for milk, some ants keep aphids for the sweet honeydew they produce.
                    Because   Just as   Although
    b. The transition indicates
                    addition   comparison   contrast

8. a. The windshield wipers squeak, _____ they don't clean well.

                  and   in short   thus

    b. The transition indicates

             illustration   cause and effect   addition

9. a. "Today we've discussed diet, exercise, and sleep as factors in stress management," the lecturer said. "_____, let's look at the role your friends can play."

            Specifically   In other words   To conclude

    b. The transition indicates

           conclusion   illustration   clarification

10. a. Freedom of religion is what drew many to the New World. _____, not all who sought such freedom were anxious to grant it to others.

            Nevertheless   Likewise   For instance

    b. The transition indicates

           contrast   comparison   illustration

SCORE

100 − 5 for each one wrong = _____%

Complete each sentence with the appropriate transition word or phrase. Then circle the kind of transition you have used.

1. a. Paula swerved to avoid hitting a squirrel sitting _____ the road.

   during   in the middle of   to the left of

   b. The transition indicates

   clarification   illustration   location

2. a. "_____ you really want that bike, _____ you'll have to earn the money for it yourself," I told my eleven-year-old.

   First . . . second   Undoubtedly . . . of course   If . . . then

   b. The transitions indicate

   time   cause and effect   emphasis

3. a. My brother, who has weird taste, likes to collect dead bugs. He _____ collects bars of soap from motels.

   equally   also   as an illustration

   b. The transition indicates

   illustration   addition   comparison

4. a. Mr. Forsyth knows Russian. _____, he can speak it fluently.

   In conclusion   For example   In fact

   b. The transition indicates

   clarification   illustration   summary

5. a. Koalas are related to kangaroos, not bears. _____, panda "bears" are related to raccoons.

   Specifically   Similarly   Undoubtedly

   b. The transition indicates

   contrast   comparison   clarification

6. a. Some scientists, _____ Roy Wolford, believe vitamins may prolong life.

   such as   last of all   after

   b. The transition indicates

   time   illustration   addition

7. a. The new night watchman is well qualified. _____, he was a security guard at a nuclear power plant.

   Previously   Ultimately   Consequently

   b. The transition indicates

   time   clarification   illustration

8. a. On our last vacation, we visited the Grand Canyon, Las Vegas,

    and San Francisco. _____, it was quite a trip.

    In short   To be specific   Immediately

    b. The transition indicates

    time   illustration   summary

9. a. Jonas has come to work late every day for the last month.

    _____, he's asking to be fired.

    Next   Clearly   For example

    b. The transition indicates

    illustration   emphasis   cause and effect

10. a. I know some of you are not looking forward to our field trip to

    the natural science museum. _____, I think you'll be

    surprised at how much you'll enjoy it.

    In a similar fashion   For example   Still

    b. The transition indicates

    location   illustration   contrast

SCORE

100 − 5 for each one wrong = _____%

Complete each sentence with the appropriate transition word or phrase. Then circle the kind of transition you have used.

1. a. We started our day at the county fair by attending a woodworking demonstration. _____, we watched a tractor-pulling contest.

    　　　　　Likewise　　As a result　　Next

    b. The transition indicates

    　　　　　time　　comparison　　conclusion

2. a. _____ there are no clocks in gambling casinos, gamblers can easily lose all sense of time.

    　　　　　Just as　　Since　　Although

    b. The transition indicates

    　　　　　cause and effect　　clarification　　time

3. a. Winetasters never swallow the wine they taste; _____, they swirl it around in their mouths and spit it out.

    　　　　　on the contrary　　in like manner　　finally

    b. The transition indicates

    　　　　　illustration　　addition　　contrast

4. a. Some women's jewelry is very expensive. _____, one diamond bracelet designed to be worn on a tennis court costs $3,500.

    　　　　　Often　　In addition　　For instance

    b. The transition indicates

    　　　　　addition　　comparison　　illustration

5. a. Joanne defrosted the meat patties _____ the refrigerator so the cat couldn't reach them.

    　　　　　like　　next to　　on top of

    b. The transition indicates

    　　　　　location　　cause and effect　　clarification

6. a. Bookbinder's is famous for its seafood dishes, _____ crabcakes and lobster.

    　　　　　just like　　first of all　　such as

    b. The transition indicates

    　　　　　illustration　　clarification　　addition

7. a. Fiberglass pools are simple to maintain; _____, they are easy to install.

    　　　　　likewise　　conversely　　finally

    b. The transition indicates

    　　　　　conclusion　　comparison　　addition

8. a. A handful of students showed up on the day of the blizzard. _____ they hadn't heard that all the schools were closed.

   In addition   Accordingly   Evidently

   b. The transition indicates

   addition   clarification   illustration

9. a. First, the pinch hitter selected a bat from the rack. Then he took a few practice swings. _____ he knelt in the on-deck circle, waiting his turn at the plate.

   Previously   Of course   Finally

   b. The transition indicates

   illustration   emphasis   addition

10. a. In a Virginia reel, the dancers form two lines, one of men and one of women. _____ each dancer is his or her partner.

   First of all   Opposite   On the contrary

   b. The transition indicates

   time   contrast   location

SCORE

100 − 5 for each one wrong = _____%

This test will check your ability to recognize the relationships (signaled by transitions) within and between sentences. Read each passage and answer the questions that follow.

A. [1]Many of today's children learn that Cinderella wore glass slippers, but the popular heroine didn't always have breakable shoes. [2]Her old and international story was accidentally slightly changed in that regard by the French writer Charles Perrault, who popularized it with his version, published in 1697. [3]Perrault referred to Cinderella's slippers as being made of "verre," the French word for glass. [4]The old French versions which were his sources, however, used the word "vair"—white squirrel fur. [5]In other words, generations of children have had the pleasure of the dramatic image of glass shoes because of a mistranslation.

    1. The relationship between the two parts of sentence 1 is one of
        a. contrast   c. cause and effect
        b. comparison d. clarification
    2. The relationship of sentence 5 to the passage is one of
        a. addition   c. comparison
        b. illustration d. summary

B. [1]Have you ever had the experience of recognizing someone's face but not being able to recall his or her name? [2]This happens because that information is split up and stored in the two different sides of your brain. [3]And each side has its own way of thinking and remembering. [4]Remembering someone's face is the task of the right side of your brain, which understands whole things at once and is responsible for visualizing, recognizing similarities, and supplying intuitions. [5]This side of your brain provides insights that are hard to put into words. [6]On the other hand, the words themselves—including the name that you have forgotten—are stored in the left side of your brain. [7]This is the side responsible for speaking, reading, writing and reasoning.

    1. The relationship of sentence 3 to sentence 2 is one of
        a. addition   c. illustration
        b. contrast   d. summary
    2. The relationship of sentence 6 to sentence 5 is one of
        a. addition   c. cause and effect
        b. contrast   d. summary

C. [1]Leaders of totalitarian movements usually have been men of great charisma who are able to motivate the masses. [2]Such leaders often seemed to be solely driven by their cause, without a care for the material things that motivate others, which undoubtedly added to their ability to gain people's confidence. [3]Fidel Castro, for example, was a superb speaker and got the backing of the majority of Cubans with his Christlike appearance, dedication to his cause, and long, eloquent television speeches. [4]Those speeches included attacks against his opponents, who often fled the country as a consequence of one of his assaults.

1. The relationship of sentence 3 to the first two sentences is one of
   a. comparison.   c. cause and effect.
   b. illustration.   d. clarification.
2. The relationship between the two parts of sentence 4 is one of
   a. addition.   c. cause and effect.
   b. illustration.   d. conclusion.

D. [1]Scientists have learned that the way we view exercise strongly influences our performance. [2]Research on Russian weightlifters, for example, demonstrated that if they were told the weights were heavy, they perceived an exercise to be more difficult. [3]If they were told the weights were light, then they considered the exercise easier. [4]Similarly, one Russian weightlifter broke a record that had eluded him after his trainer told him the weights he was lifting were not as heavy as they in fact were. [5]In another study, when people exercising on a stationary bicycle were told they were going uphill, their heart rates increased noticeably.

1. The relationship between the two parts of sentence 3 is one of
   a. contrast.   c. illustration.
   b. comparison.   d. cause and effect.
2. The relationship of sentence 4 to sentence 3 is one of
   a. addition.   c. comparison.
   b. time.   d. illustration.

E. [1]A calorie is the amount of heat required to raise the temperature of a kilogram (about a quart) of water one degree Celsius. [2]To determine the number of calories in a portion of food, a technician uses a device called a bomb calorimeter. [3]This device has a chamber that rests in a container of water. [4]The food is placed in this chamber, which is then filled with oxygen under high pressure. [5]Next, the food is set on fire. [6]As it burns, it gives off heat; the result is that the temperature of the water in the container rises. [7]Finally, the total rise in temperature is measured, giving the calorie content of the food.

1. The relationship between sentences 4 and 5 is one of
   a. time.   c. location.
   b. illustration.   d. cause and effect.

2. Sentence 6 shows relationships of
   a. addition.   c. location.
   b. time.   d. cause and effect.

SCORE

100 − 10 for each one wrong = _____%

This test will check your ability to recognize the relationships (signaled by transitions) within and between sentences. Read each passage and answer the questions that follow.

A. [1]Some of the staples of Italian-American cooking are not native to Italy. [2]For example, veal Parmesan, an American favorite, is not eaten in Italy. [3]It was invented when immigrants adapted the Italian recipe for eggplant Parmesan for use with the abundant meat available in the U.S. [4]Spaghetti and meatballs is another American dish unknown in Italy, as is pizza with everything on it. [5]Italian pizza is topped with one or two ingredients, and it is not sliced before it is served.

    1. The relationship of sentence 2 to sentence 1 is one of
        a. location.   c. illustration.
        b. contrast.   d. comparison.
    2. The word signaling the relationship of sentence 4 to sentence 3 is
        a. Another.   c. In.
        b. As.   d. On.

B. [1]The use of fire by prehistoric people probably affected wildlife both intentionally and unintentionally. [2]In all likelihood, early people used fire to drive game toward waiting hunters. [3]Later, new plant growth in the burned areas would attract more wild animals. [4]In addition, accidental fires must have also occurred frequently. [5]Because prehistoric people had trouble starting fires, they kept burning embers on hand. [6]The result must have been widespread accidental fires, especially in dry areas. [7]Certainly, these fires also would have greatly altered the habitat for wildlife.

    1. The relationship between the two parts of sentence 5 is one of
        a. contrast.   c. location.
        b. cause and effect.   d. addition.
    2. The first word in sentence 7 is used to show
        a. emphasis   c. illustration.
        b. comparison.   d. addition.

C. [1]High school seniors are expected to make crucial decisions about their future careers, yet many of them are still unrealistic about what they plan to do. [2]They seem to have little knowledge of what their chosen careers involve or how much training they require. [3]For instance, a study of more than 6,000 high school seniors in Texas showed that only about half were planning to get the appropriate amount of education for the careers they had chosen. [4]The rest were planning too many or too few years of training. [5]A more disturbing finding is that most of the students did not seem to be choosing careers that matched their interests.

1. The relationship between the two parts of sentence 1 is one of
    a. location.   c. illustration.
    b. contrast.   d. cause and effect.
2. The relationship of sentence 3 to sentence 2 is one of
    a. comparison.   c. illustration.
    b. summary.   d. time.

D.   [1]An altruistic person helps other people even when he or she expects to get nothing in return. [2]If an altruistic person walks by a car left with its lights on, then he or she is likely to try to turn them off. [3]Altruism can also motivate people to give money and time to worthy causes. [4]At its extreme, altruism means giving one's life for others, as does Mother Theresa or the person who leaps in front of a train to save a child's life. [5]In short, altruistic actions can range from the trivial to the heroic.

1. The relationship between the two parts of sentence 2 is one of
    a. location.   c. cause and effect.
    b. illustration.   d. comparison.
2. The relationship between sentence 5 and those before it is one of
    a. contrast.   c. illustration.
    b. summary.   d. cause and effect.

E.   [1]In 1850 an old pear tree stood at the corner of Third Avenue and East Thirteenth Street in New York City. [2]It still bore fruit although it had been planted more than two hundred years before by Peter Stuyvesant when he came from Holland to what was then New Amsterdam. [3]The tree was finally removed after it was destroyed in a carriage accident in 1867. [4]In that period, the streets were made of cobblestones which were hard to walk on, but pathways made of smooth, flat stones were provided for pedestrians at street corners. [5]Today one of the buildings that stood near the corner in the 1860s remains, but most of the buildings, like the old tree, are gone. [6]Likewise, the cobblestones have been replaced by smooth asphalt streets, and an electric traffic light stands today where the pear tree once stood.

1. The relationship between sentence 4 and sentence 3 is one of
    a. time.   c. cause and effect.
    b. illustration.   d. summary.
2. The signal word at the beginning of sentence 6 shows a relationship between sentence 6 and sentence 5 of
    a. clarification.   c. contrast.
    b. location.   d. comparison.

SCORE
100 − 10 for each one wrong = _____%

Circle the letter that correctly identifies the primary pattern of organization in each of the following passages.

1. Why do people daydream? One cause of daydreaming is routine or boring jobs that are tolerable only when workers imagine themselves doing something else. Deprivation also leads to daydreaming. During World War II, conscientious objectors who volunteered to go on semistarvation diets for six months focused their daydreams on food. Some even hung enticing pictures of foods on their walls to give themselves something to daydream about. Another reason people daydream is to discharge hostile feelings. For example, if an angry student imagines dropping his instructor out of a classroom window, it might help him to laugh at and dismiss his annoyance with her. Some people also daydream as a way to plan for the future, so that by the time they face the situations they imagine, they will know what to say and how to act.

   a. time order   b. contrast   c. cause and effect

2. We have progressed steadily toward outer space ever since the first supersonic jet flights of the late 1950s. The pilots who broke the sound barrier in the X-1 and X-15 planes often flew into the highest reaches of our atmosphere and almost achieved weightlessness. Following these flights, satellites began to be put into orbit, first by the Soviet Union and then by the United States. The next step was a series of manned flights in tiny space capsules launched into orbit by massive booster rockets. From the first Mercury flights to the Apollo flights that eventually landed on the moon, this stage marked humankind's efforts to reach our nearest neighbor—our moon. During the 1970s, the Pioneer and Viking programs sent unmanned probes to the planets in our solar system and even beyond. One interstellar probe has been flung out of our solar system into the space between the stars and should, theoretically, go on exploring forever.

   a. time order   b. comparison   c. cause and effect

3. Habituation is the psychological term for a common human behavior pattern: the more we are exposed to a stimulus, the less aware we become of it and, therefore, the less we respond to it. In other words, once we get used to something, we no longer notice it or try to do anything about it. During the war in Vietnam, reports and pictures from the combat zone appeared every night on television. Viewers soon became so accustomed to these stories on the network news programs that scenes of violence and escalating body counts no longer horrified them. Once the Vietnam War had entered our living rooms, it became just another television program—and just as easy to turn off.

   a. list of items   b. contrast   c. definition and example

4. A divorcing couple experiences several kinds of separations. One is a combination of legal and economic separation. At this stage the couple must decide how to divide their money and other assets. Changes in the way family members, friends and acquaintances respond to the couple as their divorce becomes known make up another, public aspect of the divorce. In the meanwhile, the divorcing couple is also separating emotionally. Sometimes this emotional distancing begins long before the legal divorce, but often even after a man and woman realize their marriage is over, they still long for each other.

   a. list of items   b. comparison   c. definition and example

5. Alcohol and marijuana have a great deal in common. People use them to relax, to become less inhibited, and to achieve a pleasant, euphoric feeling. Also, they inspire similar abuse patterns: heavy drinkers comprise about 9 percent of our population; heavy marijuana users, 10 percent. However, alcohol and marijuana have been viewed very differently in the United States. Perhaps because it has been around for thousands of years, alcohol is much more widely accepted. The attempt to outlaw its use through Prohibition lasted only fourteen years before being repealed in 1933. On the other hand, few people protested in 1937 when the Marijuana Tax Act made marijuana use illegal, and even today, only a minority of citizens favor its decriminalization.

   a. time order   b. comparison/contrast   c. cause and effect

SCORE
100 − 20 for each one wrong = _____%

Arrange the groups of scrambled sentences below into logical paragraphs by numbering them in an order that makes sense. Then circle the letter of the primary pattern of organization used.

Group 1

_____ Also, high tuitions affect the amount of time many students can put into their studies.

_____ For one thing, it undoubtedly prevents some students from attending college in the first place.

_____ Finally, those who do manage to get loans know that they must begin their careers with large debts.

_____ The high cost of college today causes problems in more ways than one.

_____ Because loans and scholarships are difficult to get, many students simply have to put in numerous hours at work in order to afford school.

a. Contrast   c. Cause and effect
b. Comparison   d. Definition and example

Group 2

_____ In either case, they are part of the society's culture.

_____ Artifacts are those objects made and used by a society.

_____ Americans, for example, use an enormous variety of artifacts, from paper clips to spaceships.

_____ They may have originated with the society or have been borrowed from others.

_____ On the other hand, in technologically advanced societies, there are numerous artifacts.

_____ In those societies whose technologies are relatively undeveloped, there are few artifacts—a few tools, cooking utensils, and so on.

a. Time order   c. Cause and effect
b. List of items   d. Definition and example

Group 3

_____ Check the classified ads and two or three real estate offices for apartments within your price range and desired locale.

_____ When you're looking for an apartment, begin by making a list of promising openings.

_____ When you have chosen your apartment, have a lawyer or other person knowledgeable about leases examine your lease before you sign it.

_____ As you inspect each apartment, make sure that faucets, toilets, stoves, and electrical wiring and outlets are functioning efficiently and safely.

_____ After you have made a solid list, visit at least five of the most promising openings.

a. Time order c. Cause and effect
b. Contrast d. Definition and example

Group 4

_____ Last, even the soaps in his bathroom are pink, white, or blue.

_____ In addition, a huge American flag hangs like a picture over the sofa in his living room.

_____ First, along the sidewalk is a picket fence that's painted red, white and blue; the blue slats of the fence are sprinkled with white stars.

_____ One of my neighbors has expressed his patriotism by decorating his home in an unusual way.

_____ Moreover, the sofa itself is bright red, with little blue pillows at either end.

a. Time order c. Comparison
b. List of items d. Definition and example

┌───┐
│   **SCORE**   │
│ **100 − 4 for each one wrong =** _____**%** │
└───┘

For each passage, put the sentence number of the main idea in the space provided. Then circle the letter of the answer that accurately identifies the primary pattern of organization of the passage.

1. ¹When you shop for sunglasses, you should do more than look for flattering frames at a bargain price. ²First, choose sunglasses that are dark enough. ³Dark colors such as green and gray provide better protection for your eyes than light colors such as pale pink and light blue. ⁴To determine whether the glasses you like are dark enough, try them on and look in a mirror. ⁵If you can see your eyes through the lenses, they are too light. ⁶You should also check for irregularities in the lenses. ⁷Hold up the sunglasses and look through them at something with straight horizontal and vertical lines on it, such as a window pane. ⁸As you move the glasses up and down, the lines should not waver. ⁹If they do, choose a different pair of sunglasses.

Sentence with the main idea: _____
Passage's pattern of organization:
a. list of items
b. comparison
c. cause and effect

2. ¹People who are continually exposed to too much noise can feel tired all the time yet be unable to sleep soundly. ²Their bodies may be plagued by digestive spasms, increased heart rates, and constricted blood vessels. ³Studies conducted on animals show that noise pollution can eventually result in damage to the ears, heart, and brain. ⁴Thus for humans, noise pollution may be one of the reasons not only for hearing loss but also for high blood pressure, ulcers, and emotional disorders.

Sentence with the main idea: _____
Passage's pattern of organization:
a. time order
b. contrast
c. cause and effect

3. ¹Jackalopes are animals said to be crosses between jack rabbits and antelopes. ²Actually, they are the fictitious creations of storytellers as well as taxidermists, who add deer antlers to stuffed rabbits. ³Tales of such animals are plentiful. ⁴For instance, African folk tales feature hares that wear false horns in order to join gatherings of horned animals, and horned hares were pictured in a book published in Europe in 1662. ⁵In American humorous tales, jackalopes are sometimes described as fierce giants. ⁶For example, the Nebraskan jackalope is known as the warrior rabbit, and Wyoming jackalopes are rumored to be as large as trees.

Sentence with the main idea: _____
Passage's pattern of organization:
a. list of items
b. cause and effect
c. definition and example

4. [1]Cities in developing countries are noticeably different from those in wealthier nations. [2]Visitors often comment on the number of younger people in the less developed countries. [3]Almost half of all city residents in these countries are children and young people as compared to less than one quarter of the population of cities in developed countries. [4]Also, many unskilled workers found jobs in European and North American cities when the economies there became industrialized. [5]In contrast, one quarter of the work force is unemployed in a typical city in a developing country. [6]Although homeless people are found in Europe and North America, many more people live on the street and in improvised shacks in the less-developed nations. [7]In Mexico City, for instance, more than four million squatters live in improvised shelters.

Sentence with the main idea: _____
Passage's pattern of organization:
a. time order
b. contrast
c. cause and effect

SCORE
100 − 12.5 for each one wrong = _____%

For each passage, put the sentence number of the main idea in the space provided. Then circle the letter of the answer that accurately identifies the primary pattern of organization of the passage.

1. ¹Mass hysteria is a type of group behavior that involves a widely held and contagious anxiety, usually as a result of a false belief. ²The medieval witch hunts were a case of mass hysteria; they were based on the belief that witches were the cause of the many problems in late medieval society, including natural disasters and illness. ³Those accused of being witches (mainly old women) were tortured until they confessed or they died. ⁴If they confessed, they were burned to death. ⁵They were also forced under torture to name accomplices, so the list of witches grew, feeding the hysteria. ⁶As many as 500,000 people were burned to death by the clergy between the fifteenth and seventeenth centuries.

Sentence with the main idea: _____
Passage's pattern of organization:
   a. time order
   b. comparison
   c. definition and example

2. ¹While management styles vary, there are certain factors that separate the good administrator from the poor one. ²A good manager anticipates problems and prepares for them, but a poor manager is often taken by surprise. ³The effective administrator recognizes repeated problems and makes changes to eliminate them; the less effective boss deals with one crisis at a time, never seeing the connections between them. ⁴In addition, a good boss delegates work to others, while the poor one prefers to take on one extra task after another rather than train employees to do the work right. ⁵The effective administrator is also flexible enough to adapt to changing situations. ⁶In contrast, the poor one often clings to the old rules whether or not they apply.

Sentence with the main idea: _____
Passage's pattern of organization:
   a. contrast
   b. cause and effect
   c. definition and example

3. ¹Advertising's main goal is, of course, to sell products, but advertising also has other effects. ²By increasing the demand for products, advertising encourages economic growth. ³It helps to maintain competition among businesses, and there is some evidence that this competition leads to lower prices for consumer goods. ⁴A case can even be made for advertising as a source of information. ⁵New products are often introduced in ads, which frequently demonstrate how the products are used

and provide information on special features and prices. [6]This information is intended to sell products, but it can also result in better-informed consumers.

Sentence with the main idea: _____
Passage's pattern of organization:
a. comparison
b. cause and effect
c. definition and example

4. [1]In January of 1954, Ernest and Mary Hemingway left Nairobi on a vacation trip on which they flew over grazing elephants, hippos bathing in the lakes, and huge flocks of feeding flamingos. [2]As they were circling a spectacular waterfall, a flock of ibis flew in front of the plane. [3]When the pilot dived to avoid the birds, he struck an abandoned telegraph wire that crossed the gorge. [4]In the crash that followed, Ernest sprained his shoulder; Mary was only slightly injured. [5]Luckily, a boat came down the river the next morning, and its crew rescued them. [6]By that evening, they were on board a small plane bound for Entebbe. [7]The plane lifted from the plowed field that served as a runway, then crashed and burst into flames. [8]Ernest escaped by breaking through a window with his head and injured shoulder, and Mary got out through another window. [9]Twice in two days they had crashed and come out alive, but Ernest had injured his head, his backbone, and a kidney, and his lower intestine had collapsed. [10]After this, even writing a letter was difficult for him.

Sentence with the main idea: _____
Passage's pattern of organization:
a. time order
b. list of items
c. contrast

SCORE
100 − 12.5 for each one wrong = _____%

For each passage, put the sentence number of the main idea in the space provided. Then circle the letter of the answer that accurately identifies the primary pattern of organization of the passage.

1. [1]Advertisers have learned that images that proved successful in the United States have not always been as successful when used in other countries. [2]"Body by Fisher," for example, was a perfectly good slogan in America, but in Flemish it was translated into "Corpse by Fisher." [3]White, which suggests cleanliness and purity in the U.S., has an entirely different meaning in Japan, where it is the color of mourning. [4]"Yellow floors," to Americans, are dingy floors, but in China yellow is a color used in religious settings. [5]"Put a Tiger in Your Tank" was an effective slogan for an oil company advertising in the U.S.; however, in Thailand it was not successful because Thais do not think of the tiger as a symbol of power.

   Sentence with the main idea: _____
   Passage's pattern of organization:
   a. contrast
   b. cause and effect
   c. definition and example

2. [1]Children master language in predictable stages. [2]At about six months, babies start to babble, which means they repeat simple sounds, such as "ma-ma-me-me." [3]About three or four months later, they can repeat sounds that others make. [4]During this stage, parents and babies often babble alternately almost as if they are carrying on little conversations. [5]These interchanges are rich in emotional meaning, although the sounds themselves are meaningless. [6]At the next stage, toddlers learn the meanings of many words, but they are not yet able to talk themselves. [7]A toddler might understand a sentence such as "Bring me your sock" but be unable to say any of the words. [8]Eventually, the child begins to talk in single words and then in two-word sentences.

   Sentence with the main idea: _____
   Passage's pattern of organization:
   a. time order
   b. comparison
   c. cause and effect

3. [1]The dance of death, which was performed in the fourteenth century in response to the Black Death, had several interesting characteristics. [2]First, it often took place in a graveyard, an appropriate place for a plague which killed one-fifth to one-half of the population of Europe, Africa, and Asia. [3]In addition, to show that the plague struck rich and poor alike, the dancers dressed to represent people from all walks of life.

[4]Perhaps the most significant aspect of this dance, however, was the part when one dancer fell down during the performance as if he or she were dead. [5]Members of the opposite sex then kissed the "victim," who rose up as if returned to life. [6]Unfortunately, this kissing often brought not life, but death, because it helped to spread the plague.

Sentence with the main idea: _____

Passage's pattern of organization:
a.   cause and effect
b.   list of items
c.   contrast

4.   [1]Plants can be surprisingly destructive. [2]Root systems can push bricks apart, lift concrete, and eventually topple buildings. [3]Plants that find niches on the surfaces of buildings are also destructive. [4]Because they must extract needed nutrients, they gradually dissolve the surfaces on which they grow. [5]Roofing tiles, plaster, and even glass cannot resist the plants. [6]Invading plants can relatively quickly turn an abandoned factory site into a field and then into woodland. [7]Especially in tropical areas, dense vegetation completely overwhelms abandoned cities; consequently, they are lost for centuries.

Sentence with the main idea: _____

Passage's pattern of organization:
a.   time order
b.   comparison
c.   cause and effect

SCORE

100 − 12.5 for each one wrong = _____%

FACT AND OPINION: Test 1

A. Some of the sentences below state facts, and some express opinions. Identify statements of fact with an **F** and statements of opinion with an **O**.

_____ 1. In 1924, the Model T Ford could be purchased for $290.

_____ 2. The Model T was the most significant invention of the first half of this century.

_____ 3. By the end of this century, electric cars will be in common use.

_____ 4. Couples should know each other for at least a year before getting married.

_____ 5. Joining the armed forces is the best way to learn a job skill.

_____ 6. No symbol is as chilling as the swastika.

_____ 7. The core of a pencil is made out of graphite and clay, not lead.

_____ 8. It's better to plant masses of flowers all in one color than in two or more colors.

_____ 9. The equator is 24,901.55 miles long.

_____ 10. It's never too early to teach children good manners.

B. Some of the sentences below state facts, and some express opinions; in addition, three include both facts and opinions. Identify statements of fact with an **F**, statements of opinion with an **O**, and the three statements of fact *and* opinion with an **F+O**.

_____ 1. Nothing is better for a stomachache than peppermint tea.

_____ 2. Every cook needs to become familiar with basil, which is a member of the mint family.

_____ 3. In laboratory experiments, peppermint extracts have counteracted some viruses in test tubes.

_____ 4. Wearing neckties is a ridiculous habit because it serves no worthwhile purpose.

_____ 5. My father bought a remnant of silk for a dollar and made it into a tie.

_____ 6. Bow ties can be bought permanently tied, but the untied type is classier.

_____ 7. The first television commercial, for a Bulova wristwatch, was broadcast in 1941.

_____ 8. Children should not be allowed to watch more than one hour of television a day.

———— 9. Johnny Carson, the greatest talk-show host of them all, became host of *The Tonight Show* in 1962.

———— 10. Watching sports events in person is better than watching them on TV.

SCORE

100 − 5 for each one wrong = ————%

FACT AND OPINION: Test 2

A. Some of the sentences below state facts, and some express opinions. Identify statements of fact with an **F** and statements of opinion with an **O**.

_____ 1. Some married couples take separate vacations.

_____ 2. In point of fact, it is always better for spouses to vacation together.

_____ 3. It's going to rain today.

_____ 4. The weather report in this morning's newspaper says that rain is likely today.

_____ 5. When my dog barks at someone she knows, she often wags her tail at the same time.

_____ 6. It would be nice to have more than twenty-four hours in a day.

_____ 7. The earth makes a complete rotation on its axis every twenty-three hours, fifty-six minutes and 4.09 seconds.

_____ 8. There is simply no excuse for being late.

_____ 9. Any student who walked into our biology class after the bell rang was marked late.

_____ 10. More American businesses should open day-care centers for their employees' children.

B. Some of the sentences below state facts, and some express opinions; in addition, three include both facts and opinions. Identify statements of fact with an **F**, statements of opinion with an **O**, and the three statements of fact and opinion with an **F + O**.

_____ 1. Cicadas, commonly called seventeen-year locusts, hibernate in the ground for seventeen years at a time.

_____ 2. After they leave the ground, male cicadas make an obnoxious buzzing sound as part of their mating pattern.

_____ 3. Clearly, cicadas are one of nature's strangest insects.

_____ 4. In Cleveland, two robbers once stole $25 from a convenience store after scaring off the cashier with a cicada.

_____ 5. Bessie Smith, known as the "Empress of the Blues," was killed in a car accident in 1937.

_____ 6. A week after the stock-market crash, Columbia released Smith's greatest recording, "Nobody Knows You When You're Down and Out."

_____ 7. Nobody can sing that song better than she did.

_____ 8. People claim to be psychic only in order to gain money and fame.

————— 9. University researchers have been investigating the possibility of psychic healing.

————— 10. Although ESP is a bunch of hogwash, my mother believes in psychic healing.

> **SCORE**
> **100 − 5 for each one wrong = _____%**

Some of the sentences in the passages below state facts, and some express opinions. Identify statements of fact with an **F** and statements of opinion with an **O**.

1. [1]There is no food that delights Americans more than the hot dog. [2]They eat frankfurters at the rate of eighty per person each year, enough to reach the moon and back to Earth two and a half times. [3]In fact, hot dogs have already been in space, as part of the diet of the Apollo astronauts who went to the moon. [4]The frankfurter dates back to 1852, when some German butchers in Frankfurt created and named it. [5]They would be astonished to know that their creation has ended up as an essential part of the American baseball scene.

   1. _____ 2. _____ 3. _____ 4. _____ 5. _____

2. [1]What people call weeds are often undeserving of such a negative name. [2]Ralph Waldo Emerson once described a weed as "a plant whose virtues have not yet been discovered." [3]He had the right attitude because weeds aren't always so bad. [4]For example, they can replenish depleted top soil with minerals. [5]Also, some plants that are called weeds are edible and nutritious.

   1. _____ 2. _____ 3. _____ 4. _____ 5. _____

3. [1]All employers should take steps to enrich the job satisfaction of their workers. [2]One program some companies have instituted is flex-time, which allows employees to write their own schedules according to their work and other needs. [3]It permits four-day work weeks for some employees. [4]Another approach that employers should definitely pursue is giving added responsibilities to all workers. [5]One researcher found that this approach raises productivity as well as worker morale.

   1. _____ 2. _____ 3. _____ 4. _____ 5. _____

4. [1]There were several queens of Egypt by the name of Cleopatra; the one who ruled in the days of Antony and Caesar was named Cleopatra VII Philopator. [2]She was born in 69 B.C. and killed herself almost forty years later. [3]The story that she killed herself with an asp is very easy to believe. [4]The asp is the Egyptian cobra, a symbol of Egyptian royalty. [5]There could have been no better way for the queen to end her life.

   1. _____ 2. _____ 3. _____ 4. _____ 5. _____

5. [1]While in the minds of many, Mickey Mouse is associated with Walt Disney, the cartoon rodent was originally drawn by Disney's old friend Ubbe Ert Iwerks. [2]Without Iwerks, Mickey Mouse would have remained a minor, forgotten character, and Disney would never have come into his own. [3]Iwerks worked for the Disney studio from 1924 to

1930 and then again from 1940 until his death in 1971. [4]During these years he worked on various animated films, including *Song of the South* (1946) and *Mary Poppins* (1964). [5]The teamwork of Disney and Iwerks was the single most important step in the success of the Disney studio.

1. _____ 2. _____ 3. _____ 4. _____ 5. _____

SCORE
100 − 4 for each one wrong = _____%

Some of the sentences below state facts, and some express opinions; in addition, *one* sentence in each passage includes both fact and opinion. Identify statements of fact with an **F**, statements of opinion with an **O**, and statements of fact and opinion with an **F + O**.

1. ¹Americans have become much too concerned about success and about owning things. ²According to a recent study, as many as 80 percent of job resumes contain false or misleading information. ³Also, it is well documented that many Americans use as much as 50 percent of their paycheck to pay back consumer loans. ⁴For their wardrobes alone, consumers each year pay out millions of dollars, dollars that should have ended up in such worthy projects as health research and in housing for the homeless. ⁵It's time for Americans to become less selfish and to contribute more to the community.

1. _____ 2. _____ 3. _____ 4. _____ 5. _____

2. ¹Identifying animal tracks is exciting and challenging. ²Finding the tracks of a coyote, fox, or wolf is far more thrilling than locating the tracks of a domestic dog, but people sometimes confuse the two types of tracks. ³One way some trackers tell them apart is to follow the tracks because domestic animals often go straight toward houses, while wild animals keep their distance. ⁴The tracks of domestic cats are often identified by the distinctive prints they make, for they place their hind feet in the marks made by their front paws. ⁵Raccoons, on the other hand, leave tracks that are shaped, in the words of one tracker, "like prints of tiny, bare human feet."

1. _____ 2. _____ 3. _____ 4. _____ 5. _____

3. ¹The worst thing an elementary teacher can do, no matter what the circumstance, is value quiet behavior at the expense of children's curiosity. ²Many educators agree that children's natural curiosity can interfere with structured class activities. ³Usually, however, satisfying students' curiosity is more important than teaching what was planned. ⁴That is why all schools should use the open-classroom system, which is designed to cater to individual student interest more than the traditional classroom does. ⁵The open classroom can give our educational system a needed shot in the arm.

1. _____ 2. _____ 3. _____ 4. _____ 5. _____

4. ¹The majority of engaged couples discuss financial issues before getting married, but fewer discuss having children. ²Yet children are the most important aspect of marriage, certainly more important than finances and work. ³Thousands of responses to a questionnaire called the Pre-Marital Inventory have shown that people often know less about their

future husband's or wife's ideas on lifestyle than they realized. [4]Specifically, many engaged people don't even know if their partner wants children and, if so, how many and what his or her ideas are on child care. [5]Thus all engaged couples should be encouraged to take the PreMarital Inventory, which was designed by a university psychologist with the help of priests and a social worker.

1. _____ 2. _____ 3. _____ 4. _____ 5. _____

5. [1]The saying "no pain, no gain" is nonsense, for experience has shown that exercising strenuously can injure some people. [2]According to experts, sports such as swimming and walking are better than activities like running and high-impact aerobics for beginners, pregnant women, the elderly, and overweight people. [3]Dr. Richard Stein, chairman of the New York Heart Association's exercise committee, says that even those in peak condition should use low-impact exercises on alternate days. [4]Walking is the low-impact exercise most commonly recommended by physicians and exercise specialists. [5]The best way to work walking into a daily schedule is to plan to walk each day with a friend.

1. _____ 2. _____ 3. _____ 4. _____ 5. _____

| **SCORE** |
| 100 − 4 for each one wrong = _____% |

Some of the sentences below state facts, and some express opinions; in addition, *one* sentence in each passage includes both fact and opinion. Identify statements of fact with an **F**, statements of opinion with an **O**, and each statement of fact *and* opinion with an **F + O**.

1. [1]School administrators should either improve our children's lunch menus or be replaced. [2]There is little value in teaching academics to children only to hurt their minds and bodies with junk food at lunch time. [3]A survey of schools throughout the country shows that school lunch menus include high-sodium, high-fat, and low-fiber foods. [4]In addition, some school districts allow sugary and high-fat foods to be sold in vending machines, which proves that school administrators really care too little about our children. [5]The first step towards improving our children's health should be to abolish vending machines from the schools.

   1. _____   2. _____   3. _____   4. _____   5. _____

2. [1]Even today, Sigmund Freud must be considered the most influential theorist in the field of psychology. [2]Before him, psychologists focused on human consciousness. [3]Freud, however, emphasized the unconscious. [4]He came to the conclusion that the personality is made up of three interrelated parts: id, ego, and superego. [5]He conceived of the id as a completely unconscious force consisting of all the basic instincts, including what must be the worst of human instincts—aggression.

   1. _____   2. _____   3. _____   4. _____   5. _____

3. [1]Hospitals across the country are facing an acute shortage of nurses, our most precious health resource. [2]According to the American Nursing Association, this crisis requires creative solutions. [3]A recent survey demonstrated that increased salaries, more benefits, and regular working hours would cause more people to enter the profession. [4]Retraining should be offered free to nurses desiring to rejoin the workforce. [5]Only in this way will more qualified and caring people be attracted to this vital profession.

   1. _____   2. _____   3. _____   4. _____   5. _____

4. [1]A common definition of retirement includes the idea of leaving the labor force, but that notion of retirement is too narrow. [2]After retiring, it is much better to remain involved in the work world part-time. [3]Some companies have recently encouraged this type of involvement for the retired by hiring two or three older part-timers in place of one full-time employee. [4]The Travelers Corporation, for example, has employed six hundred retired employees for three hundred shared jobs. [5]Another way for retirees to work part-time is to volunteer for organizations such as

hospitals and museums that would not otherwise be able to afford the help.

1. _____   2. _____   3. _____   4. _____   5. _____

5. [1]Many Americans prefer to pay the lowest taxes possible. [2]That is unfortunate, however, because people should feel honored to contribute to their own society. [3]Taxes, after all, pay for such needs as roads, police, and health research—all more important than most of what people prefer to spend their money on. [4]It is much more important, for example, for the government to have money for scholarships than for individuals to have money for luxuries. [5]If more American citizens would see that taxes are necessary for the upkeep of a great society, then no politician would ever be timid about increasing taxes when necessary.

1. _____   2. _____   3. _____   4. _____   5. _____

SCORE
100 − 4 for each one wrong = _____%

Each passage below is followed by five statements. Two of these statements are inferences that can definitely be made on the basis of the information in the selections. The three other statements are questionable—they are not fully supported by the facts given. Put **D** beside inferences that DEFINITELY CAN BE MADE and **Q** beside inferences that are QUESTIONABLE.

1. My day has not ended. When I get home I suddenly realize that I have between thirty and forty pounds of fish to clean—rockfish yet, all full of spines and pricklers and razor-sharp teeth. When I'm finished I have so many holes in me I look like a composite of George Custer, Saint Sebastian, Bonnie and Clyde, but my family comes out to view the catch and restore my faith in the whole enterprise.

   "Yuk," says my daughter.

   "That's a lot of codfish for people who aren't all that into codfish," says my wife.

   "I wouldn't eat that on a bet," says my son.

   _____ a. The family is on vacation.

   _____ b. Rockfish are difficult to clean.

   _____ c. The author's family appreciates his hard work to feed them.

   _____ d. The family will have fish for dinner.

   _____ e. When he praises his family for restoring his faith, the author is being sarcastic.

2. I guess I did it because I hadn't studied very much. And it seemed so easy—everybody knows that Mr. Brown keeps his office door unlocked. It's just too bad things didn't work out for me. Now my classmates are mad at me because they must re-study for the new test Brown is making up. My parents have taken away my car keys. And even worse, I'll have to go to summer school for biology.

   _____ a. The speaker stole a test.

   _____ b. The speaker had been failing the course.

   _____ c. The class was a biology class.

   _____ d. The speaker regrets not studying more.

   _____ e. The speaker will never cheat again.

3. Parents behave differently toward baby girls and baby boys. They are inclined to talk more to a baby girl and play more roughly with a baby boy. Boys and girls often get different types of toys and are given dif-

ferent kinds of responsibility as they grow older. When children behave like the grownups of their sex, that behavior is encouraged.

_____ a.   Parents are influenced by society's view of gender roles.

_____ b.   Parents influence their children's sense of gender identity.

_____ c.   Baby girls like to talk more than baby boys.

_____ d.   There are no inborn differences between boys and girls.

_____ e.   Parents should treat boys and girls exactly the same.

4.   A high school once offered a course called "Home Economics for Boys." Not very many boys signed up for the course. Then someone decided to rename the course instead of dropping it. So the next time the course was offered it was called "Bachelor Living," but the course otherwise remained the same. The class then drew 120 students.

_____ a.   The faculty wanted to trick the boys in their school.

_____ b.   Most of the boys did not want to sign up for a class that sounded like a class for girls.

_____ c.   The few boys who signed up for the class the first time were more interested in cooking than the others.

_____ d.   Both boys and girls signed up for the course.

_____ e.   Names can influence people.

| **SCORE** |
| **100 − 5 for each one wrong = _____%** |

Each passage below is followed by five statements. Two of these statements are inferences that can definitely be made on the basis of the information in the selections. The three other statements are questionable—they are not fully supported by the facts given. Put **D** beside inferences that DEFINITELY CAN BE MADE and **Q** beside inferences that are QUESTIONABLE.

1. We were in bed watching Johnny Carson when the doorbell rang downstairs. "What?" I said, and grabbed the remote control to mute the sound of the television. A child's voice sang out from a nearby room, "The doorbell rang."

    "Should I call the police?" I asked Jed.

    "Maybe it's a short in the house wiring," he said. "Burglars don't ring doorbells before they break in."

    I peered down to the front steps from the window, but it was too dark to see anything.

    _____ a.   Jed is afraid to go to the door.

    _____ b.   The child was awakened by the doorbell.

    _____ c.   It is nighttime.

    _____ d.   Someone is trying to break into the house.

    _____ e.   The speaker is in an upstairs room.

2. Waterbeds are not just for fun. They have been found to reduce bedsores and the breakdown of skin and tissue, possibly fatal problems for the severely paralyzed and paraplegics. Also, some doctors have found gently moving water mattresses in incubators reduce the cases of crib death. In addition, heated waterbeds have been found useful in treating lower back problems and arthritis and in helping insomniacs sleep.

    _____ a.   Waterbeds are always more comfortable than hospital beds.

    _____ b.   Some hospitals have waterbeds.

    _____ c.   All hospitals have waterbeds.

    _____ d.   All lower back problems can be cured.

    _____ e.   Doctors sometimes recommend waterbeds for insomniacs.

3. Many experts say that pink has a special charm. A California probation department that used to have trouble quieting violent juvenile offenders now puts them in bubble-gum pink cells. Within a few minutes the offenders stop screaming and banging and often even fall asleep. Also,

in a college experiment, a group of children were put in small enclosures of various colors. All of the pens became covered with graffiti—except one that was painted pink.

_____ a.   Pink paint is resistant to graffiti.

_____ b.   Colors can affect people.

_____ c.   All probation departments now use pink cells.

_____ d.   Pink seems to make people gentler.

_____ e.   Pink is the favorite color of violent juvenile offenders.

4.   My parents agreed to help me buy a car if I paid for the insurance and upkeep myself. When I found a nice used car, I added fifteen hours to my schedule at the local convenience store. That semester, my grades were lower than usual. After that, the car was sold, and I cut back on working. My grades went back up the following semester.

_____ a.   The speaker's parents pitched in to buy the used car.

_____ b.   The speaker is a high-school student.

_____ c.   The speaker worked more hours to pay for the car's insurance and upkeep.

_____ d.   The speaker preferred riding around in his car to studying.

_____ e.   The speaker's parents insisted that the car be sold.

SCORE
100 − 5 for each one wrong = _____%

Ten statements follow each of the readings below. Circle the numbers of the *five* statements which can be logically inferred from the information given.

A. They had been waiting several hours for the results. Finally, he entered the hospital room where they were sitting by the bedside. Ignoring the sleeping figure in the bed, he spoke to them matter-of-factly, without a hint of concern in his voice.

"The growth is a tumor. It's deep inside the brain. There would be enormous risk in trying to remove it. The outlook is not good."

Then he said he had to go and finish his hospital rounds, see his other patients. As he reached the door, he looked around, smiled slightly, and said, "Have a good day."

The husband jumped out of his chair. "What do you mean, 'have a good day'? he demanded. "You've just sentenced her to death. How can we have a good day after that?"

He did not flinch as he answered, "I'm just trying to give you the medical picture, Mr. Stevens. That's all. The only way I can do that is by telling the truth. I didn't mean to hurt your feelings."

A few hours later, in the hospital cafeteria, the husband remarked, "I guess he's just like anyone else. He doesn't know what to say either."

1. The first speaker is a doctor.
2. The patient is Mr. Stevens' mother.
3. The patient is elderly.
4. The patient is likely to die.
5. Mr. Stevens will not tell the patient the bad news.
6. The first speaker does not want to operate on the patient.
7. The first speaker has no emotional response to the patient's illness.
8. The husband would have preferred a warmer, less impersonal approach from the first speaker.
9. The husband dislikes doctors.
10. The husband finally forgave the first speaker for what he had said.

B. Suppose a man works six or seven days a week in a factory, trying to support his family, but never seems to be able to make ends meet. If he analyzed his situation rationally, he would probably blame the well-to-do generally and his employers specifically for failing to pay him an adequate wage. But these people have the power to cut off his income; to oppose them openly would be self-destructive. He could also blame himself for his financial problems, but this too makes him uncomfortable. Instead, he looks to the immigrants who have begun working in his factory. He doesn't really know them, but he suspects they're willing to work for low wages and that many other immigrants are eager to take his job. By a process of twisted logic, he blames these people for his poverty. Soon he is exchanging rumors about "them" with his cronies and supporting efforts to close the border. Hating immigrants makes the man and his friends feel a little better.

1. People never blame themselves for their problems.
2. Factory workers are not good at managing money.
3. All factory workers are underpaid.
4. Some people are reluctant to oppose their bosses.
5. Immigrants are eager to take other people's jobs.
6. Immigrants are now getting jobs in American factories.
7. Prejudice can be the result of wanting to blame someone for our problems.
8. The man in the example would probably be violent against immigrants.
9. The man in the example would probably oppose hiring more immigrants.
10. Some people make themselves feel better by thinking less of others.

SCORE
100 − 10 for each one wrong − _____%

Ten statements follow each of the readings below. Circle the numbers of the *five* statements which can be logically inferred from the information given.

A. A California tourist in Mexico happened to wander into a woodcarver's shop. Passing the little dolls and vases, she stopped in front of an intricately carved chair and asked its price. The woodcarver replied, "Fifty pesos." "I'd like a matched set of four chairs," the tourist explained. "What would you charge for that?" "Two hundred and fifty pesos for four matching chairs," was the answer. "That doesn't make sense," the tourist objected. "But senorita," answered the woodcarver. "It is so boring to carve four chairs that are exactly alike!"

1. The woodcarver did wonderful work.
2. The woodcarver did not make much money.
3. The tourist was wealthy.
4. She liked the carved chair.
5. The tourist thought four chairs should cost four times as much as one chair.
6. The woodcarver disliked boring work.
7. The woodcarver disliked tourists.
8. The tourist was American.
9. She bought the chairs.
10. The woodcarver worked for pleasure as well as money.

B. Parents who try to hide their arguments from their children behind closed doors may actually be depriving them of a valuable lesson in relating to others. First of all, children are very sensitive to feelings and will not be fooled by such statements as, "We aren't fighting; we're just having a discussion." Unless the argument becomes a violent battle, with extreme verbal or physical abuse, there is no harm in children looking on. In fact, parents can use such situations to teach their children that it's okay to be angry sometimes, even with someone they love and respect, that anger does not cause permanent damage to the object of the anger, and that people can use words to express their feelings and resolve conflicts. Children need to learn that the opposite of love is not anger, but indifference, and that temporary feelings of anger towards a loved one are normal and permissible. Without this lesson, they might grow into adults who have difficulty expressing anger and are frightened by their own hostile feelings.

1. Most parents try to hide their arguments from their children.
2. Some parents try to hide their arguments from their children.
3. Some parents think it can harm children to witness their arguments.
4. Parents sometimes mistakenly think they are fooling their children.

5. Violent arguments are okay as long as children are not looking on.

6. Watching nonviolent arguments can be valuable learning experiences for children.

7. All parents argue with each other.

8. Except for violent arguments, parents should never hide anything from children.

9. It's okay to be angry with someone you love.

10. People who cannot express their angry feelings never saw their parents argue.

SCORE

100 − 10 for each one wrong = _____%

Inference is at the heart of literature. While writers of factual reports tend to present their information in a straightforward manner, only some of the literary author's meaning is expressed directly. Instead, this kind of writer will use language that suggests deeper levels of interpretation beyond the surface "story." So to understand most imaginative writing—especially fiction and poetry—you must use your inference skills.

Following are two literary pieces, an excerpt from a literary biography and a poem, with each followed by a series of statements. Circle the numbers of the *five* statements which can be logically inferred in each case.

A. *From* The Silver Horn—*Thomas Sancton*

Little things that happened during these years seemed of great importance. I remember that in my first year at camp I wore an ill-fitted Boy Scout hat. One of the counselors, a boy five years my senior who seemed to me to belong already to the grown-up world of brilliance and authority, began, in a pleasant way, to tease me about the hat. Every morning for a week he led us to the abandoned logging road and clocked us as we walked and trotted a measured mile. My hat was anchored down by a heavy chin strap; it flopped and sailed about my head as I ran to the finish line. The boy began to laugh at me. He waved his arms and called out, "Come on, you rookie!" The other kids took it up and Rookie became my first nickname. I loved it. I tingled when someone called it out. I painted it on my belt, carved it on my packing case, inked it into my hatband, and began to sign it to my letters home. Years later when we were grown I knew this camp officer again. The gap between our ages had vanished and in real life now he seemed to me a rather colorless young lawyer. He did not remember about the hat.

1. The author is writing about his childhood.
2. He thought it was wonderful to be a grownup.
3. He resented being teased about his Boy Scout hat.
4. Having a nickname made Sancton feel good.
5. He liked the nickname because it was given to him by his counselor.
6. Rookie was the only nickname he ever had.
7. After they grew up, the author disliked his camp counselor.
8. After they grew up, the author no longer admired his camp counselor.
9. The author never went to camp again.
10. The hat incidents were more important to the author than they had been to his counselor.

B.   *"Richard Cory"—Edwin Arlington Robinson*

> Whenever Richard Cory went down town,
>   We people on the pavement looked at him;
> He was a gentleman from sole to crown,
>   Clean favored, and imperially slim.
>
> And he was always quietly arrayed,
>   And he was always human when he talked;
> But still he fluttered pulses when he said
>   "Good-morning," and he glittered when he walked.
>
> And he was rich—yes, richer than a king,
>   And admirably schooled in every grace;
> In fine, we thought that he was everything
>   To make us wish that we were in his place.
>
> So on we worked, and waited for the light,
>   And went without the meat, and cursed the bread;
> And Richard Cory, one calm summer night,
>   Went home and put a bullet through his head.

1.   Richard Cory treated the poor disrespectfully.
2.   Richard Cory had many personal friends.
3.   The speaker is poor.
4.   Richard Cory was extremely rich.
5.   Richard Cory did not work.
6.   The poor people in town thought Richard Cory was happy.
7.   Richard Cory had an unhappy love affair.
8.   Richard Cory was not as fortunate as he seemed.
9.   The poor preferred bread to meat.
10.   Money does not buy happiness.

SCORE

100 − 10 for each one wrong = _____%

In the space provided, indicate whether the primary purpose of each passage is to inform (**I**), to persuade (**P**), or to entertain (**E**).

_____ 1. One way to lose weight is to go on a scientific weight-loss program. These are widely advertised in those newspapers they sell at supermarket check-out lines, the ones with headlines like: BURT REYNOLDS FINDS CANCER CURE IN UFO RIDE WITH PRINCESS DIANA. You should buy one of these magazines and flip through the pages until you see a full-page advertisement with a headline that says "WOMAN LOSES 240 POUNDS IN 30 SECONDS." Under the headline are two pictures of a woman's head: in the first picture the head is on top of what appears to be an industrial boiler wearing a 1952 bathing suit; in the second picture, the head is on top of Bo Derek.

_____ 2. More and more elderly are turning to shared housing as a way to live more economically, more securely, and with more companionship. There are dozens of such projects around the country, including group homes in California, communes in Baltimore, and the "Share a Home" in Winter Park, Florida. While the latter includes 125 participants, a shared-housing project may involve only a few members. Most shared-housing projects have full- or part-time help, but members often share in such chores as shopping for food and cooking.

_____ 3. The foundation of public education has always been reading, writing and arithmetic—the three "Rs." Yet the schools insist that students who have not mastered these fundamentals continue to take all the other subjects as well. What good does it do for young people to sit in on a history or science class if they can't read or calculate well? Schools ought to require students who are very behind in the fundamentals to devote all their time to the three Rs until they are at or near grade level.

_____ 4. Aldo stopped on his way to the B deck to gaze out of one of the ship's few windows. Earth was so far away it no longer could be seen. What was Elena doing down there now? She had been so honest with him. Many women would have sworn to be faithful forever, but Elena knew that a flight to Jupiter was too long for anyone to wait. She had never wanted to make him choose between her and his career, but that was exactly what the circumstances had forced him to do. Did he regret his decision?

_____ 5. Few would argue that homes should be built in ways that encourage warm community life. Yet many housing developments are a long driving distance from community resources, which discourages neighborly interaction. If people have to enjoy parks and shop in stores far from home, they will rarely meet their neighbors. Thus when developments are planned, recreational and shopping centers should be included in the plans.

_____ 6. Until recently, it was commonly believed by intelligence experts that people reach the height of their intellectual peak by the time they're twenty. Lately, however, scientists have discovered that our minds continue to grow long after we are fully developed physically. In addition, some psychologists are expanding their notion of what makes up intelligence. Dr. Robert Sternberg of Yale University, for example, outlines seven different areas of intelligence, including musical ability and self-knowledge.

_____ 7. Prevention of mental illness is more important than its treatment, but few programs are devoted to prevention. Better education programs could lead to significant reductions in mental illnesses caused by poisoning, nutritional deficiencies, infections, and accidents. Both short-term activities, such as crisis intervention counseling, and long-term programs in schools, businesses, and communities, should be provided to promote mental health and reduce human misery.

_____ 8. Swollen glands can be uncomfortable, but they are a welcome sign that your body is working to defend itself. They are often associated with an illness such as mumps, German measles, a cold, or flu, but an insect bite or infected cut can also cause your glands to swell. A blocked duct in a salivary gland is another possible cause of a swollen gland. If swollen glands last more than a few days, they can be a sign of a serious illness, such as Hodgkin's disease.

SCORE
100 − 12.5 for each one wrong = _____%

Each of the following passages illustrates one of the five different tones identified in the box below. In the space provided, put the letter of the tone that applies to each passage.

a.	objective	d.	critical
b.	self-mocking	e.	playful
c.	pessimistic		

_____ 1. What ever happened to the practice of saving up for what you want? It seems nobody has that kind of patience any more. Many Americans buy what they want when they want it and worry about paying for it later. The average American spends significantly more than he or she earns, much to the enjoyment of the credit-card companies. Apparently people need to reach a financial crisis before they realize that it's downright stupid to neglect to balance their budgets and to save for a rainy day.

_____ 2. Machines are complete mysteries to me, which has resulted in some embarrassing service calls at my home. For example, there was the time I called in a repairman because our refrigerator was too warm. Imagine my humiliation when he told me that the cause of the problem was a dirty filter, which I didn't know existed and therefore hadn't cleaned even once in the two years we owned the refrigerator. The best example of my brilliance with machines, however, has to be the time I called for someone to fix my washing machine. The repairman's solution was simply to put the plug back in the outlet, from which it had been jarred loose by the constant vibration of the washer.

_____ 3. A sweltering summer day in Turkey resulted in a hot news story about a hot-tempered man and a dog. It seems a gunsmith named Kemal Pala was getting cranky from the heat, which is probably why he couldn't seem to warm up to the constant howling of his neighbor's dog. Perhaps the dog was hot under the collar from the heat. In any case, the howling made Pala's blood boil, so he went next door—and bit the dog three times. Is that what they mean by the dog days of summer?

_____ 4. Scientists say grilling meat creates cancer-causing substances that affect the meat in two ways. First, when fat drips onto the source of heat, the substances are formed and then carried up to the food by smoke. They are also formed when flames touch the meat. There are, however, a few ways that experts say will minimize the risk of grilling meat: (1) Use low-fat meats and non-fat sauces. (2) Partially cook meat before grilling. (3) Cover the grill with foil; punch holes in the foil to let fat drip down. (4) Avoid fire flare-ups, which cause harmful smoke. (5) Scrape off blackened material on the surface of meat before eating it. (6) Don't cook out every day.

_____ 5. Research on rats shows that when animals live in crowded conditions they live disorderly, violent lives. Humans are no exception. Crowded inner cities are models of lawlessness; the crowded highways of Los Angeles encourage driver aggression and even shootings. As our urban areas continue to grow in population density, these types of problems will surely also grow. That means more family violence and more fighting over available resources. The American dream will become just that, only a dream.

> **SCORE**
> **100 − 20 for each one wrong = _____%**

This activity will give you practice in recognizing purpose and tone. Read each of the paragraphs below. Then carefully consider the questions that follow and circle the best responses.

A. A successful doctor is scheduled to operate on a patient at 8 A.M., but it has snowed during the night, and driving is difficult. Do you think the doctor will stay home in bed? Not if he or she is professional. This attitude of professionalism is the key to being a successful college student, too. And it is within your reach, no matter how well or how poorly you have done in school up until now. You cannot undo the past, but you can adopt an attitude of professionalism from now on. All you have to do is intend to take school seriously, and the rest will follow. By attending classes, turning in assignments on time, and coming prepared for tests, you will gradually build your skills.

1. The primary purpose of this paragraph is to
   a. present facts on student behavior.
   b. persuade students to be responsible.
   c. describe to readers the virtues of professionalism.
   d. classify students.
2. In general, the tone of this paragraph can be described as
   a. critical.
   b. pessimistic.
   c. encouraging.
   d. praising.

B. According to memory experts, there are ways you can improve your chances of remembering the names of people you meet. One way is to make associations between a person's name and looks. For example, if you meet a man named Baker, you might picture him wearing a baker's hat. If the name is a difficult one, ask for the spelling and visualize the letters mentally. It's also useful to repeat the person's name as you converse, keeping your mental images in mind. And when your conversation ends, repeat the person's name as you say goodbye.

1. The primary purpose of this paragraph is to
   a. praise memory experts.
   b. teach readers how to better remember names.
   c. amuse readers with silly images.
   d. persuade readers to have better memories.
2. The overall tone of this paragraph can be described as
   a. critical and angry.
   b. obviously humorous.
   c. doubtful.
   d. straightforward and instructive.

C. Too many students treat school as a game in which they are the "good guys" and teachers are "the enemy." They turn in work far inferior to what they are capable of doing and then blame their teachers for their own failures. Such students feel assignments are impositions and tests are punishments. They think school is an institution designed to divert them from having fun, not a place intended to help them grow.

1. The author of this paragraph intends to
    a. amuse readers with student antics.
    b. present facts on student behavior.
    c. contrast types of students.
    d. persuade readers that too many students have a poor attitude.
2. The tone of this paragraph can be described as
    a. tragic.
    b. critical.
    c. pessimistic.
    d. uncertain.

D. My memory is slipping away like a greased pig in a chute, which causes me immense aggravation. This year, for instance, I forgot not only one of my kids' birthdays but also my own. That was a big boner because the only way my husband remembers my birthday is if I remember to call his secretary and remind her to remind him. In addition, last week, believe it or not, I drove the car to work and then took the bus home. Such brain bloopers often prove embarrassing. It's not unusual, for example, for me to dial a number on the phone and then have to ask the person who answers whom I have called.

1. The author's purpose in writing this paragraph is to
    a. educate readers on the problems of memory.
    b. entertain readers.
    c. persuade readers of the importance of memory.
    d. express serious concern about his or her failing memory.
2. The tone of this paragraph can be described as
    a. worried and fearful.
    b. objective and factual.
    c. intense and complex.
    d. humorous and light.

SCORE
100 − 12.5 for each one wrong = _____%

This activity will give you practice in recognizing purpose and tone. Read each of the paragraphs below. Then carefully consider the questions that follow and circle the best responses.

A. It's about time the leaders of this country stopped putting the almighty dollar ahead of the health of its citizens and confusing scientific possibilities with progress. How many Three Mile Islands must we have before they realize that just because nuclear power plants are possible doesn't mean we have to build them? It's in the nature of human beings to make stupid mistakes and be careless, so we must avoid putting them in positions where their errors will have disastrous consequences. Must it take another major accident and a generation of deformed babies before our politicians put the health of their constituents before the interests of big business?

1. The primary purpose of this paragraph is to
    a. factually inform readers about nuclear power plants.
    b. persuade readers that nuclear plants should not be built.
    c. persuade readers that humans are careless.
    d. examine for readers the problems of nuclear power.
2. The tone of this paragraph can be described as
    a. objective and factual.
    b. sympathetic and forgiving.
    c. critical and bitter.
    d. cruel and uncaring.

B. Strawberries are now available in the markets, and what a winning crop! In contrast to last year's berries, which were badly affected by poor weather conditions, these are plentiful, delicious, and relatively inexpensive. They will make the ideal climax to any meal, whether under a dollop of sour cream laced with brown sugar or crushed over a scoop of vanilla ice cream. In fact, these luscious berries are so sweet, they can stand very well on their own.

1. The primary purpose of this paragraph is to
    a. inform readers about the benefits of this year's strawberry crop.
    b. contrast this year's strawberry crop with last year's.
    c. describe to readers the many uses of strawberries.
    d. persuade readers to purchase strawberries.
2. The tone of this paragraph is best described as
    a. cheerful and enthusiastic.
    b. straightforward and factual.
    c. critical and angry.
    d. light-hearted and joking.

C. Three people were killed because a man was angry that his girlfriend wanted to break up with him. Now the state is planning to kill him, and that's as it should be. Some may argue that taking a life is always wrong, that two wrongs don't make a right. But there is nothing right about taxpayers having to give free room and board to a person who killed innocent people—because of a disappointment experienced at some point by a large percentage of the population. And there's nothing right about putting such a dangerous person in prison, from which he will probably one day be released to again threaten society.

1. The primary purpose of this paragraph is to
    a. inform readers of facts about the death penalty.
    b. advise readers about the dangers in society.
    c. persuade readers that murder is evil.
    d. persuade readers that the death penalty has merit.
2. The overall tone of this paragraph can be described as
    a. angry and vengeful.
    b. insulting.
    c. compassionate and sentimental.
    d. excited and joyous.

D. Part of the gap between thinking and feeling almost certainly comes from the lessons we learn while growing up. Usually without being aware of it, and almost inevitably, adults send message after message telling a child which emotions are acceptable and which aren't. In a house where angry words are taboo, the child gets the idea that anger is a "not OK" thing. If sex is never discussed except with great discomfort, then the child will learn to stop talking about—and even stop consciously feeling—emotions that center around the body. If the parents talk only about trivial subjects and never share their deeper feelings, the child's conversation and thinking will tend to follow the same path.

1. The purpose of this paragraph is to
    a. contrast thinking and feeling.
    b. classify known causes for the gap between thinking and feeling.
    c. persuade readers that the gap between thinking and feeling probably originates in childhood.
    d. inform readers that some parents don't share what they think and feel with their children.
2. The tone of this paragraph can be described as
    a. regretful.
    b. angry.
    c. playful.
    d. serious.

SCORE
100 − 12.5 for each one wrong = _____%

This activity will give you practice in recognizing purpose and tone. Read each of the paragraphs below. Then carefully consider the questions that follow and circle the best responses.

A. If you tend to feel tired an hour or so after you get to work, or if you feel as if your brain is moving in slow motion, the problem could be what you had for breakfast. For many of us, "breakfast" means that well-known American classic: two fried eggs with bacon or sausage, toast dripping with melted butter, and coffee with plenty of cream and sugar. But high-fat meals like this one require more digestion than usual. In the process, blood is diverted to the stomach and intestines— and away from the brain. The result is that mental processes slow down, thinking becomes sloppy, and drowsiness soon follows. To avoid this situation, researchers suggest a "brainpower breakfast" high in protein and low in fat, such as fresh fruit combined with yogurt, a bran muffin with a small portion of jelly or diet margarine, and coffee with milk.

1. The primary purpose of this paragraph is to
    a. factually inform readers about how to stay alert after breakfast.
    b. describe to readers what happens if they eat a high-fat meal.
    c. persuade readers to eat yogurt and bran instead of bacon and eggs.
    d. persuade readers to lead a more healthy lifestyle.
2. The tone of this paragraph can be described as
    a. angry.
    b. regretful.
    c. humorous.
    d. objective.

B. There are three types of people you should not trust. One type is *people who tell you God told them to tell you to send them money.* You know the guys I mean. They get on television and say: "God told me He wants you to send me some money, say $100, or even just $10, if that's all you can afford, but in all honesty I must point out that God is less likely to give you some horrible disease if your gift is in the $100 range." The theory here seems to be that God talks only to the guys on television. I always thought that if God needed money all that badly, He would get in touch with us directly.

1. The primary purpose of this paragraph is to
    a. inform readers of facts about television evangelists.
    b. advise readers of the dangers of believing everything they see on television.
    c. persuade readers that they should send money to television evangelists.
    d. persuade readers that they should not send money to television evangelists.

2. The tone of this paragraph can be described as
    a.   straight-forward and serious.
    b.   humorous and mocking.
    c.   prayerful and respectful.
    d.   sentimental and warm.

SCORE

100 − 25 for each one wrong = _____ **%**

A. Each passage below contains some examples of biased language. On the line next to the passage, write the letter of the group of words that reveals the author's bias.

_____ 1. The idea that doctors should be able to sell the drugs they prescribe to their patients is outrageous. The current situation, in which patients take prescriptions from their doctors to their pharmacists, provides a check on doctors' greed. Doctors claim they want to make acquiring drugs more convenient for their patients, but they are clearly involved in a case of conflict of interest. What prevents doctors from prescribing unneeded drugs in order to improve their profit margins? Drug salespeople tempt doctors to enter this racket by promising increased profits of $30,000 to $50,000 a year. The greedy doctors in this country are hearing the cash registers ringing, but shouldn't they be keeping their minds on the oath they took when they entered their profession?

    a. take, drugs, current
    b. involved, profit, oath
    c. patients, doctors, pharmacists
    d. outrageous, racket, greedy

_____ 2. Wonderful new materials will soon be transforming almost everything around us. Windows will darken at the flip of a switch, making blinds and drapes unnecessary. Car engines will be made of miraculous new ceramics that can run efficiently at high temperatures, removing the need for a cooling system. Because the new plastics are lighter and stronger than steel, they are ideal for everything from tennis racquets to bridges. Even the familiar plastic litter will change as marvelous new plastics that disintegrate in the sunlight replace the old ones that never wore out.

    a. materials, ceramics, plastics
    b. everything, windows, sunlight
    c. switch, cooling, familiar
    d. wonderful, miraculous, marvelous

B. Each passage below has one sentence that contains biased language. On the line next to the passage, write the number of the sentence that contains biased language.

_____ 3. [1]American businesses spend about four billion dollars a year on programs to motivate employees. [2]One goal of the motivational programs is to get all employees to agree on basic values because such agreement is believed to help a company become more successful. [3]This attempt at mind control is an outright invasion of employees' privacy and an absurd waste of stockholders' money. [4]In some programs, hypnosis and meditation are used, and others rely on encounter groups. [5]Regardless of the format, the goal is always to get employees to think in the same way—and to increase profits for employers.

———— 4. [1]Have you ever seen a geep? [2]This odd animal, which has a goat's head and neck and a sheep's body, is created when a sheep embryo is joined with a goat's embryo and implanted in a goat's womb. [3]The geep is not a very promising farm animal, but the fact that it can be created at all concerns some observers. [4]The monstrous new animals result from heartless experiments by people who do not seem to mind the horrible cruelty to animals caused by their misguided experiments. [5]The results of genetic engineering can even be patented, so more and more researchers are becoming involved in animal research in the hope of making large profits.

———— 5. [1]Network television is losing the audience its advertisers prefer: relatively young people (age 25 to 45) with good incomes and some college education. [2]Because these viewers have money to spend on advertised products, they are the people advertisers most want to reach. [3]Increasingly, however, these viewers are watching rented movies on their videocassette recorders or tuning their sets to cable television. [4]This desertion could be disastrous for the television industry and for the country as a whole, because it means the regrettable loss of the unifying experiences unselfishly provided for all Americans. [5]Network executives say that the vanishing viewers are actually recording network shows to watch later, but at the same time they are scheduling new shows aimed at attracting the lost viewers.

SCORE
100 − 20 for each one wrong = ————%

Each of the passages below illustrates a particular propaganda technique. On the line next to the passage, write the letter of the technique being used.

_____ 1. The nitwits that make up City Council have created a real crisis in town. Instead of working together to create a permanent solution for our trash-disposal problem, these political clowns and incompetents spent all their time feuding with each other.
   a. plain folks   c. bandwagon
   b. name calling   d. testimonial

_____ 2. The U. S. Heritage Committee has selected Bubble-O as the official soft drink of the Heritage Celebration to be held in six major American cities this summer. Bubble-O: an important part of your heritage.
   a. plain folks   c. transfer
   b. bandwagon   d. name calling

_____ 3. Join your neighbors and friends in a massive protest against the proposed landfill. People from all walks of life are forming the overwhelming opposition to this dangerous project. Be a part of this important movement.
   a. testimonial   c. bandwagon
   b. transfer   d. name calling

_____ 4. James Oliver, the former star of _Avenue A_, is currently talking to kids across America about the dangers of drug addiction. "You don't want drugs," he says. "You don't need them, and remember, they can kill you."
   a. glittering generalities   c. transfer
   b. testimonial   d. plain folks

_____ 5. Frank Moriarity obviously wants to send this county back to the Dark Ages. His neglect of education and other county services is irresponsible, even criminal. As a freeholder, he has been a disaster.
   a. plain folks   c. name calling
   b. glittering generalities   d. testimonial

_____ 6. Ordinary people all over the country are speaking out in support of South Dakota Senator Bob Curren's Presidential bid. Senator Curren's rough-hewn manners and casual style are popular with the little guy, who is sick and tired of big-city politicians. The people of this country are ready for a down-to-earth candidate.
   a. plain folks   c. glittering generalities
   b. name calling   d. transfer

———————   7. An Arnold Autofocus camera is the camera of your dreams. This delightful camera will make all your photography a pleasure. You'll love your new Arnold Autofocus.
    a. transfer   c. bandwagon
    b. glittering generalities   d. name calling

———————   8. Federal programs seem to be full of cheats and frauds, like the people who collect high salaries for doing no more than shuffling papers. These lazy good-for-nothings should be fired.
    a. glittering generalities   c. name calling
    b. bandwagon   d. transfer

———————   9. Buy Gordon's dental floss, the official floss of the American space program. Protect your teeth the way the astronauts do.
    a. plain folks   c. glittering generalities
    b. bandwagon   d. transfer

——————— 10. A new convention center is crucial to our great city. A stunning new facility, placed in a beautiful setting, would be the long-overdue final touch needed to usher us into the twenty-first century.
    a. plain folks   c. name calling
    b. glittering generalities   d. bandwagon

SCORE
100 − 10 for each one wrong = _____%

Read each of the passages below, and then circle the letter of the best answer to each question.

A. [1]Everyone who wants to live and work in the United States has the obligation to learn English. [2]Anything less is an insult to this country. [3]English has always been the dominant language in the United States, and this common language is what has made our country great. [4]Irresponsible critics of the legislation we propose have charged that we want to suppress the cultures of minority groups. [5]In fact, we respect and admire the diverse groups that make up this great country. [6]We ask only that these groups give up their ill-advised loyalty to their native languages.

1. Which of the following groups of words contains biased language?
   a. live, country, native
   b. insult, irresponsible, ill-advised
   c. common, critics, minority
   d. language, cultures, country
2. Which of the sentences in the passage contains a half-truth?
   a. sentence 1   c. sentence 5
   b. sentence 3   d. sentence 6

B. [1]Programs intended to encourage girls to study mathematics and pursue careers in math and science are unlikely to work. [2]Boys always do better in math and science because they are more willing to do the hard work such courses require. [3]Merely walking by a high school calculus class or a computer lab reveals that boys outnumber girls in these classes by a wide margin. [4]A closer look reveals that the top students in these courses are male. [5]The simple-minded notion that a few poorly run summer workshops for girls can reverse this situation is ridiculous.

1. Which of the sentences in the passage contains biased language?
   a. sentence 2   c. sentence 4
   b. sentence 3   d. sentence 5
2. Which sentence in the passage states a stereotype?
   a. sentence 1   c. sentence 3
   b. sentence 2   d. sentence 4

C. [1]Wouldn't a hot cup of coffee taste great right now? [2]With a Dr. Zip coffee maker, a fresh cup will be ready in minutes. [3]If you wish, you can even set Dr. Zip's automatic timer to prepare a wonderful pot of coffee to greet you first thing in the morning. [4]Dr. Zip has lots of convenient features, like the brew-strength lever that lets you decide how strong you want your coffee to be. [5]Follow the lead of Richie Martz, basketball's highest scorer this season, who says, "Every morning, I'm a beast until I get my first delicious cup of coffee from Dr. Zip."

1. Which of the following groups of words contains biased language?
   a. hot, wish, automatic
   b. features, strong, lead
   c. great, wonderful, delicious
   d. ready, minutes, first
2. Which propaganda device is used in sentence 5?
   a. testimonial   c. plain folks
   b. name calling   d. bandwagon

D. [1]Throughout the century, the percentage of students who fail to graduate from high school has been decreasing, but more than three quarters of a million students still drop out of school each year. [2]Teenagers with poor attendance, low grades, and low-income backgrounds are most at risk of dropping out. [3]Teachers who care can inspire troubled teens who might otherwise tragically end up on society's rubbish heap—dropouts without dreams and without a future. [4]By keeping a close watch on students' progress and working closely with parents and administrators, teachers can help keep these students in school. [5]A good teacher can always succeed in developing strategies designed to ensure a continued commitment to education.

1. Which propaganda technique is used in sentence 5?
   a. name calling   c. plain folks
   b. glittering generalities   d. bandwagon

2. Which of the publications listed below is most likely to be the source of this passage?
   a. a brochure distributed to students considered to be potential dropouts
   b. an open letter to all parents of students enrolled in an urban high school
   c. a textbook for college students preparing to become teachers
   d. a newspaper article about a local school system

SCORE

100 − 12.5 for each one wrong = _____%

Read each of the passages below and then circle the letter of the best answer to each question.

A.   [1]First America Bank offers a remarkable protection plan for lost or stolen credit cards. [2]For only fifteen dollars, you can buy credit card protection that covers your losses up to $10,000. [3]Isn't this impressive guarantee worth the small yearly fee? [4]Losing a credit card naturally causes some anxiety, but First America's protection plan frees you from needless worry. [5]We notify your credit card company, and we cover your losses, all for one astonishingly low fee. [6]Remember, First America Bank is as sound as the country it serves so well.

1.   Which propaganda technique is used in sentence 6?
     a.   plain folks   c.   bandwagon
     b.   transfer   d.   testimonial

2.   Which of the following missing details would the reader have to know in order to avoid being tricked?
     a.   Federal law limits a card owner's legal responsibility for lost or stolen credit cards to fifty dollars.
     b.   The First America protection plan covers no more than twenty credit cards.
     c.   A lost or stolen credit card should be reported within forty-eight hours.
     d.   The bank offers its own Red, White, and Blue Bank Card to members in the plan.

B.   [1]All babies need care, including babies born with AIDS antibodies because their mothers have AIDS. [2]Because their mothers are rarely able to care for them, foster homes must be found. [3]Some of the babies with AIDS antibodies show no signs of the disease as they grow older, but others die. [4]It takes a special kind of compassion to care for AIDS babies in the shadow of death, but a few brave people have stepped forward to accept the challenge. [5]These are ordinary people who are not necessarily well educated or well off, but they want to help these babies in need.

1.   Which sentence in the paragraph contains emotionally loaded language?
     a.   sentence 1   c.   sentence 3
     b.   sentence 2   d.   sentence 4

2.   Which propaganda technique is used in sentence 5?
     a.   testimonial   c.   bandwagon
     b.   transfer   d.   plain folks

C. [1]You probably know many people who are constantly on a diet, starving themselves and yearning for forbidden hot fudge sundaes. [2]Did you know that at least ninety-five percent of the weight that is lost through all this effort is regained? [3]A new movement is based on the belief that the vicious cycle of losing and regaining weight is worse for people than maintaining a stable (yet plump) weight. [4]Thousands of people are joining Roberta Rice, a champion of this splendid new cause, in the pledge, "I'll never diet again." [5]True, Miss Rice weighs much more than the models whose thin thighs are displayed in fashion magazines, but she is attractive, self-confident, and delighted with her role in the new movement. [6]She even reports that after she lost her obsession with food, she lost some weight.

1. Which propaganda technique is used in sentence 4?
   a. name calling   c. bandwagon
   b. transfer   d. plain folks

2. Which of the statements below expresses the author's bias?
   a. Exercising, eating wisely, and getting regular checkups are the keys to good health.
   b. Roberta Rice opposes dieting.
   c. A fat person is never a happy person.
   d. Fat people can be attractive.

D. [1]Should American businesses be allowed to have hiring and promotion policies that favor women and minorities at the expense of white men who are more qualified? [2]In 1987 the Supreme Court held that companies may follow such policies if women or minorities are underrepresented among their employees. [3]The losers in this case are white men, the people who have proven themselves most capable of doing every kind of work. [4]The Supreme Court pretends to be the champion of the rights of all, but this absurd and unjust decision discriminates against a new breed of innocent victims, well-qualified white men.

1. Which of the sentences in the paragraph contains emotionally loaded language?
   a. sentence 1   c. sentence 3
   b. sentence 2   d. sentence 4

2. Which of the sentences in the paragraph states a stereotype?
   a. sentence 1   c. sentence 3
   b. sentence 2   d. sentence 4

SCORE

100 − 12.5 for each one wrong = _____%

Read each of the passages below, and then circle the letter of the best answer to each question.

A. [1]Increasingly, nursery schools are introducing schoolwork once thought appropriate for first and second grades, proving that American educators are more interested in being trendy than following sound educational principles. [2]Preschool youngsters should not be forced to do academic work. [3]High-pressure instruction for children who just need time to play is downright crazy, and the lunatics who are teaching young children academic skills are doing more harm than good. [4]Attempting reading, writing, and arithmetic at too young an age can make small children feel like failures and lead to dislike (and even dread) of school. [5]Activities that build independence and self-esteem are far more appropriate to nursery schools than stressful academics.

1. Which propaganda technique is used in sentence 3?
    a. transfer   c. name calling
    b. glittering generalities   d. bandwagon
2. Which sentence in the paragraph contains a half-truth?
    a. sentence 1   c. sentence 3
    b. sentence 2   d. sentence 4

B. [1]Have you ever wondered why the prices at Broad Street Cameras are always twenty to forty percent lower than many of our competitors'? [2]Our magnificent discounts and amazing low prices are possible because of our wise policy. [3]That policy is to buy our products from independent importers who charge less than the companies that others choose as their offical importers. [4]As a result, we pay less than many of our competitors, and so we charge less. [5]Our warehouse is fully stocked now with cameras, computers, and video equipment, so don't buy until you see us.

1. Which of the sentences in the paragraph contains biased language?
    a. sentence 1   c. sentence 3
    b. sentence 2   d. sentence 4

2. Which of the following missing details would the reader have to know in order to avoid being tricked?
    a. Broad Street Cameras' imported goods come with English-language instructions.
    b. Products imported by companies other than officially designated importers are known as gray-market goods.
    c. Companies that are not officially chosen as importers are still legitimate businesses.
    d. Goods not ordered from manufacturers' official importers do not have a manufacturer's U.S. warranty.

C. [1]Is racism tolerated on American college campuses? [2]Of course, college students are well known for acting irresponsibly. [3]However, the latest rash of incidents demonstrates a shocking return to racial intolerance. [4]At one campus, a battle between mostly white Red Sox fans and mostly black Mets fans turned into a destructive race riot. [5]At another, white students dressed in sheets burned a paper cross in a black student's room. [6]Similar shameful incidents have been reported recently on campuses across the country.

1. Which of the following groups of words contains emotionally loaded language?
   a. college, acting, demonstrates
   b. students, campus, Red Sox
   c. acting, latest, sheets
   d. shocking, destructive, shameful
2. Which of the following sentences in the passage states a stereotype?
   a. sentence 1   c. sentence 3
   b. sentence 2   d. sentence 4

D. [1]Isn't it a shame that men are so often fearful of commitment and true communication? [2]Women have increasingly gained self-confidence and established flourishing careers, but many men today seem scared and confused. [3]Anger and jealousy because of women's success is hard for men to admit to themselves, but men who deny these feelings are dishonest and cowardly. [4]Many men avoid closeness with successful women because they fear that women will rob them of their masculinity. [5]We need not accept these glaring weaknesses in men any longer.

1. Which of the following groups of words contains emotionally loaded language?
   a. commitment, communication
   b. women, careers, avoid
   c. scared, cowardly, glaring
   d. gained, admit, accept
2. The author of this passage reveals a bias
   a. in favor of men.
   b. in favor of women.
   c. against men with successful careers.
   d. against women with successful careers.

SCORE
100 − 12.5 for each one wrong =   %

A. Three statements in each cluster below are reasons. One is a conclusion. Label each as a reason (**R**) or a conclusion (**C**).

1. _____ The record shop was darkened and empty.

   _____ Its door was padlocked.

   _____ Its display window was empty except for a sign reading "Bankruptcy Sale: Friday."

   _____ The record shop's owner had gone bankrupt.

2. _____ My sister must prefer shopping at home to going to a store.

   _____ She sends away for every catalogue that's printed.

   _____ She orders items from department store circulars.

   _____ She watches the Home Shopping Network ten hours a day.

3. _____ My dog has been scratching more than usual.

   _____ His paws are covered with little black specks.

   _____ While I was petting him, a flea jumped onto my arm and bit me.

   _____ My dog has fleas.

4. _____ The news anchors on Channel 1 spend more time on small talk than those on Channel 2.

   _____ Channel 2 features important local and world issues.

   _____ Channel 2's newscasts are better than Channel 1's.

   _____ Channel 1 emphasizes sensational stories, such as local fires and highway accidents.

B. Circle the letter of the sentence that states a valid conclusion based on the evidence in each group below.

Group 1

- A woman was robbed and beaten on her way home from the bus.
- She did not get a very good look at her attacker, but she said it was a man wearing jeans and a sweat shirt.
- The woman was taken to the hospital to have her injuries treated; she was released very quickly.

Which of the following is a valid conclusion that can be drawn from the evidence above?

   a. The woman was careless about where she walked.
   b. Her attacker will never be found.
   c. Her injuries were not terrible.
   d. She will never take that bus at that time again.

Group 2

- A dozen children who were at the shore last weekend came down with viral infections.
- A pipe on the waste-disposal system of a nearby city broke, and waste was spilled in waters near the shore.
- The waste-processing system does not totally clean all city waste.

Which of the following is a valid conclusion that can be drawn from the evidence above?

   a. The children's infections had nothing to do with the waste spill.
   b. The children's infections were certainly the result of the waste spill.
   c. The children's infections might have resulted from the waste spill.
   d. The city waste workers were careless.

Group 3

- My father will turn forty in a couple of months.
- Lately, he has been bad-tempered and very moody.
- Also, he has been talking about quitting his job and has argued quite a bit with my mother.

Which of the following is a valid conclusion that can be drawn from the evidence above?

   a. The speaker's father is certainly having a mid-life crisis.
   b. The cause of the personality changes in the father is his job.
   c. The speaker's mother is not very understanding.
   d. Something is troubling the father.

Group 4

- Vitamin C is not stored in the body fat like some other vitamins.
- Any vitamin C not used by the body is excreted within a few hours.
- In addition, vitamin C is an acid, and thus it's best not to take large doses of it on an empty stomach.

Which of the following is a valid conclusion that can be drawn from the evidence above?

   a. Everyone should take supplemental doses of vitamin C.
   b. For people who take vitamin C pills, it is more efficient to take one pill a day.
   c. People should spread out vitamin C intake through the day.
   d. People should never take vitamin C pills on an empty stomach.

SCORE
100 − 5 for each one wrong = _____%

A. In each item below, circle the letter of the most dependable source of evidence for that statement.

1. "Public speaking is the easiest course this college offers. If you want an easy 'A,' take public speaking."
   a. The college newspaper
   b. The person ahead of you in line at registration
   c. Your roommate, who is planning to take a public speaking course this semester
   d. An alumnus who graduated several years ago

2. "It's almost impossible to earn a living as a country-and-western musician. Very few singers make it to the top. If I were you, I'd put away that guitar and start practicing something that will earn you a decent living."
   a. Your parents
   b. The owner of a record store
   c. Kitty Denver, a well-known country-and-western star
   d. Your older sister, who is a country music fan

3. "Next year's Paris fashions will have an athletic look and even shorter hemlines."
   a. A local journalist
   b. The *Times's* fashion reporter, just returned from a trip to Paris
   c. A salesperson in J. C. Penney, a large department store
   d. A fortune teller at the county fair

B. For each item below, write *S* on the line if the evidence given is sufficient to be convincing. Write *N* if there is not enough evidence given to support the conclusion.

_____ 1. This cabin is full of mosquitoes. Close your eyes, and you can hear them whining. In fact, one just bit me.

_____ 2. It makes much more sense to shop at a supermarket than at a convenience store. Prices are twenty per cent lower, you can buy any brand you want, and most supermarkets are now open in the evening, too.

_____ 3. A poll of several readers of *Today's World* revealed that not one of them ever reads what's on the editorial page. Obviously the owners and editors of that newspaper have a lot to learn about their readers' tastes.

C. Circle the letter of the sentence in each paragraph that does not support the conclusion of the argument.

1. [1]When your body begins sending you signals that you're pushing yourself too hard, it's time to slow down and relax. [2]If you are under too much stress, you may feel tired all the time. [3]Even after

a good night's sleep, you are likely to feel exhausted. [4]In fact, scientists say it's possible for people to get too much sleep. [5]Stress also causes numerous other physical problems, such as backaches, headaches, poor digestion, and high blood pressure.

Which sentence does not support the author's conclusion that stress has a bad effect on people's physical condition?

a. sentence 2   c. sentence 4
b. sentence 3   d. sentence 5

2.   [1]Renting a movie on videocassette makes much more sense these days than going to see a movie at a theater. [2]First of all, the large selection of video movies will always be many times greater than the available choices at all the neighborhood theaters and malls. [3]The rental stores even offer cassettes of made-for-television movies, foreign films, and classics like the legendary comedies of Charlie Chaplin. [4]Also, the low cost of film rental is well below the price of admission to a movie these days. [5]And you won't have to put up with noisy patrons drowning out the sound track with their personal conversations or comments on the action on the screen. [6]These ill-mannered moviegoers should be ejected from a theater when they create a disturbance.

Which sentence is not valid evidence for the conclusion that renting a movie makes more sense than going out to see one?

a. sentence 3   c. sentence 5
b. sentence 4   d. sentence 6

SCORE
100 − 12.5 for each one wrong = _____%

Each argument below contains a logical fallacy. Circle the letter of the statement which best expresses the type of fallacy contained in the argument.

1. The French woman next door to me makes the best stews and sauces I've ever tasted. It must be true that the French are all great cooks.
   a. Generalization based on insufficient evidence (hasty generalization)
   b. Assumption that order of events alone shows cause and effect (false cause)
   c. Assumption that things being compared are more alike than different (false comparison)
   d. Assumption that there are only two sides to a question (either-or fallacy)

2. Those who want to stand in the way of our plans to build housing on prairie land obviously don't care about the prosperity of this area.
   a. Statement repeats itself (circular reasoning)
   b. Shifts argument to irrelevant personal criticism (personal attack)
   c. Attributes to opponent a position not actually held (straw man)
   d. Evidence sounds good but has nothing to do with argument (changing the subject)

3. Earl will make a lousy class treasurer because he's just a conceited jerk.
   a. Statement repeats itself (circular reasoning)
   b. Shifts argument to irrelevant personal criticism (personal attack)
   c. Attributes to opponent a position not actually held (straw man)
   d. Evidence sounds good but has nothing to do with argument (changing the subject)

4. A few weeks after my old boss left the company, I got a promotion. He must have been holding me back.
   a. Generalization based on insufficient evidence (hasty generalization)
   b. Assumption that order of events alone shows cause and effect (false cause)
   c. Assumption that things being compared are more alike than different (false comparison)
   d. Assumption that there are only two sides to a question (either-or fallacy)

5. Harry Fleming is not the kind of man for our school board. Don't forget that his father was a convicted forger.
   a. Statement repeats itself (circular reasoning)
   b. Shifts argument to irrelevant personal criticism (personal attack)
   c. Attributes to opponent a position not actually held (straw man)
   d. Evidence sounds good but has nothing to do with argument (changing the subject)

6. Trapping is a cruel practice because it is unkind to animals.
   a. Statement repeats itself (circular reasoning)
   b. Shifts argument to irrelevant personal criticism (personal attack)
   c. Attributes to opponent a position not actually held (straw man)
   d. Evidence sounds good but has nothing to do with argument (changing the subject)

7. If you don't buy your food at Buy Rite, you aren't getting your money's worth.
   a. Statement repeats itself (circular reasoning)
   b. Assumption that order of events alone shows cause and effect (false cause)
   c. Assumption that things being compared are more alike than different (false comparison)
   d. Assumption that there are only two sides to a question (either-or fallacy)

8. Treat your children like flowers—feed them, let them have plenty of sunshine, and they'll grow up hardy and beautiful.
   a. Generalization based on insufficient evidence (hasty generalization)
   b. Assumption that order of events alone shows cause and effect (false cause)
   c. Assumption that things being compared are more alike than different (false comparison)
   d. Assumption that there are only two sides to a question (either-or fallacy)

SCORE
100 − 12.5 for each one wrong = _____%

Read each of the passages below. Then circle the letter of the best answer to each of the questions that follow.

1. [1]A high-fiber diet is a healthier diet. [2]In agricultural societies where vegetables and grains form a large part of the diet, there is less cancer of the colon and less heart disease. [3]In addition, because fiber is filling but not digested by the body, high-fiber diets discourage obesity. [4]Some health specialists also believe that low-fiber diets can lead to peptic ulcers, diabetes, and gum disease. [5]Finally, a high-fiber diet featuring fresh vegetables and nutty-flavored grains can be as delicious and satisfying as any.

    1. Which of the following is not relevant to the author's conclusion that a high-fiber diet is healthier than a low-fiber diet?
        a. sentence 2   c. sentence 4
        b. sentence 3   d. sentence 5

    2. Which of the following suggests that a high-fiber diet might help people lose weight?
        a. sentence 2   c. sentence 4
        b. sentence 3   d. sentence 5

2. [1]The proposal to allow casino gambling in town should be defeated. [2]Its defenders claim that casinos will bring substantial improvements to our town, but one has only to glance at Atlantic City to know that it hasn't benefited much from its casinos. [3]Besides, the defenders of this bill are more interested in their investments than in the possible benefits to the town. [4]It's possible that casinos would provide employment for some of our residents, but that gain is a lot to pay for bringing Las Vegas-type mobsters to town. [5]And any increase we gain in municipal taxes will be substantially reduced by the need for a bigger police force and maintenance staff.

    1. Which of the following is not relevant to the author's conclusion that casino gambling should not be allowed?
        a. sentence 2   c. sentence 4
        b. sentence 3   d. sentence 5

    2. Which of the following would have strengthened the author's case against casino gambling?
        a. figures on the town's current municipal taxes
        b. information on the spread of mobster activity in other gambling towns
        c. The largest amount of money ever won in Atlantic City
        d. The number of casinos in Atlantic City

3.   [1]Smoking should be forbidden in all places of work. [2]Smokers may have the right to hurt themselves, but they do not have the right to hurt others, and the smoke non-smokers inhale is widely believed to be harmful. [3]This is an especially important point for smokers with asthmatic children to keep in mind. [4]Even if occasional exposure is not particularly harmful, exposure to smoke in the workplace can be constant. [5]In addition, by limiting the amount that smokers smoke, the ban will benefit employers. [6]As a group, smokers take more sick days than others, so it is reasonable to assume that if they smoke less, they will take fewer sick days.

1.   Which of the following is not relevant to the author's conclusion that smoking should be banned from the workplace?
     a.   sentence 3   c.   sentence 5
     b.   sentence 4   d.   sentence 6

2.   Which of the following supports the point that a ban on smoking would benefit employers as well as employees?
     a.   sentence 3   c.   sentence 5
     b.   sentence 4   d.   sentence 6

4.   [1]Everyone should have a living will, which is a legal document that states you do not want useless life-prolonging medical treatment when a major illness leaves no hope for recovery. [2]A living will means your wishes will be followed even if you become too ill to communicate. [3]That means you will be protected from being forced to painfully extend your death. [4]Without such an arrangement, your family is bound to suffer the financial and emotional stress of prolonging your death. [5]You can draw up your own living will, but because laws are complicated you should at least have an attorney review the will.

1.   Which of the following does not contribute to the soundness of the author's conclusion that everyone should have a living will?
     a.   sentence 2   c.   sentence 4
     b.   sentence 3   d.   sentence 5

2.   Which of the sentences in the passage is an example of the either-or fallacy?
     a.   sentence 2   c.   sentence 4
     b.   sentence 3   d.   sentence 5

SCORE

100 − 12.5 for each one wrong = _____%

Read each of the passages below. Then circle the letter of the best answer to each of the questions that follow.

1. [1]Most people who do not pay their credit-card debts have no intention of swindling anyone. [2]Calling them deadbeats is heartless and wrong. [3]When they used their credit cards to make purchases, they fully intended to pay their bills, but bad luck interfered. [4]Losing a job is one brutal blow that makes people unable to pay their bills. [5]Divorce and illness are other painful situations that have led to defaults on credit-card debts.

    1. Which of the following does not provide valid support for the author's main point (stated in sentence 1)?
        a. sentence 2   c. sentence 4
        b. sentence 3   d. sentence 5

    2. Based on the evidence in the passage, we can conclude that
        a. there are no credit-card swindlers.
        b. people with bad financial luck should never have to pay their credit-card bills.
        c. people should not use credit cards.
        d. many people would pay their debts upon getting back on their feet financially.

2. [1]About one and a half million students are paddled in public schools each year, many for minor offenses such as circling rather than underlining answers on a worksheet. [2]Some schools even have a special discipline officer who performs this function. [3]Sometimes the paddlings are so severe that the students are injured. [4]Judging from studies that link paddling with juvenile delinquency, this kind of violence breeds more violence. [5]In addition, students who have been paddled often suffer from anxiety and stress-related problems. [6]These studies prove that as a disciplinary technique, paddling students can do more harm than good.

    1. Which of the following sentences does not provide valid support for the author's conclusion that paddling does more harm than good?
        a. sentence 2   c. sentence 4
        b. sentence 3   d. sentence 5

    2. Another valid conclusion that can be drawn from this passage is that students who are paddled
        a. learn very little in school.
        b. learn not to misbehave in school.
        c. always become juvenile delinquents.
        d. sometimes learn to use violence as a way to solve problems.

3. [1]Keeping up with the news is an important part of good citizenship. [2]First of all, it's only by watching the policies of our elected officials that we can make judgments about their performance. [3]If we are not satisfied, we can then write them letters to try to influence them. [4]We can also use what we learn about their performance to determine how we vote in the coming elections. [5]Knowing about current events can also make us more interesting conversationalists. [6]Finally, we can occasionally learn from the news about how we can be useful to society. [7]Perhaps we can serve a family in need of help by sending a few dollars or offer to volunteer at a shelter for the homeless that we learn is opening nearby.

    1. Which of the following does not support the author's conclusion that keeping up with the news contributes to good citizenship?
        a. sentence 4   c.   sentence 6
        b. sentence 5   d.   sentence 7

    2. Which of the following provides valid support for the author's point that knowing the policies of elected officials contributes to good citizenship?
        a. sentence 4   c.   sentence 6
        b. sentence 5   d.   sentence 7

4. [1]Individual and family stress would be lessened if families would assign work more evenly among family members. [2]Often wives who work full-time also do most of the work around the house, which makes their lives more stressful than necessary. [3]According to a recent survey, a majority of women feel a lot of strain, and more than a third say they are chronically tired. [4]This stress certainly creates tension between husbands and wives, thereby single-handedly causing our high divorce rate. [5]The fact that women still do most of the family chores shows that they are not fully liberated. [6]If household work was more fairly divided between wives, husbands, and children, everyone's lives would undoubtedly be improved.

    1. Which of the following does not support the author's point that women are under a great deal of stress?
        a. sentence 2   c.   sentence 4
        b. sentence 3   d.   sentence 5

    2. Which of the sentences is an example of the fallacy of false cause?
        a. sentence 2   c.   sentence 4
        b. sentence 3   d.   sentence 5

SCORE
100 − 12.5 for each one wrong = _____%

Part III

SEVENTEEN READING SELECTIONS

1

The Yellow Ribbon
Pete Hamill

Preview

When is a yellow ribbon like a pair of open arms? For the answer, read this selection, which first appeared in a *New York Post* newspaper column by Pete Hamill. After reading it, you'll understand why this story was the inspiration for a television movie and the popular song "Tie a Yellow Ribbon 'Round the Old Oak Tree."

Words to Watch

cocoon (2):   protective covering
bluntness (13):   abruptness
exaltation (22):   joy

They were going to Fort Lauderdale, the girl remembered later. There were 1 six of them, three boys and three girls, and they picked up the bus at the old terminal on 34th Street, carrying sandwiches and wine in paper bags, dreaming of golden beaches and the tides of the sea as the gray cold spring of New York vanished behind them. Vingo was on board from the beginning.

As the bus passed through Jersey and into Philly, they began to notice that 2 Vingo never moved. He sat in front of the young people, his dusty face masking his age, dressed in a plain brown ill-fitting suit. His fingers were stained from cigarettes and he chewed the inside of his lip a lot, frozen into some personal <u>cocoon</u> of silence.

Somewhere outside of Washington, deep into the night, the bus pulled into a 3 Howard Johnson's, and everybody got off except Vingo. He sat rooted in his seat, and the young people began to wonder about him, trying to imagine his life: Perhaps he was a sea captain, maybe he had run away from his wife, he could be an old soldier going home. When they went back to the bus, the girl sat beside him and introduced herself.

"We're going to Florida," the girl said brightly. "You going that far?"   4

"I don't know." Vingo said.   5

"I've never been there," she said. "I hear it's beautiful."   6

"It is," he said quietly, as if remembering something he had tried to forget.   7

"You live there?"   8

"I did some time there in the Navy. Jacksonville."   9

"Want some wine?" she said. He smiled and took the bottle of Chianti and   10
took a swig. He thanked her and retreated again into his silence. After a while, she
went back to the others, as Vingo nodded in sleep.

In the morning they awoke outside another Howard Johnson's, and this time   11
Vingo went in. The girl insisted that he join them. He seemed very shy and ordered
black coffee and smoked nervously, as the young people chattered about sleeping
on the beaches. When they went back on the bus, the girl sat with Vingo again,
and after a while, slowly and painfully and with great hesitation, he began to tell his
story. He had been in jail in New York for the last four years, and now he was
going home.

"Four years!" the girl said. "What did you do?"   12

"It doesn't matter," he said with quiet <u>bluntness</u>. "I did it and I went to jail.   13
If you can't do the time, don't do the crime. That's what they say and they're right."

"Are you married?"   14

"I don't know."   15

"You don't know?" she said.   16

"Well, when I was in the can I wrote to my wife," he said. "I told her, I said,   17
Martha, I understand if you can't stay married to me. I told her that. I said I was
gonna be away a long time, and that if she couldn't stand it, if the kids kept askin'
questions, if it hurt her too much, well, she could just forget me. Get a new guy—
she's a wonderful woman, really something—and forget about me. I told her she
didn't have to write me or nothing. And she didn't. Not for three-and-half years."

"And you're going home now, not knowing?"   18

"Yeah," he said shyly. "Well, last week, when I was sure the parole was coming   19
through I wrote her. I told her that if she had a new guy, I understood. But if she
didn't, if she would take me back she should let me know. We used to live in this
town, Brunswick, just before Jacksonville, and there's a great big oak tree just as
you come into town, a very famous tree, huge. I told her if she would take me back,
she should put a yellow handkerchief on the tree, and I would get off and come
home. If she didn't want me, forget it, no handkerchief, and I'd keep going on
through."

"Wow," the girl said. "Wow."   20

She told the others, and soon all of them were in it, caught up in the approach   21
of Brunswick, looking at the pictures Vingo showed them of his wife and three
children, the woman handsome in a plain way, the children still unformed in a
cracked, much-handled snapshot. Now they were 20 miles from Brunswick and the
young people took over window seats on the right side, waiting for the approach
of the great oak tree. Vingo stopped looking, tightening his face into the ex-con's
mask, as if fortifying himself against still another disappointment. Then it was 10
miles, and then five and the bus acquired a dark hushed mood, full of silence, of

absence, of lost years, of the woman's plain face, of the sudden letter on the break-fast table, of the wonder of children, of the iron bars of solitude.

Then suddenly all of the young people were up out of their seats, screaming   22
and shouting and crying, doing small dances, shaking clenched fists in triumph and exaltation. All except Vingo.

Vingo sat there stunned, looking at the oak tree. It was covered with yellow   23
handkerchiefs, 20 of them, 30 of them, maybe hundreds, a tree that stood like a banner of welcome blowing and billowing in the wind, turned into a gorgeous yellow blur by the passing bus. As the young people shouted, the old con slowly rose from his seat, holding himself tightly, and made his way to the front of the bus to go home.

SKILL-DEVELOPMENT QUESTIONS

Vocabulary in Context

1. The word *fortifying* in "tightening his face into the ex-con's mask, as if fortifying himself against still another disappointment" (paragraph 21) means
   a. strengthening.
   b. watching.
   c. hurrying.
   d. losing.

2. The word *acquired* in "the bus acquired a dark hushed mood" (paragraph 21) means
   a. needed.
   b. gained.
   c. stopped.
   d. lost.

Central Point and Main Ideas

3. Which sentence best expresses the main idea of this selection?
   a. Prison sentences can ruin marriages.
   b. A bus ride to Florida can be an interesting experience.
   c. Vingo did not know what to expect.
   d. Vingo returned from prison to find that his wife still loved him.

4. Which sentence best expresses the main idea of paragraph 3?
   a. The bus stopped at a Howard Johnson's.
   b. The young people began to be curious about Vingo.
   c. Vingo might have been a sea captain.
   d. Everyone got off the bus except Vingo.

Key Details

_____   5.   TRUE OR FALSE? Vingo felt he should not have been put in prison.

Transitions

6.   The relationship of the first four words in the sentence below to the rest of the sentence is one of
     a.   emphasis.
     b.   location.
     c.   time.
     d.   cause and effect.

     Somewhere outside of Washington, deep into the night, the bus pulled into a Howard Johnson's, and everybody got off except Vingo. (Paragraph 3)

7.   The transition words *as, when, after, now,* and *then,* which Hamill uses throughout this selection, all signal
     a.   cause and effect.
     b.   location.
     c.   emphasis.
     d.   time.

8.   The relationship expressed in the phrase "a tree that stood like a banner of welcome" (paragraph 23) is one of
     a.   contrast.
     b.   comparison.
     c.   cause and effect.
     d.   time.

Patterns of Organization

9.   The main pattern of organization of paragraph 2 is
     a.   cause and effect.
     b.   comparison and contrast.
     c.   list of items.
     d.   time order.

10. The main pattern of organization of the entire selection is
     a.   cause and effect.
     b.   comparison and contrast.
     c.   list of items.
     d.   time order.

Fact and Opinion

11. In telling this narrative, Hamill
    a. stresses his own opinions.
    b. leaves out any of Vingo's opinions.
    c. leaves out any of the young people's opinions.
    d. includes some of Vingo's and some of the young people's opinions.

12. Judging by the first sentence of the selection, Hamill got some facts for this non-fiction narrative by
    a. observing everything as a passenger on the bus ride.
    b. only imagining what might have happened on such a ride.
    c. interviewing at least one passenger.
    d. using a tape recording of the bus ride.

Inferences

13. We can infer that the young people were going to Florida
    a. on business.
    b. to visit family.
    c. on vacation.
    d. to get married.

14. The author implies that Vingo thought
    a. he would someday be in prison again.
    b. there might be no yellow handkerchief on the tree.
    c. his wife was wrong for not writing to him in prison.
    d. his wife was sure to want him back.

_____ 15. TRUE OR FALSE? The statement that Vingo "rose from his seat, holding himself tightly" (last paragraph) implies that Vingo was trying to contain his emotions.

Purpose and Tone

16. The purpose of "The Yellow Ribbon" is to
    a. inform readers that a convict's life can be rebuilt after prison.
    b. persuade readers to avoid a life of crime.
    c. entertain readers with a heartwarming story.

17. In paragraphs 17 through 21, the author's tone becomes increasingly
    a. bitter.
    b. amused.
    c. suspenseful.
    d. disbelieving.

Bias and Propaganda

18. Which of the following sentences based on the selection (paragraph 21) contains the *least* number of emotionally loaded words?
    a. The bus acquired a dark hushed mood.
    b. The bus was filled with silent anticipation.
    c. The bus became quiet.
    d. The bus was as still as a tomb.

Evaluating Arguments

19. Which of the following is a valid conclusion that can be drawn from the evidence below?
    a. Vingo was nervous about something.
    b. Vingo was on the verge of a nervous breakdown.
    c. Vingo had a hostile personality.
    d. Vingo disliked young people.

    [Vingo's] fingers were stained from cigarettes and he chewed the inside of his lip a lot, frozen into some personal cocoon of silence. (Paragraph 2)

20. Which of the following is *not* a valid conclusion that can be drawn from the evidence below?
    a. The young people were interested in seeing if a yellow handkerchief would be on the oak tree.
    b. Vingo had been a good father.
    c. Vingo didn't mind sharing his story with the young people.
    d. Vingo had held and looked at the photos a lot.

    She told the others, and soon all of them were in it, caught up in the approach of Brunswick, looking at the pictures Vingo showed them of his wife and three children, the woman handsome in a plain way, the children still unformed in the cracked, much-handled snapshot. (Paragraph 21)

THINKING ACTIVITIES

Outlining

Complete the following outline of Hamill's narrative by filling in the letters of the missing details. The details appear in random order in the following list.

Central Point: After being in prison, Vingo discovered that his wife wanted him back.

1. _____
2. _____
3. _____
4. _____
5. _____

Items Missing from the Outline
a. The bus ride begins.
b. Everyone waits to reach Brunswick.
c. They reach the oak tree.
d. Vingo tells his story.
e. The young people become curious about Vingo.

Summarizing

Following is an incomplete summary of "The Yellow Ribbon." Circle the letter (**a**, **b**, or **c**) of the sentence below that *best* completes the summary.

A man named Vingo had just been released from prison and was on a bus headed home. Some young people were also on the bus, and they got Vingo to tell his story. He said he had written to his wife when he went to prison to explain he would understand if she found another man. He hadn't heard from her since but still loved her very much. So he recently wrote to her, telling her to put a yellow handkerchief on a well-known oak tree in town if she wanted him to come home. If the handkerchief wasn't on the tree, he wouldn't get off the bus there.

_____ After a tense ride to Vingo's hometown, he and his fellow travelers finally got his wife's answer: not one, but scores of handkerchiefs fluttering on the tree.

a. Vingo felt his wife would be making a big mistake if she didn't want him home again.
b. Vingo showed pictures of his wife and children to the young people, who got caught up in waiting to see the oak tree.
c. Vingo would just continue on the bus to Florida, which is where the young people were going.

DISCUSSION QUESTIONS

1. From whose point of view is Vingo's story told? Why do you think Hamill chose to tell it from that point of view?

2.   What do you think might be the reason or reasons that Vingo's wife never wrote him while he was in prison?

3.   While there is much we don't learn about Vingo in this very short narrative, Hamill does provide us with clues to some important aspects of his personality. What can we infer about the kind of man Vingo is?

4.   Many people are thrilled, some even to tears, by this story. What makes "The Yellow Ribbon" have such a powerful effect on readers?

Check Your Performance   THE YELLOW RIBBON

Skill	Number Right	Points	Total
Vocabulary in Context (2 items)	_____	× 4 :	_____
Central Point and Main Ideas (2)	_____	× 4 :	_____
Key Details (1)	_____	× 4 :	_____
Transitions (3)	_____	× 4 :	_____
Patterns of Organization (2)	_____	× 4 :	_____
Fact and Opinion (2)	_____	× 4 :	_____
Inferences (3)	_____	× 4 :	_____
Purpose and Tone (2)	_____	× 4 :	_____
Bias and Propaganda (1)	_____	× 4 :	_____
Evaluating Arguments (2)	_____	× 4 :	_____

(total of 20 questions)

Outlining (5)	_____	× 2 :	_____
Summarizing (1)	_____	× 10 :	_____

FINAL SCORE (OF POSSIBLE 100)   _____

Enter your final score into the reading performance chart on page 454.

2

The Fast-Food Phenomenon
Lila Perl

Preview

Are you hungry? Why not join the crowd at a local fast-food restaurant? A Whopper or Chicken McNuggets might make a convenient meal, and at a fast-food restaurant you can be sure of what you are getting. Or can you? Lila Perl points out in this article that fast food isn't necessarily good food, and she urges readers to think twice before biting into that burger.

Words to Watch

grappling (5):   struggling
rancid (7):   spoiled
carcinogenic (7):   cancer-causing
common denominator (11):   something agreeable to all
rendered (11):   made
lair (12):   hideaway
replica (12):   copy

Americans have been described as a people who are always "on the move." 1
Speed that up a little to "on the run," and you can easily see why fast food has become a way of life for most of us.

The Eating-Out Society

What makes Americans spend nearly half their food dollars on meals away 2
from home? The answers lie in the way Americans live today. During the first few

decades of the twentieth century, canned and other convenience foods freed the family cook from full-time duty at the kitchen range. Then, in the 1940s, work in the wartime defense plants took more women out of the home than ever before, setting the pattern of the working wife and mother.

Today about half of the country's married women are employed outside the   3
home. But, unless family members pitch in with food preparation, women are not fully liberated from that chore. Instead many have become, in a sense, prisoners of the completely cooked convenience meal. It's easier to pick up a bucket of fried chicken on the way home from work or take the family out for pizzas, heroes, or burgers than to start opening cans or heating up frozen dinners after a long, hard day.

Also, the rising divorce rate means that there are more single working parents   4
with children to feed. And many young adults and elderly people, as well as unmarried and divorced mature people, live alone rather than as part of a family unit and don't want to bother cooking for one.

Fast food is appealing because it *is* fast, it doesn't require any dressing up, it   5
offers a "fun" break in the daily routine, and the outlay of money seems small. It can be eaten in the car—sometimes picked up at a drive-in window without even getting out—or on the run. Even if it is brought home to eat, there will never be any dirty dishes to wash because of the handy disposable wrappings. Children, especially, love fast food because it's finger food, no grappling with knives and forks, no annoying instructions from adults about table manners.

As for traveling Americans, a traditionally mobile people in a very large coun-   6
try, the familiar golden arches, Mexican "taco" hats, and "leaning towers" of pizza are reassuring signs that make them feel at home away from home. Even boring, repetitious food is okay, Americans seem to have decided, as long as it is recognizable and dependable. No wonder Ray Kroc unashamedly titled his McDonald's success-story autobiography *Grinding It Out*.

Fast Food Nutrition

What about the nutrition in a standard fast food meal of a burger, fries, and a   7
Coke or shake? Fast feeders argue that the meat patty, lettuce and tomato, enriched bun, and potatoes are honest foods offering protein, carbohydrates, vitamins, and minerals. But let's take a closer look. The beef patty is shockingly expensive protein on a cost per ounce basis, the lettuce and tomato are minimal, a token gesture toward supplying a ration of salad for the guilt-ridden, the bun is basically bleached white flour and air, and the fries are overloaded with grease and salt. They are also low in the nutriment that a baked or boiled potato would supply because high-heat frying and long standing tend to destroy their vitamin C and other nutrients. One particular fast food risk is the too-often reheated fat used in deep frying. Smoking or rancid oil commonly causes only indigestion, but recent studies indicate that it may also have carcinogenic effects.

No one seems able to defend the cola drink with its sugar (or saccharin) and   8
caffeine. And the fast food shake, which is carefully *not* called a milkshake, contains mainly water, saturated fat, emulsifiers, thickeners, sugar, and artificial flavoring.

Nor do the brine-soaked pickle slices or "special" sauces thickened with gum traga-canth add any nutritive pluses. In short, the typical fast food meal is high in sugar, salt, saturated fat, and additives. Although it may offer some protein, it is generally low in calcium, iron, fiber, and vitamins A, C, D, and E.

At the same time, it contributes about 1,000 calories to our daily intake, more 9 than one-third of the average requirement for males eleven years and up, and nearly half of the daily requirement for females aged eleven and up. An occasional binge at the burger stand isn't going to ruin one's health, but it's pretty clear that a too-steady fast food diet is poorly balanced and carries a lot of empty calories—far too many for the food value it provides.

Of course, all fast food isn't hamburgers. But it's questionable whether the 10 typical fried chicken, fried fish, hot dog, chili, or taco meal can be any better bal-anced nutritionally, for most lack whole grains, fresh fruits and vegetables, and milk.

In addition, the flavors of the food specialities presented tend to have been 11 processed out by design. In order to appeal to the widest possible range of eaters, the industry has had to find an acceptable <u>common denominator</u>. So fish, which has had a bad name with many Americans because of its "fishy" taste, has been <u>rendered</u> almost flavorless by the seafood chains and is served up in slabs that taste more of breading and fat than of fish. And Mexican food, which the chains considered too "hot" for the average American taste, has lost its character and been "de-spiced" into an unauthentic blandness.

Eating the Scenery

What their food may lack in the way of flavor and character, many of the new 12 sit-down eateries try to make up for in the decor. The "theme restaurant" is one of the latest developments in the fast food industry. A fish-and-chips outlet may be done as a sea pirate's <u>lair</u> or a family-style steak house may be a <u>replica</u> of an Old West gambling parlor. English pubs, Mexican haciendas, and even <u>Victorian</u> railroad stations are among today's most popular "dinner house" themes. Usually molded plastic masquerades as rough oak beams, yet the scenery tries hard to make the food taste more authentic than it is. Nevertheless, the chain-run dinner houses serve the same kind of assembly-line meals that the fast food takeouts do. Food arrives in the restaurant kitchen prepackaged, in individual portions, and often precooked, requir-ing just a quick browning or a few seconds heating in a microwave oven. No chef presides over the kitchen, merely a staff of attendants who work from printed timing instructions.

Even some of the more elite restaurants, with fancy menus, formal waiters, 13 and high prices are not above serving prefrozen beef burgundy and lobster à la Newburg supplied by the same corporate kitchens that prepare airline meals.

How can you tell, short of visiting the kitchen, if you're getting mass- 14 produced glop at gourmet prices? Small, family-run restaurants more often prepare honest food from scratch. And critical taste buds, not dulled by a regular diet of unimaginative, standardized food, can usually spot the difference between the thinly disguised TV dinner and a well-cooked meal prepared with quality ingredients.

To help restaurant patrons know what they're paying for, several American 15 cities have recently proposed "truth-in-menu" bills. Restaurants would have to indicate on their menus any dish that wasn't made in their own kitchens, and would also have to reveal the additives they used, such as MSG, in preparing various dishes. Such proposals may not pass easily into law, but through alerting the public to deceptive practices they may help to stem the advance of high-priced fast food served on white tablecloths.

SKILL-DEVELOPMENT QUESTIONS

Vocabulary in Context

1. The word *mobile* in "As for traveling Americans, a traditionally mobile people in a very large country, the familiar golden arches, Mexican 'taco' hats, and 'leaning towers' of pizza are reassuring signs that make them feel at home away from home" (paragraph 6) means
   a. hungry.
   b. frequently traveling.
   c. lonely.
   d. stay-at-home.

2. The word *presides* in "No chef presides over the kitchen, merely a staff of attendants who work from printed timing instructions" (paragraph 12) means
   a. supervises.
   b. argues.
   c. makes excuses.
   d. relaxes.

Central Point and Main Ideas

3. Which sentence best expresses the central point of this selection?
   a. Fast food is familiar and dependable.
   b. Fast food has become a way of life for many Americans.
   c. More American cities need "truth-in-menu" laws.
   d. Americans are eating too much fast food, a situation that can be improved with greater awareness.

4. Which sentence best expresses the main idea of paragraph 12?
   a. Chain-run restaurants try to make food taste better.
   b. Sit-down restaurants offer attractive decors.
   c. Mexican haciendas are among the popular "dinner-house" themes.
   d. Despite their elaborate decor, chain sit-down restaurants are simply fast-food places.

Key Details

_____ 5. TRUE OR FALSE? The popularity of fast food is the result of changes in the American lifestyle.

6. According to the author, fast food provides all of the following *except*
    a. low-salt content.
    b. a quickly available meal.
    c. fun.
    d. dependability.

Transitions

7. The signal words in paragraph 4 that show addition are
    a. also, and.
    b. more, than.
    c. means, part of.
    d. with, for one.

8. The sentence below
    a. compares fast food to other food.
    b. contrasts fast food to other food.
    c. gives the causes for the appeal of fast food.
    d. gives illustrations of fast food.

   Fast food is appealing because it *is* fast, it doesn't require any dressing up, it offers a "fun" break in the daily routine, and the outlay of money seems small. (Paragraph 5)

Patterns of Organization

9. The pattern of organization in the supporting sentences of paragraph 2 is
    a. time order.
    b. definition and example.
    c. list of items.
    d. comparison.

10. The main pattern of organization in paragraph 11 is
    a. comparison.
    b. definition and example.
    c. time order.
    d. cause and effect.

Fact and Opinion

11. The sentence below states
    a. a fact.
    b. an opinion.
    c. a fact and an opinion.

    And many young adults and elderly people, as well as unmarried and divorced mature people, live alone rather than as part of a family unit and don't want to bother cooking for one. (Paragraph 4)

12. Paragraph 15 contains
    a. facts that contradict the author's conclusion.
    b. facts that support the author's conclusions about take-out food.
    c. facts and the author's opinion about what might be done to help solve the problems she has described.
    d. conflicting opinions from which readers may choose the ones with which they agree.

Inferences

13. The author implies that a steady diet of fast food is
    a. low in fat.
    b. nutritionally sound.
    c. low in calories.
    d. unhealthy.

_____ 14. TRUE OR FALSE? The author implies that people have a right to know exactly what they are eating.

Purpose and Tone

15. The author's primary purpose is to
    a. inform.
    b. persuade.
    c. entertain.

16. The author's tone when discussing fast food is
    a. amused.
    b. totally objective.
    c. approving.
    d. disapproving.

Bias and Propaganda

17. Which group of words from paragraph 14 contains biased language?
    a. glop, unimaginative, thinly disguised
    b. kitchen, restaurants, spot
    c. visiting, prices, family-run
    d. prepare, diet, ingredients

18. Which propaganda technique is the author using when she describes fast food as "almost flavorless"?
    a. plain folks.
    b. transfer.
    c. testimonial.
    d. name calling.

Evaluating Arguments

19. Which of the following best supports the author's implication that fast food is not nutritious?
    a. The fast-food beef patty is an expensive source of protein.
    b. High-heat frying lowers the amount of vitamin C in French fries.
    c. Fast food is almost flavorless.
    d. Restaurants decorated in themes have increased lately.

20. In paragraph 7, the author supports her claim that "the beef patty is shockingly expensive protein on a cost per ounce basis"
    a. with facts that compare the cost of protein in beef patties with the cost of other sources of protein.
    b. with expert opinions.
    c. with facts on the percentage of people's food budget that goes toward beef patties.
    d. with no facts or opinions.

THINKING ACTIVITIES

Outlining

Following is an incomplete outline of "The Fast-Food Phenomenon." Complete it by filling in the letters of the items below the outline.

Central Point: Because Americans are eating out more and paying more for poor quality food, they should become more aware of what they are eating.

A. _____
    1. More working women
    2. More single-parent families and singles
    3. Convenience of fast-food restaurants

    4. _____
B. Poor quality of fast food
    1. Low in nutrition

    2. _____
    3. Poor flavor
C. Sit-down restaurants
    1. Theme decors

    2. _____

D. _____
    1. Check out family-run restaurants
    2. Become more critical about food
    3. Support truth-in-menu laws

Items Missing from the Outline
a. High in calories
b. Why people eat so much fast food
c. Need for more consumer awareness
d. Prepackaged and prefrozen meals
e. Dependability of fast food

Summarizing

1. Circle the letter of the statement that best summarizes the set of supporting details in paragraphs 1 through 6.
    a. Americans are eating out more than ever.
    b. Americans are eating restaurant meals more than ever for reasons that make them frequently choose fast food.
    c. Fast-food restaurants serve boring but dependable meals.

2. Circle the letter of the statement that best summarizes the set of supporting details in paragraphs 7 through 11.
    a. Fast food is more nutritious than most people realize.
    b. Fast food is unhealthy and dull tasting.
    c. Cola drinks and fast-food shakes contain harmful additives.

3. Circle the letter of the statement that best summarizes the set of supporting details in paragraphs 12 through 13.
   a. Many sit-down restaurants serve the same kind of prepackaged foods as fast-food takeouts do, but they try to make up for it with fancy decors.
   b. Sit-down restaurant chains are being decorated in various themes, such as a sea pirate's lair or an English pub.
   c. The kitchens in chain-run dinner houses are staffed by people who don't really cook.

4. Circle the letter of the statement that best summarizes the set of supporting details in paragraphs 14 through 15.
   a. People who don't let their taste become dulled by poor food can often distinguish a quality meal from a bad one.
   b. Several American cities are considering "truth-in-menu" laws to help patrons better know what kinds of food restaurants offer.
   c. Consumers can avoid fast food by checking out family-run restaurants, becoming more critical about their food, and demanding menus that give relevant information on restaurant food.

DISCUSSION QUESTIONS

1. Do you ever eat fastfood? What are its appeals for you?

2. If the author is trying to convince us that fast food is not good food, why do you think she begins her article by explaining why fast food is so popular? Also, why do you think she doesn't suggest that Americans should eat home-cooked meals more often?

3. What does the author imply by the sentence "No wonder Ray Kroc unashamedly titled his McDonald's success-story autobiography *Grinding It Out*" (paragraph 6)?

4. At the beginning of the article, Perl implies that Americans are "on the run," thereby explaining fast food's popularity. What else in our society—besides fast food—is caused by our always being in such a hurry? And which of these other "fast" things might not be so good for us?

Check Your Performance   THE FAST FOOD PHENOMENON

Skill	Number Right		Points		Total
Vocabulary in Context (2 items)	_____	×	4	:	_____
Central Point and Main Ideas (2)	_____	×	4	:	_____
Key Details (2)	_____	×	4	:	_____
Transitions (2)	_____	×	4	:	_____
Patterns of Organization (2)	_____	×	4	:	_____
Fact and Opinion (2)	_____	×	4	:	_____
Inferences (2)	_____	×	4	:	_____
Purpose and Tone (2)	_____	×	4	:	_____
Bias and Propaganda (2)	_____	×	4	:	_____
Evaluating Arguments (2)	_____	×	4	:	_____

(total of 20 questions)

Outlining (5)	_____	×	2	:	_____
Summarizing (4)	_____	×	2.5	:	_____

FINAL SCORE (OF POSSIBLE 100)   _____

Enter your final score into the reading performance chart on page 454.

3

A BLIND WOMAN'S GRIM INSIGHT
Dan Chu

Preview

Have you always assumed that people go out of their way to help the handicapped? Ever since Millicent Collinsworth was blinded by an accident, she has learned the hard way that people are not always considerate. Through her story, this article from *People* magazine tells about some of the obstacles the blind must face in our society and how one person works to overcome them.

Words to Watch

stifling (1): suffocating
claustrophobic (3): afraid of being shut up in a small space
vulnerable (6): open to attack
dabbled (7): got involved in a casual way
annuity (8): a sum of money paid at regular intervals
contemplated (8): thought about

The afternoon was hot and muggy, and rush hour in Los Angeles was at full 1 boil when Millicent Collinsworth, 39, started home to Hollywood earlier this month with her guide dog, Eeyore. She boarded a city bus, sat down a few feet behind the driver and settled the black Labrador retriever between her feet. With each stop the overcrowded bus became more stifling; passengers shoved and cursed. Suddenly, a man went berserk. "I've got to breathe!" he yelled, groping wildly toward the door.

In his panic he struck Collinsworth in the face. "He hit me so hard that he 2 knocked off my dark glasses and split open my lip," she recalls. Worse, the shoving

287

crowd was trampling Eeyore's harness, and she could hear the dog choking as the leash tightened around his throat. When Collinsworth bent over to free the dog, she was knocked to the floor. No one came to her aid.

Hastily the driver stopped the bus to let the claustrophobic man off. Though   3
still 15 blocks from home, Collinsworth wanted out, too, and had to push and elbow her way to the door. "Nobody helped," she says. Shaken and crying, she began to stumble home, trusting Eeyore to lead the way. Collinsworth felt a wetness on her face, hands and clothes, and assumed it was her own tears. No one on the busy stretch of Sunset Boulevard stopped to ask if she needed assistance.

Only as she fumbled with the lock of her apartment did Collinsworth realize   4
that her hands were slippery with blood, not tears. She rushed to the phone and called her boyfriend of six months, Gary Williams, 31, as neighbors, alarmed by the bloody streaks on her door, began to gather outside. One of them, Dan Schwab, "thought that someone was dead in there, and he got the manager," Collinsworth recalls. Paramedics were summoned to take her to the hospital, where she received four stitches on her lip.

The cut will heal. The wound to Collinsworth's self-confidence may not. Her   5
injury was a minor one, but the dozens of people who saw her on the street, covered with blood, had no way of knowing that, because none of them bothered to ask. It's that cold indifference that has left Collinsworth afraid to move around the city alone—a victim less of a crazed commuter than of society's shocking blind spot when it comes to the handicapped. "It was like a nightmare where you scream and no sound comes out," she says of her walk home. "To be in the dark and hurt and not have anyone help is the most terrifying thing of all." In the eight years since she lost her sight, Collinsworth has learned that for the old or infirm, such terror is all too common.

It was not the first time Collinsworth had been assaulted. Last year, she says,   6
a man jumped her from behind as she was leaving the Braille institute. "He grabbed for my purse and ripped open my blouse," she says. "I screamed. Some people came around a corner and the man fled, though he got my purse." A few months later another mugger snatched a bag of groceries out of her arms. "It becomes a way of life with the handicapped," she says. "You get to know that the world knows you're vulnerable."

That bitter lesson may seem particularly cruel to one who loses her sight sud-   7
denly, as Collinsworth did, in the midst of a thriving career. In 1979 the Arkansas native, once married and divorced, was an energetic, high-profile executive, traveling the country as a public relations director for W. R. Grace & Co. She also dabbled in acting and ran a children's theater near her home in Irvine, Calif. It was there, in June of 1979, that Collinsworth came to the aid of a workman teetering on his ladder and was hit between the eyes by a falling hammer. Within five years despite nine operations, she was totally blind.

"I'd always been a go-getter, and then my script was destroyed," says Collins-   8
worth, who describes herself as emotionally devastated by the accident. The $1,500-a-month annuity she won from the construction company, along with a payment of $25,000 every five years, doesn't begin to compensate for the destruction of the life she had enjoyed before blindness. Prior to the accident, she says, "It never occurred

to me not to go anywhere whenever I wanted. I prided myself on my independence." After being struck blind, Collinsworth admits, she briefly <u>contemplated</u> suicide.

Instead, with the help of family, friends, sympathetic doctors and her religious 9 faith, Collinsworth gradually reclaimed her life. One friend helped her buy clothes and arrange them systematically in her closet so that she doesn't mix stripes with polka-dots; another helped her memorize the layout of the local grocery store. The first time she shopped alone, "I got all my groceries and I got to the check-out stand, and the whole store burst into applause," she says. She hadn't realized that concerned clerks and puzzled patrons were watching her every move.

Collinsworth, who has never returned to work, did take up acting again late 10 last year, joining a workshop called HAPPI—Handicapped Artists, Performers and Partners Inc. That's where she met Williams, one of several nonhandicapped actors in the group. Last October she got Eeyore. "I can't tell you the feeling I had when I first grabbed Eeyore's harness—the feeling of dignity restored in independence," she says.

Now she must fight to get that feeling back. "I'm a lousy loser," says Collins- 11 worth. "To be honest, the only way I could accept blindness was to try to be the best blind lady around." Discovering, as she puts it, that "the world itself has become emotionally blind" is a grave setback. "But I have my whole life ahead of me. If I give up now, I'll have an awful lot of time to sit alone in the dark."

SKILL-DEVELOPMENT QUESTIONS

Vocabulary in Context

1. The word *infirm* in "for the old or infirm, such terror is all too common" (paragraph 5) means
   a. weak.
   b. strong.
   c. young.
   d. careless.

2. The word *devastated* in "Collinsworth . . . describes herself as emotionally devastated by the accident" (paragraph 8) means
   a. strengthened.
   b. reassured.
   c. destroyed.
   d. unconcerned.

Central Point and Main Ideas

3. Which sentence best expresses the central point of this selection?
   a. Blindness changed Collinsworth's life.

     b. Since becoming blind, Collinsworth's struggle to become indepen-
dent has been hindered by indifference and cruelty.

     c. Collinsworth has tried to be "the best blind lady around."

     d. With the help of others and a guide dog, the blind can lead a full
and independent life.

4. Which sentence best expresses the main idea of paragraph 5?
     a. Collinsworth's injury from the bus incident was minor.
     b. Society has a blind spot when it comes to the handicapped.
     c. Because of people's indifference after the bus incident, Collins-
worth is afraid to get around alone.
     d. The walk home after the bus incident was the worst part of the
experience for Collinsworth.

5. Which sentence best expresses the main idea shared by paragraphs 9
and 10?
     a. Collinsworth no longer works.
     b. Collinsworth started acting again.
     c. After becoming blind, Collinsworth rebuilt her life with the help
of others.
     d. When Collinsworth got her dog, Eeyore, she felt she gained the
dignity of independence.

Key Details

6. Collinsworth lost her sight
     a. while she was traveling for her job.
     b. while living in Arkansas.
     c. when she tried to help someone.
     d. as the result of an assault.

_____ 7. TRUE OR FALSE? The author feels that Collinsworth's physical injury from the bus incident was less serious than the injury to her self-
confidence.

Transitions

8. The relationship of the second sentence on page 291 to the first sentence is one of
     a. contrast.
     b. addition.
     c. location.
     d. time.

In 1979 the Arkansas native, once married and divorced, was an energetic, high-profile executive, traveling the country as a public relations director for W.R. Grace & Co. She also dabbled in acting and ran a children's theater near her home in Irvine, Calif. (Paragraph 7)

9. The relationship of the second sentence below to the first sentence is one of
   a. addition.
   b. illustration.
   c. contrast.
   d. summary.

After being struck blind, Collinsworth admits, she briefly contemplated suicide.

    Instead, with the help of family, friends, sympathetic doctors and her religious faith, Collinsworth gradually reclaimed her life. (Paragraphs 8–9)

Patterns of Organization

10. The pattern of organization of paragraph 1 is
    a. list of items.
    b. comparison/contrast.
    c. cause and effect.
    d. time order.

Fact and Opinion

11. Which of the following statements is an opinion?
    a. "When Collinsworth bent over to free the dog, she was knocked to the floor."
    b. "The wound to Collinsworth's self-confidence may not [heal]."
    c. "It was not the first time Collinsworth had been assaulted."
    d. Within five years despite nine operations, she was totally blind.

12. Which of the following statements contains both a fact and an opinion?
    a. "Paramedics were summoned to take her to the hospital, where she received four stitches on her lip."
    b. "A few months later another mugger snatched a bag of groceries out of her arms."
    c. "The $1,500-a-month annuity she won from the construction company, along with a payment of $25,000 every five years,

doesn't begin to compensate for the destruction of the life she had enjoyed before blindness."
d. "She hadn't realized that concerned clerks and puzzled patrons were watching her every move."

Inferences

13. From the article, we can conclude that the handicapped
a. may be more likely to be mugged because they are easy targets.
b. are no more likely to be assaulted than anyone else.
c. cannot safely use public transportation.
d. have enough support from society.

14. The author implies that Collinsworth
a. needs more money.
b. is worse off than most handicapped people.
c. is trying very hard to rebuild her life.
d. can no longer have a rich life.

Purpose and Tone

15. The main purpose of this article is to
a. inform.
b. persuade.
c. entertain.

16. The tone of this article is
a. sentimental.
b. totally objective.
c. prayerful.
d. serious and sympathetic.

Bias and Propaganda

17. Which of the following groups of words and phrases from paragraph 5 contains biased language?
a. cut, wound, Collinsworth's self-confidence
b. cold indifference, society's shocking blind spot
c. blood, in the dark, hurt
d. alone, old or infirm, common

Evaluating Arguments

18. According to the evidence given in the article, the author's statement that "The wound to Collinsworth's self-confidence may not [heal]" is most strongly supported by
    a. the author's background in psychology.
    b. statistics on the handicapped who have been assaulted.
    c. Collinsworth's remarks on the incident.
    d. Collinsworth's attitude toward her blindness in general.

19. Which of the following best supports the comment that society has a "shocking blind spot when it comes to the handicapped" (paragraph 5)?
    a. Collinsworth's annuity from the construction company does not begin to compensate for her blindness.
    b. Numerous people were indifferent to Collinsworth on the bus and as she bled on her way home.
    c. Collinsworth was assaulted outside the Braille institute.
    d. A mugger once snatched a bag of groceries out of her arms.

20. Judging by the article, the facts in it were obtained by the author
    a. from bystanders.
    b. from friends of Collinsworth.
    c. from Collinsworth herself.
    d. from Collinsworth's family

THINKING ACTIVITIES

Outlining

Following is a general outline of the article. Complete the outline by filling in the letters of the missing supporting details, provided in random order below the outline.

A. People's indifference to Millicent Collinsworth's injury on a bus ride weakened her confidence in her ability to get around independently.
   1. A claustrophic man hit her face in his panic, and in the scuffle that followed, she was knocked down; no one came to her aid.
   2. _____
   3. When she finally got home, neighbors called paramedics, who took her to the hospital, where she received stitches for a split lip.

B. _____

1. The year before, a man mugged her and got away with her purse.

2. _____

C. Ever since Collinsworth was blinded while trying to help a workman falling from a ladder, she has worked to regain her independence.

1. She receives payments from an insurance company as a result of the accident.

2. _____

3. As a result of the bus incident, she must again fight for her self-confidence, which she is determined to do.

Items Missing from the Outline

a. Collinsworth had been attacked before.
b. Bleeding, she got off the bus and let her dog lead her home; on the way, no one asked if she needed assistance.
c. Later, a mugger stole a bag of groceries she was carrying.
d. With the help of others and a Seeing Eye dog, she became more independent, joined an acting workshop, and met her boyfriend.

Summarizing

Complete the following summary of the article by filling in the missing words.

A blind woman, Millicent Collinsworth, was hurt on a bus when another passenger went berserk on a Los Angeles bus. Although she was _____ noticeably and knocked down, no one on the bus or on the busy street where she walked to get home offered to help her. Collinsworth had also been _____ twice before that incident as a result, she believes, of her vulnerability. Earlier, she had been blinded in an _____ when she tried to help a workman teetering on a ladder, and had worked hard to adjust to being blind. Payments from an insurance company and help from others enabled her to become more independent. She joined a workshop for handicapped _____, where she met her boyfriend. She also got a Seeing Eye dog, who made it possible for her to get around on her own. Now she is determined to regain the self-confidence she had in her ability to be _____.

DISCUSSION QUESTIONS

1. How can you explain the fact that so many people could be indifferent to a blind woman's injuries?

2. This article emphasizes the fact that Collinsworth feels more vulnerable because people have been indifferent to her at a time of need. But it also points out that many have responded to her needs. When did people come to her aid, and why do you think they did that?

3. The author emphasizes Collinsworth's desire for independence. Why do you think independence is so important to her?

4. Do you know any handicapped people? What special challenges do they face? Have people taken advantage of their vulnerability, been indifferent to their needs, or provided some genuine help?

Check Your Performance   A BLIND WOMAN'S GRIM INSIGHT

Skill	Number Right	Points	Total
Vocabulary in Context (2 items)	_____	× 4 :	_____
Central Point and Main Ideas (3)	_____	× 4 :	_____
Key Details (2)	_____	× 4 :	_____
Transitions (2)	_____	× 4 :	_____
Patterns of Organization (1)	_____	× 4 :	_____
Fact and Opinion (2)	_____	× 4 :	_____
Inferences (2)	_____	× 4 :	_____
Purpose and Tone (2)	_____	× 4 :	_____
Bias and Propaganda (1)	_____	× 4 :	_____
Evaluating Arguments (3)	_____	× 4 :	_____

(total of 20 questions)

Outlining (4)	_____	× 2.5 :	_____
Summarizing (5)	_____	× 2 :	_____

FINAL SCORE (OF POSSIBLE 100)   _____

Enter your final score into the reading performance chart on page 454.

4

Bubba Smith's Decision
Scott Ostler

Preview

Football great Bubba Smith, a former defensive end for two professional teams, became a star for the second time after he began appearing in Miller Lite beer commercials. Eventually, students of all ages were yelling Miller Lite slogans whenever they saw him. Smith then grew uncomfortable about his job as Miller's spokesman. The commercials were important to him, both financially and emotionally, so he faced a very difficult decision. Should he continue to promote a product he thought was doing some people harm?

Words to Watch

stupendously (3): extremely, greatly
verbatim (10): word for word

Bubba Smith has sworn off booze. Not drinking it, but selling it. 1

Bubba never did drink, but he sold a ton of beer by making cute television 2
ads. Not anymore. Bubba has kicked the habit.

As far as I know, Bubba Smith is the first athlete ever, maybe the first *person* 3
ever, to give up a very lucrative, <u>stupendously</u> easy and really amusing job making
beer commercials, just because he decided it was wrong.

Here's how it happened: 4

"I went back to Michigan State for the homecoming parade last year," Bubba 5
said. "I was the grand marshal and I was riding in the back seat of this car. The
people were yelling, but they weren't saying, 'Go, State, go!' One side of the street
was yelling 'Tastes great!' and the other side was yelling 'Less filling!'

"Then we go to the stadium. The older folks are yelling 'Kill, Bubba, kill!' But 6
the students are yelling 'Tastes great! Less filling!' Everyone in the stands is drunk.

296

It was like I was contributing to alcohol, and I don't drink. It made me realize I was doing something I didn't want to do.

"I was with my brother, Tody, who is my agent. I told him, 'Tody, I'll never 7 do another Lite beer commercial.' He almost [bleeped] on himself."

At the time, the Smith brothers had been dickering with the brewery over a 8 new contract for Bubba.

"[The beer people] thought it was because of the money," Bubba said. "But it 9 didn't have anything to do with the money. That was hard to give up, especially me, being a black athlete, it's hard to get stuff [commercial endorsements].

"I loved doing the commercials, but I didn't like the effect it was having on a 10 lot of little people. I'm talking about people in school. Kids would come up to me on the street and recite lines from my commercials, <u>verbatim</u>. They knew the lines better than I did. It was scary. Kids start to listen to things you say, you want to tell 'em something that is the truth.

"I loved doing the commercials, it's like me telling everyone in school, hey, 11 it's cool to have a Lite beer. I'd go to places like Daytona Beach and Fort Lauderdale on spring breaks [as a spokesman for the brewery], and it was scary to see how drunk those kids were. It was fun talking to the fans, until you see people lying on the beach because they can't make it back to their room, or tearing up a city."

The irony of Bubba making all those beer commercials was that he doesn't 12 drink. Never did. OK, he did drink twice in his life. He remembers those two times vividly, in a hazy sort of way.

His first night as a freshman at Michigan State, Bubba went to a party. He 13 mixed himself a drink. Then the drink mixed him.

"I poured in some vodka, gin, beer, a little bourbon, all in a big glass," Smith 14 says. "I didn't like the taste, so I drank it all in one gulp. It was a real trip. I started to get dizzy. Some guy was dancing with the girl I brought to the party. I weighed about 325 at the time, and I grabbed him, took him out on the porch and threw him off the porch. Then the ground came up and hit me in the face. I went back to my room, laid down, and fell out of the top bunk. I said, 'Never again.'

"I did drink one other time. It was the night before we were shooting a com- 15 mercial. The ad agency wanted me to hang out with Billy Martin, so he wouldn't get into trouble. We were sitting at the hotel bar and he was drinking vodka martinis. I asked him how they were, and he ordered me a double. We sat there about two hours and I had about 10 of 'em.

"I felt OK, then I got up and looked at the lobby, and it was turning. By the 16 time we got to the elevator we were almost on our knees."

The obvious question is, why would a nondrinker like Bubba spend eight years 17 making beer ads?

The beer people came to him just after he retired from football. He had been 18 a big star—6-8 and 285 pounds—a fast and ferocious defensive end for the Baltimore Colts and then the Raiders. His career was cut about half a decade short by a freak knee injury.

For nearly a year Bubba was a hermit, holed up in his apartment, ordering 19 pizzas, edging up over the 300-pound mark again, feeling lonely and unloved. He had made a lot of money in football, but he had spent a lot. He needed a job. This one looked fine.

"Making those commercials, that was a joy to me," Bubba said. "I told myself 20
I couldn't be doing anything wrong. It seemed so innocent. You don't see things
sometimes until you step back from it. Making those commercials, we were a *team*.
It was like football, without the pain. That was an important part of my life, especially the [annual] reunion commercials. It would be five days of sheer laughter—at
the shoot, after the shoot, every night.

"Also, it was also a prideful thing with me. I wanted to make sure we went 21
after Budweiser. So I'm out there hustling like a dog, and we became the third-
largest selling brand. Dick [Butkus, Smith's partner in many of the commercials]
and I knew the formula. We could go in and run off a commercial in three hours."

When Bubba quit, the brewery went out and hired L. C. Greenwood, another 22
huge, intimidating, black former football player who wears eyeglasses and a mus-
tache. Bubba ripped the tops off beer cans. L. C. rips trees out of the ground.

"[The ad people] don't miss a beat," Bubba said. 23

Smith lives in L. A., gets a lot of movie and TV acting roles. He lifts weights 24
now, which he never did as a football player, and he weighs about 245 pounds, well
below his playing weight.

He has learned how to keep himself in shape. He has learned something 25
else, too.

"As the years wear on, you stop compromising your principles," Bubba said. 26

SKILL-DEVELOPMENT QUESTIONS

Vocabulary in Context

1. The word *lucrative* in "a very lucrative, stupendously easy, and really
   amusing job making beer commercials" (paragraph 3) means
   a. difficult.
   b. poorly paid.
   c. nasty.
   d. profitable.

2. The word *dickering* in "the Smith brothers had been dickering with the
   brewery over a contract" (paragraph 8) means
   a. crying.
   b. bargaining.
   c. lying.
   d. penalizing.

3. The word *intimidating* in "the brewery hired . . . another huge, intimidating, black former football player" (paragraph 22) means
   a. personable.
   b. threatening.
   c. gentle.
   d. fancy.

Central Point and Main Ideas

4. Which sentence best expresses the central point of the selection?
   a. Bubba Smith decided that having principles is more important than making money.
   b. Bubba Smith doesn't approve of drinking.
   c. Bubba Smith helped to sell a lot of beer.
   d. Bubba Smith wants kids to stop drinking.

5. Which sentence best expresses the main idea of paragraph 6?
   a. The homecoming drunkenness made Bubba see he wanted no more part in encouraging people to drink.
   b. Older people remember Bubba as a football player.
   c. The kids knew all the words in the beer commercial.
   d. Everyone in the stadium was drunk.

Key Details

6. Bubba started doing beer commercials
   a. while playing in Baltimore.
   b. at Michigan State.
   c. because he needed the work.
   d. because it seemed like fun.

_____ 7. TRUE OR FALSE? Bubba became depressed after his retirement from football.

8. Which of the reasons below did NOT influence Smith's decision to stop appearing in beer advertisements?
   a. Young people on the street knew the lines of the commercials better than Smith did.
   b. The beer companies seemed to be too competitive and wanted to make too much money.
   c. Smith does not drink himself and does not like influencing others to drink.
   d. Drunkenness at a football game at Michigan State University made Smith think he was encouraging drinking.

Transitions

9. The relationship between the first half and the second half of the sentence on page 300 is one of
   a. time.
   b. contrast.
   c. addition.
   d. cause and effect.

Bubba never did drink, but he sold a ton of beer by making cute television ads. (Paragraph 2)

10. The signal word "also" in the sentence below shows
    a. addition.
    b. contrast.
    c. emphasis.
    d. cause and effect.

    Also, it was a prideful thing with me. (Paragraph 21)

Patterns of Organization

11. Paragraph 14 is organized according to which of the following patterns?
    a. list of items
    b. time order
    c. comparison
    d. definition and example

Fact and Opinion

12. Paragraph 10 includes
    a. only facts.
    b. only opinions.
    c. both facts and opinions.

Inferences

13. The author implies that
    a. Smith's injury did not force him to retire.
    b. Smith is happier now that he is no longer doing the commercials.
    c. Smith never took a drink.
    d. the brewery understood why Bubba stopped doing the commercials.

_____ 14. TRUE OR FALSE? From the article we can conclude that Smith handled his "retirement" from beer commercials better than he handled his retirement from football.

Purpose and Tone

15. The primary purpose of this article is to
    a. persuade everyone to stop drinking.
    b. entertain readers with stories about the times Smith got drunk.
    c. inform readers about the reason for Smith's decision to stop doing beer commercials.

16. The author's tone when referring to Bubba Smith is one of
    a. anger.
    b. sentimentality.
    c. confusion.
    d. admiration.

Bias and Propaganda

17. Bubba Smith reveals, in paragraphs 9–11, a bias
    a. against doing commercials.
    b. against drinking.
    c. in favor of beer commercials.
    d. in favor of Lite beer.

18. Which propaganda device can be found in the words of the Miller Lite commercial "Less filling!"?
    a. plain folks
    b. bandwagon
    c. glittering generalities
    d. testimonial

Evaluating Arguments

19. Which of the following statements is a valid conclusion that can be drawn from the excerpt below?
    a. The brewery was glad that Bubba Smith left so that Greenwood could be hired.
    b. Unlike Bubba Smith, L.C. Greenwood is willing to compromise his principles.
    c. L.C. Greenwood makes more effective ads than Bubba Smith did.
    d. The brewery's advertising policy was unaffected by Bubba Smith's principles.

    When Bubba quit, the brewery went out and hired L.C. Greenwood, another huge, intimidating, black former football player who wears eyeglasses and a mustache. Bubba ripped the tops off beer cans. L.C. rips trees out of the ground. (Paragraph 22)

20. What conclusion can be drawn from the fact that Smith enjoyed making beer commercials and the money he earned from them?
    a. Standing up for what he believed was not easy for him.
    b. There was no reason for Smith to stop making the commercials.
    c. Anyone can make an effective beer commercial.
    d. Working in advertising is very similar to playing football.

THINKING ACTIVITIES

Outlining

Following is an incomplete outline of the article. Complete it by filling in the letters of the missing main and secondary supporting details. The details appear in random order in the list below.

Central Point: As former professional football player Bubba Smith learned, doing what one believes in is more important than making money.

A. Smith began to realize the effects his commercials were having on young people.
   1. College students chanted beer slogans at him wherever he went.
   2. He saw that many college students were getting drunk on beer.

   3. _____

B. Smith's personal experiences with alcohol were negative.

   1. _____
   2. He was drunk again the night before shooting one of the commercials and could hardly get back to his hotel room.

C. _____
   1. When the brewery offered him the job, he needed the money.

   2. _____
   3. He took pride in how much beer his commercials were selling.
D. Smith feels better about himself after he quit making the commercials.
   1. He has now found work as a movie and TV actor.

   2. _____

Items Missing from the Outline

a. The commercials meant a great deal to Smith.
b. He was drunk once as a freshman and got into a fight.
c. He has learned to stop compromising his principles.
d. He enjoyed making the commercials because of the teamwork involved.
e. Therefore, he told his agent he would no longer make beer commercials.

Summarizing

Add the words needed to complete the following summary of the article.

Bubba Smith no longer makes lite beer commercials. He became alarmed about the _____ his commercials were having on young people when he heard college students chanting beer _____ and saw them getting drunk. He told his agent that he would never make another beer commercial. Smith felt that by making the commercials, he was _____ college students to drink, even though he did not drink himself. He had begun making the commercials for the _____ but soon found that he also enjoyed making them, so quitting was doubly difficult for him. The brewery quickly replaced him with another football player, but Smith did not let quitting the ad get him down. He learned to stay in shape and found acting work. And he has learned it's best to stop _____ his principles.

DISCUSSION QUESTIONS

1. What do you think of Smith by the end of the article? Do you admire him, or do you think he was a fool? Would you have made the same decision? Why or why not?

2. Smith states that making the Miller Lite commercials " was a joy to me" and " was also a prideful thing." What do these remarks reveal about Smith's personality and about his attitude to his work?

3. How is appearing in a television commercial like playing professional football? Where in the selection does Smith reveal, through his feelings about the beer ads, that he recognizes this similarity?

4. Which is more important to you—making money or doing what you believe in? Which do you think is more important to most people?

Check Your Performance   BUBBA SMITH'S DECISION

Skill	Number Right	Points	Total
Vocabulary in Context (3 items)	_____	× 4 :	_____
Central Point and Main Ideas (2)	_____	× 4 :	_____
Key Details (3)	_____	× 4 :	_____
Transitions (2)	_____	× 4 :	_____
Patterns of Organization (1)	_____	× 4 :	_____
Fact and Opinion (1)	_____	× 4 :	_____
Inferences (2)	_____	× 4 :	_____
Purpose and Tone (2)	_____	× 4 :	_____
Bias and Propaganda (2)	_____	× 4 :	_____
Evaluating Arguments (2)	_____	× 4 :	_____

(total of 20 questions)

Outlining (5)	_____	× 2 :	_____
Summarizing (5)	_____	× 2 :	_____

FINAL SCORE (OF POSSIBLE 100)   _____

Enter your final score into the reading performance chart on page 454.

5

Coping with Santa Claus
Delia Ephron

Preview

Children can't continue to believe in Santa Claus forever. Still, their parents often seem unwilling to tell them the truth about Santa. How do you think parents should respond when children say, "I know who really brings the presents"? In this article, Delia Ephron tells how she and her husband reacted when they were confronted with that situation.

Words to Watch

hedgy (2):   misleading
pretentious (2):   overly dignified
deceit (8):   dishonesty
squiggliest (8):   waviest
modicum (10):   small amount
diplomatically (18):   tactfully
reproachfully (32):   disapprovingly

Julie had turned 8 in October and as Christmas approached, Santa Claus was 1 more and more on her mind. During the week before Christmas, every night she announced to her father, "I know who really brings the presents. You do!" Then, waiting a moment, she added, "Right?"

Jerry didn't answer. Neither he nor I, her stepmother, was sure she really 2 wanted the truth. We suspected she did, but couldn't bring ourselves to admit it to her. And we both felt uncomfortable saying something <u>hedgy</u>. Something <u>pretentious</u>. Something like, "But Santa does exist dear, he exists in spirit—in the spirit of giving in all of us." That sounded like some other parents in some other house with some other child.

I actually resented Julie for putting us on the spot. Wasn't the truth about Santa something one learned from a classmate? The same classmate who knows a screwed-up version of the facts of life. Or else from a know-it-all older sister—as I did. Mine sneaked into my room on Christmas Eve, woke me and said, "Go into the hall and look. You'll see who really puts out the presents." 3

There was another problem. Jerry and I were reluctant to give up Santa Claus ourselves. We got to tell Julie and her younger brother, Adam, to put out the cookies in case Santa was hungry. We made a fuss about the fire being out in the fireplace so he wouldn't get burned. We issued a few threats about his list of good children and bad. It was all part of the tension and thrill of Christmas Eve—the night the fantasy comes true. And that fantasy of a fat jolly man who flies through the sky in a sleigh drawn by reindeer and arrives via chimney with presents—that single belief says everything about the innocence of children. How unbearable to lose it. For them and for us. So Jerry and I said nothing. And the next night Julie announced it again. 4

Christmas Eve Julie appeared with a sheet of yellow, lined paper. At the top she had written, "If you are real, sign here." It was, she said, a letter to Santa. She insisted that on this letter each of us—her father, Adam and I—write the words "Santa Claus," so if Santa were to sign it, she could compare our handwriting with his. Then she would know she had not been tricked. 5

Jerry signed. I signed. Adam, who was 5 and couldn't write, gave up after the letter "S." Julie folded the paper into quarters, wrote "Santa Claus" on the outside and stuck it on a ledge inside the chimney along with two Christmas cookies. 6

After much fuss, Julie and Adam were tucked into bed. Jerry and I put out the presents. We were not sure what to do about the letter. 7

After a short discussion, and mostly because we couldn't resist, we opted for deceit. Jerry took the note and, in the squiggliest printing imaginable, wrote "Merry Christmas, Santa Claus." He put the note back in the fireplace and ate the cookies. 8

The next morning, very early, about 6, we heard Julie and Adam tear down the hall. Jerry and I, in bed, listened for the first ecstatic reactions to the presents. Suddenly, we heard a shriek. "He's real! He's real! He's really real!!!!" The door to our room flew open. "He's REAL!!!" she shouted. Julie showed us the paper with the squiggly writing. 9

Somehow, this was not what we had bargained for. I had expected some mod-icum of disbelief—at least a "Dad, is this for real?" 10

Julie clasped the note to her chest. Then she dashed back to the presents. 11

That afternoon, our friend Deena came over to exchange gifts. "Santa Claus is real," said Julie. 12

"Oh," said Deena. 13

"I know for sure, for really, really sure. Look!" And Julie produced the proof. 14

Just then the phone rang. Knowing it was a relative calling with Christmas greetings, Julie rushed to answer it. "Santa Claus is real," I heard her say to my sister Nora, the same sister who had broken the bad news about Santa Claus to me 30 years ago. Julie handed me the phone. 15

"What is this about?" asked Nora.   16

I told her the story, trying to make it as funny as possible, hoping she wouldn't   17
notice how badly Jerry and I had handled what I was beginning to think of as "the
Santa issue." It didn't work.

"We may have made a mistake here," said Nora, <u>diplomatically</u> including her-   18
self in the mess.

"You're telling me!" I said. "Do you think there's any chance Julie will forget   19
all this?" That was what I really wanted, of course—for the whole thing to go away.

"I doubt it," said Nora.   20

We had a wonderful day—good food, good presents, lots of visitors. Then it   21
was bedtime.

"Dad?" said Julie, as he tucked her in.   22

"What?"   23

"If Santa's real, then Rudolph must be real, too."   24

"What!"   25

"If Santa's real—"   26

"I heard," said Jerry. He sat down on her bed and took a deep breath. "You   27
know, Julie," and then he stopped. I could see he was trying to think of a way, any
way, to explain our behavior so it wouldn't sound quite as deceptive, wrong and
stupid as it was. But he was stumped.

"Yeah," said Julie.   28

"I wrote the note," said Jerry.   29

She burst into tears.   30

Jerry apologized. He apologized over and over while Julie sobbed into her   31
pillow. He said he was wrong, that he shouldn't have tricked her, that he should
have answered her questions about Santa Claus the week before.

Julie sat up in bed. "I thought he was real," she said <u>reproachfully</u>. Then sud-   32
denly she leaned over the bed, pulled out a comic from underneath and sat up again.
"Can I read for five minutes?" she said.

"Sure," said Jerry.   33

And that was it. One minute of grief at Santa's death, and life went on.   34

Jerry and I left Julie's room terribly relieved. I immediately got a craving for   35
leftover turkey and headed for the kitchen. I was putting the bird back in the refrigerator when I heard Adam crying. I went down the hall. The door to his room was
open and I heard Julie, very disgusted, say: "Oh, Adam, you don't have to cry! Only
babies believe in Santa Claus."

SKILL-DEVELOPMENT QUESTIONS

Vocabulary in Context

1. The words *opted for* in "because we couldn't resist, we opted for deceit"
    (paragraph 8) means
    a. questioned.
    b. decided in favor of.
    c. decided against.
    d. admired.

2. The word *ecstatic* in "Jerry and I . . . listened for the first ecstatic re-
    actions to the presents" (paragraph 9) means
    a. quiet.
    b. joyful.
    c. frightened.
    d. disappointed.

Central Point and Main Ideas

3. Which sentence best expresses the central point of this selection?
    a. Children will eventually learn that Santa Claus does not exist.
    b. When children seriously ask who brings the Christmas presents,
        it's time to tell them the truth.
    c. Jerry made a mistake in eventually telling Julie the truth.
    d. Parents should always tell their children the truth.

4. Which sentence best expresses the main idea of paragraph 3?
    a. Delia did not want to be the one to tell Julie that Santa Claus did
        not exist.
    b. Children learn about Santa Claus and sex from their classmates.
    c. Delia resented her older sister for telling her the truth about Santa
        Claus.
    d. Most kids learn the truth about Santa Claus in school.

Key Details

_____ 5. TRUE OR FALSE? Delia and Jerry did not tell Julie the truth partly
    because they themselves liked the fantasy of Santa Claus.

6. Delia and Jerry
    a. felt Julie reacted in an immature way.
    b. never told Julie that the signature was a fake.
    c. realized that they had handled the problem poorly.
    d. thought it was best that Adam also know the truth.

Transitions

7. The two parts of the sentence below show a relationship of
    a. cause and effect.
    b. time.
    c. comparison.
    d. contrast.

    . . . mostly because we couldn't resist, we opted for deceit. (Para-
    graph 8)

8. The sentence below begins with a
   a. cause-effect signal.
   b. contrast signal.
   c. comparison signal.
   d. location signal.

   At the top she had written, "If you are real, sign here." (Paragraph 5)

Patterns of Organization

9. The sentence "So Jerry and I said nothing" reveals that the main pattern of organization of paragraph 4 is
   a. time order.
   b. cause and effect.
   c. comparison/contrast.
   d. definition and example.

10. The main pattern of organization of paragraphs 5 through 35 is
    a. time order.
    b. list of items.
    c. cause and effect.
    d. comparison/contrast.

Fact and Opinion

_____ 11. TRUE OR FALSE? The sentence below is a
   a. fact.
   b. opinion.
   c. fact and opinion.

   The door to his room was open and I heard Julie, very disgusted, say: "Oh, Adam, you don't have to cry!"

12. Which of the following is a statement of opinion?
    a. "We made a fuss about the fire being out in the fireplace so he wouldn't get burned."
    b. "We issued a few threats about his list of good children and bad."
    c. "And that fantasy of a fat jolly man who flies through the sky in a sleigh drawn by reindeer and arrives via chimney with presents— that single belief says everything about the innocence of children."
    d. "Christmas Eve Julie appeared with a sheet of yellow, lined paper."

Inferences

13. The author implies that she
    a. dislikes being a stepmother.
    b. was influenced by her own childhood experiences with Santa Claus.
    c. disapproved of Jerry faking Santa Claus's signature.
    d. was not surprised by anything the children did.

14. The author implies that Jerry
    a. finally knew he had to tell Julie the truth.
    b. is not a caring father.
    c. never realized they had misjudged how to deal with Julie.
    d. felt Julie had reacted badly to the truth about Santa Claus.

Purpose and Tone

15. The author's primary purpose in this narration is to
    a. inform readers about how difficult it can be for parents to know the right thing to do.
    b. entertain readers with warm memories of her family's experiences with Santa Claus.
    c. persuade, through her own family's experiences, that it's better to tell children the truth about Santa when they seriously ask.

16. The best description of the tone of paragraph 3 is
    a. joyful.
    b. frustrated.
    c. mysterious.
    d. optimistic.

17. The author writes about her and her husband's mistakes in a tone of
    a. great shame.
    b. honesty.
    c. bitterness.
    d. pride.

Bias and Propaganda

18. Which of the following phrases based on the selection (paragraph 3) uses unbiased language?
    a. know-it-all older sister
    b. bossy older sister
    c. well-meaning older sister
    d. older sister

Evaluating Arguments

19. Which of the following best supports the statement that "as Christmas approached, Santa Claus was more and more on [Julie's] mind"?
    a. "During the week before Christmas, every night she announced to her father, 'I know who really brings the presents. You do!'"
    b. "Christmas Eve Julie appeared with a sheet of yellow, lined paper."
    c. "Neither he nor I, her stepmother, was sure she really wanted the truth."
    d. "I actually resented Julie for putting us on the spot."

20. The author supports her view that she and Jerry handled "the Santa issue" badly with
    a. quotations from child psychologists.
    b. personal observations.
    c. a study of how many families handled the issue.
    d. statistics.

THINKING ACTIVITIES

Outlining

Note: As you have seen, the central point of a selection may be wholly or partially implied by the author. In the case of a narrative, this is much more likely to be so. The author mainly tells readers what happened, leaving them to come to conclusions about the central point, just as they would do if they had witnessed the events personally. That is the case with this selection. Ephron does tell readers that she and her husband did not handle the situation with Julie very well, but she only implies what they should have done to handle the situation better. That inference is included in the statement of the central point in the outline below.

Following is an incomplete outline of the selection. Complete the outline by filling in the letters of the episodes mixed below.

Central Point: Julie should have been told the truth about Santa Claus when she showed she was ready for it.

1. _____

2. _____

3. _____

4. _____

5. _____

Items Missing from the Outline

    a.   Julie's response to being "told" there is a Santa Claus

    b.   Julie's question about who brings the presents and her parents' reactions

    c.   Jerry's confession and Julie's reaction to the truth

    d.   Julie's scheme to verify Santa and her parents' reaction

    e.   Telephone conversation revealing Delia's understanding of her and Jerry's misjudgement

Summarizing

1.   Circle the letter of the statement that best summarizes the first set of supporting details for the central point of "Coping With Santa Claus" (paragraphs 1–4).

    a.   Julie believed in Santa Claus, but she wanted to make sure.

    b.   Delia wished Julie had asked someone else about Santa Claus.

    c.   Julie asked her parents about Santa Claus, but they did not tell her the truth because they did not want her or them to give Santa up.

2.   Circle the letter of the statement that best summarizes the second set of supporting details for the central point (paragraphs 5–8).

    a.   Julie thought up a test to see if Santa Claus was real, but her parents decided to deceive her so she would still believe in Santa.

    b.   Jerry wrote Julie a note and signed it "Santa Claus."

    c.   Julie wrote a note asking Santa Claus to sign his name and then had her family sign it too so she could see if there really was a Santa.

3.   Circle the letter of the statement that best summarizes the third set of supporting details for the central point (paragraphs 9–15).

    a.   Julie's response to the results of her test was an unquestioning belief in and great joy over the existence of Santa Claus.

    b.   Delia expected Julie to respond differently to the results of her test to see if there was a Santa Claus.

    c.   Julie told her aunt that Santa Claus is real.

4. Circle the letter of the statement that best summarizes the fourth set of supporting details for the central point (paragraphs 16–20).
    a. Delia spoke on the phone to her sister, who, as a child, had told her the truth about Santa Claus.
    b. Delia told her sister the story about Julie's search for the truth about Santa Claus.
    c. In a conversation with her sister, Delia revealed she understood that she and Jerry had mishandled Julie's search for the truth about Santa Claus.

5. Circle the letter of the statement that best summarizes the final set of supporting details for the central point (paragraphs 21–35).
    a. Jerry finally told his daughter he had written the Santa Claus note.
    b. Julie was very upset when she finally learned the truth about Santa Claus from her father.
    c. Julie was only briefly upset after learning the truth about the note and about Santa Claus from her father.

DISCUSSION QUESTIONS

1. Why didn't Ephron end her story at paragraph 34? In other words, what did she add to the story by including paragraph 35? How does paragraph 35 relate to what Ephron tells us early in the selection?

2. Ephron never directly tells her readers why she came to the conclusion that her and her husband's behavior was "wrong and stupid." She expects readers to understand the mistakes through the details of her narrative. Which details could persuade readers that she and her husband had made mistakes?

3. How does Ephron keep her story from being a heavy treatment of the question of how and when to tell children about Santa Claus?

4. What experiences have you had as a child that involved asking your parents for the truth about something? Were you always ready to hear the truth when you asked?

Check Your Performance   COPING WITH SANTA CLAUS

Skill	Number Right	Points	Total
Vocabulary in Context (2 items)	_____	× 4 :	_____
Central Point and Main Ideas (2)	_____	× 4 :	_____
Key Details (2)	_____	× 4 :	_____
Transitions (2)	_____	× 4 :	_____
Patterns of Organization (2)	_____	× 4 :	_____
Fact and Opinion (2)	_____	× 4 :	_____
Inferences (2)	_____	× 4 :	_____
Purpose and Tone (3)	_____	× 4 :	_____
Bias and Propaganda (1)	_____	× 4 :	_____
Evaluating Arguments (2)	_____	× 4 :	_____

(total of 20 questions)

Outlining (5)	_____	× 2 :	_____
Summarizing (5)	_____	× 2 :	_____

FINAL SCORE (OF POSSIBLE 100)   _____

Enter your final score into the reading performance chart on page 454.

6

If I'm So Smart, How Come I Flunk All the Time?

Charles W. Slack

Preview

Have you ever had the feeling that no matter how hard you studied, your teacher was not going to raise your grades? If so, you may feel this selection was written just for you. It confirms such feelings by pointing out that teachers can be biased when they grade. But that doesn't mean you're helpless. According to this article, there are ways to sell teachers on the idea that you're a successful student, and you can even learn more in the process.

Words to Watch

varying (1):   differing
standardized tests (3):   tests designed to measure performance accurately
sour grapes (5):   saying something is worthless just because it is hard to get (from an Aesop fable in which a fox cannot reach some tempting grapes and thus decides they must be too sour to eat anyway)
bluff (9):   pretend

Can twenty flunking students of <u>varying</u> intelligence raise their math and English a full year's level in only thirty working days?   1

Dr. Lloyd Homme, chief of a special educational "fix-it" laboratory in Albuquerque, New Mexico, said yes and put teams of behavioral scientists together with the flunking students to work on the problem. Any available technology could be   2 used—teaching machines, programmed instruction, computer-assisted methods—to cram a year's knowledge into the boys.

Were the experiments a success? The scientists said yes but the students said 3 no. When grades were measured using <u>standardized</u> tests under strict laboratory conditions, marks went up more than one year on the average. Meanwhile, back at the school, the students were still barely passing, at best. "The experiment was fine for the scientists. They proved their theory on paper and made a name for themselves, but most of us were still flunking in class," remarked one seventeen-year-old.

The only clue to the mystery was this common remark: "The teachers ignore 4 us—they've got it in for us."

At first the scientists on the team thought the complaint was just <u>sour grapes</u> 5 and told the boys to work harder. When grades still failed to rise, the scientists felt there might be some truth in what the young team members were saying. Not that teachers were to blame, necessarily, but there still might be some negative bias. "You should see what goes on in class!" said the boys.

"The only thing to do was to take them up on it, go into the classroom with 6 them and see what was holding back their grades," said Dr. Homme.

Hence, bearded behavioral scientists ended up in the back row of math and 7 English classes and made observations about the behavior of students and teachers. Homme was surprised to discover that two simple actions made the difference.

"With few exceptions, our students acted like dummies," said Dr. Homme, 8 "even though we knew they were ahead of the rest in knowledge. They were so used to playing the class idiot that they didn't know how to show what they knew. Their eyes wandered, they appeared absent-minded or even belligerent. One or two read magazines hidden under their desks, thinking, most likely, that they already knew the classwork. They rarely volunteered and often had to have questions repeated because they weren't listening. Teachers, on the other hand, did not trust our laboratory results. Nobody was going to tell them that 'miracles' could work on Sammy and Jose."

In the eyes of teachers, students seemed to fall into three groups. We'll call 9 them: *bright-eyes, scaredy-cats* and *dummies.*

Bright-eyes had perfected the trick of:
1. "eyeballing" the instructor at all times, even from the minute he entered the room.
2. never ducking their eyes away when the instructor glanced at *them.*
3. getting the instructor to call on them when they wanted *without* raising their hands.
4. even making the instructor go out of his way to call on someone else to "give others a chance" (especially useful when bright-eyes themselves are uncertain of the answer).
5. readily admitting ignorance so as not to <u>bluff</u>—but in such a way that it sounds as though ignorance is rare.
6. asking many questions.

Scaredy-cats [the middle group]:
1. looked toward the instructor but were afraid to let him "catch their eyes."
2. asked few questions and gave the impression of being "underachievers."

3.   appeared uninvolved and had to be "drawn out," so they were likely to be criticized for "inadequate participation."

Dummies (no matter how much they really knew):

1.   never looked at the instructor.
2.   never asked questions.
3.   were stubborn about volunteering information in class.

To make matters worse, the tests in school were not standardized and not   10
given nearly as frequently as those given in the laboratory. School test-scores were open to teacher bias. Classroom behavior of students counted a lot toward their class grades. There was no doubt that teachers were biased against the dummies. The scientists concluded that no matter how much knowledge a dummy gained on his own, his grades in school were unlikely to improve unless he could somehow change his image into a bright-eyes. This would mean . . .

1.   Look the teacher in the eye.
2.   Ask questions and volunteer answers (even if uncertain).

"Teachers get teacher-training in how to play their roles. Why shouldn't stu-   11
dents get student-training in how to play bright-eyes?" asked Homme. Special train-ing sessions were held at the laboratory. Dummies were drilled in eyeballing and hand-raising, which, simple as they sound, weren't easy to do. "I felt so square I could hardly stand it," complained one of the dummies. "That was at first. Later, when I saw others eyeballing and hand-raising and really learning more, I even moved my seat to the front. It flipped the teacher out of her skull. She couldn't get over it."

Those who found eyeballing especially difficult were taught to look at the   12
instructor's mouth or the bridge of his nose. "Less threatening to the student," explained Homme. "It seems less aggressive to them."

Unfortunately, not all of the dummies were able to pick up new habits during   13
the limited training period. Some learned in the laboratory but couldn't do it in the classroom. These became scaredy-cats—at least a step up. But for the majority, grades improved steadily once they got the hang of their new techniques. The stu-dents encouraged and helped each other to hand-raise and eyeball.

Teachers' comments reflected the improvement. "There is no doubt that stu-   14
dent involvement was increased by the program and as a result grades went up."

By way of advice to others wishing to improve their own eyeballing and hand-   15
raising, student Jose Martinez suggests: "Don't try to do it all at once. You'll shock the teacher and make it tough for yourself. Begin slowly. Work with a friend and help each other. Do it like a game. Like exercising with weights—it takes practice but it's worth it."

Homme agrees. "In fact, results are guaranteed for life," he says.   16

SKILL-DEVELOPMENT QUESTIONS

Vocabulary in Context

1. The word *belligerent* in "they didn't know how to show what they knew. . . . .they appeared absent-minded or even belligerent" (paragraph 8) means
   a. eager.
   b. hostile.
   c. alert.
   d. peaceful.

2. The word *inadequate* in "Scaredy-cats . . . appeared uninvolved and had to be 'drawn out,' so they were likely to be criticized for 'inadequate participation'" (paragraph 9) means
   a. not enough
   b. not easy
   c. rapid
   d. frequent

Central Point and Main Ideas

3. Which sentence best expresses the central point of this article?
   a. Several students raised their math and English levels in thirty days.
   b. Grades improve when students learn to combine study with "eyeballing" the teacher and class participation.
   c. Laboratory results are not always repeated in the classroom.
   d. Teachers ignore the weaker students.

4. Which sentence best expresses the main idea of paragraph 11?
   a. Training sessions were held at the laboratory.
   b. "Dummies" were trained to improve their classroom skills.
   c. It is not easy for "dummies" to learn eyeballing and hand-raising.
   d. Better students sit in the front of the classroom.

Key Details

5. After being trained in math and English, the flunking students did not know
   a. their math.
   b. their English.
   c. how to show what they knew.
   d. how to take a standardized test.

_____ 6. TRUE OR FALSE? The classroom teachers expected that the boys would get better grades after the thirty-day training.

Transitions

7. The signal words in the sentences below show
    a. time.
    b. contrast.
    c. illustration.
    d. addition.

    "That was at first. Later, when I saw others eyeballing and hand-raising and really learning more, I even moved my seat to the front . . ." (Paragraph 11)

8. The relationship between the second half of the sentence below and the first half is one of
    a. addition.
    b. contrast.
    c. time.
    d. illustration.

    Some learned in the laboratory but couldn't do it in the classroom.

Patterns of Organization

9. The pattern of organization of paragraph 3 is
    a. list of items.
    b. time order.
    c. contrast.
    d. definition and example.

10. Paragraph 9 is organized with both
    a. cause and effect and time order.
    b. contrast and time order.
    c. a list of items and time order.
    d. a list of items and definitions.

Fact and Opinion

11. Which of the following is a statement of opinion?
    a. "When grades were measured using standardized tests under strict laboratory conditions, marks went up more than one year on the average."
    b. "[Eyeballing and hand-raising are] 'like exercising with weights—it takes practice but it's worth it.' "
    c. "Special training sessions were held at the laboratory."
    d. "Teachers' comments reflected the improvement [in student involvement and grades]."

12. Paragraph 11 includes
    a. only facts about student-training.
    b. only opinions about student-training.
    c. both facts and opinions about student-training.

Inferences

13. The author implies that at first the scientists
    a. believed the boys' complaints.
    b. thought the boys were doing well enough in school.
    c. believed the boys' problem was that they weren't working hard enough.
    d. disliked the teachers.

_____ 14. TRUE OR FALSE? The author implies that standardized tests are more biased than the tests the teachers used.

Purpose and Tone

15. The author's main purpose is to
    a. inform readers how students can improve their grades.
    b. persuade readers that teachers do not treat students fairly.
    c. entertain readers with student stunts.

16. The author's tone when discussing the three groups of students is
    a. solemn and formal.
    b. informal.
    c. angry.
    d. regretful.

Bias and Propaganda

17. The author uses the word "dummies" to reflect
    a. his bias against those students.
    b. the teachers' bias against those students.
    c. the scientists' bias against those students.
    d. the fact that those students are not smart.

18. Homme's remark at the end of the article that "results are guaranteed for life" might be considered
    a. a bandwagon appeal.
    b. a glittering generality.
    c. a plain-folks appeal.
    d. name calling.

Evaluating Arguments

19.   Which of the following evidence from the article supports the conclusion that students benefit from looking teachers in the eye and raising their hands?
a.   Under strict laboratory conditions, students who had been trained by behavioral scientists raised their grades on standardized tests.
b.   Students who found it hard to look teachers in the eye were trained to focus on their noses or mouths instead.
c.   Training in a lab helped students learn the classroom techniques.
d.   Teachers reported that the students' increased involvement in class raised their grades.

20.   The statement that students must be trained to look teachers in the eye and speak up in class or they will fail their courses would be an example of which logical fallacy?
a.   Assumption that there are only two sides to a question (either-or fallacy)
b.   Assumption that order of events alone shows cause and effect (false cause)
c.   Assumption that things being compared are more alike than different (false comparison)
d.   Evidence sounds good but has nothing to do with the argument (changing the subject)

THINKING ACTIVITIES

Outlining

Following is an incomplete brief outline of the article. Complete it by filling in the letters of the items below the list.

Central Point: By increasing class participation, students can improve their grades.

1.   _____

2.   _____

3.   _____

4.   They found that students could be classified into three groups: those that were constantly involved, those that participated only rarely, and those that never looked at their teachers or spoke in class.

5.   _____

6.   _____

Items Missing from the Outline

a. Behavioral scientists worked with flunking students to increase their knowledge of math and English.
b. Most of them improved steadily and raised their grades.
c. Training helped the students learn to look their teachers in the eye and raise their hands.
d. The students increased their scores on standardized tests in the lab, but they were not doing any better at school.
e. The scientists visited the school to find out what was wrong.

Summarizing

Following is an incomplete summary of "If I'm So Smart, How Come I Flunk All the Time?" Circle the letter (**a**, **b**, or **c**) of the sentence below that <u>best</u> completes the summary.

Using a variety of techniques, a team of scientists worked with failing students to improve their math and English skills. Although the scientists believed they were successful, many of the students were still failing their courses, so the scientists visited classes to find out what was wrong. _____

_____.

A middle group acted uninvolved and scared, and the successful students were so involved in the class that they seemed more knowledgeable than they really were. Changing the approach of the less successful students was not easy, but most of them were able to improve their grades by trying the new techniques.

a. To their surprise, they found that some students who knew the information were acting like dummies, rarely volunteering answers or looking at their teachers.
b. In the classrooms they discovered that, despite their training, the teachers were treating some students unfairly.
c. They could not find out why one group of students consistently did poorly on all the tasks they were given.

DISCUSSION QUESTIONS

1. According to Slack, teachers see students as either bright-eyes, scaredy-cats, or dummies. Do you agree? Are there other categories you would add?

2. Have you noticed any difference between the attitudes of teachers in classes in which you participate less and in classes in which you participate more? Are there any differences in how much you learn in those classes?

3. An important aspect of this article is the difference between what students really know and what teachers think they know. How did this difference affect the way Slack named the three group of students?

4. By training the students in class-participation techniques, the scientists helped many of the students to change the teachers' bias against them. Do you think there is any way teachers can be trained to be less biased in the first place?

Check Your Performance   IF I'M SO SMART,
                                HOW COME I FLUNK
                                ALL THE TIME?

Skill	Number Right	Points	Total
Vocabulary in Context (2 items)	_____	× 4 :	_____
Central Point and Main Ideas (2)	_____	× 4 :	_____
Key Details (2)	_____	× 4 :	_____
Transitions (2)	_____	× 4 :	_____
Patterns of Organization (2)	_____	× 4 :	_____
Fact and Opinion (2)	_____	× 4 :	_____
Inferences (2)	_____	× 4 :	_____
Purpose and Tone (2)	_____	× 4 :	_____
Bias and Propaganda (2)	_____	× 4 :	_____
Evaluating Arguments (2)	_____	× 4 :	_____

(total of 20 questions)

Outlining (5)	_____	× 2 :	_____
Summarizing (1)	_____	× 10 :	_____

FINAL SCORE (OF POSSIBLE 100)   _____

Enter your final score into the reading performance chart on page 454.

7

Shame
Dick Gregory

Preview

Upon receiving help, most of us feel grateful. But what if the help is given in an inconsiderate way? In this autobiographical piece, comedian and social activist Dick Gregory shows that the good intentions of a giver are not enough if they don't take the recipient's pride into account.

Words to Watch

complected (1):   complexioned
stoop (2):   an outside stairway, porch, or platform at the entrance to a house
mackinaw (28):   a short, plaid coat or jacket
googobs (29):   Gregory's slang for *gobs*, a large amount

I never learned hate at home, or shame. I had to go to school for that. I was 1 about seven years old when I got my first big lesson. I was in love with a little girl named Helene Tucker, a light-complected little girl with pigtails and nice manners. She was always clean and she was smart in school. I think I went to school then mostly to look at her. I brushed my hair and even got me a little old handkerchief. It was a lady's handkerchief, but I didn't want Helene to see me wipe my nose on my hand. The pipes were frozen again, there was no water in the house, but I washed my socks and shirt every night. I'd get a pot, and go over to Mister Ben's grocery store, and stick my pot down into his soda machine. Scoop out some chopped ice. By evening the ice melted to water for washing. I got sick a lot that winter because the fire would go out at night before the clothes were dry. In the morning I'd put them on, wet or dry, because they were the only clothes I had.

Everybody's got a Helene Tucker, a symbol of everything you want. I loved 2 her for her goodness, her cleanness, her popularity. She'd walk down my street and my brothers and sisters would yell, "Here comes Helene," and I'd rub my tennis sneakers on the back of my pants and wish my hair wasn't so nappy and the white folks' shirt fit me better. I'd run out on the street. If I knew my place and didn't come too close, she'd wink at me and say hello. That was a good feeling. Sometimes I'd follow her all the way home, and shovel the snow off her walk and try to make friends with her Momma and her aunts. I'd drop money on her stoop late at night on my way back from shining shoes in the taverns. And she had a Daddy, and he had a good job. He was a paper hanger.

I guess I would have gotten over Helene by summertime, but something happened in that classroom that made her face hang in front of me for the next twenty-two years. When I played the drums in high school it was for Helene and when I broke track records in college it was for Helene and when I started standing behind microphones and heard applause I wished Helene could hear it, too. It wasn't until I was twenty-nine years old and married and making money that I finally got her out of my system. Helene was sitting in that classroom when I learned to be ashamed of myself. 3

It was on a Thursday. I was sitting in the back of the room, in a seat with a chalk circle drawn around it. The idiot's seat, the troublemaker's seat. 4

The teacher thought I was stupid. Couldn't spell, couldn't read, couldn't do arithmetic. Just stupid. Teachers were never interested in finding out that you couldn't concentrate because you were so hungry, because you hadn't had any breakfast. All you could think about was noontime, would it ever come? Maybe you could sneak into the cloakroom and steal a bite of some kid's lunch out of a coat pocket. A bite of something. Paste. You can't really make a meal of paste, or put it on bread for a sandwich, but sometimes I'd scoop a few spoonfuls out of the big paste jar in the back of the room. Pregnant people get strange tastes. I was pregnant with poverty. Pregnant with dirt and pregnant with smells that made people turn away, pregnant with cold and pregnant with shoes that were never bought for me, pregnant with five other people in my bed and no Daddy in the next room, and pregnant with hunger. Paste doesn't taste too bad when you're hungry. 5

The teacher thought I was a troublemaker. All she saw from the front of the room was a little black boy who squirmed in his idiot's seat and made noises and poked the kids around him. I guess she couldn't see a kid who made noises because he wanted someone to know he was there. 6

It was on a Thursday, the day before the Negro payday. The eagle always flew on Friday. The teacher was asking each student how much his father would give to the Community Chest. On Friday night, each kid would get the money from his father, and on Monday he would bring it to the school. I decided I was going to buy a Daddy right then. I had money in my pocket from shining shoes and selling papers, and whatever Helene Tucker pledged for her Daddy I was going to top it. And I'd hand the money right in. I wasn't going to wait until Monday to buy me a Daddy. 7

I was shaking, scared to death. The teacher opened her book and started calling out names alphabetically. 8

"Helene Tucker?" 9

"My Daddy said he'd give two dollars and fifty cents." 10

"That's very nice, Helene. Very, very nice indeed." 11

That made me feel pretty good. It wouldn't take too much to top that. I had almost three dollars in dimes and quarters in my pocket. I stuck my hand in my 12 pocket and held onto the money, waiting for her to call my name. But the teacher closed her book after she called everybody else in the class.

I stood up and raised my hand. 13

"What is it now?" 14

"You forgot me?" 15

She turned toward the blackboard. "I don't have time to be playing with you, Richard." 16

"My Daddy said he'd . . ." 17

"Sit down, Richard, you're disturbing the class." 18

"My Daddy said he'd give . . . fifteen dollars." 19

She turned around and looked mad. "We are collecting this money for you and your kind, Richard Gregory. If your Daddy can give fifteen dollars you have no business being on relief." 20

"I got it right now, I got it right now, my Daddy gave it to me to turn in today, my Daddy said . . ." 21

"And furthermore," she said, looking right at me, her nostrils getting big and her lips getting thin and her eyes opening wide, "we know you don't have a Daddy." 22

Helene Tucker turned around, her eyes full of tears. She felt sorry for me. Then I couldn't see her too well because I was crying, too. 23

"Sit down, Richard." 24

And I always thought the teacher kind of liked me. She always picked me to wash the blackboard on Friday, after school. That was a big thrill, it made me feel important. If I didn't wash it, come Monday the school might not function right. 25

"Where are you going, Richard!" 26

I walked out of school that day, and for a long time I didn't go back very often. There was shame there. 27

Now there was shame everywhere. It seemed like the whole world had been inside that classroom, everyone had heard what the teacher had said, everyone had turned around and felt sorry for me. There was shame in going to the Worthy Boys Annual Christmas Dinner for you and your kind, because everybody knew what a worthy boy was. Why couldn't they just call it the Boys Annual Dinner, why'd they have to give it a name? There was shame in wearing the brown and orange and white plaid <u>mackinaw</u> the welfare gave to three thousand boys. Why'd it have to be the same for everybody so when you walked down the street the people could see you were on relief? It was a nice warm mackinaw and it had a hood, and my Momma beat me and called me a little rat when she found out I stuffed it in the bottom of a pail full of garbage way over on Cottage Street. There was shame in running over to Mister Ben's at the end of the day and asking for his rotten peaches, there was shame in asking Mrs. Simmons for a spoonful of sugar, there was shame in running out to meet the relief truck. I hated that truck, full of food for you and your kind. I ran into the house and hid when it came. And then I started to sneak through alleys, to take the long way home so the people going into White's Eat Shop wouldn't see me. Yeah, the whole world heard the teacher that day, we all know you don't have a Daddy. 28

It lasted for a while, this kind of numbness. I spent a lot of time feeling sorry for myself. And then one day I met this wino in a restaurant. I'd been out hustling 29 all day, shining shoes, selling newspapers, and I had googobs of money in my pocket. Bought me a bowl of chili for fifteen cents, and a cheeseburger for fifteen cents, and a Pepsi for five cents, and a piece of chocolate cake for ten cents. That was a good meal. I was eating when this old wino came in. I love winos because they never hurt anyone but themselves.

The old wino sat down at the counter and ordered twenty-six cents worth of 30 food. He ate it like he really enjoyed it. When the owner, Mister Williams, asked him to pay the check, the old wino didn't lie or go through his pocket like he suddenly found a hole.

He just said: "Don't have no money." 31

The owner yelled: "Why in hell you come in here and eat my food if you 32 don't have no money? That food cost me money."

Mister Williams jumped over the counter and knocked the wino off his stool 33 and beat him over the head with a pop bottle. Then he stepped back and watched the wino bleed. Then he kicked him. And he kicked him again.

I looked at the wino with blood all over his face and I went over. "Leave him 34 alone, Mister Williams. I'll pay the twenty-six cents."

The wino got up, slowly, pulling himself up to the stool, then up to the 35 counter, holding on for a minute until his legs stopped shaking so bad. He looked at me with pure hate. "Keep your twenty-six cents. You don't have to pay, not now. I just finished paying for it."

He started to walk out, and as he passed me, he reached down and touched 36 my shoulder. "Thanks, sonny, but it's too late now. Why didn't you pay it before?"

I was pretty sick about that. I waited too long to help another man. 37

SKILL-DEVELOPMENT QUESTIONS

Vocabulary in Context

1. The word *pledged* in "Whatever Helene Tucker pledged for her Daddy, I was going to top it" (paragraph 7) means
   a. repeated.
   b. studied.
   c. promised to give.
   d. brought home.

2. The word *hustling* in "I'd been out hustling all day, shining shoes, selling newspapers, and I had googobs of money in my pocket" (paragraph 29) means
   a. complaining.
   b. relaxing.
   c. studying hard.
   d. working energetically.

Central Point and Main Ideas

3. Which sentence best expresses the central point of this selection?
    a. Dick Gregory had a long-standing crush on a girl named Helene Tucker.
    b. The charity Gregory received was given in a way that labeled him as poor, which made him ashamed.
    c. From both the giving and receiving ends, young Gregory learned that *how* something is given is as important as *what* is given.
    d. Gregory grew up in a fatherless, poor family.

4. Which sentence best expresses the main idea of paragraph 5?
    a. Gregory liked to eat paste.
    b. The teacher assumed Gregory was stupid.
    c. The teacher never realized that Gregory was hungry all the time.
    d. The teacher assumed Gregory was stupid and never realized his poor work was the result of hunger.

Key Details

———— 5. TRUE OR FALSE? Helene Tucker represented a way of life that Gregory wished he had.

6. After the teacher told him he was the type of person the Community Chest helped and that he was fatherless,
    a. Gregory never went back to school.
    b. Gregory felt sorry for himself for a while.
    c. Gregory stopped working.
    d. Gregory felt Helene Tucker did not feel sorry for him.

Transitions

7. The relationship of the second sentence below to the first is one of
    a. addition.
    b. comparison.
    c. contrast.
    d. illustration.

    I stuck my hand in my pocket and held onto the money, waiting for her to call my name. But the teacher closed her book after she called everybody else in the class. (Paragraph 12)

8. The sentence on page 329 contains a
    a. contrast signal.
    b. location signal.

c. time signal.
d. cause-effect signal.

I love winos because they never hurt anyone but themselves. (Paragraph 29)

Patterns of Organization

9. Paragraphs 30–36 are organized according to
    a. list of items.
    b. time order.
    c. cause and effect.
    d. comparison/contrast.

Fact and Opinion

10. Which of the following is a statement of opinion?
     a. "I was sitting in the back of the room, in a seat with a chalk circle drawn around it."
     b. "Paste doesn't taste too bad when you're hungry."
     c. "She turned toward the blackboard."
     d. "Helene Tucker turned around, her eyes full of tears."

11. The sentence below is a statement of
     a. fact.
     b. opinion.
     c. fact and opinion.

Teachers were never interested in finding out that you couldn't concentrate because you were so hungry, because you hadn't had any breakfast.

Inferences

_____ 12. TRUE OR FALSE? In the classroom scene, the author implies that Helene is a sensitive girl.

13. In paragraph 5, the author implies that
     a. he is stupid.
     b. teachers understood him well.
     c. it was difficult for him to concentrate in school.
     d. he felt alone and ignored in school.

_____ 14. TRUE OR FALSE? The author implies that the wino taught him a valuable lesson.

Purpose and Tone

_____ 15. TRUE OR FALSE? The author's primary purpose was to inform readers of how he learned what shame is.

16. The word that best describes the tone of the last paragraph of the selection is
   a. angry.
   b. objective.
   c. sentimental.
   d. ashamed.

Bias and Propaganda

17. Of the following statements, which is the least biased?
   a. Gregory was an idiot.
   b. Gregory was stupid.
   c. Gregory lacked academic skills.
   d. Gregory was a troublemaker.

Evaluating Arguments

_____ 18. TRUE OR FALSE? The teacher's conclusion that Gregory was stupid did not take into account all the relevant evidence.

19. To support his point of view, the author uses several
   a. statistics.
   b. expert opinions.
   c. personal experiences.
   d. famous quotations.

20. Which evidence from the selection supports Gregory's statement that, after the school incident, he felt shame everywhere?
   a. Helene Tucker's eyes were full of tears.
   b. Gregory was always chosen to wash the blackboards on Fridays.
   c. Gregory stuffed the plaid mackinaw in a garbage can.
   d. Gregory wanted to pay for the wino's dinner.

THINKING ACTIVITIES

Outlining

The following outline of "Shame" is missing two major supporting details and three minor supporting details. Complete the outline by filling in the missing details, which are listed on page 331.

Central point: Young Gregory learned both the shame of being let down by those who were supposed to help him and the shame of letting down another person.

1. _____

    a. Intention to impress Helene Tucker by pledging to Community Chest

    b. _____

    c. _____

2. _____

    a. Earns a lot of money one day and goes to a restaurant for a good meal

    b. Sees wino being beaten for not being able to pay for his meal

    c. _____

Items Missing from the Outline

- Offers to pay for meal, but too late
- Becoming ashamed of his own failure to help another
- Is humiliated by teacher
- Becoming ashamed of his poverty
- Leaves school and avoids it in the future

Summarizing

Complete the following summary of "Shame" by filling in the blank spaces.

To impress Helene Tucker, a girl he adored, Gregory decided one day in school to make a pledge on behalf of his father to the Community Chest. In fact, Gregory planned to use money he had earned himself, for he had no father, and his family was very poor. The teacher's response to Gregory's pledge, however, was to point out _____

_____

Gregory felt shamed in front of the world; he walked out of class and did not return to school often for a long time. He felt very sorry for himself until one day he happened to earn a lot of money and decided to go to a restaurant for a good meal. At the restaurant he witnessed an incident in which a wino ordered a meal and then got severely beaten for not being able to pay. Gregory later offered to pay for the meal, but, as the wino said, _____

_____

Gregory saw then that he too was capable of letting someone else down.

DISCUSSION QUESTIONS

1. Why did Gregory include both the classroom and the restaurant anecdotes in one piece? What is the difference between the shame he felt in the first incident and the shame he felt in the second? What are the similarities between the two incidents?

2. What does Gregory mean by the sentence "The eagle always flew on Friday" (paragraph 7)? What does this fact reveal about his world?

3. One type of irony is an event or an effect that is the opposite of what might be expected. In what ways are the following parts of "Shame" ironic?

   I never learned hate at home, or shame. I had to go to school for that.

   If I knew my place and didn't come too close, she'd wink at me and say hello. That was a good feeling.

   I looked at the wino with blood all over his face and I went over. "Leave him alone, Mister Williams. I'll pay the twenty-six cents."

   The wino got up. . . . He looked at me with pure hate.

4. Has anyone ever tried to help you in a way that didn't take all your needs into account? If so, how did you feel toward that person? What are some ways activities that are meant to help people might also hurt them?

Check Your Performance   SHAME

Skill	Number Right	Points	Total
Vocabulary in Context (2 items)	_____	× 4 :	_____
Central Point and Main Ideas (2)	_____	× 4 :	_____
Key Details (2)	_____	× 4 :	_____
Transitions (2)	_____	× 4 :	_____
Patterns of Organization (1)	_____	× 4 :	_____
Fact and Opinion (2)	_____	× 4 :	_____
Inferences (3)	_____	× 4 :	_____
Purpose and Tone (2)	_____	× 4 :	_____
Bias and Propaganda (1)	_____	× 4 :	_____
Evaluating Arguments (3)	_____	× 4 :	_____

(total of 20 questions)

Outlining (5)	_____	× 2 :	_____
Summarizing (2)	_____	× 5 :	_____

FINAL SCORE (OF POSSIBLE 100)   _____

Enter your final score into the reading performance chart on page 454.

8

Guarding Against Crime
Denise Worthington

Preview

Have you ever been the victim of a crime—or do you know someone who has? These days, your answer is likely to be "yes," for there has been a dramatic increase in crime over the last decade. That increase has made many fearful of physical harm and loss of property. But, as you'll learn from this article, Americans are not taking it lying down.

Words to Watch

bunker (4): an underground protected space, often used for military purposes
elaborate (8): complicated
vulnerable (8): exposed
array (9): impressive list
improvised (9): created to fill a need

Celebrity-watchers, take note: a new fad has hit the entertainment world— 1
crime-fighting.

In Hollywood, California, stars such as comedienne Joan Rivers host wine- 2
and-tear-gas parties. The guest of honor is a security expert who teaches other guests
the proper technique involved in discharging a canister of tear gas.

Country-pop singer Kenny Rogers has built a 30-foot-high electric fence 3
around his million-dollar Athens, Georgia estate. A small band of security men patrol the grounds twenty-four hours a day.

Movie star Goldie Hawn's home was built to withstand a minor invasion. 4
There are reinforced steel bars on all the windows, the doors are bullet-proof, and
the bathroom resembles a small <u>bunker</u>. Hawn swears by her two guard dogs, large
and ferocious Rottweillers.

But it's not only the wealthy and famous who are worried about their security. 5

Among Americans of all economic levels, concern for protecting ourselves and our property has never been greater. There's good reason we're afraid of crime. In the last 10 years the number of residential burglaries has increased dramatically. The FBI estimates a home is broken into every 13 seconds. The average value of property stolen has more than doubled in the last decade. The number of crimes against our person, such as rape and murder, has also increased. There's a growing feeling that nobody's safe anymore. In a recent survey 1,000 homeowners were asked if they knew someone whose home had been robbed in the last three years. Over 65% answered yes. In the same survey, almost 90% of respondents expressed fears that they might be burglarized.

Clearly, Americans are worried about crime. But just as clearly, we're fighting 6 back—with crime watch programs, more efficient home security systems, handguns, guard dogs, tear gas, and a host of other products and techniques designed to win the war against crime.

First, neighborhood crime watch programs are springing up all across the 7 country. New York City alone has over 150,000 residents involved in community watch groups. These groups are usually trained by the local police department and come to serve as the eyes and ears of the police, not to replace them. These groups help residents develop a greater awareness of what's going on in the neighborhood. They also serve to renew community spirit, bringing neighbors together in a way that is reminiscent of life on the frontier. In town after town, city after city, crime watches are working. One law enforcement expert estimates neighbor watch teams reduce residential burglaries by 90%. Statistics indicate that the odds of being victimized by a break-in in a community without a watch are one in 45. However, with a watch operating within a community, the odds of being burglarized drop all the way to one in 1000.

Second, Americans have become much more home security conscious. It's es- 8 timated that we spend between $2 billion and $3 billion on personal security, much of that going in attempts to make the home safer. For example, in 1986 we purchased more than 240 million burglar alarms, spending anywhere from a few hundred dollars on a basic trip-switch mechanism to $10,000 or more for a highly elaborate system. We are also much more careful about the entrances to our homes. Americans have added one or more tamper-resistant deadbolt locks to the standard locks on their doors; in addition, we have reinforced the doors themselves with metal or plywood to prevent a would-be burglar from breaking through. We have also adopted much better ways of safeguarding the parts of our homes most vulnerable to a break-in: the basement windows and the fire escape. We now bar and gate these areas, and we know that even something as simple and inexpensive as a tenpenny nail, driven on a slight angle at the point where the top and bottom sashes of a window come together, makes entry much more difficult than the easily-jimmied interlocking catch. And we no longer hide a spare key under the doormat or on top of the door frame . . . we've realized that burglars know about those places, too. A third popular method of safeguarding the home is Project Identification. Under this program, valuables are marked with an identification number. The number is then recorded by the police, making the resale of stolen goods more risky and difficult. Finally, we have learned to take precautions at vacation time. Americans now place timers on radios and lights, notify the neighbors and the local police department, and discontinue mail and newspaper delivery before they leave for a trip.

Third, Americans are resorting to handguns, guard and attack dogs, and tear 9 gas, as well as many other methods in efforts to achieve personal security. Handgun sales are at an all-time high. In California, for example, the number of legally registered handguns is close to 400,000. Add to that figure the number of unregistered guns held by Californians, which law enforcement officials believe could be around a half-million, and the total approaches a staggering stockpile of one million guns in one state alone. The sale of guard and attack dogs is also at a record level. Preferred breeds include German shepherds and Doberman pinschers, and prices for a well-trained dog can range from $1,000 to $5,000. Millions of us routinely carry knives, baseball bats, crowbars, hatpins, and an <u>array</u> of other <u>improvised</u> weapons that almost defies imagination.

In conclusion, it looks as if we're not going to take it anymore. We're willing 10 to spend large amounts of money and invest considerable time and energy to fight an epidemic of crime. And while it's not taking place overnight, progress is being made. There's a new awareness among Americans that we can't expect the police to be entirely responsible for our protection. We're starting to take action, cooperatively and individually, to watch out for ourselves. The signs are everywhere. Americans are fighting back.

SKILL-DEVELOPMENT QUESTIONS

Vocabulary in Context

1. The word *reminiscent* in "They renew community spirit, bringing neighbors together in a way that is reminiscent of life on the frontier" (paragraph 7) means
   a. unlike.
   b. a reminder.
   c. respectful.
   d. hopeful.

2. The word *resorting* in "Americans are resorting to handguns, guard and attack dogs, and tear gas" (paragraph 9) means
   a. reacting.
   b. unattracted.
   c. turning for aid.
   d. reversing.

Central Point and Main Ideas

3. Which sentence best expresses the central point of the selection?
   a. Crime-fighting is a new fad in Hollywood.
   b. Many Americans are fighting increased crime by protecting their property and themselves.

    c.   Burglaries can be prevented in various ways.

    d.   Americans are spending billions to safeguard their homes.

4. Which sentence best expresses the main idea of paragraph 5?

    a.   Americans are concerned about protecting their property.

    b.   Over the last decade, residential robberies have increased greatly.

    c.   Because of a high rate of crime, Americans of all incomes are worried about security.

    d.   A recent survey shows how much Americans worry about crime.

5. Which sentence best expresses the main idea of paragraph 8?

    a.   Americans are buying various types of alarm systems.

    b.   Locks are better than ever before.

    c.   Americans are trying harder to make their homes secure.

    d.   Project Identification is a new and popular program.

Key Details

6. According to the article, crime-watch programs usually do *not*

    a.   increase residents' awareness of their communities.

    b.   renew community spirit.

    c.   replace police efforts.

    d.   work outside of New York City.

_____ 7. TRUE OR FALSE? All methods of adding to the security of a home are expensive.

Transitions

8. The relationship of the sentence below to the information that comes before it is one of

    a.   addition.

    b.   clarification.

    c.   contrast.

    d.   comparison.

Clearly, Americans are worried about crime. (Paragraph 6)

9. The relationship of the sentence below to the information that comes before it is one of

    a.   contrast.

    b.   comparison.

    c.   illustration.

    d.   summary.

In conclusion, it looks as if we're not going to take it anymore. (Paragraph 10)

Patterns of Organization

10. The pattern of organization of paragraph 4 is
    a. list of items.
    b. time order.
    c. comparison/contrast.
    d. definition/example.

———————— 11. TRUE OR FALSE? Paragraph 5 is organized in a combined pattern: cause-and-effect and list of items.

Fact and Opinion

12. Which of the following is a statement of opinion?
    a. "There's good reason we're afraid of crime."
    b. "New York City alone has over 150,000 residents involved in community-watch programs."
    c. "Handgun sales are at an all-time high."
    d. "The sale of guard and attack dogs is also at a record level."

13. The sentence below is a statement of
    a. fact.
    b. opinion.
    c. fact and opinion.

    For example, in 1986 we purchased more than 240 million burglar alarms, spending anywhere from a few hundred dollars on a basic trip-switch mechanism to $10,000 or more for a highly elaborate system.

Inferences

14. From the article we can conclude that
    a. burglars look for an empty house.
    b. fire escapes cannot be made secure.
    c. people protect themselves in only legal ways.
    d. it is safe to leave a spare key outside the front door.

Purpose and Tone

15. The main purpose of this article is to
    a. inform readers about how Americans are fighting crime.
    b. persuade readers to take all of the crime-fighting actions named in the article.
    c. entertain readers with anecdotes about celebrities.

16. The tone of paragraph 2 is best described as
    a. serious with a humorous touch.
    b. frightening.
    c. angry.
    d. compassionate with a hint of sadness.

Bias and Propaganda

17. By using the word *fad* in the sentence below, the author reveals her opinion that
    a. crime-fighting will be a passing interest among celebrities.
    b. celebrities don't do a good job of fighting crime.
    c. celebrities should not worry about crime.
    d. the high rate of crime will soon pass like a fad.

    Celebrity-watchers, take note: a new fad has hit the entertainment world—crime-fighting.

18. Which of the following statements based on the article (paragraph 9) uses the least biased language?
    a. The total approaches a staggering stockpile of one million handguns in one state alone.
    b. The total approaches a stockpile of one million handguns in one state alone.
    c. The total approaches one million handguns in one state alone.
    d. The total approaches one million handguns in California.

Evaluating Arguments

19. In paragraph 5, the author supports the statement below with
    a. a personal anecdote.
    b. interviews with crime victims.
    c. statistics on crime.
    d. none of the above.

    There's good reason we're afraid of crime.

20. Which of the following pieces of information would best support the central point of this article?
    a. The name of the company that teaches celebrities how to use tear gas.
    b. The names of companies who manufacture tear gas.
    c. Statistics on a growing amount of tear-gas sold to homeowners in recent years.
    d. Expert opinions on the best burglar alarms to use.

THINKING ACTIVITIES

Outlining

Following is an incomplete outline of "Guarding Against Crime." Complete the outline by filling in the letters of the missing central point, primary supporting detail, and minor supporting details, given in random order below.

Central Point: _____

A. Communities are forming neighborhood crime-watch programs, which have greatly reduced local burglaries.
    1. Neighborhood crime-watchers are usually trained by the police, whom they assist, not replace.

    2. _____
    3. An expert estimate and statistics show that these programs are highly successful.

B. _____

    1. _____
    2. We are protecting the entrances to our homes.
    3. Many safeguard their homes with Project Identification.
    4. Americans are taking precautions when they go on vacation.
C. Americans are buying weapons and guard dogs for greater personal security.
    1. More handguns are being bought than ever before.
    2. Guard and attack dogs are also more popular than ever.

    3. _____

Items Missing from the Outline

a. We are buying more burglar alarms.
b. Many people routinely carry weapons of all sorts.
c. Americans, concerned about the epidemic of crime, are protecting themselves in various ways.
d. These programs renew community spirit.
e. There has been an increase of home-security measures.

Summarizing

1. Circle the letter of the statement that best summarizes the central point of "Guarding Against Crime" as expressed in the introduction (paragraphs 1–6).
    a. Celebrities are fighting crime with wine-and-tear-gas parties and extensive security measures.

    b.   There has been a dramatic increase in crime over the last decade.

    c.   Because of a dramatic increase in crime over the last decade, Americans of all economic levels are fighting against crime.

2.   Circle the letter of the statement that best summarizes the first set of supporting details for the central point (paragraph 7)

    a.   More and more communities are forming neighborhood crime-watch programs, which greatly reduce neighborhood burglaries.

    b.   Over 150,000 residents are involved in crime-watch programs in New York City.

    c.   The presence of a crime-watch program decreases the odds of a community break-in from one in 45 to one in 1,000.

3.   Circle the letter of the statement that best summarizes the second set of supporting details for the central point (paragraph 8).

    a.   Americans bought over 240 million burglar alarms in 1986.

    b.   Americans are making their homes more secure with various devices and techniques.

    c.   Americans are taking more security precautions when they go on vacations.

4.   Circle the letter of the statement that best summarizes the third set of supporting details for the central point (paragraph 9).

    a.   Americans are concerned about their personal security.

    b.   More guard and attack dogs are being bought than ever before.

    c.   Americans are using weapons and dogs in their effort to gain greater personal security.

5.   Circle the letter of the statement that best summarizes the restatement of the central point in the concluding paragraph.

    a.   Americans are being motivated by the epidemic of crime.

    b.   Americans are spending the time and money needed to protect themselves against the epidemic of crime.

    c.   The fight against crime will not be won overnight.

DISCUSSION QUESTIONS

1.   Are you among those who are worried about crime? If so, why? Did you get any useful ideas on fighting crime from the article? Have you already used any?

2.   Why do you think the author introduced her article with the anecdotes about celebrities? How do these anecdotes relate to her central point?

3.   The author writes that neighborhood crime-watch programs "also serve to renew community spirit, bringing neighbors together in a way that

is reminiscent of life on the frontier." What do you think she means by this statement? How could the crime-watch programs "renew community spirit"?

4. According to the article, an important part of Americans' crime-fighting efforts involves handguns. Many people, however, are against the sale of handguns. Do you think private ownership of handguns is a good way to fight crime? Why or why not?

Check Your Performance   GUARDING AGAINST CRIME

Skill	Number Right	Points	Total
Vocabulary in Context (2 items)	_____	× 4 :	_____
Central Point and Main Ideas (3)	_____	× 4 :	_____
Key Details (2)	_____	× 4 :	_____
Transitions (2)	_____	× 4 :	_____
Patterns of Organization (2)	_____	× 4 :	_____
Fact and Opinion (2)	_____	× 4 :	_____
Inferences (1)	_____	× 4 :	_____
Purpose and Tone (2)	_____	× 4 :	_____
Bias and Propaganda (2)	_____	× 4 :	_____
Evaluating Arguments (2)	_____	× 4 :	_____

(total of 20 questions)

Outlining (5)	_____	× 2 :	_____
Summarizing (5)	_____	× 2 :	_____

FINAL SCORE (OF POSSIBLE 100)   _____

Enter your final score into the reading performance chart on page 454.

9

The No-Fat Nation
James Fallows

Preview

Many Americans rely on working out to improve health and to feel good. It is hard, then, for us to imagine a country in which few people exercise. We might expect such a country to be full of unhealthy people struggling with weight problems. Yet James Fallows, the author of this article from *Atlantic* magazine, found almost no fat people in Japan, where exercise is the exception rather than the rule. Why are people who rarely exercise so healthy—and so slim? In this article based on his experiences in Japan, Fallows provides his answer.

Words to Watch

longevity (3):   long life
cardinal (6):   basic, fundamental
sedentary (7):   characterized by much sitting
vigor (9):   energy
omnipresent (9):   constant
bestirring (10):   making oneself take energetic action
frugal (10):   thrifty
atavistic (12):   backsliding
stupefying (14):   astonishing
girth (16):   fatness
satiation (18):   a condition of extreme fullness

This may seem a small thing, but it sums up many of the differences between 1 us and the Japanese: they can live practically forever in circumstances that Americans have come to regard as fatal.

I'm not talking about the threat of beriberi or industrial wastes or anything so 2 exotic—only about exercise. Most Japanese, judging by the ones I have seen during a four-and-a-half-month stay in Tokyo, live in happy ignorance of aerobics, health clubs, and Nautilus machines—and they live, and live, and live. Last summer the government released the latest set of statistics showing that Japanese people are living even longer than they used to, and easily longer than we are. The average life expectancy for Japanese women is now more than 80 years, and for men it's in the mid-70s. Yet during those long years the average Japanese person will rarely work up a sweat.

I should perhaps explain why this mystery is so intriguing to me. I have 3 reached a stage in life (I've just turned 37) at which practical steps toward longevity are more interesting than they used to be. For 20 or so years before arriving in Japan I'd placed my hopes for health and heartiness where many other Americans have: on exercise and sports. Long ago I played on school tennis teams and ran cross-country. He-man activities these may not be, but I enjoyed them, and kept on enjoying them until a few months ago. I also thought it must do at least some good to be out there, breathing hard, several times a week. Wasn't that, in fact, precisely what all the health experts recommended?

The only thing I'm now sure of is that exercise used to make me feel better. 4 These days I don't get any, and I feel like hell. In Japan I walk a lot—to and from train stations, up and down the endless subway stairs—but almost never run, swim, play tennis or basketball, or engage in any other forms of exercise that tax lungs and sweat glands. Last month, on a trip to Hiroshima, I rowed my family around in a little boat. Three months ago I sneaked onto the British Embassy's tennis court and played tennis for half an hour—mixed doubles. That's about it.

The reason for my new indolence is perfectly simple: Tokyo is so crowded that 5 it doesn't have space for sports. I once read that Frank Shorter, the famous marathoner, never missed a day of running, even when on the road. He'd change his clothes in an airport bathroom and head outside to put in a few miles. No doubt he would have found a way to make even Tokyo into a sports paradise. I frequently see a few people like him—Westerners, mainly, who push their way down the jammed sidewalks as they attempt to "run" a few miles.

Conceivably I could have followed their example—running late at night after 6 my trip home on the train. My wife could theoretically have gone swimming, if she'd been willing to wait in line several hours at the pool built for the 1964 Olympic Games. We could have tried harder, could have joined the foreign madmen dodging down the street, could have shown more of that cardinal Japanese virtue, fighting spirit. My point is that most Japanese—who, after all, are going to outlive us—take Tokyo's limits for granted and don't even try.

The few exercise clubs that exist in Tokyo are well beyond the reach of the 7 average Japanese family. One extremely well-off Japanese friend told me that he had recently joined a swimming club with a $10,000 initiation fee. The club has 1,500 members, who compete for use of one 25-meter pool. When they stop working and are ready to have a good time, most Japanese still prefer more or less sedentary activities—purposeful drinking, fancy restaurant meals, parties to view the cherry blossoms or maple leaves or even the new-fallen snow. Teenage girls in Tokyo have lately favored carrying black nylon tennis-racket bags, labeled Dunlop or Donnay, as fashion accessories and statements of self. From the way they hang on the girls' shoulders and feel when they jab into my kidneys on the subway car, I assume that the bags actually contain rackets. But I would bet that most of them have never been used—unless, of course, being carried and admired is in fact their primary function.

Many Japanese youngsters take up gymnastics, *kendo*, or other aerobic activi- 8
ties, but as grown-up "salarymen" or housewives, they tend to leave these childish pursuits behind. In America I often talked sports with my friends—not sports we watched so much as sports we played. In Japan I've had many conversations about the sumo *bashos* (tournaments) and Japan-league baseball, but the only friends who have mentioned their own athletic interests are those who have lived in America and come to think of exercise as something they "should" have.

So why are they all so healthy? Why, even before outliving us, do they look 9
so much fresher and less shopworn than Westerners of similar age? (My rule of thumb when meeting a Japanese man is to guess his age by Western standards of wrinkles and hair loss—and then add 10 years to come up with his real age. The misjudgment runs the other way, too: people here are always guessing that I am older than I am.) Maybe they look so young because Tokyo's cheerless climate spares them the withering effects of the sun. But there must be more to Japanese vigor and longevity than the near omnipresent cloud cover over Tokyo, which has a copious annual rainfall.

The answer, of course, is the Japanese diet. By living so long while bestirring 10
themselves so little, the Japanese prove that their diet is healthier than ours—and that diet matters more than exercise does. But there is an emotional significance to this statement that is hard to appreciate until you've lived it. Japanese food is on the whole superb, one of the adornments of the culture. Yet merely by eating it one begins to feel part of a society that is frugal, competitive, keen-edged.

Like most other Americans, I've heard for years that our national cuisine con- 11
tains too much fat. But I never took this personally until I came to Japan. For the first month or two after arrival my wife and children and I felt constantly fam-ished—even after we had gotten over the price shock that at first made us reluctant to buy anything at all. Although it took us a while to realize it, we were being starved for fat: a meal couldn't leave us feeling really full unless it laid down a rime of fat globules in our mouths and stomachs. (Let's not talk about our arteries.) Japanese food is varied and flavorful, and when accompanied by mounds of rice it can even seem filling. But for us it lacked staying power, because it had so little fat.

A week or two after arrival we suddenly grasped what was wrong when we 12
passed one of Tokyo's countless McDonald's outlets and, overcome by atavistic crav-ings, turned back and rushed in. We ate Big Macs and drank milkshakes, felt the grease on our lips and fingers, and carried a full feeling with us the rest of the day.

We've adjusted more gracefully after our several months here. We live on rice, 13
fish, pickles, noodles, and miso soup, made from soybeans. Most of the time we feel satisfied. We tell ourselves that Japan is making us healthier, even though we puff and trudge when we climb subway steps and generally feel like we're falling apart. But the idea that fat distinguishes the two cultures stays with us, like the fat from an order of fries.

It's not that the Japanese are uninterested in greasy, fat-drenched food. They 14
are wild about McDonald's, Kentucky Fried Chicken, Mr. Donut, and other Amer-

ican-style fat mines. Their own cuisine features one cheap, popular item that approximates the hot dog in nutritional value: *ton katsu*, a fatty pork cutlet, breaded and prepared like a Texas chicken-fried steak. I need hardly add that the local *ton katsu* outlet is my family's favorite haunt. Sushi eaters pay a premium for *toro*, the oiliest part of the tuna. Some of the most expensive food to be had in Japan (which is saying something) is its domestic beef, which is so thickly marbled with fat that every bite is a swirl of red and white. For sheer stupefying obesity, the biggest Japanese sumo wrestlers, at 400 pounds and up, make William "The Refrigerator" Perry look like an overpublicized fake.

But while recognizing that fat has its place, and even according it some dignity, the Japanese somehow avoid getting carried away. After we'd been going to a local public bath for several weeks, one of my sons looked around the room, inspecting the bodies one by one. Then he asked, in his loudest voice, "Daddy, why aren't there any fat people in Japan?" His question made me realize why I felt so at home in the baths. In America the typical locker-room situation always made me think of myself as an underdeveloped weakling. Here I was merely tall.   15

About a month later I visited Yokosuka, a port town south of Tokyo where the U.S. Navy has a base. For the first time in Japan I saw dozens of American families on the street, not just the scattered businessmen and consultants of Tokyo. I stared goggle-eyed at my countrymen, amazed not at how tall they were or what a variety of colors they came in but at how many of them were fat. How do they do it? I found myself wondering. How can they possibly eat enough to become so much fatter than the Japanese? (The Japanese Ministry of Agriculture says that there's no mystery at all about the difference in girth. The average American is said to ingest 800 calories a day more than a Japanese—3,393 calories versus 2,593.)   16

Because fat in America runs along class lines, it should not be surprising that sailors' wives were fatter than the downtown sharpies from IBM. Still, I marveled at us as Americans, regardless of class. Every tank town in America has better sports facilities than can be found practically anywhere in Japan—but we take it for granted that we and our friends will get bigger and heavier with each passing year. Why did this happen to us? How do the cooped-up Japanese remain so fit?   17

Primitive cultures attach moral and political significance to body size—powerful chiefs had better look well fed—and I'm afraid that I am starting to do the same thing. Forty years ago the physical contrast between Americans and Japanese was between the tall, strong victors and the short, weak vanquished. Now it looks to me like a contrast between a soft culture and a hard one—between people who eat to satiation and those whose portions are small.   18

The Japanese do permit themselves excesses: each night on the subway I see businessmen who are fall-down, throw-up drunk. But they generally curb their appetites and channel their energies into production, not mere exercise. On a trip outside Japan I watched a bodybuilder from UCLA work out in a hotel gym. I thought about the hours of hard work his physique had cost him. There are very few who resemble him in Japan. His counterparts spend their time not in the gym but with the work group.   19

Some Japanese friends tell me that things are changing. Kids are overeating now; adults are starting to worry about weight. I don't believe it, but I take heart   20 from their concern. When *Jane Fonda's Workout Book* becomes a best-seller in Japan, we'll know that our industries have a chance.

SKILL-DEVELOPMENT QUESTIONS

Vocabulary in Context

1. The word *indolence* in "The reason for my new indolence is . . . Tokyo . . . doesn't have space for sports" (paragraph 5) means
   a. activity.
   b. laziness.
   c. conditioning.
   d. sport.

2. The word *famished* in "my wife and children and I felt constantly famished. . . . we were being starved for fat" (paragraph 11) means
   a. very hungry.
   b. satisfied.
   c. stuffed.
   d. poor.

3. The word *copious* in "But there must be more to Japanese vigor and longevity than the near omnipresent cloud cover over Tokyo, which has a copious annual rainfall" (paragraph 9) means
   a. small.
   b. rare.
   c. welcome.
   d. plentiful.

Central Point and Main Ideas

4. Which sentence best expresses the central point of the selection?
   a. There are no fat people in Japan.
   b. Though the Japanese rarely exercise, they live longer lives than Americans because of their low-fat diet.
   c. The average Japanese eats 800 calories a day less than the average American.
   d. Exercising in Tokyo is difficult because it is so crowded and health clubs are very expensive.

5. Which sentence best expresses the main idea of paragraph 2?
   a. The Japanese exercise less but live longer than Americans.
   b. Japanese men live until their mid-70s.
   c. Japanese women live until their 80s.
   d. Most Japanese exercise rarely.

Key Details

6. Many Japanese exercise
   a. in health clubs.
   b. when they are young.
   c. by jogging.
   d. by wrestling and playing baseball.

7. According to the article, the Japanese combination of long life, little exercise and a low-fat diet proves
   a. exercise is harmful.
   b. exercise makes no contribution to health.
   c. diet is more important to good health than exercise.
   d. watching sports is better than playing them.

Transitions

8. The signal words in the sentence below show
   a. illustration.
   b. addition.
   c. location.
   d. emphasis.

   The answer, of course, is the Japanese diet. (Paragraph 10)

Patterns of Organization

9. The main pattern of organization of paragraph 8 is
   a. cause and effect.
   b. definition and example.
   c. comparison/contrast.
   d. time order.

10. The relationship between paragraphs 9 and 10 is one of
    a. time order.
    b. cause and effect.
    c. definition and examples.
    d. list of items.

Fact and Opinion

11. The sentence on page 349 is a statement of
    a. fact.
    b. opinion.
    c. both fact and opinion.

The average American is said to ingest 800 calories a day more than a Japanese—3,393 calories versus 2,593. (Paragraph 16)

12. Which of the following is a statement of fact?
    a. "Maybe they look so young because Tokyo's cheerless climate spares them the withering effects of the sun."
    b. "Japanese food is on the whole superb, one of the adornments of the culture."
    c. "Last month, on a trip to Hiroshima, I rowed my family around in a little boat."
    d. "Now it looks to me like a contrast between a soft culture and a hard one."

Inferences

13. The author implies that the Japanese diet is
    a. a reflection of the nature of the Japanese people.
    b. inexpensive.
    c. made up of food that is less tasty than American food.
    d. easy for Americans to adjust to.

_____ 14. TRUE OR FALSE? The author implies that the Japanese people have less time for leisure activities than Americans.

Purpose and Tone

15. The author's main purpose is to
    a. inform Americans about the Japanese culture.
    b. entertain readers with amusing stories of his Japanese adventures.
    c. persuade Americans that a low-fat diet is more important to good health than exercise.

16. In general, the author's tone is
    a. angry but understanding.
    b. self-pitying and hopeless.
    c. critical and ridiculing.
    d. serious but good-humored.

Bias and Propaganda

_____ 17. TRUE OR FALSE? The following selections from the article reveal that the author feels the Japanese are more competitive than Americans.

Yet merely by eating [Japanese food] one begins to feel part of a society that is frugal, competitive, keen-edged.

[The Japanese] spend their time not in the gym but with the work group.

When *Jane Fonda's Workout Book* becomes a best-seller in Japan, we'll know that our industries have a chance.

18.   In the sentence below, the biased words are
a.   "even before outliving us."
b.   "they look."
c.   "much fresher and less shopworn."
d.   "Westerners of similar age."

Why, even before outliving us, do they look so much fresher and less shopworn than Westerners of similar age? (Paragraph 9)

Evaluating Arguments

19.   Which of the following statements is a valid conclusion based on the information in paragraph 14?
a.   All Japanese love McDonald's food.
b.   Fatty foods are expensive in Japan because foreigners increase the demand for them.
c.   Chain restaurants selling Japanese fast food would certainly be successful in the United States.
d.   The Japanese eat some food that is high in fat.

20.   Which of the following evidence does *not* support the author's conclusion that the Japanese are healthier than we are?
a.   "[The Japanese] can live practically forever in circumstances that Americans have come to regard as fatal."
b.   "The few exercise clubs that exist in Tokyo are well beyond the reach of the average Japanese family."
c.   "But while recognizing that fat has its place . . . the Japanese somehow avoid getting carried away."
d.   "The average American is said to ingest 800 calories a day more than a Japanese."

THINKING ACTIVITIES

Outlining

Following is an incomplete outline based on "The No-Fat Nation." Complete it by filling in the letters of the missing primary and secondary details. The details appear in random order below the outline.

Central Point: In contrast to Americans, the Japanese rarely exercise, yet they live longer, healthier lives because of their low-fat diets.

A. The Japanese way of life
   1. Little exercise for adults

      a. _____
      b. Expense of health clubs
   2. Low-fat diet
   3. Effects on health

      a. _____
      b. _____

B. _____
   1. Belief in regular exercise for adults
   2. High-fat diet

   3. _____
      a. Look older than Japanese
      b. Shorter lives than Japanese

Items Missing from the Outline

(1) Healthier looks than Americans
(2) Lack of space in Tokyo
(3) Effects on health
(4) Longer lives than Americans
(5) The American way of life

Summarizing

Add the words needed to complete the following summary of "The No-Fat Nation."

The Japanese live longer than Americans, yet they rarely _____ . Americans enjoy sports and health clubs, but there is too little

_____ in Tokyo for sports. In addition, health clubs are too expensive for most Japanese. Nevertheless, to Americans the Japanese

look _____ than they are. The main reason for their good

health is their _____ . In contrast, Americans crave foods

that are rich in _____ . As a result, Americans live shorter lives and are fatter. In comparison to the Japanese, on the whole, the American culture seems self-indulgent.

DISCUSSION QUESTIONS

1. What facts does Fallows give to show that the Japanese are healthier than Americans? Has he left anything out?

2. While the Japanese diet is central to Fallows' essay, he doesn't mention it until paragraph 10. Why do you think he didn't mention diet earlier in the article?

3. Besides the facts that the Japanese live longer than Americans, don't exercise much, and eat a low-fat diet, what do we know about life in Japan after reading "The No-Fat Nation"?

4. Should all Americans be asked to read this article? Why or why not?

Check Your Performance		THE NO-FAT NATION		
Skill	*Number Right*		*Points*	*Total*
Vocabulary in Context (3 items)	_____	× 4 :		_____
Central Point and Main Ideas (2)	_____	× 4 :		_____
Key Details (2)	_____	× 4 :		_____
Transitions (1)	_____	× 4 :		_____
Patterns of Organization (2)	_____	× 4 :		_____
Fact and Opinion (2)	_____	× 4 :		_____
Inferences (2)	_____	× 4 :		_____
Purpose and Tone (2)	_____	× 4 :		_____
Bias and Propaganda (2)	_____	× 4 :		_____
Evaluating Arguments (2)	_____	× 4 :		_____
(total of 20 questions)				
Outlining (5)	_____	× 2 :		_____
Summarizing (5)	_____	× 2 :		_____
FINAL SCORE (OF POSSIBLE 100)				_____

Enter your final score into the reading performance chart on page 454.

10

The Bystander Effect
Dorothy Barkin

Preview

A few years ago, thirty-eight people witnessed a brutal attack—and hardly raised a finger to stop it. That kind of unwillingness to get involved is the topic of this article by Dorothy Barkin, who analyzes the confusion and lack of responsibility bystanders often feel when witnessing a crime or medical emergency. She begins by describing four crisis situations—and placing you right there at the scene. How would you react?

Words to Watch

intervene (2):   interfere
phenomena (4):   facts
apathy (23):   indifference
paralysis (32):   inability to act
diffusion (32):   spreading

It is a pleasant fall afternoon. The sun is shining. You are heading toward the 1 parking lot after your last class of the day. All of a sudden, you come across the following situations. What do you think you'd do in each case?

Situation One: A man in his early twenties dressed in jeans and a T-shirt is using a coat hanger to pry open a door of a late-model Ford sedan. An overcoat and camera are visible on the back seat of the car. You're the only one who sees this.

Situation Two: A man and woman are wrestling with each other. The woman is in tears. Attempting to fight the man off, she screams, "Who are you? Get away from me!" You're the only one who witnesses this.

Situation Three: Imagine the same scenario as in Situation Two except that this time the woman screams, "Get away from me! I don't know why I ever married you!"

Situation Four: Again imagine Situation Three. This time, however, there are a few other people (strangers to you and each other) who also observe the incident.

Many people would choose not to get involved in situations like these. By-   2
standers are often reluctant to <u>intervene</u> in criminal or medical emergencies for reasons they are well aware of. They may fear possible danger to themselves or getting caught up in a situation that could lead to complicated and time-consuming legal proceedings.

There are, however, other, less obvious factors which influence the decision to   3
get involved in emergency situations. Complex psychological factors, which many are unaware of, play an important part in the behavior of bystanders; knowing about these factors can help people to act more responsibly when faced with emergencies.

To understand these psychological <u>phenomena</u>, it is helpful to look at what   4
researchers have learned about behavior in the situations mentioned at the beginning of this article.

Situation One: Research reveals a remarkably low rate of bystander intervention to protect property. In one study, more than 3,000 people walked past 214 staged car break-ins like the one described in this situation. The vast majority of passers-by completely ignored what appeared to be a crime in progress. Not one of the 3000 bothered to report the incident to the police.

Situation Two: Another experiment involved staging scenarios like this and the next situation. In Situation Two, bystanders offered some sort of assistance to the young woman 65 percent of the time.

Situation Three: Here the rate of bystander assistance dropped down to 19 percent. This demonstrates that bystanders are more reluctant to help a woman when they believe she's fighting with her husband. Not only do they consider a wife in less need of help; they think interfering with a married couple may be more dangerous. The husband, unlike a stranger, will not flee the situation.

Situation Four: The important idea in this situation is being a member of a group of bystanders. In more than fifty studies involving many different conditions, one outcome has been consistent: bystanders are much less likely to get involved when other witnesses are present than when they are alone.

Thus, membership in a group of bystanders lowers the likelihood of each   5
member of the group becoming involved. This finding may seem surprising. You might think there would be safety in numbers and that being a member of a group would increase the likelihood of intervention. How can we explain this aspect of group behavior?

A flood of research has tried to answer this and other questions about emer- 6
gency bystanders ever since the infamous case of the murder of Kitty Genovese.

In 1964 in the borough of Queens in New York City, Catherine "Kitty" Gen- 7
ovese, twenty-eight, was brutally murdered in a shocking crime that outraged the
nation.

The crime began at 3 A.M. Kitty Genovese was coming home from her job as 8
manager of a bar. After parking her car in a parking lot, she began the hundred-
foot walk to the entrance of her apartment. But she soon noticed a man in the lot
and decided instead to walk toward a police call box. As she walked by a bookstore
on her way there, the man grabbed her. She screamed.

Lights went on and windows opened in the ten-story apartment building. The 9
attacker then went to his car and drove off. Struggling, Genovese made her way
inside the building.

Next, the attacker stabbed Genovese. She shrieked, "Oh, my God, he stabbed 10
me! Please help me! Please help me!"

From an upper window in the apartment house, a man shouted, "Let that girl 11
alone!"

The assailant, alarmed by the man's shout, started toward his car, which was 12
parked nearby. However, the lights in the building soon went out, and the man
returned. He found Genovese struggling to reach her apartment—and stabbed her
again.

She screamed, "I'm dying! I'm dying!" 13

Once more lights went on and windows opened in the apartment building. 14
The attacker then went to his car and drove off. Struggling, Genovese made her
way inside the building.

But the assailant returned to attack Genovese yet a third time. He found her 15
slumped on the floor at the foot of the stairs and stabbed her again, this time fatally.

The murder took over a half hour, and Kitty Genovese's desperate cries for 16
help were heard by at least thirty-eight people. Not a single one of the thirty-eight
who later admitted to having witnessed the murder bothered to pick up the phone
during the attack and call the police. One man called after Genovese was dead.

Comments made by bystanders after this murder provide important insight 17
into what group members think when they consider intervening in an emergency.

These are some of the comments: 18

"I didn't want my husband to get involved." 19

"Frankly, we were afraid." 20

"We thought it was a lovers' quarrel." 21

"I was tired." 22

The Genovese murder sparked a national debate on the questions of public 23
apathy and fear and became the basis for thousands of sermons, editorials, classroom
discussions, and even a made-for-television movie. The same question was on everybody's mind—how could thirty-eight people have done so little?

Nine years later, another well-publicized incident provided additional infor- 24
mation about the psychology of a group witnessing a crime.

On a summer afternoon in Trenton, New Jersey, a twenty-year-old woman 25
was brutally raped in a parking lot in full view of twenty-five employees of a nearby

roofing company. Though the workers witnessed the entire incident and the woman repeatedly screamed for help, no one came to her assistance.

Comments made by witnesses to the rape were remarkably similar to those made by the bystanders to the Genovese murder. For example, one witness said, "We thought, well, it might turn out to be her boyfriend or something like that." 26

It's not surprising to find similar excuses for not helping in cases involving a group of bystanders. The same psychological principles apply to each. Research conducted since the Genovese murder indicates that the failure of bystanders to get involved can't be simply dismissed as a symptom of an uncaring society. Rather, the bystander effect, as it is called by social scientists, is the product of a complex set of psychological factors. 27

Two factors appear to be most important in understanding the reactions of bystanders to emergencies. 28

First is the level of ambiguity involved in the situation. Bystanders are afraid to endanger themselves or look foolish if they take the wrong action in a situation they're not sure how to interpret. A person lying face down on the floor of a subway train may have just suffered a heart attack and be in need of immediate medical assistance—or he may be a dangerous drunk. 29

Determining what is happening is especially difficult when a man is attacking a woman. Many times lovers do quarrel, sometimes violently. But they may strongly resent an outsider, no matter how well-meaning, intruding into their affairs. 30

When a group of bystanders is around, interpreting an event can be even more difficult than when one is alone. Bystanders look to others for cues as to what is happening. Frequently other witnesses, just as confused, try to look calm. Thus bystanders can mislead each other about the seriousness of an incident. 31

The second factor in determining the reactions of bystanders to emergencies is what psychologists call the principle of moral diffusion. Moral diffusion is the lessening of a sense of individual responsibility when someone is a member of a group. Responsibility to act diffuses throughout the crowd. When a member of the group is able to escape the collective paralysis and take action, others in the group tend to act as well. But the larger the crowd, the greater the diffusion of responsibility, and the less likely someone is to intervene. 32

The more social scientists are able to teach us about how bystanders react to emergencies, the better the chances that we will take appropriate action when faced with one. Knowing about moral diffusion, for example, makes it easier for us to escape it. If you find yourself witnessing an emergency with a group, remember that everybody is waiting for someone else to do something first. If you take action, others may also help. 33

Also realize that any one of us could at some time be in desperate need of help. Imagine what it feels like to need help and have a crowd watching you suffer and do nothing. Remember Kitty Genovese. 34

SKILL-DEVELOPMENT QUESTIONS

Vocabulary in Context

1. The word *scenario* in "Imagine the same scenario as in situation two except that this time the woman screams, 'Get away from me! I don't know why I ever married you!'" (paragraph 1) means
   a. fight.
   b. relationship.
   c. suggested scene.
   d. quotation.

2. The word *ambiguity* in "First is the level of ambiguity involved . . . . Bystanders are afraid to endanger themselves or look foolish . . . in a situation they're not sure how to interpret" (paragraph 29) means
   a. argument.
   b. uncertainty.
   c. bragging.
   d. crowding.

Central Point and Main Ideas

3. Which sentence best expresses the central point of this selection?
   a. People don't want to get involved in emergencies.
   b. Kitty Genovese was murdered because no one helped enough.
   c. People don't care what happens to others.
   d. Understanding why bystanders react as they do in a crisis can help people act more responsibly.

4. Which sentence best expresses the main idea of paragraph 27?
   a. Bystanders always have the same excuses for not helping.
   b. There has been research on bystanders since the Genovese murder.
   c. The "bystander effect" is a symptom of an uncaring society.
   d. A number of psychological factors, not a simple lack of caring, keeps bystanders from getting involved.

Key Details

Bystanders are most likely to help
   a. a woman being attacked by her husband.
   b. in any emergency when others are around.
   c. a woman being attacked by a stranger.
   d. when property is being stolen.

6. According to the author, when there is a group of bystanders,
    a. everyone is more likely to help.
    b. it is easier to understand what is happening.
    c. each is more likely to act after someone else takes action.
    d. they are not influenced at all by each other.

Transitions

7. The first word of the second sentence below serves as
    a. an addition signal.
    b. an illustration signal.
    c. a contrast signal.
    d. a cause-effect signal.

    Frequently other witnesses, just as confused, try to look calm. Thus bystanders can mislead each other about the seriousness of an incident. (Paragraph 31)

8. The relationship between the two parts of the sentence below is one of
    a. cause and effect.
    b. comparison.
    c. contrast.
    d. illustration.

    If you take action, others may also help. (Paragraph 33)

Patterns of Organization

9. The pattern of organization of paragraph 8 is
    a. cause and effect.
    b. time order.
    c. list of items.
    d. comparison/contrast.

10. The pattern of organization of paragraph 32 is
    a. comparison/contrast.
    b. list of items.
    c. definition and example.
    d. time order.

Fact and Opinion

11. Which sentence is a statement of opinion?
    a. "The crime began at 3 A.M."

   b. "From an upper window in the apartment house, a man shouted, 'Let that girl alone!'"

   c. "Though the workers witnessed the entire incident and the woman repeatedly screamed for help, no one came to her assistance."

   d. "Two factors appear to be most important in understanding the reactions of bystanders to emergencies."

12. The following sentence is a statement of

   a. fact.

   b. opinion.

   c. fact and opinion.

     In more than fifty studies involving many different conditions, one outcome has been consistent: bystanders are much less likely to get involved when other witnesses are present than when they are alone.

Inferences

13. From the article, we can conclude that Kitty Genovese's killer

   a. knew his victim.

   b. was unaware of the witnesses.

   c. stabbed her too quickly for her to get help.

   d. kept attacking when he realized no one was coming to help her.

14. From the article, we can conclude that of the following situations, the bystander is most likely to get involved when

   a. a man passes a house that is being burglarized.

   b. a high-school student sees a man collapsing on a street when no one else is present.

   c. a neighbor sees a father and son fighting in their yard.

   d. a softball team sees a man chasing a woman.

Purpose and Tone

15. The main purpose of this article is to

   a. simply inform readers about the bystander effect and the factors contributing to it.

   b. persuade people to be more helpful in emergency situations by informing them about the true nature of the problem.

   c. entertain people with strange facts about human behavior.

16. The tone of the last paragraph of this article can be described as

   a. angry.

   b. confused.

     c.   pleading.

     d.   light-hearted.

Bias and Propaganda

17. Which version of the sentence below does *not* contain emotionally loaded language?

     a.   "A twenty-one-year-old woman was brutally raped in a parking lot."

     b.   "A twenty-one-year-old woman was viciously attacked in a parking lot."

     c.   "A helpless twenty-one-year-old woman was assaulted in a public place."

     d.   "A twenty-one-year-old woman was assaulted in a parking lot."

Evaluating Arguments

18. The author supports his statement that "bystanders are much less likely to get involved when other witnesses are present" with

     a.   opinions.

     b.   quotations from experts.

     c.   research and examples.

     d.   no evidence.

19. The sentence below is an example of

     a.   a hasty generalization.

     b.   a half-truth.

     c.   an either-or fallacy.

     d.   a personal attack.

A person lying face down on the floor of a subway train may have just suffered a heart attack . . .—or he may be a dangerous drunk. (Paragraph 29)

20. The author supports her statement that "The more social scientists are able to teach us about how bystanders react to emergencies, the better the chances that we will take appropriate action when faced with one" (paragraph 33) with

     a.   statistics.

     b.   an opinion.

     c.   a research experiment.

     d.   an example.

THINKING ACTIVITIES

Outlining

Here is an outline that shows the central point and primary supporting details of "The Bystander Effect." Only two secondary supporting details are given. Complete the outline by filling in the two missing secondary supporting details.

Central Point: There are patterns to the behavior of bystanders, and understanding those patterns can help people be more responsible bystanders.

1.   Experiments have shown a general pattern to witnesses' responses to emergency situations.
   a.   There is a low rate of witness intervention on behalf of property.
   b.   Bystanders are more willing to help a woman being assaulted by a stranger than one being assaulted by her husband.
   c.   Bystanders are much less likely to help in an emergency when other witnesses are present.
2.   Two cases of witnesses being particularly unhelpful have also provided information on bystander behavior.
   a.   Thirty-eight people heard Kitty Genovese being stabbed but no one called the police until she was dead.

   b.   _____

   _____

3.   Two factors seem to be largely responsible for the reluctance of bystanders to help at times.
   a.   One is the bystanders' fear of taking the wrong action if they are not sure of what is really happening.

   b.   _____

   _____ .

Summarizing

Add the ideas needed to complete the following summary of "The Bystander Effect."

Witnesses to crisis situations are less likely to help when only property is at risk and when a woman is being attacked by a man who seems to be her husband. Numerous studies have shown that their resistance to

helping is increased when they are _____ . A famous example is the case of Kitty Genovese, who was stabbed to death at 3 A.M. while returning to her apartment. The attack went on for over half an hour. Thirty-eight people listened to her cries for help, but

_____ . In another example, employees of a roofing company ignored a rape taking place on a nearby parking lot. Two psycho-

logical factors seem to explain _____ . One is the level of uncertainty in the situation. If the bystanders don't know how to

_____ , they don't want to take action. The other factor is the principle of moral diffusion. The larger the crowd that is watching,

the less responsibility _____ . Understanding these factors can help people be more useful in emergency situations.

DISCUSSION QUESTIONS

1. Have you ever been in a situation where the bystander effect played a part? Would your behavior be any different in light of what you have learned from this article?

2. Why might fewer people intervene in a car break-in than in an assault such as those described in Situations 2, 3, and 4? What do the research findings suggest about our concern for private property—as opposed to our concern for people's well-being?

3. In paragraph 33, the author suggests that if you understand what causes "the bystander effect," you can act appropriately in an emergency: "If you take action, others may also help." If, say, you were in a group of onlookers while a fight was in progress, what are some specific things you could do that would encourage others to intervene?

4. How does the conclusion of this article clarify the author's purpose for the reader? How does the article's beginning fit in with that purpose?

Check Your Performance THE BYSTANDER EFFECT

Skill	Number Right	Points	Total
Vocabulary in Context (2 items)	_____	× 4 :	_____
Central Point and Main Ideas (2)	_____	× 4 :	_____
Key Details (2)	_____	× 4 :	_____
Transitions (2)	_____	× 4 :	_____
Patterns of Organization (2)	_____	× 4 :	_____
Fact and Opinion (2)	_____	× 4 :	_____
Inferences (2)	_____	× 4 :	_____
Purpose and Tone (2)	_____	× 4 :	_____
Bias and Propaganda (1)	_____	× 4 :	_____
Evaluating Arguments (3)	_____	× 4 :	_____

(total of 20 questions)

Outlining (2)	_____	× 5 :	_____
Summarizing (5)	_____	× 2 :	_____

FINAL SCORE (OF POSSIBLE 100)   _____

Enter your final score into the reading performance chart on page 454.

11

Fifteen
Bob Greene

Preview

Do you remember what it was like to be fifteen years old? At fifteen, boys are too old to do much of what they used to enjoy but too young to drive. As a result, many of them find little to do on the weekend besides hanging around the shopping mall. In this article from *Esquire* magazine, columnist Bob Greene describes the seeming aimlessness of an afternoon at the mall for two boys, both fifteen, and reminds us that being young involves frustration as well as freedom.

Words to Watch

dilemma (22):   a difficult situation with no good alternatives
concoction (37):   combination
octave (48):   eight tones
persists (52):   continues
caddy (61):   carry clubs for golf players

"This would be excellent, to go in the ocean with this thing," says Dave Gem- 1
butis, fifteen.

He is looking at a $170 Sea Cruiser raft. 2

"Great," says his companion, Dan Holmes, also fifteen. 3

This is at Herman's World of Sporting Goods, in the middle of the Woodfield 4
Mall in Schaumburg, Illinois.

The two of them keep staring at the raft. It is unlikely that they will purchase 5
it. For one thing, Dan has only twenty dollars in his pocket, Dave five dollars. For
another thing—ocean voyages aside—neither of them is even old enough to drive.
Dave's older sister, Kim, has dropped them off at the mall. They will be taking the
bus home.

Fifteen. What a weird age to be male. Most of us have forgotten about it, or have idealized it. But when you are fifteen . . . well, things tend to be less than perfect. 6

You can't drive. You are only a freshman in high school. The girls your age look older than you and go out with upperclassmen who have cars. You probably don't shave. You have nothing to do on the weekends. 7

So how do you spend your time? In 1982, most likely at a mall. Woodfield is an enclosed shopping center sprawling over 2.25 million square feet in northern Illinois. There are 230 stores at Woodfield, and on a given Saturday those stores are cruised in and out of by thousands of teenagers killing time. Today two of those teenagers are Dave Gembutis and Dan Holmes. 8

Dave is wearing a purple Rolling Meadows High School Mustangs windbreaker over a gray M*A*S*H T-shirt, jeans, and Nike running shoes. He has a red plastic spoon in his mouth, and will keep it there for most of the afternoon. Dan is wearing a white Ohio State Buckeyes T-shirt, jeans, and Nike running shoes. 9

We are in the Video Forum store. Paul Simon and Art Garfunkel are singing "Wake Up Little Susie" from their Central Park concert on four television screens. Dave and Dan have already been wandering around Woodfield for an hour. 10

"There's not too much to do at my house," Dan says to me. 11

"Here we can at least look around," Dave says. 12

"At home I don't know what we'd do." 13

"Play catch or something," Dan says. "Here there's lots of things to see." 14

"See some girls or something, start talking," Dave says. 15

I ask them how they would start a conversation with girls they had never met. 16

"Ask them what school they're from," Dan says. "Then if they say Arlington Heights High School or something, you can say, 'Oh, I know somebody from there.'" I ask them how important meeting girls is to their lives. 17

"About forty-five percent," Dan says. 18

"About half your life," Dave says. 19

"Half is girls," Dan says. "Half is going out for sports." 20

An hour later, Dave and Dan have yet to meet any girls. They have seen a girl from their own class at Rolling Meadows High, but she is walking with an older boy, holding his hand. Now we are in the Woodfield McDonald's. Dave is eating a McRib sandwich, a small fries, and a small Coke. Dan is eating a cheeseburger, a small fries, and a medium root beer. 21

In here, the <u>dilemma</u> is obvious. The McDonald's is filled with girls who are precisely as old as Dave and Dan. The girls are wearing eye shadow, are fully developed, and generally look as if they could be dating the Green Bay Packers. Dave and Dan, on the other hand . . . well, when you're a fifteen-year-old boy, you look like a fifteen-year-old boy. 22

"They go with the older guys who have the cars," Dan says. 23

"It makes them more popular," Dave says. 24

"My ex-girlfriend is seeing a junior," Dan says. I ask him what happened. 25

"Well, I was in Florida over spring vacation," he says. "And when I got back I heard that she was at Cinderella Rockefella one night, and she was dancing with this guy, and she liked him, and he drove her home and stuff." 26

"She two-timed him," Dave says. 27

"The guy's on the basketball team," Dan says. I ask Dan what he did 28
about it.

"I broke up with her," he says, as if I had asked the stupidest question in the 29
world.

I ask him how he did it.

"Well, she was at her locker," he says. "She was working the combination. 30
And I said, 'Hey, Linda, I want to break up.' And she was opening her locker door
and she just nodded her head yes. And I said, 'I hear you had a good time while I
was gone, but I had a better time in Florida.'"

I ask him if he feels bad about it. 31

"Well, I feel bad," he says. "But a lot of guys told me, 'I heard you broke up 32
with her. Way to be.'"

"It's too bad the Puppy Palace isn't open," Dan says. 33

"They're remodeling," Dave says. 34

We are walking around the upper level of Woodfield. I ask them why they 35
would want to go to the Puppy Palace.

"The dogs are real cute and you feel sorry for them," Dan says. 36

We are in a fast-food restaurant called the Orange Bowl. Dave is eating a 37
frozen <u>concoction</u> called an O-Joy. They still have not met any girls.

"I feel like I'd be wasting my time if I sat at home," Dan says. "If it's Friday 38
or Saturday and you sit home, it's considered . . . low."

"Coming to the mall is about all there is," Dave says. "Until we can drive." 39

"Then I'll cruise," Dan says. "Look for action a little farther away from my 40
house, instead of just riding my bike around."

"When you're sixteen, you can do anything," Dave says. "You can go all the 41
way across town."

"When you have to ride your bike . . ." Dan says. "When it rains, it ruins 42
everything."

In the J.C. Penney store, the Penney Fashion Carnival is under way. Wally the 43
Clown is handing out favors to children, but Dave and Dan are watching the young
female models parade onto a stage in bathing suits.

"Just looking is enough for me," Dan says. 44

Dave suggests that they head out back into the mall and pick out some girls 45
to wave to. I ask why.

"Well, see, even if they don't wave back, you might see them later in the day," 46
Dan says. "And then they might remember that you waved at them, and you can
meet them."

We are at the Cookie Factory. These guys eat approximately every twenty min- 47
utes.

It is clear that Dan is attracted to the girl behind the counter. He walks up, 48
and his voice is slower and about half an <u>octave</u> lower than before.

The tone of voice is going to have to carry the day, because the words are not 49
all that romantic:

"Can I have a chocolate-chip cookie?" 50

The girl does not even look up as she wraps the cookie in tissue paper. 51

Dan persists. The voice might be Clark Gable's: 52

"What do they cost?"   53

The girl is still looking down.   54

"Forty-seven," she says and takes his money, still looking away, and we   55
move on.

Dave and Dan tell me that there are lots of girls at Woodfield's indoor ice-   56
skating rink. It costs money to get inside, but they lead me to an exit door, and
when a woman walks out we slip into the rink. It is chilly in here, but only three
people are on the ice.

"It's not time for open skating yet," Dan says. "This is all private lessons."   57

"Not much in here," Dave says.   58

We sit on benches. I ask them if they wish they were older.   59

"Well," Dan says, "when you get there, you look back and you remember.   60
Like I'm glad that I'm not in the fourth or fifth grade now. But I'm glad I'm not
twenty-five, either."

"Once in a while I'm sorry I'm not twenty-one," Dave says. "There's not much   61
you can do when you're fifteen. This summer I'm going to caddy and try to save
some money."

"Yeah," Dan says. "I want to save up for a dirt bike."   62

"Right now, being fifteen is starting to bother me a little bit," Dave says. "Like 63
when you have to get your parents to drive you to Homecoming with a girl."

I ask him how that works.   64

"Well, your mom is in the front seat driving," he says. "And you're in the back   65
seat with your date."

I ask him how he feels about that.   66

"It's embarrassing," he says. "Your date understands that there's nothing you   67
can do about it, but it's still embarrassing."

Dave says he wants to go to Pet World.   68

"I think they closed it down," Dan says, but we head in that direction anyway.   69
I ask them what the difference is between Pet World and the Puppy Palace.

"They've got snakes and fish and another assortment of dogs," Dan says. "But   70
not as much as the Puppy Palace."

When we arrive, Pet World is, indeed, boarded up.   71

We are on the upper level of the mall. Dave and Dan have spotted two girls   72
sitting on a bench directly below them, in the mall's main level.

"Whistle," Dan says. Dave whistles, but the girls keep talking.   73

"Dave, wave to them and see if they look," Dave says.   74

"They aren't looking," Dave says.   75

"There's another one over there," Dan says.   76

"Where?" Dave says.   77

"Oh, that's a mother," Dan says. "She's got her kid with her."   78

They return their attention to the two downstairs.   79

Dan calls to them: "Would you girls get the dollar I just dropped?"   80

The girls look up.   81

"Just kidding," Dan says.   82

The girls resume their conversation.   83

"I think they're laughing," Dan says.   84

"What are you going to do when the dumb girls won't respond," Dave says.   85

"At least we tried," Dan says.   86

I ask him what response would have satisfied him.   87

"The way we would have known that we succeeded," he says, "they'd have   88
looked up here and started laughing."

The boys keep staring at the two girls.   89

"Ask her to look up," Dan says. "Ask her what school they go to."   90

"I did," Dave says. "I did."   91

The two boys lean over the railing.   92

"Bye, girls," Dave yells.   93

"See you later," Dan yells.   94

The girls do not look up.   95

"Too hard," Dan says. "Some girls are stuck on themselves, if you know what   96
I mean by that."

We go to a store called the Foot Locker, where all the salespeople are dressed   97
in striped referee's shirts.

"Dave!" Dan says. "Look at this! Seventy bucks!" He holds up a pair of New   98
Balance running shoes. Both boys shake their heads.

We move on to a store called Passage to China. A huge stuffed tiger is placed   99
by the doorway. There is a PLEASE DO NOT TOUCH sign attached to it. Dan
rubs his hand over the tiger's back. "This would look so great in my room," he
says.

We head over to Alan's TV and Stereo. Two salesmen ask the boys if they are   100
interested in buying anything, so they go back outside and look at the store's window. A color television set is tuned to a baseball game between the Chicago Cubs
and the Pittsburgh Pirates.

They watch for five minutes. The sound is muted, so they cannot hear the   101
announcers.

"I wish they'd show the score," Dave says.   102

They watch for five minutes more.   103

"Hey, Dave," Dan says. "You want to go home?"   104

"I guess so," Dave says.   105

They do. We wave goodbye. I watch them walk out of the mall toward the   106
bus stop. I wish them girls, dirt bikes, puppies, and happiness.

SKILL-DEVELOPMENT QUESTIONS

Vocabulary in Context

1. The word *sprawling* in "Woodfield is an enclosed shopping center
    sprawling over 2.25 million square feet . . . There are 230 stores at
    Woodfield" (paragraph 8) means
    a. beneath.
    b. spread out.
    c. less than.
    d. planned for.

2. The word *muted* in "The sound is muted, so they cannot hear the
    announcers" (paragraph 101) means
    a. increased.
    b. improved.
    c. loud.
    d. turned off.

Central Point and Main Ideas

3. Which sentence best expresses the central point of the selection?
    a. Kids spend too much time at the mall.
    b. Boys of fifteen are caught in a difficult stage between boyhood and
        manhood, with apparently little to do on weekends.
    c. Fifteen-year-old boys are always eating.
    d. Bob Greene met two boys at the mall, a place where teenage boys
        can pass time looking for girls, looking at stores, and eating.

4. Which sentence best expresses the main idea of paragraph 22?
    a. Fifteen-year-old boys have trouble attracting girls their age because
        the girls are more mature.
    b. Fifteen-year-old girls look as if they could date the Green Bay
        Packers.
    c. McDonald's is filled with fifteen-year-old girls.
    d. Fifteen-year-old girls wear too much make-up.

Key Details

5. The boys go to the mall mainly
    a. to find long-term girlfriends.
    b. to shop.
    c. because they can think of nothing better to do.
    d. to eat.

_____ 6. TRUE OR FALSE? Dave and Dan are perfectly satisfied being fifteen.

Transitions

7. In the second sentence below, the word "but" shows
    a. illustration.
    b. location.
    c. contrast.
    d. addition.

    It costs money to get inside, but they lead me to an exit door, and
    when a woman walks out we slip into the rink. (Paragraph 56).

8. The relationship between the first and second parts of the sentence below is one of
    a. addition.
    b. cause and effect.
    c. contrast.
    d. time.

    Two salesmen ask the boys if they are interested in buying anything, so they go back outside. . . . (Paragraph 100)

Patterns of Organization

9. The relationship between paragraphs 7 and 8 is one of
    a. comparison.
    b. time order.
    c. definition and example.
    d. cause and effect.

10. The details in paragraph 22 show a
    a. time order.
    b. list of items.
    c. cause and effect.
    d. contrast.

Fact and Opinion

11. From paragraph 9 on, the author supports his argument mainly with
    a. facts and statistics about teenaged boys.
    b. facts about Dave and Dan's afternoon at the mall.
    c. opinions about teenagers and their problems.
    d. facts and opinions about Dave and Dan's use of spare time.

12. The sentence "But when you are fifteen . . . well, things tend to be less than perfect" (paragraph 6) gives
    a. the author's opinion.
    b. Dave and Dan's opinion.
    c. a fact that could be checked and proven.
    d. both a fact and an opinion.

Inferences

13. The author implies that the boys
    a. have never had girlfriends.
    b. have no money.
    c. look forward to driving.
    d. are afraid to talk to girls.

_____ 14. TRUE OR FALSE? The author implies that he wrote about Dave and Dan because they are different from most boys their age.

Purpose and Tone

15. The author's primary purpose is to
    a. inform readers about fifteen-year-old boys through an entertaining and persuasive narration.
    b. persuade readers that fifteen-year-old boys should not spend so much time in shopping malls.
    c. entertain readers with the antics of fifteen-year-old boys.

16. The tone of this article is
    a. bitter.
    b. sympathetic.
    c. envious.
    d. sentimental.

Bias and Propaganda

17. The author's last line suggests that he
    a. is biased in favor of the boys.
    b. is biased against the boys.
    c. has no bias about the boys.
    d. is biased against dirt bikes.

18. Which of the statements below is a half-truth?
    a. Dave and Dan are only fifteen, so they cannot drive yet.
    b. Because older boys have cars, they are more popular with the girls.
    c. At fifteen boys have little to do, so they often hang out at the shopping mall.
    d. Dave and Dan often wander aimlessly through the mall, proving they are lazy and unambitious.

Evaluating Arguments

19. From the article, we can conclude that the author
    a. believes the boys shouldn't hang out at malls.
    b. believes the boys should hang out at malls.
    c. is simply observing that boys do hang out at malls.
    d. believes the boys will always hang out at malls.

20. Which of the following best supports the author's opinion that in 1982 fifteen-year-old boys are most likely to spend their free time in a mall?
    a. "Woodfield is an enclosed shopping center. . . ."
    b. ". . . on a given Saturday those stores are cruised in and out of by thousands of teenagers killing time."
    c. "Today two of those teenagers are Dave Gembutis and Dan Holmes."
    d. "There is not too much to do at my house," Dan says to me.

THINKING ACTIVITIES

Outlining

Complete the following outline of the article by filling in the letters of the missing details. The details appear in random order in the list below the outline.

Central point: For boys, fifteen is a difficult in-between age, which includes the feeling there is little to do on weekends except hanging out at the shopping mall.

1. _____

2. _____

3. _____

4. _____

5. _____

Items Missing from the Outline
a. Dave and Dan wander the mall eating, looking at stores, and looking for girls and puppies without much luck.
b. Having little to do on weekends, fifteen-year-old boys, specifically Dave and Dan, hang out at shopping malls.
c. They go home.
d. They watch a baseball game without sound for ten minutes.
e. Dave and Dan admire a Sea Cruiser raft they cannot afford to buy.

Summarizing

Add the words needed to complete the following summary of "Fifteen."

Fifteen-year-old boys are in an in-between stage during which they feel they have little to do on weekends besides wandering around shopping malls. Good examples are Dave Gembutis and Dan Holmes. Because they are too young to _____ and can find little to do at home, they hang out at a shopping mall on weekends. At the mall, they hope to meet some _____ , but older boys with cars attract the fifteen-year-old girls, such as Dan's former _____ . Dave and Dan wander from store to store, stopping frequently to buy something to _____ . As they walk around, they are unable to get any girls interested in them or even to see any _____ in the pet shops. After watching a baseball game on a soundless TV for a while, they decide they might as well go home.

DISCUSSION QUESTIONS

1. Just as paragraphs are organized in patterns, so are longer pieces. What is the main pattern of organization of this article? Why do you think Greene chose to organize it in this way?

2. Greene obviously could not include in his article every single event and remark that occurred when he was with Dave and Dan. On what basis did he select the events he did include? For example, what was Greene's purpose in presenting the anecdote about the Puppy Palace (paragraphs 33–36)? About how Dave and Dan watch the models in bathing suits rather than watch Wally the Clown? About stops at the Orange Bowl restaurant and the Cookie Factory?

3. Can you remember when you were fifteen? How did you spend your spare time? What were your interests then?

4. What do you think are the positive aspects of teenagers hanging around malls? The negative aspects? What do you feel the boys should be doing?

Check Your Performance FIFTEEN

Skill	Number Right	Points	Total
Vocabulary in Context (2 items)	_____	× 4 :	_____
Central Point and Main Ideas (2)	_____	× 4 :	_____
Key Details (2)	_____	× 4 :	_____
Transitions (2)	_____	× 4 :	_____
Patterns of Organization (2)	_____	× 4 :	_____
Fact and Opinion (2)	_____	× 4 :	_____
Inferences (2)	_____	× 4 :	_____
Purpose and Tone (2)	_____	× 4 :	_____
Bias and Propaganda (2)	_____	× 4 :	_____
Evaluating Arguments (2)	_____	× 4 :	_____

(total of 20 questions)

Outlining (5)	_____	× 2 :	_____
Summarizing (5)	_____	× 2 :	_____

FINAL SCORE (OF POSSIBLE 100) _____

Enter your final score into the reading performance chart on page 454.

12

Nonverbal Communication
Anthony F. Grasha

Preview

When we think of communication, we usually think of language. But a great deal of human communication takes place without speaking. When we are angry, we may make a fist. When we are happy, our faces give us away. The extent to which we reveal our feelings without words, however, goes much further than we are often aware of. In this selection, Anthony F. Grasha provides an overview of just how much we really say without words.

Words to Watch

enhance (1): strengthen
norms (2): normal standards
culprit (6): guilty one
manipulate (7): use
utterances (7): verbal expressions
quivering (8): trembling

The way we dress, our mannerisms, how close we stand to people, eye contact, touching, and the ways we mark our personal spaces convey certain messages. *Such nonverbal behaviors communicate certain messages by themselves and also <u>enhance</u> the meaning of our verbal communications.* Pounding your fist on a table, for example, suggests anger without anything being spoken. Holding someone close to you conveys the message that you care. To say "I don't like you" with a loud voice or waving fists increases the intensity of the verbal message. Let us examine the concepts of *personal space* and *body language* to gain additional insights into the nonverbal side of interpersonal communication. 1

Nonverbal Messages: The Use of Personal Space

Edward Hall notes that we have personal spatial territories or zones that allow   2
certain types of behaviors and communications. We only allow certain people to
enter or events to occur within a zone. Let us look at how some nonverbal messages
can be triggered by behaviors that violate the <u>norms</u> of each zone. The four personal
zones identified by Hall are as follows:

1 *Intimate distance*. This personal zone covers a range of distance from body   3
contact to one foot. Relationships between a parent and child, lovers, and close
friends occur within this zone. As a general rule, we only allow people we know
and have some affection for to enter this zone. When someone tries to enter without
our permission, they are strongly repelled by our telling them to stay away from us
or by our pushing them away. Why do you think we allow a doctor to easily violate
our intimate distance zone?

2 *Personal distance*. The spatial range covered by this zone extends from one to   4
four feet. Activities like eating in a restaurant with two or three other people, sitting
on chairs or on the floor in small groups at parties, or playing cards occur within
this zone. Violations of the zone make people feel uneasy and act nervously. When
you are eating at a restaurant, the amount of table space that is considered yours is
usually divided equally by the number of people present. I can remember becoming
angry and generally irritated when a friend of mine placed a plate and glass in my
space. As we talked I was visibly irritated, but my anger had nothing to do with the
topic we discussed. Has this ever happened to you?

3 *Social distance*. Four to twelve feet is the social distance zone. Business meet-   5
ings, large formal dinners, and small classroom seminars occur within the boundaries
of the social distance zone. Discussions concerning everyday topics like the weather,
politics, or a best seller are considered acceptable. For a husband and wife to launch
into a heated argument during a party in front of ten other people would violate
the accepted norms for behavior in the social zone. This once happened at a formal
party I attended. The nonverbal behaviors that resulted consisted of several people
leaving the room, others looking angry or uncomfortable, and a few standing and
watching quietly with an occasional upward glance and a rolling of their eyeballs.
What would violate the social distance norms in a classroom?

4 *Public distance*. This zone includes the area beyond twelve feet. Addressing a   6
crowd, watching a sports event, and sitting in a large lecture section are behaviors
we engage in within this zone. As is true for the other zones, behaviors unacceptable
for this zone can trigger nonverbal messages. At a recent World Series game a young
male took his clothes off and ran around the outfield. Some watched with amuse-
ment on their faces, others looked away, and a few waved their fists at the <u>culprit</u>.
The respective messages were, "That's funny," "I'm afraid or ashamed to look," and
"How dare you interrupt the game." What would your reaction be in this situation?

Nonverbal Messages: The Use of Body Language

Body language refers to the various arm and hand gestures, facial expressions,   7
tone of voice, postures, and body movements we use to convey certain messages.
According to Erving Goffman, they are the things we "give off" when talking to

other people. Goffman notes that our body language is generally difficult to <u>manip-</u><u>ulate</u> at will. Unlike our verbal <u>utterances</u>, we have less conscious control <u>over the</u> specific body gestures or expressions we might make while talking. Unless we are acting on a stage or purposely trying to create a certain effect, they occur automatically without much thought on our part.

Michael Argyle notes that body language serves several functions for us. *It* *helps us to communicate certain emotions, attitudes, and preferences.* A hug by someone close to us lets us know we are appreciated. A friendly wave and smile as someone we know passes us lets us know we are recognized. A <u>quivering</u> lip tells us that someone is upset. Each of us has become quite sensitive to the meaning of various body gestures and expressions. Robert Rosenthal has demonstrated that this sensitivity is rather remarkable. When shown films of people expressing various emotions, individuals were able to identify the emotion correctly 66 percent of the time even when each frame was exposed for one twenty-fourth of a second. *Body language* *also supports our verbal communications.* Vocal signals of timing, pitch, voice stress, and various gestures add meaning to our verbal utterances. Argyle suggests that we may speak with our vocal organs, but we converse with our whole body. *Body lan-* *guage helps to control our conversations.* It helps us to decide when it is time to stop talking, to interrupt the other person, and to know when to shift topics or elaborate on something because our listeners are bored, do not understand us, or are not paying attention. 8

SKILL-DEVELOPMENT QUESTIONS

Vocabulary in Context

1. The word *convey* in "the ways we mark our personal space convey certain messages" (paragraph 1) means
    a. prevent.
    b. carry.
    c. entertain.
    d. deny.

2. The word *repelled* in "When someone tries to enter without our permission, they are strongly repelled by our telling them to stay away from us" (paragraph 3) means
    a. greeted.
    b. turned away.
    c. encouraged.
    d. ignored.

Central Point and Main Ideas

3. Which sentence best expresses the central point of the selection?
    a. It is difficult to communicate without words.

b.   People communicate with each other in various ways.

c.   Nonverbal behavior both communicates messages and emphasizes verbal messages.

d.   The way we use personal space can trigger nonverbal messages.

4.   Which sentence best expresses the main idea of paragraph 7?
a.   We must plan our body language.
b.   It is hard to control body language.
c.   Actors use body language to create an effect.
d.   Body language, which we normally cannot control, reveals our feelings.

5.   The main idea of paragraph 8 is expressed in
a.   the first sentence.
b.   the second sentence.
c.   the next-to-last sentence.
d.   the last sentence.

Key Details

_____   6.   TRUE OR FALSE? Nonverbal behavior helps us make our conversations more effective.

7.   According to Rosenthal's work, we
a.   frequently understand body language.
b.   rarely understand body language.
c.   always understand body language.
d.   never understand body language.

Transitions

8.   The relationship of the second part of the sentence below to the first part is one of
a.   illustration.
b.   summary.
c.   contrast.
d.   addition.

Such nonverbal behaviors communicate certain messages by themselves and also enhance the meaning of our verbal communications. (Paragraph 1)

9.   The signal word at the beginning of the sentence below shows
a.   emphasis.
b.   comparison.

     c.   contrast.

     d.   time.

Unlike our verbal utterances, we have less conscious control over the specific body gestures or expressions we might make while talking. (Paragraph 7)

Patterns of Organization

10. The pattern of organization in paragraphs 3, 4, 5, and 6 is
    a.   time order.
    b.   comparison/contrast.
    c.   definition and example.
    d.   list of items.

11. On the whole, paragraph 8
    a.   compares and contrasts body language to verbal expression.
    b.   lists the functions of body language.
    c.   defines body language and gives examples of it.
    d.   uses time order to narrate an incident about body language.

Fact and Opinion

12. The sentence below contains
    a.   facts that contradict the general idea of the paragraph.
    b.   facts to support the idea that body language communicates feelings.
    c.   opinions supporting the idea that body language communicates feelings.
    d.   facts and opinions on how body language communicates.

When shown films of people expressing various emotions, individuals were able to identify the emotion correctly 66 percent of the time even when each frame was exposed for one twenty-fourth of a second. (Paragraph 8)

Inferences

_____ 13. TRUE OR FALSE? Just as body language generally occurs automatically, so does the use of personal space.

14. Goffman's ideas on body language (paragraph 7) imply that
    a.   we usually are aware of our own body language.
    b.   our body language might reveal emotions we wish to hide.
    c.   we can never manipulate our body language.
    d.   we should learn to manipulate our body language.

Purpose and Tone

15. The author's primary purpose is to
    a. entertain readers with anecdotes of nonverbal behavior.
    b. inform readers about different kinds of nonverbal communication.
    c. persuade readers to become more aware of the nonverbal messages they send.

16. On the whole, the author's tone is
    a. humorous.
    b. objective.
    c. scornful.
    d. enthusiastic.

Bias and Propaganda

17. The most likely source of this article is
    a. a newspaper editorial.
    b. an encyclopedia article.
    c. an introductory psychology textbook.
    d. a personnel manual used by employers as a guide to hiring.

18. Which of the statements below is a half-truth?
    a. Body language helps people control conversations because it shows when listeners are bored or inattentive.
    b. People at a restaurant table usually divide space up equally, so they feel annoyed when others take more than their share of the space.
    c. Many people feel repelled when strangers enter their personal space, so they should see a doctor to help them overcome their fears.
    d. Body language usually occurs without people being aware of it, so it is generally hard to control.

Evaluating Arguments

19. Which of the following statements is a valid conclusion that can be drawn from the evidence below?
    a. Families should eat at large tables.
    b. Business people should sit as close to their clients as possible.
    c. Formal dinners should not take place in rooms larger than twelve feet across.
    d. Discussing your recent divorce at a formal dinner will make others uncomfortable.

    Four to twelve feet is the social distance zone. Business meetings, large formal dinners, and small classroom seminars occur within the boundaries of the social distance zone. Discussions concerning everyday topics like the weather, politics, or a best seller are considered acceptable. (Paragraph 5)

20. To support his central point, the author uses
    a. examples.
    b. research.
    c. opinions of other experts.
    d. all of the above.

THINKING ACTIVITIES

Outlining

Complete the following outline of "Nonverbal Communication" by using the information in the boldface headings, italics, and numbers in the selection.

Central Point: Our use of personal space and body language communicates meaning and emphasizes verbal communication.

A. Nonverbal messages and interpersonal communication

B. _____
    1. Intimate distance
    2. Personal distance

    3. _____

    4. _____
C. Nonverbal messages: the use of body language
    1. Definition and explanation of body language
    2. Functions of body language

        a. _____

        b. _____
        c. Helps control our conversations

Summarizing

Add the words needed to complete the following summary of the article.

The ways people use space and the ways they act can _____ messages on their own and as emphasis to what is spoken. In the space around them, people allow only certain kinds of activities, which vary according to how _____ they are to each other. Usually only people who are fond of each other are allowed to approach each other at an intimate distance. People who are at restaurants and parties are expected to stay further away, at a _____ distance. Business meetings and formal dinners take place at a social distance, which is within a boundary of four to twelve feet. Finally, the _____ distance involves areas of anything over twelve feet. People also communicate nonverbally through body movements and facial expressions.

This body _____ helps reveal feelings, adds meaning to speech, and helps control conversations.

DISCUSSION QUESTIONS

1. What are your answers to the following questions from the selection? Why do you think the author included these questions?

   Why do you think we allow a doctor to easily violate our intimate distance zone?

   I can remember becoming angry and generally irritated when a friend of mine placed a plate and glass in my space. . . . Has this ever happened to you?

   What would violate the social distance norms in a classroom?

2. This selection includes headings, italics, labels and numbered items. How are these related to the author's purpose?

3. What are some examples of situations in which someone's body language might contradict his or her verbal communication?

4. How useful is the concept of personal space? In what real-life situations could this knowledge be helpful?

Check Your Performance　　　NONVERBAL COMMUNICATION

Skill	Number Right	Points	Total
Vocabulary in Context (2 items)	_____	× 4 :	_____
Central Point and Main Ideas (3)	_____	× 4 :	_____
Key Details (2)	_____	× 4 :	_____
Transitions (2)	_____	× 4 :	_____
Patterns of Organization (2)	_____	× 4 :	_____
Fact and Opinion (1)	_____	× 4 :	_____
Inferences (2)	_____	× 4 :	_____
Purpose and Tone (2)	_____	× 4 :	_____
Bias and Propaganda (2)	_____	× 4 :	_____
Evaluating Arguments (2)	_____	× 4 :	_____

(total of 20 questions)

Outlining (5)	_____	× 2 :	_____
Summarizing (5)	_____	× 2 :	_____

FINAL SCORE (OF POSSIBLE 100)　　_____

Enter your final score into the reading performance chart on page 454.

13

On Her Own in the City
George Will

Preview

"The dog ate my baby." Just another sensational headline in a supermarket tabloid, you might think. But you'd be wrong. Read the following true story by nationally syndicated columnist George Will to realize the full human tragedy of what happened to one young mother alone in a big city.

Words To Watch

intermittently (4):   on and off
prenatal (4):   before childbirth
succor (7):   assistance
arraigned (7):   charged, officially accused
inevitably (9):   unavoidably
indispensable (10):   necessary

When police, responding to her call, arrived at her East Harlem tenement, she 1
was hysterical: "The dog ate my baby." The baby girl had been four days old, twelve
hours "home" from the hospital. Home was two rooms and a kitchen on the sixth
floor, furnished with a rug, a folding chair, and nothing else, no bed, no crib.

"Is the baby dead?" asked an officer. "Yes," the mother said, "I saw the baby's 2
insides." Her dog, a German shepherd, had not been fed for five days. She explained: "I left the baby on the floor with the dog to protect it." She had bought
the dog in July for protection from human menaces.

She is twenty-four. She went to New York three years ago from a small Ohio 3
community. She wanted to be on her own. She got that wish.

She was employed <u>intermittently</u>, until the fifth month of her pregnancy, 4
which she says was the result of a rape she did not report to the police. She wanted
the baby. She bought child-care books, and had seven <u>prenatal</u> checkups at Bellevue

Hospital. Although she rarely called home or asked for money, she called when the baby was born. Her mother mailed twenty-five dollars for a crib. It arrived too late.

When labor began she fed the dog with the last food in the apartment and 5 went alone to the hospital. The baby was born on Wednesday. When she left Bellevue Sunday evening, the hospital office holding her welfare payment was closed. With six dollars in her pocket and a baby in her arms, she took a cab home. The meter said four dollars and the driver demanded a dollar tip. When she asked his assistance in getting upstairs, he drove off.

The hospital had given her enough formula for three feedings for the baby. 6 Rather than spend her remaining dollar that night on food for herself and the dog, she saved it for the bus ride back to Bellevue to get her welfare money. Having slept with the baby on a doubled-up rug, she left the baby and dog at 7 A.M. It was 53 degrees, too cold she thought to take the baby. She had no warm baby clothes and she thought the hospital had said the baby was ailing. She got back at 8:30 A.M. Then she called the police.

Today the forces of law and order and <u>succor</u> are struggling to assign "blame" 7 in order to escape it. Her attorney and Bellevue are arguing about how she was released, or expelled, on Sunday evening. Welfare officials are contending with charges that they are somehow culpable for her failure to receive a crib before giving birth, and for her living conditions. (She was receiving payment of $270 a month; her rent was $120.) She has been <u>arraigned</u> on a charge of negligent homicide, but no one seems anxious to prosecute.

Late in New York's U.S. Senate primary, Daniel P. Moynihan, talking like a 8 senator prematurely, said that this case dramatizes weaknesses of the welfare system, and indicated that it also dramatizes the need for him in Washington. Perhaps.

But because cities are collections of strangers, they are, <u>inevitably</u>, bad places 9 to be poor. Not that there are good places, but cities, being <u>kingdoms</u> of the strong, are especially hellish for the poor.

Cities have their <u>indispensable</u> purposes, and their charms, not the least of 10 which is that you can <u>be alone in</u> a crowd. But that kind of living alone is an acquired taste, and not for the weak or unfortunate. They are apt to learn that no city's institutions can provide protective supports like those of an extended family or real community. No metropolis can provide a floor of support solid enough to prevent the bewildered—like the woman from Ohio—from falling through the cracks.

Through those cracks you get an occasional glimpse of what George Eliot 11 meant: "If we had a keen vision and feeling of all ordinary human life, it would be like hearing the grass grow and the squirrel's heartbeat, and we should die of that roar which lies on the other side of silence."

SKILL-DEVELOPMENT QUESTIONS

Vocabulary in Context

1. The word *menaces* in "she had bought the dog . . . for protection from human menaces" (paragraph 2) means
    a. visitors.
    b. threats.
    c. concern.
    d. friendship.

2. The word *culpable* in "Welfare officials are contending with charges that they are somehow culpable" (paragraph 7) means
    a. efficient.
    b. innocent.
    c. worthy of blame.
    d. grateful.

Central Point and Main Ideas

3. Which sentence best expresses the central point of the selection?
    a. People should live alone in the city.
    b. Cities are not good places to live for those who are alone, weak, and poor.
    c. German shepherds are vicious animals.
    d. The welfare system is filled with weaknesses.

4. Which sentence best expresses the main idea of paragraph 7?
    a. The woman's attorney is arguing with people at Bellevue Hospital.
    b. Everyone involved in the woman's case is blaming someone else for the tragedy.
    c. The woman receives too little welfare money.
    d. The woman herself is mainly at fault for the tragedy.

Key Details

5. The woman left Ohio and went to New York because
    a. she had family in New York.
    b. she wanted to establish an independent life.
    c. she needed money.
    d. she had no family in Ohio.

6. Before the baby was born, the woman had trouble with all of the following except
   a. people.
   b. money.
   c. jobs.
   d. the police.

Transitions

7. The relationship between the two parts of the sentence below is
   one of
   a. comparison.
   b. contrast.
   c. addition.
   d. illustration.

   Although she rarely called home or asked for money, she called when
   the baby was born. (Paragraph 4)

8. The relationship between the two sentences below is one of
   a. addition.
   b. contrast.
   c. time.
   d. conclusion.

   She got back at 8:30 A.M. Then she called the police. (Paragraph 6)

Patterns of Organization

9. Paragraph 5 is organized according to
   a. time order.
   b. a list of items.
   c. comparison/contrast.
   d. cause and effect.

10. Paragraph 9 is organized according to
    a. time order.
    b. a list of items.
    c. comparison/contrast.
    d. cause and effect.

Fact and Opinion

_____ 11. TRUE OR FALSE? The first six paragraphs of this selection consist
              mainly of facts about the woman's tragedy and what caused it.

_____ 12.   TRUE OR FALSE? The sentence below contains both a fact and an opinion.

Today the forces of law and order and succor are struggling to assign "blame" in order to escape it. (Paragraph 7)

Inferences

13.   In paragraph 3, the author implies that the woman
   a.   was too young to leave Ohio.
   b.   was not very intelligent.
   c.   was more on her own than she had wanted to be.
   d.   was pleased that she got her wish.

14.   The author implies that Moynihan's remarks on this case (paragraph 8)
   a.   show that Moynihan never heard of the woman.
   b.   are totally without merit.
   c.   miss the point that New York City was simply not a good place for this woman to live.
   d.   are the answer to this woman's problems.

Purpose and Tone

_____ 15.   TRUE OR FALSE? Will's primary purpose in writing this selection was to attack the city's welfare system for not helping the woman.

16.   The tone of this selection can best be described as
   a.   outraged.
   b.   detached.
   c.   concerned.
   d.   sentimental.

Bias and Propaganda

17.   Which sentence best reveals the author's personal judgment of the mother?
   a.   "She had bought the dog in July for protection from human menaces."
   b.   "She wanted the baby."
   c.   "She has been arraigned on a charge of negligent homicide, but no one seems anxious to prosecute."
   d.   "No metropolis can provide a floor of support solid enough to prevent the bewildered—like the woman from Ohio—from falling through the cracks."

_____ 18. TRUE OR FALSE? By putting the word *home* in quotation marks in the first paragraph, the author makes a personal judgment about the mother's home.

Evaluating Arguments

19. Which of the following evidence from the article supports the conclusion that the city is too impersonal for people without financial and human resources?
    a. The woman's pregnancy was the result of a rape.
    b. The welfare office was closed when the woman left the hospital.
    c. When the woman asked the cab driver to help her get upstairs, he drove away.
    d. The woman had no warm clothing for the baby.

20. Which of the following logical fallacies seems present in Daniel Moynihan's statement, in paragraph 8, that this case shows the weaknesses of the welfare system?
    a. Shifts argument to irrelevant personal criticism (personal attack)
    b. Generalization based on insufficient evidence (hasty generalization)
    c. Assumption that order of events alone shows cause and effect (false cause)
    d. Assumption that there are only two sides to an issue (either-or fallacy)

THINKING ACTIVITIES

Outlining

Following is an incomplete brief outline of "On Her Own in the City." Complete it by filling in the letters of the items below the outline.

Central Point: _____

    A. A poor woman could not cope well by herself with a large, impersonal city.

       1. Her hysterical call to the police revealed her dog ate her baby.

       2. _____

       3. After the birth of her baby, she couldn't stretch her welfare check to cover both bus fare to pick up her next check and dog food.

       4. _____

       5. With all the impersonal institutions involved, placing blame for this tragedy was difficult.

B.   The city is too impersonal for people without financial and human resources.

Items Missing from the Outline

a.   She had employment problems and was so poor that her apartment had no furniture.
b.   Having no warm baby clothes or furniture, she left her baby on the floor with her dog when she left.
c.   A big city is a terrible place to be poor and alone.

Summarizing

Add the words needed to complete the following summary of "On Her Own in the City."

In New York City, a young woman from a small town returned from

picking up her _____ to find her dog had eaten her new-born baby. She was alone, unemployed, and too poor to afford furniture. She had been released from the hospital with the baby after the

office with her welfare check had _____ . So the next day she used her last dollar for the bus ride to pick up her check. Having no warm baby clothes, she left the baby on her apartment floor with the dog. When she got back and saw what had happened, she called

the _____ . The various authorities involved aren't sure

whom to _____ , but the woman was charged with negli-gent homicide. This case shows why _____ , where life is impersonal, are bad places for the poor and alone.

DISCUSSION QUESTIONS

1.   What (if anything) do you think should be done to the mother of the baby? Should she be punished? If so, of what crime is she guilty?

2.   If the woman had remained in her Ohio hometown, how might her story have been different? What can small towns do for their residents that large cities do not—or cannot?

3.   What changes might be made in our governmental system to prevent more tragedies like this one from happening? Do you think the system has enough people and money to put these reforms into practice?

4.   What does the George Eliot quotation at the end of this selection mean? Why do you think Will chose to end this piece with that quotation?

Check Your PerformanceON HER OWN IN THE CITY

Skill	Number Right	Points	Total
Vocabulary in Context (2 items)	_____	× 4 :	_____
Central Point and Main Ideas (2)	_____	× 4 :	_____
Key Details (2)	_____	× 4 :	_____
Transitions (2)	_____	× 4 :	_____
Patterns of Organization (2)	_____	× 4 :	_____
Fact and Opinion (2)	_____	× 4 :	_____
Inferences (2)	_____	× 4 :	_____
Purpose and Tone (2)	_____	× 4 :	_____
Bias and Propaganda (2)	_____	× 4 :	_____
Evaluating Arguments (2)	_____	× 4 :	_____

(total of 20 questions)

Outlining (3)	_____	× 3.3 :	_____
Summarizing (5)	_____	× 2 :	_____

FINAL SCORE (OF POSSIBLE 100)   _____

Enter your final score into the reading performance chart on page 454.

14

Death on the Road
Albert R. Karr

Preview

Do you consider yourself a better-than-average driver? If you do, you have plenty of company, according to this article from the *Wall Street Journal*. In fact, most drivers consider their skills to be above average. Then what is the cause of all the accidents? And what can be done to improve traffic safety? The answers in this selection may surprise you.

Words to Watch

reverting (2): returning
ingrained (2): deep-seated
proneness (6): tendency
inducing (8): causing
embargo (9): ban on trade

In 1904, the story goes, there were just two automobiles in Kansas City, Mo. 1
They crashed into each other at an intersection.

Many of today's 155 million U.S. drivers continue to have trouble avoiding 2
collisions, and traffic-safety experts continue to search for ways to make driving safer. After an emphasis on improving the designs of cars and roads in recent years, the auto-safety focus now is reverting to what used to be called "the nut behind the wheel." But it isn't easy to improve the ingrained behavior of drivers, whom some analysts blame for more than 90% of all traffic accidents.

The problem is that pinpointing which drivers are to blame for crashes, why 3
accidents happen and how to stop them remains elusive. For example, drivers with the worst accident or violation records do account for more than their share of accidents, but their numbers are relatively few, and they cause only a small percentage of all crashes. "The largest part of the traffic-accident problem has been shown to involve lapses by normal drivers rather than errors by just a few problem cases,"

according to Theodore Forbes, a Michigan State University psychology professor and highway-safety research adviser.

Changing driver habits is so difficult partly because "people just don't take driving seriously," says Frank Kramer, an accident investigator for the California Highway Patrol. "They grow up with it and take it as second nature. They never stop to think they're driving 3,000 to 4,000 pounds of steel down the road at 40 to 50 miles per hour." 4

The leading cause of accidents, an Indiana University study concluded, is failure to look for or see hazards before pulling into traffic, changing lanes or passing. Other causes include excessive speed; improper evasive action in an emergency, such as locking the brakes instead of steering around an obstacle; inattention; and distractions within the car. (Distraction from stereo tapes rose steadily during the four-year period studied.) 5

According to General Motors Corp. researchers, following other cars too closely is an important factor in accident proneness. And it's estimated that 40% to 50% of fatal traffic accidents involve drinking drivers. 6

Combination of Causes

What prevents easy solutions is the fact that although various unsafe acts, such as speeding or tailgating, can lead to a collision, they usually don't. Other things generally have to be wrong, too: poor judgment or slow reactions by more than one driver, car-design features that impair a driver's vision or otherwise increase the hazard, or perhaps a tricky road. A number of these problems combine to produce an accident. 7

Many safety experts say the car and the road play bigger roles than often realized in inducing bad driving and are easier to improve than driver behavior. Nevertheless, a new wave of driver-training programs is springing up around the country to teach traffic-law violators and others to drive more safely. More states are cracking down on drunk drivers. And the federal government is pushing driver-related programs. 8

Ironically, the most effective driver-control measure has been one aimed at saving fuel rather than lives—the 55-mile-per-hour national speed limit first imposed during the 1974 Arab oil embargo. The speed limit is cited as the major factor in a drop in U.S. traffic fatalities from a peak of 54,600 in 1972 to a recent low 44,500 in 1975. One reason is that between 45 and 60 mph, the chances of death in a crash double, and they double again from 60 to 70 mph. 9

Concerned that compliance with the law has slipped, many states are renewing efforts to enforce the 55-mph limit. In Missouri, for example, speeding citations climbed from 51,000 in 1973 to 182,000 in 1974 after the new speed limit was imposed, and highway deaths fell 26% to 1,075. But later, as speeds crept up, so did fatalities. Thus, a new effort was begun in 1978, using aircraft and other means, along with a lot of publicity, to show that the crackdown was "serious," says Lt. Ralph Biele, a Missouri Highway Patrol spokesman. The crackdown, along with a recent campaign against drunk driving, has helped cut road deaths again, by 14% between 1978 and 1981. 10

Enforcement of the 55-mph limit, however, is facing resistance in many states, 11 especially Western states, where road speeds have long been high. Safety experts warn that reduced speeding penalties could increase highway fatalities; indeed, when Maryland troopers seeking a pay raise engaged in a ticket-writing slowdown for several months last year, road deaths climbed. Since 1975, federal figures show, most of the U.S. increase in deaths has occurred in the West.

A growing number of states also are stepping up highway enforcement and 12 passing laws requiring stiffer penalties to combat drunk driving. In the past, however, such efforts haven't permanently reduced alcohol-related fatalities substantially. One reason might be that in many crashes with alcohol involvement, bad-driving practices that aren't tied to alcohol are also involved.

Undoubtedly, police traffic-law enforcement keeps roads safer than they would 13 be without it. But the kind of driving—such as tailgating—that can lead to serious accidents often differs from driving that produces traffic violations. So, in Chicago, police are cracking down on tailgating as a major case of fatalities, says Paul L. Tasch, the commander of the Chicago Police Department's traffic-enforcement division. "It's a difficult charge to enforce," he says, "but we've zeroed in on it and are trying to increase the number of arrests."

Mixed Results

Other driver-related programs have produced mixed results. Many states and 14 localities have installed government and private driver-improvement programs for frequent traffic violators, older drivers and others. These programs include the National Safety Council's "defensive driving" course and an attitude-mending, eight-hour session offered in about a dozen states by the National Traffic Safety Institute, a Salem, Ore., company formed in 1975.

Studies of such programs frequently show a small improvement in violators' 15 safety records and sometimes a reduction in traffic convictions; but accident frequency changes little. In California, an improvement program for frequent violators trims accidents and violations about 10% for six months after the sessions, says Raymond Peck, a California Department of Motor Vehicles research specialist. But the effect on road safety is "very minor," he concedes—preventing about 1,200 accidents a year, or only 0.2% of the state's yearly reported total.

Longstanding high-school driver-education courses also have fallen short of 16 safety planners' goals. A recent four-year federal demonstration project in Georgia's DeKalb County, which includes Atlanta, was designed to assess whether an advanced driver-ed course could clearly result in safer driving. But the analysis so far shows that although traffic violations by the course's graduates were lower than for others, there was little reduction in accidents—a typical result for many driver-improvement programs.

Educational Hazard?

Some studies conclude that high-school driver-education actually reduces high- 17 way safety by encouraging the licensing of high-risk young drivers and putting them on the road earlier than otherwise. Leon Robertson, a Yale University safety researcher, found that when Connecticut eliminated financing for driver-ed and nine school systems dropped the courses, licensing and crash involvement of 16-year-olds and 17-year-olds dropped sharply.

Predictions Difficult

Though some drivers have more traffic violations and accidents than others, 18 past records often are of little help in predicting who will have accidents. Most offenders in any one year invariably turn out to be crash- and violation-free for, say, the next three years, and for the previous three years, too. Studies show that if an "accident-prone" group can be identified and millions of persons screened out from being licensed, those who would actually have accidents would be a small part of that group.

Other studies show that most drivers involved in crashes blame others for the 19 accidents and that 90% of those surveyed consider their driving to be better than average. The difficulty of changing such attitudes prompts some experts to conclude that more significant safety gains can be made by making cars more protective or by designing highways that make safe driving easier.

"We have no empirical evidence that trying to change the behavior of the 20 driver is effective, and we have a lot of evidence that improving the vehicle and the highway is very effective," says David Klein, a professor of social science at Michigan State University and a veteran highway-safety analyst.

Even those who advocate increased attention to the driver, such as Mr. Knaff 21 of the federal traffic-safety agency, concede that any gains will come slowly. "There's no such thing," he says, "as a silver bullet."

SKILL-DEVELOPMENT QUESTIONS

Vocabulary in Context

1. The word *elusive* in "The problem is that pinpointing . . . why accidents happen and how to stop them remains elusive" (paragraph 3) means
   a. confusing.
   b. clear.
   c. critical.
   d. alone.

2. The word *empirical* in "We have no empirical evidence that trying to change the behavior of the driver is effective, and we have a lot of evidence that improving the vehicle and the highway is very effective" (paragraph 20) means
   a. unreliable.
   b. strange.
   c. discouraging.
   d. factual.

Central Point and Main Ideas

3. Which sentence best expresses the central point of this article?
    a. Accidents are caused by unsafe actions.
    b. Most traffic accidents are caused by poor vehicle and highway design.
    c. Drunk drivers may be involved in as many as half of fatal traffic accidents.
    d. There seems to be no easy solution to the problem of driver error, the main cause of traffic accidents.

4. Which sentence best expresses the main idea of paragraph 16?
    a. According to one study, driver-education courses for high-school students have not significantly reduced accidents.
    b. The federal government sponsored an advanced driver-education course in DeKalb County, Georgia.
    c. Graduates of the federal driver-education project in Georgia committed fewer traffic violations than others.
    d. Graduates of the federal driver-education project in Georgia had almost as many traffic accidents as others.

Key Details

————   5. TRUE OR FALSE? Accidents are usually caused by a combination of problems.

6. According to the article, the 55-mile-per-hour speed limit
    a. was originally designed to save lives.
    b. eliminates crashes.
    c. has resulted in fewer fatal crashes.
    d. has always been fully enforced.

7. According to a California accident investigator, drivers
    a. are not mindful of the fact that they drive up to 4,000 pounds of steel at highway speeds.
    b. easily change their driving habits.
    c. take driving very seriously.
    d. are usually aware of the potential dangers of driving a large vehicle at high speeds.

8. TRUE OR FALSE? The most common cause of highway accidents is driving too fast.

Transitions

9. The relationship between the sentences below is one of
    a. cause and effect.
    b. time.
    c. illustration.
    d. contrast.

    Many safety experts say the car and the road . . . are easier to improve than driver behavior. Nevertheless, a new wave of driver-training programs is springing up. . . . (Paragraph 8)

10. The relationship between the second part of the sentence below to the first part is one of
    a. contrast.
    b. addition.
    c. clarification.
    d. time.

    Safety experts warn that reduced speeding penalties could increase highway fatalities; indeed, when Maryland troopers seeking a pay raise engaged in a ticket-writing slowdown for several months last year, road deaths climbed. (Paragraph 11)

Patterns of Organization

11. In paragraph 10, the author presents
    a. a definition and example about driving (definition and example).
    b. a listing of many programs enforcing the 55-mph speed limit (list of items).
    c. a comparison of states' enforcement programs (comparison).
    d. the results of some efforts to enforce the 55-mph speed limit (cause and effect).

Fact and Opinion

12. The following is a statement of
    a. fact.
    b. opinion.
    c. fact and opinion.

    In Missouri, for example, speeding citations climbed from 51,000 in 1973 to 182,000 in 1974 after the new speed limit was imposed, and highway deaths fell 26% to 1,075. (Paragraph 10)

13. Which of the following is a statement of opinion?
    a. "According to General Motors Corporation researchers, following other cars too closely is an important factor in accident proneness."
    b. "More states are cracking down on drunk drivers."
    c. "One reason might be that in many crashes with alcohol involvement, bad-driving practices that aren't tied to alcohol are also involved."
    d. "Longstanding high-school driver-education courses also have fallen short of safety planners' goals."

Inferences

14. From the article, we can conclude that an accident is more likely to happen when a driver
    a. leaves a parking lot.
    b. approaches a street sign.
    d. goes 27 miles per hour in a 25-mile-per-hour zone.
    e. tries to find a good station on the radio while driving.

15. The author implies that driver-training programs
    a. succeed only with older drivers.
    b. are producing disappointing results.
    c. are growing because of their great success in improving driver behavior.
    d. are more effective than the 55-mile-per-hour speed limit.

Purpose and Tone

16. The purpose of this article is
    a. to inform readers about the causes of traffic accidents and the efforts to make driving safer.
    b. to persuade readers that driver-training programs should be abolished.
    c. to entertain readers with anecdotes about drivers.

17. The tone of this article can be described as
    a. pleading.
    b. objective.
    c. annoyed.
    d. optimistic.

Bias and Propaganda

18. The author uses name-calling when he
    a. states, "Many of today's 155 million U. S. drivers continue to have trouble avoiding collisions."
    b. refers to a driver as "the nut behind the wheel."
    c. quotes Frank Kramer's statement that "people just don't take driving seriously."
    d. reports, "More states are cracking down on drunk drivers."

Evaluating Arguments

19. The central point of this article is supported by
    a. opinions.
    b. statistics.
    c. factual examples.
    d. all of the above.

20. The author's statement that "the most effective driver-control measure has been . . . the 55-mile-per-hour national speed limit" is supported by all the following statements *except*
    a. "The speed limit is cited as the major factor in a drop in U. S. traffic fatalities from a peak of 54,600 in 1972 to a recent low 44,500 in 1975."
    b. "Concerned that compliance with the law has slipped, many states are renewing efforts to enforce the 55-mph limit."
    c. "But later, as speeds crept up, so did fatalities."
    d. "The crackdown [on speed], along with a recent campaign against drunk driving, has helped cut road deaths again, by 14 percent between 1978 and 1981."

THINKING ACTIVITIES

Outlining

Following is an incomplete outline of paragraphs 10–17 of the article. Complete it by filling in the letters of the missing items, which are shown in random order below the outline.

Central Idea: Types of driver-related programs aimed at improving traffic safety.

1. _____

2. _____

3. _____

Items Missing from the Outline

a. High-school driver-education courses
b. Enforcement of speed, drunk-driving, and other traffic laws
c. Driver-improvement programs for frequent traffic violators, older drivers, and others

Summarizing

Below is the first part of a summary of "Death on the Road" followed by three different ways of completing it. Circle the letter (**a**, **b**, or **c**) of the best ending to the summary.

> Improving driving behavior—the leading cause of highway accidents— is not easy. So many factors are involved in accidents, including carelessness, poor driver attitudes, and non-driver-related elements like a poor road, that experts cannot predict or control driver behavior very well. Nevertheless, there is an increasing emphasis on driver-related programs. The most effective so far has been the 55-mile-an-hour speed limit.

a. Many states are now strictly enforcing this limit with notable success. In Missouri, for example, an increase in speeding tickets combined with a campaign against drunk driving cut road deaths by 14 percent within about three years.
b. However, there is much resistance to this law, especially in the Western states. In contrast to the speed limit, driver-improvement and driver-education programs have had mixed and limited success. Some experts feel that because of the poor results with most driver-related programs, the emphasis should be on improving car and road design.
c. Because of the difficulty of predicting just who will cause an accident, however, one program that is not being attempted is the refusing of licenses to accident-prone drivers. Because so much more has been learned about improving cars and highways, some experts feel efforts in those areas should be emphasized.

DISCUSSION QUESTIONS

1. Why did Karr begin with the brief anecdote about two automobiles in Kansas City, Missouri? What point is he making? How effectively does that anecdote pull the reader into the article?

2. Think about the accidents you have been in, have witnessed, or have heard about. What factors were involved in causing each accident?

3. Karr writes, "The difficulty of changing such attitudes prompts some experts to conclude that more significant safety gains can be made by making cars more protective or by designing highways that make safe driving easier." In what ways could cars and highways be improved?

4. According to accident-investigator Frank Kramer, "People just don't take driving seriously." Do you agree? Why?

Check Your Performance		DEATH ON THE ROAD		
Skill	Number Right		Points	Total
Vocabulary in Context (2 items)	_____	×	4 :	_____
Central Point and Main Ideas (2)	_____	×	4 :	_____
Key Details (4)	_____	×	4 :	_____
Transitions (2)	_____	×	4 :	_____
Patterns of Organization (1)	_____	×	4 :	_____
Fact and Opinion (2)	_____	×	4 :	_____
Inferences (2)	_____	×	4 :	_____
Purpose and Tone (2)	_____	×	4 :	_____
Bias and Propaganda (1)	_____	×	4 :	_____
Evaluating Arguments (2)	_____	×	4 :	_____
	(total of 20 questions)			
Outlining (3)	_____	×	3.3 :	_____
Summarizing (1)	_____	×	10 :	_____
	FINAL SCORE (OF POSSIBLE 100)			_____

Enter your final score into the reading performance chart on page 454.

15

Shyness
Richard Wolkomir

Preview

Have you ever not raised your hand in class because you would be embarrassed to draw attention to yourself? Does it sometimes take courage for you to pursue a new friendship? If so, like many people, you know what it's like to feel shy. Fortunately, as this magazine article by writer Richard Wolkomir explains, no one has to suffer such distress forever.

Words to Watch

equate (5):   make equal
initiated (9):   started
attributes (10):   credits
genetic (11):   inherited at birth
extroverted (15):   friendly, outgoing
encroaching (19):   trespassing, taking without permission
perceptions (25):   ideas
invariably (25):   always

He's tall and interesting looking, dressed in a business suit. He smiles and says 1
"Hi" when Carol Johnson, a twenty-five-year-old typist in Rochester, New York, gets on the bus, but her tongue freezes and she glances away, hating herself. It's a familiar reaction. Since speaking at staff meetings also makes her nervous, she lets co-workers take credit for her new ideas; at parties, she stands to one side, wishing someone would notice her, and praying he won't.

Carol suffers from a problem that almost everyone experiences at some time: 2
shyness. For her, shyness is neither cute nor sweet, nor easy to overcome. It makes her distant when she wants to be friendly; cold when she wants to be warm—and lonely when she wants company.

It was four years ago, when Carol broke up with her boyfriend, that her shy- 3
ness began to bother her. "He was talkative and very domineering in conversations, so I sort of sat back, not talking much," she says. "We'd been going together since high school, and after we split I suddenly found I didn't have much to say to people."

For three years, Carol had little social life. Then, one day, she told herself, "If 4
you don't try something, you'll just slip further and further back." She forced herself to become more active. She volunteered for the Special Olympics, and began to meet other people who shared her interest in handicapped children. It was an important first step. "I'm making progress . . . slowly," she says.

Carol is not alone. At some time in their lives, over 80 percent of all Americans 5
report feeling shy, according to Stanford University psychologist Philip Zimbardo, Ph.D., a shyness authority and author of *The Shy Child*. It's a special problem for women, many of whom are still raised to equate bashfulness with femininity.

Yet, in today's intensely competitive work place, shyness can be a severe hand- 6
icap. What will happen if your stomach knots every time you meet a new client? How far will you rise if you're too shy to be assertive with the workers you supervise?

"Whenever I had to talk to new people I'd get sick to my stomach and sweat," 7
recalls Sylvia Madden, now a Purdue University counselor in her late twenties, who conducts a shyness workshop for college students. "It used to be awful to make a speech—forget about talking to boys."

Sylvia says her shyness began in childhood. Her parents were quiet people 8
who kept to themselves, and she was a tall, awkward and self-conscious girl who was never encouraged to socialize with others. Throughout college, she depended upon her boyfriend for her social life. But when she moved away for graduate school, she resolved not to become isolated.

"I made myself go to parties—I had a miserable time at first, but I was deter- 9
mined to do it," she says, recalling that it took all her courage to invite someone out for coffee. "For the first time, I actively initiated friendships and I could feel myself changing." Oddly enough, it was a rejection that convinced her she'd won her battle. "I invited a guy to go to a party," she says. "When he turned me down, instead of being crushed, I decided that the loss was his—it felt wonderful!"

Sylvia Madden attributes her own early shyness to poorly developed social 10
skills and a negative self-image—two common causes of the problem. Sometimes teenagers develop poor self-images because they're physically different from their peers, whether they're shorter or taller, fatter or thinner—or even prettier, says Dr. Zimbardo. But often shyness develops because parents' expectations make a child feel self-conscious regardless of her attributes. A parent's love may depend on a child's performance—such as a good report card, or trying to meet unrealistic expectations. A mother, trying to fulfill her own fantasies, for instance, may want her daughter to become a ballerina, even though the girl has no special talent for dance. "Failing as a dancer, she may feel she's failed completely as a person," says Dr. Zimbardo.

According to recent studies, shyness is one of a number of behavioral charac- 11
teristics that can even be hereditary. Jerome Kagan, a Harvard University psychologist, found that up to one-third of all shy children are born bashful. And a study of

identical and fraternal twins by Robert Plomin, Ph.D., of the University of Colorado at Boulder, and David C. Rowe, Ph.D., of the University of Oklahoma at Norman, shows that shyness, which is evident in infancy, is largely genetic.

However or whenever shyness develops, it can be debilitating. Fortunately, it 12 can be overcome. The first step is invariably the same: a sudden decision to change.

Angela Dix, for example, a forty-year-old publicist for a New England health 13 agency, was a painfully shy child of a shy mother. When her parents divorced and her mother became dependent on her, Angela's shyness increased. But subconsciously she knew she had to break out into a larger world; against her mother's wishes, she enrolled in a large, urban university.

"By the time we drove up to the dormitory, my mother was so upset about 14 'losing' me that we were barely speaking," Angela remembers. "I was terrified of being alone in this large, strange place, but I knew that meeting people and making a life for myself were completely up to me, and I resolved right then to do something about it."

She forced herself to walk through the dormitory, cheerfully saying, "Hi!" to 15 the other freshmen. A few nights later she was nominated floor president. "At first, I thought they had made a mistake—they were voting for the fake, outgoing me," she says. "But it was then that I realized that if I acted extroverted, then that's what I was."

Shyness is so common that psychologists have recently been focusing consid- 16 erable attention on the problem. There are now over forty "shyness workshops" at universities around the country. Many of the participants are women, often because men are reluctant to admit they *have* a problem.

At her Purdue University workshops, Sylvia Madden starts each session with 17 exercises to help participants become comfortable with one another. For instance, each member of the group talks about herself to another member who takes notes. Then the note-taker introduces her partner to the group as a whole.

She also leads the participants in such psychological games as "sculpting," in 18 which participants pretend they are statues that express the feeling of shyness or its opposite. "Often, when they express how it feels *not* to be shy, they will reach out a hand toward someone else," she says.

Group members also work on conversational skills, discussing the physical 19 symptoms of shyness and how to say things more effectively in situations that bother them. For instance, a woman who wants to ask a co-worker to stop encroaching on her area of responsibility acts out the scene, asking another member to take the part of the "villain."

All participants sign a "behavioral contract" that specifies their own goals. For 20 instance, one goal might be, "I want to say hello to three strangers every day."

Such techniques *do* work. A twenty-year-old woman majoring in mathematics 21 recently enrolled in a shyness workshop at Pennsylvania State University, where these programs developed, after she'd dropped out of the university's public-speaking course for her sixth time.

Her first assignment was to return a bulky, blue wristwatch she'd just bought. 22 She really wanted a small watch, but had been too shy to tell the clerk. With the help of her counselor, she wrote out a precise plan of action: "At 3:30 this afternoon

I will go to the store, find the clerk who sold me the blue watch and explain that I want a small one."

At the next class, proudly wearing a delicate wristwatch, she had enough con- 23 fidence to try public speaking. "Afterward, she just stood at the lectern whispering, 'Wow, wow!'" says Herman Cohen, Ph.D., a professor of speech communication who ran the workshop. "Even after she sat down, I could still hear her saying, 'Wow!'"

Even if there's no workshop near you, you can use some of these techniques. 24 Dr. Zimbardo suggests becoming your own friendly coach. Instead of telling yourself bad things about yourself—"I'm dumb"; "I'm fat"; "I have nothing to say"— give yourself compliments: "My hair looks good today"; "I'm a good cook." And, try to improve. "Although I started off just right—what can I do next time to get the results I want? Speak louder? Look her right in the eye? Reveal a little about myself before I ask questions?"

"I'm fascinated by the distorted perceptions shy people have of themselves," 25 says Dr. Cohen. "For instance, almost invariably they consider themselves far less attractive or talkative than they actually are. You're responsible for no more than fifty percent of any conversation—if a conversation is a dud, why are you so sure it's all your fault?"

Gerald Phillips, Ph.D., who directs the shyness program at Pennsylvania State 26 University, tells people to put their goals in writing. "'I will become an interesting conversationalist' is an unrealistic goal," he says. "You can't be sure what others will find interesting; some people actually find nothing interesting except themselves. It's much better to say: 'At the office tomorrow I'll start a conversation with Bill and I'll talk to him for at least three minutes.' Include in your plan of action three or four subjects to talk about."

Afterward, he says, check off the goals you accomplish and celebrate each vic- 27 tory with a reward to boost your self-confidence.

Dr. Phillips also advises shy people to imitate particular traits they admire. 28 Does the woman you respect look people in the eye? Speak loudly enough to be heard? How does she use her expressions and body language to make what she says seem lively? How does she make transitions from one subject to another? He also suggests "active listening" to master conversation. If you look attentive when the other person talks, and ask appropriate questions, it puts the burden of conversation on them, rather than on you. And it makes you less self-conscious.

"Even if you hardly say two words all evening, the other person will probably 29 think you're a terrific conversationalist," says Dr. Phillips. "And most people worth knowing will reciprocate by asking you questions."

A bit of bashfulness can be an asset: "The people who join our program are 30 much more considerate, much more sensitive to the needs of others, than most people," says Dr. Phillips. And that's no compliment to shy away from.

SKILL-DEVELOPMENT QUESTIONS

Vocabulary in Context

1. The word *domineering* in "He was talkative and very domineering in conversations, so I sort of sat back" (paragraph 3) means
   a. quiet.
   b. controlling.
   c. pale.
   d. sour.

2. The word *debilitating* in "whenever shyness develops, it can be debilitating. Fortunately, it can be overcome," (paragraph 12) means
   a. encouraging.
   b. weakening.
   c. stylish.
   d. catching.

Central Point and Main Ideas

3. Which sentence best expresses the central point of the selection?
   a. More shyness workshops are available than ever before.
   b. Shyness is hereditary.
   c. Shy people are likely to be failures.
   d. Shyness, a common problem with various causes, can be overcome.

4. Which sentence best expresses the main point of paragraph 11?
   a. All shy children are born bashful.
   b. Some studies have concluded that people can be born shy.
   c. A Harvard psychologist found that up to one-third of shy children are born bashful.
   d. A study of identical and fraternal twins was conducted by several researchers.

5. Which sentence best expresses the main point of paragraph 26?
   a. Shy people have unrealistic goals, according to one expert.
   b. Most shy people are uninteresting.
   c. According to one expert, putting realistic goals in writing helps people overcome shyness.
   d. One expert says that some people are only interested in themselves.

Key Details

_____ 6. TRUE OR FALSE? According to the author, many women are raised to feel being shy is feminine.

7. According to one shyness expert, shy people
   a. are good supervisors.
   b. don't recognize all the good things about themselves.
   c. are happy being shy.
   d. are unable to boost their own self-confidence.

Transitions

8. The relationship of the second sentence below to the one before it is one of
   a. cause and effect.
   b. comparison.
   c. contrast.
   d. illustration.

   Throughout college, she depended upon her boyfriend for her social life. But when she moved away for graduate school, she resolved not to become isolated. (Paragraph 8)

9. The sentence below begins with
   a. a contrast signal.
   b. an illustration signal.
   c. a clarification signal.
   d. an emphasis signal.

   "For instance, almost invariably they consider themselves far less attractive or talkative than they actually are." (Paragraph 25)

Patterns of Organization

10. Paragraph 10 uses the pattern of
    a. time order.
    b. cause and effect.
    c. comparison and contrast.
    d. definition and example.

11. The main pattern of organization in paragraphs 22–23 is that of
    a. time order.
    b. list of items.
    c. comparison and contrast.
    d. definition and example.

Fact and Opinion

12. Which of the following contains *both* fact and opinion?
    a. "He's tall and interesting looking, dressed in a business suit."

b.   "Jerome Kagan, a Harvard University psychologist, found that up to one-third of all shy children are born bashful."

c.   "There are now over forty 'shyness workshops' at universities around the country."

d.   "Dr. Phillips also advises shy people to imitate particular traits they admire."

_____ 13.   TRUE OR FALSE? Paragraph 11 consists of a series of facts.

Inferences

14.   The author implies that overcoming shyness
a.   is easy.
b.   is impossible.
c.   can only be done at workshops.
d.   takes determination.

15.   In paragraph 29, Dr. Phillips implies that
a.   all shy people are good conversationalists.
b.   shy people shouldn't try to speak much.
c.   many people's idea of a good conversationalist is someone who listens to them.
d.   shy people should avoid talking to people who aren't worth knowing.

Purpose and Tone

16.   The tone of this selection can be described as
a.   pessimistic.
b.   regretful.
c.   humorous.
d.   optimistic.

17.   The author's main purpose in writing "Shyness" is probably to
a.   entertain us with anecdotes of people who overcame shyness.
b.   inform us of successful techniques in overcoming shyness.
c.   persuade us that any problem can be solved if we work at it.

Bias and Propaganda

18.   Which of the following statements in the selection contains an example of a half-truth?
a.   "When he turned me down, instead of being crushed, I decided that the loss was his. . . ."

b. "Whenever I had to talk to new people I'd get sick to my stomach and sweat. . . ."

c. ". . . I knew that meeting people and making a life for myself were completely up to me. . . ."

d. "Failing as a dancer, she may feel she's failed completely as a person."

Evaluating Arguments

19. Which of the following evidence from the article does NOT support the author's conclusion that shyness can be overcome?
    a. Sylvia Madden, a shy child, now leads shyness workshops for college students.
    b. Studies of twins show that shyness can be inherited.
    c. Angela Dix was elected floor president of her dormitory after forcing herself to greet the other freshmen.
    d. The math major succeeded in returning a large wristwatch to the store.

20. Which of the following evidence from the article provides valid support for the conclusion that shyness can be a handicap in school?
    a. Carol's boyfriend was domineering in conversations.
    b. Sylvia Madden forced herself to go to parties and start new friendships.
    c. The math major had dropped out of her public speaking course six times.
    d. The math major kept saying "Wow!" after making a speech.

THINKING ACTIVITIES

Outlining

Complete the outline of "Shyness" by filling in the missing supporting details. Choose the details from the list below the outline.

A. Background on shyness
  1. A common and difficult problem.

  2. _____
    a. Poorly developed social skills
    b. Negative self-image
      (1) Physical differences from peers
      (2) Unrealistic parental expectations
  c. _____

B. Ways to overcome shyness
   1. Decide to change and be more social

   2. _____
   3. Use workshop techniques on your own
      a. Compliment yourself

      b. _____

      c. _____
      d. Listen actively

Items Missing from the Outline

- Inherited from parents
- Put goals in writing
- Causes of shyness
- Imitate traits you admire
- Attend a shyness workshop

Summarizing

1. Circle the letter of the statement that best summarizes the central point of "Shyness," as expressed in the first twelve paragraphs.
   a. Shyness is a special problem for women in our society.
   b. Shyness, which is a common problem caused by various factors, can be defeated.
   c. Nearly everyone experiences shyness at some time or other.

2. Circle the letter of the statement that best summarizes the first set of supporting details (paragraphs 12–15) for the central point.
   a. A forty-year-old publicist was painfully shy.
   b. To overcome shyness, people must be determined to change.
   c. To overcome shyness, people must understand their subconscious goals.

3. Circle the letter of the statement that best summarizes the second set of supporting details (paragraphs 16–23) for the central point.
   a. Attending shyness workshops is a good way to learn to overcome shyness.
   b. A Purdue University workshop uses psychological games to help shy people.
   c. One shyness workshop helped a woman exchange a wristwatch she didn't want.

4. Circle the letter of the statement that best summarizes the third set of supporting details (paragraphs 24–30) for the central point.
   a. One expert feels shy people have distorted images of themselves.
   b. Some techniques used at shyness workshops are useful even if people don't attend a workshop.
   c. Shy people can benefit by imitating qualities of people they admire.

DISCUSSION QUESTIONS

1. Are there certain situations—such as a job interview, a particular classroom or workplace, or a party most of whose guests you don't know—where you become shy or feel shyness taking over? If so, what techniques mentioned in the article might help you combat your shyness?

2. What are the similarities and differences between Carol Johnson (paragraphs 1–4) and Sylvia Madden (paragraphs 7–10)? Consider the causes of their shyness and their approaches to overcome it.

3. The author uses many examples of shy people and workshop exercises throughout his article. Why do you think he chose to use so many examples? What would the article be like without any examples?

4. Do you feel that a person should deal with his or her problems alone, or with other people, as in a workshop, helping out? Does the group approach make it easier—or harder—to deal with personal problems?

Check Your Performance   SHYNESS

Skill	Number Right	Points	Total
Vocabulary in Context (2 items)	_____	× 4 :	_____
Central Point and Main Ideas (3)	_____	× 4 :	_____
Key Details (2)	_____	× 4 :	_____
Transitions (2)	_____	× 4 :	_____
Patterns of Organization (2)	_____	× 4 :	_____
Fact and Opinion (2)	_____	× 4 :	_____
Inferences (2)	_____	× 4 :	_____
Purpose and Tone (2)	_____	× 4 :	_____
Bias and Propaganda (1)	_____	× 4 :	_____
Evaluating Arguments (2)	_____	× 4 :	_____

(total of 20 questions)

Outlining (5)	_____	× 2 :	_____
Summarizing (4)	_____	× 2.5 :	_____

FINAL SCORE (OF POSSIBLE 100)   _____

Enter your final score into the reading performance chart on page 454.

16

Getting My Act Together
Christina Plutzer

Preview

Perhaps we all sometimes feel that the saying "Where there's a will, there's a way" refers to others and that for us, there is no way. At such moments, experiences like Christina Plutzer's are especially inspiring, for they remind us that there's more than one way or time to reach a goal. They also teach us that getting help along the way can signify wisdom, not weakness.

Words to Watch

legion (1):   large number
sporadic (1):   in scattered single instances
psychedelics (1):   drugs
staccato (6):   brief and sharp
listless (6):   dull
prim (10):   very proper
delve (14):   search deeply
rifled (27):   searched persistently
privy to (30):   in on
incoherent (35):   not logical
formidable (38):   impressive
genteelly (38):   in a refined way
implementing (43):   putting into effect

After two marriages, four children, a legion of self-aborted careers, and many 1
attempts to escape social accountability, I concluded at 38 that either my life was

over, or had never actually begun. Sporadic ventures into self-help books (written, I decided, for those who didn't need much help at all), and psychedelics (which increased my cosmic awareness of the world's beauty and my own uselessness) didn't help. In desperation, I showed up at the office of the county mental health clinic to announce that I was a homicidal, suicidal, passive-aggressive psychotic who could not afford to be put on their waiting list. The intake counselor apparently agreed with some of this, and after a biographical interview, gave me an appointment the following day.

Dr. Pellman introduced himself the next morning with a warm handshake. His   2
voice was deep, and his eyes held intense, visible concern. He was about 40 and darkly attractive. I immediately wondered how he was in bed. Having come this far, I chose not to take any chances.

"I'm sorry," I muttered, "but I really don't relate too well to men. Is there any   3
chance I could see a female therapist?"

His concerned warmth gave way to professional detachment, as he asked me   4
to wait in his office while he saw whether my preference could be accommodated. Great, I thought, over a hundred emotionally distraught people in this area dying to see a shrink, and I've got to be picky about gender. Dr. Pellman returned to tell me that I would be seen the following week by Mrs. Victoria Smith, Room 209, 1 P.M., and good luck.

Mrs. Smith was a trim, gray-haired woman in her late 50s. She wore a crisp   5
conservative suit and no makeup, and reminded me of every English teacher and nun I'd ever feared. This lady, I thought glumly, had never done drugs, evaded a landlord, or fallen in love with a Black musician. She has a cat, a house, the correct stock portfolios, and the traditional morals of "Good Family."

She had not had time to read my intake biography, and therefore, I was in-   6
formed, our first session would cover some personal history. This was accomplished with staccato questions and listless answers since, by this time, I'd become more bored than depressed by my dismal childhood. She took tidy, undecipherable notes, nodding her head occasionally at her paperwork. When she at last looked at me, she asked what I thought my strengths were.

"I think I'm a good parent," I responded hesitantly.   7

"What makes you think so?" she asked.   8

Oh fine, I groaned. She's going to challenge what little I think I have? "Well,"   9
I answered sullenly, "they don't kill baby animals or practice witchcraft."

"That's a good start, considering your own childhood." For the first time, she   10
smiled. I had made this prim, efficient lady smile. Maybe if I couldn't be sane or interesting, I could at least be amusing.

"And what," she continued, smile gone, "do you consider your major weak-   11
nesses to be?"

"It would take me years to list those," I said.   12

Mrs. Smith's voice was businesslike and abrupt. "I intend to be here for quite   13
some time, and I suspect you will be too. We'll examine the realities of your situation, and see how each issue can be handled with whatever strengths you currently have."

Her practical approach was beginning to scare me. I longed for a couch and a   14
bearded Freudian with a German accent. He would delve wisely into my soul, ferret

out hidden answers to my fears and failures, then face me with the "Truth" that would save me forever from the flames of self-hatred.

"What do you want to do that you feel you can't?" she asked calmly.　15

I want to become a screaming, raging success, I howled inwardly. I want to 16 wake up and be glad I'm me. I want to be a board chairman, a rock star, a woman who's sure. I want to radiate worth and confidence for miles around, you dry, prim tower of togetherness.

"I don't know," I said.　17

"Then that's the first thing we have to find out. Our time is up for today. We 18 will meet twice a week, Monday and Wednesday, at this time. Next time you come, I expect you to have some ideas on what you want to do with your life." Mrs. Smith peered over her glasses and said a bit more softly, "There must be something you want, and that you sense you can accomplish. Otherwise, you wouldn't have found your way here."

At the next session, I repeated stubbornly that I thought I was a good parent, 19 and might eventually like to work with children. My daughters and their friends liked being with me. I listened to them without judging, respected their opinions, and interceded only when I felt their activities might be potentially dangerous. Mrs. Smith introduced the possibility of a career in child care or counselling. "But," she said, "there isn't much money there unless you have a degree."

My education had consisted of graduating from high school, then heading 20 straight for Greenwich Village, living day-to-day, and taking infrequent jobs when I was forced, by some unfair social criterion, to pay my own rent. Then marriage, kids, divorce, remarriage, kids, and redivorce.

"You could consider registering at the community college," she suggested.　21

Sure I could, lady, I thought. I could also consider taking over IBM. I've got 22 no money and a car that needs to coast a mile before it starts. Serve me some more fantasies.

"Do you think you would be able to handle college level work and four chil- 23 dren at the same time?" she asked.

"Probably," I answered, more out of pride than conviction.　24

Mrs. Smith said she thought so, too. However, she was obviously not going 25 to do any of the legwork for me. She simply gave me the address of the college. "Get their brochure, select the Freshman courses that interest you, and next meeting, we'll go over your choices." We managed during the remaining time to talk some about my family, ex-husbands, lovers and drug use, but it seemed to me to be almost incidental conversation. Except she was always taking those damned notes.

"Look," I said at the next session, "I have the brochure and I've looked over 26 the courses, but there's no way I can afford this on welfare, and my car refuses to go to college."

Mrs. Smith <u>rifled</u> through her briefcase and handed me financial aid forms. 27 "You should have picked these up, too," she said sternly. "There is also a cheap, county mini-bus service to the college. This is the phone number."

Together we worked on the financial papers, and I began to get an uneasy 28 feeling that she actually assumed I would go to college. A 38-year-old Betty Coed? Would someone carry my books? Would I be asked to the prom? Am I crazier than

I thought, or is this well-bred lady imposing her own values and expecting them to be mine?

I registered for the fall term. My routine of readying the kids for school, then being terrified because they weren't home to justify my existence, was shattered. I had to take English, and chose to take psychology courses. My sessions with Mrs. Smith became erratic, depending on our mutual schedules. Between meetings with her, tending to my daughters, and adjusting to such alien activities as reading and writing, I had much less time to sabotage my personal life.   29

At the end of my second semester, Mrs. Smith concluded that I was too poor, a fact I'd been privy to for years. I was doing well in school and had a part-time position at an adolescent counseling center. But I was always behind on rent, food, kids' clothing, and other petty survival needs. She mentioned two possibilities— either working a full-time job, taking classes at night, or applying for OVR funds. On the basis of my family, I chose the latter.   30

The Office of Vocational Rehabilitation is a state organization that offers funding and training to the physically and emotionally handicapped. To be psychiatrically handicapped, and at the same time, trainable, is difficult to prove, especially if one's goal is a liberal arts program. Mrs. Smith, for the first time, did the groundwork for me, finding a counselor there who was new to the system, and eager for his first cases.   31

She wrote a psychiatric evaluation, diagnosing me as having "low self-esteem." The letter was carefully worded, she explained, because if I were flagrantly psychotic, they would judge me incapable of completing an educational program. However, I had to be crazy enough to qualify, not just depressed or nervous.   32

I was on my own as far as the interview with the OVR psychiatrist, who spoke briefly with me. He then showed me the Rorschach Test (Psychology 101) and after my first interpretation, "the devil tearing out the liver of an angel," he put away the remaining ink blots. He simply wrote that, in his opinion, I would qualify for state funding for educational expenses, in addition to those provided by the school. Thereafter, life became a little easier financially.   33

For the next two years, Mrs. Smith and I met at her house, my apartment, restaurants (always individual tabs), and at the mental health clinic. During this time, she had worked out an agreement with the county that allowed her to be paid through the clinic without billing me. At least, that's what she told me.   34

Depending on my day, I would come to her depressed and self-pitying, triumphant with new achievements, demanding solutions, or sometimes, high and incoherent. She was always there, listening, suggesting, laughing and, very rarely, sympathizing. Some sessions were emotional explosions. Others were as dry and practical as stockholders' meetings. The demands of school and dealing with rapidly growing children were leaving me less and less time for recreational self-destruction.   35

I don't remember when I first wondered what it was like for her to live completely alone on a three-acre estate, and whether she had a family or a personal life. When I was ready to ask, it seemed natural for her to talk. She told me her husband had died 14 years ago, three months after they had adopted an infant son. Her only sister lived 400 miles away. Although she had friends in the profession, her work was her passion.   36

I began to spend weekends, when my children were visiting their fathers in 37
the City, at her home helping with the gardening and cleaning, which she grimly
and compulsively did herself. Her home's formal elegance was interrupted only by
two chaotic areas—a recess with a mammoth desk overflowing with reports, research articles and correspondence, and an adjoining room which was a busy combination of greenhouse, sewing room and dining space.

Evenings, I'd help myself to her <u>formidable</u> library while she watched TV. Or 38
we'd discuss her job, our children (her son was in boarding school), or various
articles in professional journals. I'd select albums from her husband's enormous record collection, and she'd remark that she hadn't heard those particular records in
years. I suspected that she just didn't listen to music any more. Later, she would
drink herself <u>genteelly</u>, but determinedly, to sleep. I'd gently help her to bed before
retiring to the guest room.

With my own children, she was a brisk, bustling aunt. One of Mrs. Smith's 39
patients was a dance teacher, and in lieu of payment, my daughters were enrolled in
her classes. They enjoyed Mrs. Smith's breezing in occasionally to hand out advice,
praise, and sometimes, a small, practical gift. At some point, Mrs. Smith became
Victoria to me.

In late 1981, my friend Bill wrote to tell me that he was giving up his apart- 40
ment in the Village, and would I be interested? Three weeks later, my closest friend
Diane, with whom I corresponded regularly, called from New York City and said
her agency was looking for people with experience and education in counseling
emotionally disturbed children.

I mentioned the coincidence to Victoria, who I knew considered the City a 41
place one visited once a year for a Broadway show and a French dinner. We talked
about it continually after the letter and phone call. She knew how small I thought
the county was, and that I'd come with my husband to live in the country, mainly
for my kids. I'd already sent an inquiry to Diane's agency, and asked Bill how much
time I had to decide. I think Victoria and I both knew I was going.

Victoria constantly reminded me that I had to stay in school, and advised me 42
not to start working right away. It was the only time she ever offered me money,
to stay unemployed for a while, to ease the kids' adjustment to city life. She gathered
material on the City's community resources and educational institutions. She also
told me rather stuffily that she had checked out Diane's agency, and had received
"satisfactory" reports on it. On the other hand, she quoted the latest crime statistics
in New York City whenever she had the chance, and frequently in conversation
brought up the high cost of living there.

I was busy taking finals, making moving arrangements, signing, closing, pack- 43
ing, notifying, and investigating neighborhood schools. Vaguely I realized that three
years ago I hadn't felt capable of moving from one apartment to another. I'd been
too helpless to handle even trivial issues. Now I had made a monstrously risky
decision, and was efficiently <u>implementing</u> it.

After three years of crying, confiding my sins, and arguing with this woman, 44
I was amazed at how inarticulate I became saying good-bye to her. I knew it was
pointless to tell her I couldn't have come this far without her; she would have
reacted with scorn. She'd persistently believed in me, and that belief had been my
anchor.

"Thank you for teaching me how to sew," I said the morning we left.   45
"Thank you for all your help with the gardening," Victoria said.   46
We held each other tightly, until the train pulled in.   47

SKILL-DEVELOPMENT QUESTIONS

Vocabulary in Context

1. The word *ferret* in "he would . . . ferret out hidden answers to my fears and failures, then face me with the 'Truth' " (paragraph 14) means
   a. search.
   b. leave.
   c. throw.
   d. cut.

2. The word *flagrantly* in "if I were flagrantly psychotic, they would judge me incapable of completing an educational program" (paragraph 32) means
   a. calmly.
   b. wisely.
   c. never.
   d. very obviously.

Central Point and Main Ideas

3. Which sentence best expresses the central point of this selection?
   a. Christina Plutzer needed the kind of help that self-help books could not supply.
   b. A college education is necessary in today's world.
   c. With her own will and the help of a caring professional, Plutzer put her life on the right track.
   d. Professional relationships can develop into friendships.

4. Which sentence best expresses the main idea of paragraph 1?
   a. At age 38, Christina Plutzer thought her life was over.
   b. Plutzer was depressed and desperate.
   c. Because Plutzer wanted to straighten out her life, she got an appointment at a mental health clinic.
   d. Plutzer, who was married twice and had four children, had not built a career for herself.

Key Details

5. TRUE OR FALSE? Plutzer had previously tried to escape from her problems by using drugs.

6. The author
   a. was positive that she could both handle college work and care for her children.
   b. did not need financial aid.
   c. eventually recognized and appreciated Mrs. Smith's strong support.
   d. found it easy to say good-bye to Victoria.

Transitions

7. The relationship between the first and second parts of the sentence below is one of
   a. time.
   b. cause and effect.
   c. contrast.
   d. comparison.

   She had not had time to read my intake biography, and therefore, I was informed, our first session would cover some personal history. (Paragraph 6)

8. The relationship between the first and second parts of the sentence below is one of
   a. comparison.
   b. contrast.
   c. time.
   d. cause and effect.

   Although she had friends in the profession, her work was her passion. (Paragraph 36)

Patterns of Organization

9. The pattern of organization of paragraph 5 is
   a. cause and effect.
   b. definition and example.
   c. list of items.
   d. time order.

10. The pattern of organization of paragraph 20 is
    a. comparison.
    b. time order.
    c. list of items.
    d. definition and example.

Fact and Opinion

_____ 11. TRUE OR FALSE? The sentence below is a statement of fact.

I had to take English, and chose to take psychology courses. (Paragraph 29)

12. The sentence below
    a. is a factual description that everyone would agree on.
    b. is purely an opinion.
    c. is both opinion and fact.

I began to spend weekends, when my children were visiting their fathers in the city, at her home helping with the gardening and cleaning, which she grimly and compulsively did herself.

Inferences

13. The author implies in paragraphs 2 and 3 that she
    a. never really wanted a female therapist.
    b. was afraid that a male therapist would be a distraction to her.
    c. disliked men.
    d. disliked women.

14. We can infer from the last sentence of paragraph 34 that Plutzer thought Dr. Smith
    a. was untrustworthy.
    b. had lied to her all along.
    c. was getting money from the county.
    d. may have been giving Plutzer free therapy.

Purpose and Tone

15. The author's purpose is
    a. to inform readers in an entertaining and persuasive way that it's possible to improve one's life.
    b. to persuade readers that the way to improve one's life is through professional counseling.
    c. to entertain readers with anecdotes of her experience with therapy.

16. The author's tone when she writes about herself is
    a. usually arrogant, but sometimes objective.
    b. largely self-mocking at first, and then proud.
    c. totally objective.
    d. uncaring.

Bias and Propaganda

17. The author includes
    a. only the details that show her own efforts to improve her life.
    b. only details that show the strong side of Mrs. Smith.
    c. only details that show Mrs. Smith as unsympathetic.
    d. details that show both her own and Mrs. Smith's weaknesses.

18. The sentence below contains a
    a. glittering generality.
    b. stereotype.
    c. half-truth.
    d. testimonial.

    I longed for a couch and a bearded Freudian with a German accent. (Paragraph 14)

Evaluating Arguments

19. In the passage below, the third sentence includes
    a. the assumption that registering at college is much like taking over IBM (a false comparison).
    b. the assumption that the order of events in her life alone show cause and effect (false cause).
    c. irrelevant personal criticism of Mrs. Smith (personal attack).
    d. a generalization about IBM based on too little evidence (hasty generalization).

    "You could consider registering at the community college," [Mrs. Smith] suggested.
    Sure I could, lady, I thought. I could also consider taking over IBM. (Paragraphs 21–22)

20. Which of the following statements provides evidence that Plutzer at least partly understands how Mrs. Smith helped her?
    a. "I suspected that she just didn't listen to music any more."
    b. "I think Victoria and I both knew I was going."
    c. "She'd persistently believed in me, and that belief had been my anchor."
    d. "We held each other tightly, until the train pulled in."

THINKING ACTIVITIES

Outlining

Following is an incomplete outline of the article. Complete it by filling in the letters of the missing details. The details appear in random order below the outline.

Central Point: With personal motivation and insightful, caring help, Christina Plutzer strengthened her self-image and her life.

1. _____

2. _____

3. _____

4. _____

5. _____

6. Plutzer and Smith part sadly.

Items Missing from the Outline

a. Plutzer seeks professional help and gets Mrs. Smith as a counselor.
b. Plutzer becomes strong enough to attempt being on her own and takes advantage of opportunities to rebuild her life.
c. Mrs. Smith's approach begins to work.
d. Plutzer doubts Mrs. Smith's concern and approach.
e. Plutzer and Mrs. Smith become friends, and they help each other.

Summarizing

Complete the following summary by filling in the missing idea.

At 38, Christina Plutzer felt the need for help to build a rewarding life. So she found a counselor, Mrs. Victoria Smith, who at first seemed too practical and unsympathetic to Plutzer. But Smith's approach of encouraging Plutzer to find an interest and go to school gave Plutzer's life a positive direction. Smith's true interest in Plutzer was revealed as she did the little things that were necessary to insure Plutzer's plans would succeed. They continued to have meetings when possible, and their relationship developed into a deep friendship in which Plutzer was also able to help Smith. After about three years, _____

_____

She decided to take those opportunities and found she had the strength to follow through on her decision efficiently and competently. Smith wished Plutzer did not have to leave her but did whatever she could to help. When they parted it was with great regret but pleasure in their progress and friendship.

DISCUSSION QUESTIONS

1. Just as patterns are used to organize paragraphs, they are used to organize larger pieces. What is the basic pattern of organization of this selection: *time order, list of items, comparison/contrast, cause and effect, or definition and example*? Why did Plutzer choose this pattern?

2. Plutzer writes that Dr. Smith's belief in her had been her "anchor." What do you think she means by that? How did that belief help Plutzer achieve her goals?

3. How does Plutzer's growing personal strength show up in her relationship with Victoria Smith? Use specific parts of the selection to back up your points.

4. Throughout her narration, Plutzer uses surprise and exaggeration. For example, at the clinic, Plutzer calls herself "a homicidal, suicidal passive-aggressive psychotic." Find some other places in which Plutzer uses surprise or exaggeration. Why do you think she includes this style of writing?

Check Your Performance   GETTING MY ACT TOGETHER

Skill	Number Right	Points	Total
Vocabulary in Context (2 items)	_____	× 4 :	_____
Central Point and Main Ideas (2)	_____	× 4 :	_____
Key Details (2)	_____	× 4 :	_____
Transitions (2)	_____	× 4 :	_____
Patterns of Organization (2)	_____	× 4 :	_____
Fact and Opinion (2)	_____	× 4 :	_____
Inferences (2)	_____	× 4 :	_____
Purpose and Tone (2)	_____	× 4 :	_____
Bias and Propaganda (2)	_____	× 4 :	_____
Evaluating Arguments (2)	_____	× 4 :	_____

(total of 20 questions)

Outlining (5)	_____	× 2 :	_____
Summarizing (1)	_____	× 10 :	_____

FINAL SCORE (OF POSSIBLE 100)   _____

Enter your final score into the reading performance chart on page 454.

17

Why People Are Not Assertive
Ronald B. Adler

Preview

Have you ever been angry with yourself for not speaking up for your rights? Do you do things you don't want to just to please others? If so, you have difficulty—like many of us—being assertive. In this selection from a communications textbook, the author explains some of the myths that prevent us from being assertive. Once we understand the myths, he suggests, we may be able to please ourselves as well as others.

Words to Watch

complements (1): balances
stifle (1): hold back
assertiveness (1): the quality of having self-confidence and determination in stating one's opinions
gregarious (2): sociable
veneer (3): appearance
succumb (4): give in
speculate on (5): form a theory about
subscribing (6): agreeing
adherence to (7): believing in
ludicrous (7): ridiculous
acknowledging (19): admitting
naïve (21): unsophisticated
blithely (21): cheerfully

Almost from the time they learn to speak, children are taught to accept the belief system of their society. Many of the beliefs that compose this system are useful ones: for example, the idea that physical violence is not an acceptable way of resolving conflicts or the principle that a healthy body complements a healthy mind. On the other hand, there are a number of irrational beliefs—called "myths" here—that actually inhibit effective social functioning. We shall discuss five myths that stifle assertiveness.

The Myth of Perfection

People who accept this myth believe that a worthwhile communicator should be able to handle any situation with complete confidence and skill. While such a standard of perfection might serve as a target and source of inspiration (rather like making a hole in one for a golfer), it's totally unrealistic to expect that one can reach or maintain such a level of behavior; people simply aren't perfect. Perhaps the myth of the perfect communicator comes from believing too strongly in novels, television, or films. In these places we are treated to descriptions of such characters as the perfect mate or child, the totally controlled and gregarious host, and the incredibly competent professional. While these images are certainly appealing, it's inevitable that we will come up short when compared to them.

Once you accept the belief that it's desirable and possible to be a perfect communicator, the thought follows that people won't appreciate you if you are imperfect. Admitting one's mistakes, saying "I don't know," or sharing feelings of uncertainty or discomfort become social defects when viewed in this manner. Given the desire to be valued and appreciated, it is a temptation to try at least to *appear* perfect. Thus, many people assemble a variety of social masks, hoping that if they can fool others into thinking that they are perfect, perhaps they'll find acceptance. The costs of such deception are high. If others ever detect that this veneer of confidence is a false one, then the actor is seen as a phony, and regarded accordingly. Even if the unassertive actor's role of confidence does go undetected, such a performance uses up a great deal of psychological energy and thus makes the rewards of approval less enjoyable.

The alternative way of behaving for persons who succumb to the myth of perfection and fail to measure up to the impossible standard they have set for themselves is to withdraw from interaction with others—in effect, to state that "If I can't communicate well, I won't do it at all." Needless to say, these sad individuals suffer as much as do their insecure, pretending cousins who claim to be perfect.

The irony for these communicators who fruitlessly strive for acceptance through perfection is that their efforts are unnecessary. Research and common sense both suggest that the people we regard most favorably are those who are competent but not perfect. It is easy to speculate on why this is so. First, many people see the acts of others as the desperate struggle that they are. In these cases it's obviously easier to like someone who is not trying to deceive you than one who is. Second, most of us become uncomfortable around someone we regard as perfect. Knowing we don't measure up to these standards, the temptation may be to admire this superhuman, but from a distance.

Not only can <u>subscribing</u> to the myth of perfection keep others from liking 6
you, it also acts as a force to diminish your own self-esteem. How can you like
yourself when you don't measure up to the way you ought to be? How liberated
you become when you can comfortably accept the idea that you are not perfect,
that:

> like everyone else, you sometimes have a hard time expressing yourself;

> like everyone else, you make mistakes from time to time, and there is no reason
> to hide this;

> you are honestly doing the best you can to realize your potential, to become
> the best person you can be.

The Myth of Acceptance.

The myth of acceptance states that the way to judge the worth of one's actions 7
is by the approval they bring. Communicators who subscribe to this belief go to
incredible lengths to seek acceptance from people who are significant to them, even
when they must sacrifice their own principles and happiness to do so. <u>adherence</u> to
this irrational myth can lead to some <u>ludicrous</u> situations:

> remaining silent in a theater when others are disturbing the show for fear of
> "creating a scene";

> buying unwanted articles so that the salespeople won't think you have wasted
> their time or think you are cheap;

> ridiculing individuals or ideas merely to gain stature as "one of the group";

> greatly inconveniencing yourself by running errands, lending money, and the
> like, not because you genuinely want to, but so that others will think you are
> nice.

In addition to the obvious dissatisfaction that comes from denying your own 8
principles and needs, the myth of acceptance is irrational because it implies that
others will respect and like you more if you go out of your way to please them.
Often this simply isn't true. How is it possible to respect people who have compro-
mised important values only to gain acceptance? How is it possible to think highly
of people who repeatedly deny their own needs as a means of buying approval?
While others may find it tempting to use these individuals to suit their ends or
amusing to be around them, genuine affection and respect are hardly due such characters.

In addition, striving for universal acceptance is irrational because it is simply 9
not possible. Sooner or later a conflict of expectations is bound to occur: one person
will approve if you behave only in a certain way, while another will only accept the
opposite course of action. What are you to do then?

Don't misunderstand: eschewing the myth of approval does not mean living a 10
life of selfishness. It's still important to consider the needs of others and to meet
them whenever possible. It's also pleasant—one might even say necessary—to strive

for the respect of those people we value. The point here is that when you must abandon your own needs and principles in order to seek these goals, the price is too high.

The Myth of Causation

People who live their lives in accordance with this myth believe that it is their 11 duty to do nothing that might possibly hurt or in any way inconvenience others. This attitude leads to behaviors such as:

visiting one's friends or family out of a sense of obligation rather than a genuine desire to see them;

keeping to yourself an objection to another person's behavior that is in some way troublesome to you;

pretending to be attentive to a speaker when you are already late for another engagement or are feeling ill;

praising and reassuring others who ask for your opinion, even when your honest response is a negative one.

A reluctance to speak out in situations like these is often based on the assump- 12 tion that you are the cause of others' feelings: that you hurt, confuse, or anger them. Actually, such a position is not correct. You don't *cause* feelings in others; rather, they *respond* to your behavior with feelings of their own. To recognize the truth of this statement, consider how strange it sounds to suggest that we make others fall in love with us. Such a statement simply doesn't make sense. It would be more correct to say that we act in one way or another, and that some people might fall in love with us as a result of these actions, while others wouldn't. In the same way, it's incorrect to say that we *make* others angry, upset, sad—or happy, for that matter. Behavior that upsets or pleases one person might not bring any reaction from another. It's more accurate to state that others' responses are as much or more a function of their own psychological makeup as they are determined by our own behavior.

Restricting your communication because of the myth of causation can result 13 in three types of damaging consequences. First, as a result of your caution you often will fail to have your own needs met; there's little likelihood that others will change their behavior unless they know that it's affecting you in a negative way.

A second consequence of keeping silent is that you are likely to begin resenting 14 the person whose behavior you find bothersome. Obviously this reaction is illogical, since you never have made your feelings known, but logic doesn't change the fact that keeping your problem buried usually leads to a buildup of hostility.

Even when your withholding of feelings is based on the best of intentions, it 15 often damages relationships in a third way; for once others find out about your deceptive nature, they will find it difficult ever to know when you really are upset with them. Even your most fervent assurances that everything is fine become suspect, since the thought is always present that you may be covering up for resentments you are unwilling to express. Thus, in many respects, taking responsibility for others' feelings is not only irrational—it is also counterproductive.

The Myth of Helplessness

This irrational idea suggests that satisfaction in life is determined by forces 16 beyond your control. People who continuously see themselves as victims make statements such as:

"There's no way a woman can get ahead in this society. It's a man's world, and the best thing I can do is to accept it."

"I was born with a shy personality. I'd like to be more outgoing, but there's nothing I can do about that."

"I can't tell my boss that she is putting too many demands on me. If I did, I might lose my job."

The error in statements like these becomes apparent when you recall the point 17 made in the introduction of this book: there are very few things you can't do if you really want to. Most "can't" statements can more correctly be rephrased in one of two ways.

The first of these ways is to say that you *won't* act in a certain way, that you 18 *choose not* to do so. For instance, you may choose not to stand up for your rights or not to say no to unwanted requests, but it is probably inaccurate to claim that some outside force keeps you from doing so. The second phrase that can often more accurately replace "can't" is the assertion that you *don't know how* to do something. Examples of this sort of situation include not knowing how to state a complaint in a way that reduces defensiveness or being unaware of how best to carry on a conversation. Like these two problems, many difficulties that you might claim can't be solved do have solutions; the task is to find out what those solutions are and to work diligently and learn how to apply them.

When viewed in this light, it's apparent that many "can'ts" are really rational- 19 izations to justify one's not wanting to change. Once you've persuaded yourself that there's no hope for you, it's easy to give up trying. On the other hand, acknowledging that there is a way to change—even though it may be difficult—puts the responsibility for your predicament on your shoulders. Knowing that you can move closer to your goals makes it difficult to complain about your present situation. You *can* become a better communicator—this book is one step in your movement toward that goal. Don't give up or sell yourself short!

The Myth of Catastrophic Failure

Communicators who subscribe to this irrational belief operate on the assump- 20 tion that if something bad can possibly happen, it will happen. Typical catastrophic fantasies include:

"If I invite them to the party, they probably won't want to come."

"If I speak up in order to try and resolve a conflict, things will probably get worse."

"If I apply for the job I want, I probably won't be hired."

"If I tell them how I really feel, they'll probably think I'm a fool."

While it's undoubtedly <u>naïve</u> to <u>blithely</u> assume that all of your interactions 21 with others will meet with success, it's equally damaging to assume you will fail. The first consequence of such an attitude is that you'll be less likely even to attempt to express yourself at important times. This is a clear illustration of the avoidance behavior described in the previous section: by behaving in a manner that reduces the possibility of anticipated punishment, you never discover whether your expectations of catastrophe are, in fact, realistic. To see the folly of such an attitude, simply carry the concept of avoidance behavior to its logical extreme. Imagine people who fear *everything;* how would they live their lives? They couldn't step outside in the morning to see what kind of day it is for fear they would be struck by lightning or a falling airplane. They couldn't drive in a car for fear of a collision. They couldn't engage in any exercise for fear the strain might cause a heart attack. If this example seems ridiculous, consider whether you have ever withdrawn from communicating because you were afraid of consequences that weren't likely to occur. A certain amount of prudence is wise, but carrying caution too far can lead to a life of lost opportunities.

Even when one acts in spite of catastrophic fantasies, problems occur. In many 22 cases the fact that you expect to fail can make that failure more likely. The principle behind this fact has been termed the "self-fulfilling prophecy," and it will be discussed in detail in a few pages. For now, realize that you may be sabatoging your own chances of success simply by expecting that you won't succeed.

One way to escape from the myth of catastrophic failure is to reassess the 23 consequences that would follow even if you don't succeed in your efforts to communicate successfully. Keeping in mind the folly of trying to be perfect and of living only for the approval of others, realize that failing in a given instance usually isn't as bad as it might seem. What if people do laugh at you? Suppose you don't get the job? What if others do get angry at your remarks? Are these matters really *that* serious?

SKILL-DEVELOPMENT QUESTIONS

Vocabulary in Context

1. The word *resolving* in "physical violence is not an acceptable way of resolving conflicts" (paragraph 1) means
   a. strengthening.
   b. avoiding.
   c. solving.
   d. starting.

2. The word *eschewing* in "eschewing the myth of approval does not mean living a life of selfishness" (paragraph 10) means
   a. accepting.
   b. explaining.
   c. avoiding.
   d. analyzing.

Central Point and Main Ideas

3. Which sentence best expresses the central point of the selection?
   a. Trying to achieve perfection is useless.
   b. It is possible for everyone to move closer to his or her goals.
   c. Some irrational beliefs prevent people from being effective, confident communicators.
   d. Avoidance behavior can lead to fears.

4. Which sentence best expresses the main idea of paragraph 12?
   a. We can be the cause of other people's feelings.
   b. It sounds strange to suggest we make others fall in love with us.
   c. Others may fall in love with us as a result of our actions.
   d. We don't cause other people's feelings.

5. The first sentence of paragraph 13 ("Restricting your communication because of the myth of causation can result in three types of damaging consequences") contains the main idea for
   a. paragraphs 12 and 13.
   b. paragraph 13.
   c. paragraphs 13 and 14.
   d. paragraphs 13, 14, and 15.

Key Details

6. Research shows the people we regard most favorably
   a. are competent but not perfect.
   b. can handle any situation with complete confidence and skill.
   c. try to appear perfect.
   d. always wants others' approval.

_____ 7. TRUE OR FALSE? One way to escape the myth of catastrophic failure is to imagine what will happen if you do fail.

Transitions

8. The relationship of the second sentence below to the first is one of
   a. emphasis.
   b. addition.
   c. contrast.
   d. comparison.

   It is easy to speculate on why [we regard most favorably those who are competent but not perfect]. First, many people see the acts of others as the desperate struggle that they are. (Paragraph 5)

9. The relationship between the two parts of the sentence below is one of
    a. illustration.
    b. addition.
    c. comparison.
    d. contrast.

    A certain amount of prudence is wise, but carrying caution too far can lead to a life of lost opportunities. (Paragraph 21)

Patterns of Organization

10. The pattern of organization of paragraph 7 is
    a. time order.
    b. definition and example.
    c. comparison.
    d. contrast.

11. The pattern of organization of paragraphs 13–15 is a combination of
    a. cause and effect and list of items.
    b. time order and contrast.
    c. cause and effect and time order.
    d. definition and example and comparison.

Fact and Opinion

12. The sentences below
    a. are totally factual.
    b. are all opinion.
    c. contain both fact and opinion.

    Research and common sense both suggest that the people we regard most favorably are those who are competent but not perfect. It is easy to speculate on why this is so. First, many people see the acts of others as the desperate struggle that they are.

13. The following and other statements set off in quotation marks in paragraphs 16 and 20 are all
    a. facts.
    b. opinions.
    c. both fact and opinion.

    "There's no way a woman can get ahead in this society. It's a man's world, and the best thing I can do is to accept it." (Paragraph 16) "If I apply for the job I want, I probably won't be hired." (Paragraph 20)

Inferences

_____ 14. TRUE OR FALSE? The author implies that it would be useful to teach children *not* to accept the entire belief system of society.

15. The author implies that
    a. all your interactions with others can meet with success.
    b. everyone fails at times.
    c. taking responsibility for others' feelings is productive.
    d. perfect communicators on TV or in films are good examples of what's possible.

Purpose and Tone

_____ 16. TRUE OR FALSE? The author's purpose is to inform communication students about five myths that interfere with assertiveness *and* to persuade students that accepting those myths is foolish.

17. The author's tone is
    a. playful.
    b. serious.
    c. depressed.
    d. angry.

Bias and Propaganda

18. Which of the following (based on paragraph 7) has the least emotionally loaded language?
    a. Believing in this irrational myth can lead to some ridiculous situations.
    b. Believing in this irrational myth can lead to some uncomfortable situations.
    c. Believing in this irrational point of view can lead to some uncomfortable situations.
    d. Believing in this point of view can lead to some uncomfortable situations.

Evaluating Arguments

19. Which of the following is a valid conclusion that can be drawn from paragraph 18?
    a. There is really much one cannot do in life.
    b. People following the myth of helplessness avoid taking responsibility.

    c.   All difficulties can be solved.

    d.   There is no "cure" for helplessness.

20.   The author supports his points throughout with

    a.   research.

    b.   case histories.

    c.   personal experiences.

    d.   explanations and examples.

THINKING ACTIVITIES

Outlining

Complete the following very general outline of "Why People Are Not Assertive."

Central Point: Five of the irrational "myths" of our society's belief system interfere with assertiveness.

1. _____

2. _____

3. _____

4. _____

5. _____

Summarizing

Complete the following summary on the myth of causation.

The myth of causation says that _____

_____

But this belief is based on the false notion that we can cause others' feelings. Also, keeping one's own feelings in because of this myth can result in three

harmful results. First, _____

A second harmful result is that a believer begins to_____

_____. Third, _____.

DISCUSSION QUESTIONS

1.   The author mainly uses explanations and very general examples to make his points. How persuasive is his evidence and why? Do you think it could have been made more persuasive? How?

2. Adler writes: "Perhaps the myth of the perfect communicator comes from believing too strongly in novels, television, or film." Give some examples of characters that show how those media might reinforce the myth of perfection.

3. One way to break away from the myth of catastropic failure, writes Adler, is to realize "that failing in a given instance usually isn't as bad as it might seem." What failure have you experienced that wasn't as bad as you thought it might be? Did you learn anything from the experience that helped you to succeed later?

4. Probably we all at one time or another have given in to one of the five myths Adler writes about. Which one are you most likely to give in to? Which do you see practiced around you? Give some examples from your experience.

Check Your Performance WHY PEOPLE ARE NOT ASSERTIVE

Skill	Number Right	Points	Total
Vocabulary in Context (2 items)	_____	× 4 :	_____
Central Point and Main Ideas (3)	_____	× 4 :	_____
Key Details (2)	_____	× 4 :	_____
Transitions (2)	_____	× 4 :	_____
Patterns of Organization (2)	_____	× 4 :	_____
Fact and Opinion (2)	_____	× 4 :	_____
Inferences (2)	_____	× 4 :	_____
Purpose and Tone (2)	_____	× 4 :	_____
Bias and Propaganda (1)	_____	× 4 :	_____
Evaluating Arguments (2)	_____	× 4 :	_____

(total of 20 questions)

Outlining (5)	_____	× 2 :	_____
Summarizing (4)	_____	× 2.5 :	_____

FINAL SCORE (OF POSSIBLE 100) _____

Enter your final score into the reading performance chart on page 454.

Limited Answer Key

Understanding Vocabulary in Context

Practice 1

1. Example: *only a spoonful*
   Definition: small
   (*Note:* Here and below, related words expressing the same definition can also be considered correct.)

2. Examples: *City Hall, schoolhouse, bank*
   Definition: buildings

3. Examples: *What sign are you?, How do you like this place?*
   Definition: conversation starters

4. Examples: *gardening, long-distance bike riding*
   Definition: hobbies

5. Examples: *two heads, webbed toes*
   Definition: abnormalities

Practice 2

1. a person who habitually postpones doing things)

2. carefully examine)

3. practical)

4. isolating infected patients)

5. mercy-killing)

Practice 3

Synonyms of the definitions given are also correct.

1. Antonym: *rich*
   Definition: poverty

2. Antonym: *long, vague*
   Definition: brief and to the point, concise

3. Antonym: *openly*
   Definition: secretly

4. Antonym: *weak*
   Definition: strong

5. Antonym: *plainly*
   Definition: fancy, or flashy

Practice 4

Synonyms of the definitions given are also correct.

1. main points

2 Recognizing Main Ideas

Practice 1

1. flavor
2. office machines
3. floor covering
4. footwear
5. building
6. painkiller
7. wall covering
8. fruit
9. desserts
10. apple tree

Practice 2

1. exercise
2. holidays
3. emotions, or feelings
4. kitchen appliances, small appliances, or appliances
5. science
6. punctuation marks
7. religions

2. inactive

3. lie

4. secret (Given the context, "spy" could also be an acceptable choice, though a less accurate one.)

5. mystery

8. classes
9. life stages
10. riddles

Practice 3

1. b
2. c
3. d
4. a
5. c

Practice 4

Group 1.	a.	SD
	b.	T
	c.	MI
	d.	SD
Group 2.	a.	T
	b.	SD
	c.	MI
	d.	SD
Group 3.	a.	SD
	b.	SD
	c.	T
	d.	MI

Group 4.   a.   SD
            b.   T
            c.   SD
            d.   MI

Group 5.   a.   SD
            b.   SD
            c.   MI
            d.   T

Practice 5

A.   1

B.   4

C.   2

D.   1, 5

Practice 6

1.   b

2.   a

3.   c

3   Identifying Key Supporting Details

Practice 1

List 1:
(The order of points a. and b. can vary.)

1. Bad location

2. Poor advertising
   a. Relied on word of mouth
   b. No display ad in Yellow Pages

3. a. Unexpected rise in wholesale prices
   b. High salaries for workers

List 2:
(The order of the major and minor details can vary.)

1. The Wolfers
   a. Order large, deluxe, supreme pizzas
   b. Fold and swallow slices whole

2. The Sparrows
   a. Order slivers of pizza
   b. Nibble at the edges

3. The Clean-Up Crew
   a. Eat leftover crusts
   b. Eyeball other people's pizza after theirs is gone

List 3:
(The order of points a. and b. can vary.)

1. Love addicts
   a. Cannot function without a boyfriend or girlfriend
   b. Are unable to break off a damaging personal relationship

2. Television addicts
   a. Always turn television on when home
   b. Arrange their schedules around favorite shows

3. Sports addicts
   a. Spend weekends during football season in front of the television or at games
   b. Make their summers revolve around baseball

Practice 2

1. a, c, d

2. a, c, e

3. a, c, d

Practice 3

1. a. Hepatitis A, or infectious hep-
        atitis—source: fecal contami-
        nation
    b. Hepatitis B, or serum hepati-
        tis—source: blood transfu-
        sions, contaminated needles

2. a. Parents' need: to satisfy their
        unfulfilled dreams

    b. Children's need: to feel their
        parents are unquestionably de-
        pendable

3. a. Pigs are not as dirty as they are
        made out to be.
    b. Pigs are smarter than most
        people think.

4 Understanding Relationships I: Transitions

Answers to some of these exercises will vary.

Practice 1

1. also

2. First of all

3. In addition

4. another

5. Finally

Practice 2

1. After

2. before

3. While

4. often

5. Next

Practice 3

1. in contrast

2. Although

3. but

4. in spite of

5. nevertheless

Practice 4

1. Similarly

2. in like manner

3. in the same way

4. In like manner

5. Just as

Practice 5

1. For example

2. for instance

3. To illustrate

4. as an illustration

5. For example

Practice 6

1. Above

2. under

3. across

4. the top of

5. inside

Practice 7

1. Because

2. therefore

3. Since

4. As a result

5. thus

Practice 8

1. To sum up

2. in conclusion

3. All in all

4. To conclude

5. In short

Practice 9

1. undoubtedly

2. Clearly

3. Of course

4. in fact

5. Truly

5 Understanding Relationships II: Patterns of Organization

Practice 1

A. 1. Lie down with arms at sides and fingers open
   2. Close eyes and put distracting thoughts out of mind
   4. Take deep breath, hold it, let it out slowly, and breathe slowly and easily
   5. Concentrate on pleasant scene

B. 1 . First explosion
   2b. Herculaneum is buried under mud and ash

C. Main idea: There are several steps to remembering your dreams.
   2. Put a pen and notebook near your bed.
   3. Turn off alarm and wake up gradually.
   4. Write down any dream you remember before getting out of bed in the morning.

Practice 2

A. Number of items: 3
   Type of item: advantages for children of owning a pet

B. Number of items: 3
   Type of item: ways to be an active listener

C. Number of items: 3
   Type of item: ways of reacting to children's untruthfulness

Practice 3

A. Comparison: mysteries and science fiction

B. Comparison and contrast: humans and other primates

C. Contrast: federal government's and journalists' roles in society (in relation to their attitudes towards secrecy).

Practice 4

A. 1. Cause: the 5-percent fall in unemployment
      Effect: more people can afford expensive consumer goods
   2. Cause: slipping and falling on ice
      Effect: I twisted my ankle
   3. Cause: Mr. Coleman's compulsive gambling
      Effect: his bankruptcy
   4. Cause: Melba's boss not appreciating her work habits
      Effect: Melba's work became careless

5. Cause: late spring freeze
Effect: poor Florida orange crop

B. 6. Uncontrolled high blood pressure: cause
Stroke: effect
Heart attack: effect

7. Valid objection: cause
Thrown-out evidence: effect
Dismissed case: effect

8. Ammunition was low: cause
Food supplies were low: cause
General surrendered: effect

9. The company needed more space: cause
The boss rented an additional floor: effect
The boss moved the shipping room to the basement: effect

10. The start of the baseball season: cause
People called in sick to work: effect
People played hooky: effect

C. 1. Inability to listen carefully all the time: effect
Message overload: cause
Preoccupation with personal concerns: cause
Surrounding noise: cause

2. Meditation: cause
Decrease or elimination of drug use: effect
Cardiovascular improvements: effect
Stress relief: effect

3. Children's names: cause
Popularity: effect
Self-image: effect
Behavior: effect

Practice 5

A. Definition: 1   Example: 2

B. Definition: 1   Example: 4

C. Definition: 2   Example 1: 4

Example 2: 5

6 Distinguishing Facts from Opinions

Practice 2

1. O
2. F
3. O
4. F
5. O
6. F
7. F
8. O
9. F
10. O

Practice 3

1. O
2. F
3. F + O
4. F + O
5. O
6. F
7. O
8. F
9. F + O
10. O

7 Drawing Inferences

Practice 1

1. c
2. b
3. c
4. c
5. c
6. c
7. a
8. b
9. c
10. d

Practice 2

1. c
2. b
3. b
4. c
5. b

Practice 3

1, 6, 8

8 Understanding Purpose and Tone

Purpose: Practice

1. I
2. P
3. E
4. P
5. E
6. E
7. I
8. E
9. P
10. I

Tone: Practice 2

A.   1.   disbelieving
2.   delighted
3.   hostile
4.   objective
5.   cautious

B.   6.   admiring
7.   objective
8.   critical
9.   sympathetic
10.   ironic

Tone: Practice 3

1. c
2. b
3. d
4. a
5. e

9 Detecting Bias and Propaganda

Practice 1

1. a

2. b

3. a

4. b

5. b

Practice 2

1. a

2. c

3. b

Practice 3

The following should be crossed out:

1. Sharon Hogan is a genius

2. proving that modern democracy is a far stronger force than Communism

3. An excellent day-care program is guaranteed

4. proving that they will never be a successful team

5. which shows that students today are more cynical and apathetic than they were in the past

Practice 4

1. Group being stereotyped: motor-cycle gang members
   Assumption: they are badly be-haved

2. Group being stereotyped: redheads
   Assumption: they have hot tempers

3. Group being stereotyped: girls
   Assumption: they are too delicate for "rough" sports

4. Group being stereotyped: doctors
   Assumption: they spend too much time playing golf

5. Group being stereotyped: welfare recipients
   Assumption: they prefer not to work

Practice 5

1. c

2. c

3. b

Practice 6

1. a

2. c

3. a

Practice 7

1. d

2. a

3. c

4. a

5. c

6. c

7. d

8. b

9. a

10. c

10 Evaluating Arguments

Practice 1

1. R, C
2. R, C
3. R, C
4. C, R
5. C, R, R
6. R, C, R
7. R, R, R, C
8. R, R, C, R
9. C, R, R, R
10. R, R, C, R

Practice 2

Group 1. d
Group 2. b
Group 3. a

Practice 3

A. 1. d
   2. a
   3. b

B. 1. N
   2. N
   3. S

C. 1. c
   2. c
   3. a

Practice 4

1. d
2. a
3. b
4. b
5. c

Practice 5

1. a
2. b
3. d
4. c
5. a

ANSWERS TO FOUR SELECTED READINGS

An Important Note: To strengthen your reading skills, you must do more than simply find out which of your answers are right and which are wrong. You also need to figure out (with the help of this book, the teacher, or other students) *why* you missed the questions you did. By using each of your wrong answers as a learning opportunity, you will gradually improve your scores as you work through this book. To help you learn, this section includes both answers and information to help you understand the answers. Don't forget to reread the appropriate parts of the selections as you analyze your errors.

Bubba Smith's Decision, Scott Ostler

Skill-Development Questions (pages 298–302)

1. d

2. b

3. b

4. a   The author makes it clear early in this piece (paragraph 3) and in the last sentence that the article centers on why Smith decided to give up his job doing beer ads. Answers *b, c,* and *d* are each too narrow to be the central point—they are included in it.

5. a   Answers *b, c,* and *d* are too narrow.

6. c   See paragraph 19.

7. True   See paragraph 19.

8. b   Answer *b* was not mentioned in the article; answers *a, c,* and *d* all relate to Smith's concern about encouraging people to drink too much, which is why he decided to stop appearing in beer ads.

9. b   The fact that Smith never drank contrasts with the fact that he made beer ads.

10. a   The word "also" introduces an *additional* point Smith makes about the beer commercials.

11. b   Being a narration of a series of events, this paragraph naturally follows a time order; it includes one time-order signal: *then* ("Then the ground came up and hit me in the face").

12. c   It is a fact that Smith "loved doing the commercials" but "didn't like the effect it was having on a lot of little people." His comments about the kids who approached him are also factual, but it is Smith's opinion that such experiences are "scary" and that "you want to tell 'em something that is the truth."

13. b   We can conclude that Smith is happier now for several reasons: 1. He is no longer acting against his conscience, 2. he is in good physical shape (paragraphs 24–25), and 3. he hasn't gone without work (paragraph 24).

14. True   The descriptions of Smith's lifestyles right after retirement from football (Paragraph 19) and after quitting beer commercials (paragraphs 24–26) show that he made a happier and healthier adjustment after his second "retirement."

15. c

16. d   While the author allows Smith to speak for himself through much of the article, Ostler reveals his admiration for Smith's moral behavior when discussing him in paragraph 3 and paragraphs 24–26.

17. b

18. c   What does "Less filling" really mean to a beer drinker? Not much. Although many beer drinkers may prefer a less-fattening beer, probably none have ever wished for a less-filling one. The phrase, then, is a glittering generality—an important-sounding claim that really says very little.

19. d   Answers *a* and *c* are wrong because nothing in the passage supports them. While it's true that L. C. Greenwood is willing to do something that goes against Bubba Smith's principles, we don't know that it goes against Greenwood's own principles—perhaps he is not against drinking; therefore answer *b* is wrong.

20. a   In order for Smith to stand up for what he believed, he had to give up a lot.

Thinking Activities (pages 302–303)

Outlining
A-3.:   e
B-1.:   b
  C: a
C-2.:   d
D-2.:   c

Summarizing
(Any words with the same or very similar meaning to the following answers are also correct.)
effects
ads
encouraging
money
compromising

Guarding Against Crime, Denise Worthington

Skill-Development Questions (pages 336–339)

1. b

2. c

3. b   The central point is stated in paragraph 6. Answers *a, c,* and *d* are too narrow to be the central point—they are included in it.

4.   c   To find this implied main idea, you had to find a statement that would cover all or most of the details of paragraph 5; responses *a, b,* and *d* are each too narrow.

5.   c   Paragraph 8 includes a topic sentence (which, remember, expresses the main idea): ". . . Americans have become much more home security conscious." Response *c* uses different words to say pretty much the same thing.

6.   c   See paragraph 7.

7.   False   In paragraph 8, we learn that "something as simple and *inexpensive* as a tenpenny nail" can make a home more secure.

8.   b   The signal word "clearly" announces a clarification here.

9.   d   The signal words "in conclusion" introduce a summary statement.

10.   a   The details of Goldie Hawn's security efforts could be rearranged in this paragraph without changing the meaning very much. This tells us that the paragraph is a list of items. If it used a time order (*b*), the details could not be logically rearranged. In addition, nothing is being compared or contrasted (*c*) here, and no new term is being defined and illustrated (*d*).

11.   True   This paragraph provides the "good *reason* we're afraid of crime," which means it deals with cause and effect. The details of increased crime, however, are presented in a list of items.

12.   a   Responses *b, c,* and *d* can all be proven by checking the correct records, but answer a gives a judgement that cannot be proven. Even though *a* may be a widely accepted judgement, some people may feel Americans are exaggerating the dangers of crime and should not be fearful.

13.   a   All of the facts in this statement (the number of burglar alarms purchased in 1986 and the costs of those alarms) can be proven either true or false by checking the business records of the burglar-alarm industry.

14.   a   In paragraph 8 we learn that "Americans now place timers on radios and lights." The reason for such an action would be to turn the radios and lights on even when no one was home. We can conclude, therefore, that an occupied house deters burglars. Response *b* is wrong because paragraph 8 says there are ways to safeguard fire escapes. From the fact that Californians have unregistered guns (paragraph 9), we can conclude that *c* is incorrect. And from the statement "we no longer hide a spare key under the doormat" (paragraph 8) we can infer that *d* is also incorrect.

15.   a

16.   a   While paragraph 2 discusses a serious subject, an event that combines instruction about tear gas with a wine party will seem somewhat humorous to many.

17. a The word "fad" refers to something that is popular for a short time. So we can conclude that the author expects something to be popular only briefly. Because your experience tells you that the high rate of crime is unlikely to pass like a fad (*d*), you can assume that the correct response is *a*.

18. d The words in *a*, *b*, and *c* that suggest a personal judgement about the number of handguns are "staggering," "stockpile," and "in one state alone." In *d*, the fact is presented in a straightforward way, with no judgements.

19. c If you missed this one, reread the paragraph.

20. c Growing sales in tear gas to homeowners would show that Americans are increasingly protecting themselves against crime.

Thinking Activities (pages 340–341)

Outlining
Central Point: c
      A-2.: d
        B: e
      B-1.: a
      C-3.: b

Summarizing
1. c
2. a
3. b
4. c
5. b

Nonverbal Communication, Anthony F. Grasha

Skill-Development Questions (pages 377–381)

1. b

2. b

3. c This selection includes a clear statement of the central point—it is even italicized for emphasis (see paragraph 1). Answer *a* is wrong according to the article. Answer *b* is too broad—it could include writing letters, making phone calls, etc. Answer *d* is too narrow to be the central point.

4. d The paragraph does not include answer *a;* answers *b* and *c* are too narrow to be the main idea.

5. a The first sentence tells us "that body language serves several functions." Then the paragraph goes on to name and discuss the three functions, highlighted by italics.

6. True   This point is part of the central point (stated in paragraph 1) and is explained further in paragraph 8.

7. a   See paragraph 8.

8. d   The first part of the sentence gives one function of nonverbal behaviors; the second part of the sentence (beginning with the word *and*) *adds* another function of nonverbal behaviors.

9. d   "Unlike" implies that things are somehow different; in other words, they contrast in some ways. In this case, "verbal utterances" are being contrasted with "body gestures or [facial] expressions."

10. c   Paragraphs 3–6 all begin with an italicized term which is then defined and illustrated.

11. b   The first sentence of this paragraph (the topic sentence) suggests that the paragraph is a list of "several functions" of body language. As we read on, we see a list does follow. In fact, as noted for question 5, the author has emphasized that list by italicizing the major supporting details of the paragraph.

12. b   The details of this sentence are facts that emerged from Rosenthal's experiment; they are used to support the first detail of the paragraph, which is that body language communicates "certain emotions, attitudes, and preferences."

13. True   Personal experience tells us that when people react to personal space in the ways Hall suggests, they are usually unaware of the issue of personal space.

14. b   If our body language occurs "automatically without much thought on our part," it is reasonable to conclude that we sometimes move in ways that reveal our true feelings even when we don't want to. An example of this could occur when a child says she has not gone into the cookie jar but her expression or posture says otherwise.

15. b

16. b

17. c   An editorial (*a*), meant to express an opinion, would not be objective, as this is. While an encyclopedia article (*b*) would also be written in a straightforward, objective manner with the intention to inform, it would not include all the teaching devices (italicizing, numbering, boldface headings) that this article includes. Because this selection does not intend to persuade or instruct people in how to behave and provides a broad, academic overview, it would not be appropriate for use in a personnel manual (*d*).

18. c This statement mistakenly equates the idea of being repelled by strangers entering one's personal space (a common experience, according to Hall) with "fears" that require professional attention.

19. d According to the statements from paragraph 5, "everyday topics" are acceptable topics at formal dinners; we can thus conclude that a guest's recent divorce would be much too intimate of a topic for such an event.

20. d Among the *examples* given are those used to illustrate the four personal zones (paragraphs 3–6). Rosenthal's experiment with films (paragraph 8) was a *research* study on recognizing expressions; also, Hall's personal zones suggest that he probably did research on that topic. Among the possible *opinions* in this selection is Goffman's observation that "our body language is generally difficult to manipulate at will." In addition, the four categories of personal zones represent Hall's *opinions* on how to categorize personal space.

Thinking Activities (pages 381–382)

Outlining
   2:   Nonverbal Messages: The Use of Personal Space
   2-c.:   Social distance
   2-d.:   Public distance
   3-b.-1):   Helps communicate certain emotions, attitudes, and preferences
   3-b.-2):   Supports our verbal communications

Summarizing
communicate, or a similar word, such as *tell*
near, or a similar word, such as *close*
personal
public
language

Getting My Act Together, Christina Plutzer

Skill-Development Questions (pages 418–421)

1. a

2. d

3. c This central point is implied by the selection. Responses *a* and *d* are true according to the selection, but they are too narrow to cover the whole narrative and thus to be its central point; response *b* is a hasty generalization based on one person's (Plutzer's) experience.

4. c Any statement of the main idea of this paragraph must include the idea that she made an appointment at the clinic, for that is the link to the rest of the narrative.

5. True   See paragraph 1

6. c   See paragraph 44

7. b   The *cause* here is: "she had not had time to read my intake biography"; the *effect* is: "our first sessions would cover some personal history." The signal word used here is "therefore."

8. b   The fact that Mrs. Smith's passion centered on her work contrasts with the fact that she had personal friends (because we would expect Mrs. Smith to feel at least as much passion for friends as for work).

9. c   These details could be presented in a different order and still make sense. Being a description of Mrs. Smith, this paragraph shows little cause and effect (*a*), no definition and example (*b*), and is not based on time order (*d*), which requires a specific order.

10. b   In this paragraph, the author gives a very broad account of her personal history in the order in which it happened; she uses the signal word "then" twice here.

11. True   That the school required the author to take English and that she elected to take psychology courses are not opinions, but events that either happened or did not happen.

12. c   Everyone would easily agree that it is a fact that Plutzer spent weekends, when her children were gone, helping Mrs. Smith do her gardening and cleaning. It's also a fact that Mrs. Smith otherwise did that work herself; but that she did that work "grimly and compulsively" is Plutzer's opinion—others might characterize the way Mrs. Smith did the work as, for example, quiet and efficient.

13. b

14. d

15. a

16. b   Compare, for example, paragraphs 14 and 28 to paragraph 43.

17. d

18. b   Plutzer characterizes psychoanalysts as having beards and being German (both like Sigmund Freud, the famous and stereotypical psychoanalyst).

19. a

20. c   Plutzer realized that Mrs. Smith's belief in her was crucial to her ability to find "worth and confidence" (paragraph 16).

Thinking Activities (pages 422–423)

Outlining
1. a
2. d
3. c
4. b
5. e

Summarizing
Plutzer learned that an apartment in her old neighborhood and a job working with children in New York were both available.

PRONUNCIATION GUIDE FOR THE WORDS ON PAGES 157-175

Next to each vowel sound is a common word that contains the sound.

ā	play	ī	high	o͞o	fool
ă	pat	ĭ	pit	o͝o	book
ä	calm	ō	go	ŭ	cut
ē	be	ŏ	pot	ûr	fur
ĕ	ten	ô	raw	uh	about

READING PERFORMANCE CHART

Mastery Tests

	Context Clues	Main Idea	Key Details	Transitions	Patterns
1	_____	_____	_____	_____	_____
2	_____	_____	_____	_____	_____
3	_____	_____	_____	_____	_____
4	_____	_____	_____	_____	_____
5	_____	_____	_____	_____	_____

	Inferences	Fact/ Opinion	Purpose/ Tone	Bias/ Propaganda	Reasoning
1	_____	_____	_____	_____	_____
2	_____	_____	_____	_____	_____
3	_____	_____	_____	_____	_____
4	_____	_____	_____	_____	_____
5	_____	_____	_____	_____	_____

Reading Selections

1	_____	6	_____	11	_____	16	_____
2	_____	7	_____	12	_____	17	_____
3	_____	8	_____	13	_____	18	_____
4	_____	9	_____	14	_____		
5	_____	10	_____	15	_____		

Acknowledgments

Adler, Ronald B. "Why People Are Not Assertive," from *Talking Straight*. Copyright © 1977 by Holt, Rinehart and Winston. Reprinted by permission of CBS College Publishing.

Barkin, Dorothy. "The Bystander Effect." Copyright © 1986 by Trend Publications. Reprinted by permission.

Chu, Dan. "A Blind Woman's Grim Insight." Copyright © 1987 by *People*. Reprinted by permission.

Ephron, Delia. "Coping with Santa Claus," *Funny Sauce* by Delia Ephron. Copyright © 1982, 1983, 1986 by Delia Ephron. All rights reserved. Reprinted by permission of Viking Penguin, Inc.

Fallows, James. "The No-Fat Nation." Copyright © 1986 by James Fallows. Reprinted by permission of the *Atlantic Monthly* and James Fallows.

Greene, Bob. "Fifteen." Copyright © 1983 by John Deadline Enterprises, Inc. Reprinted by permission of Sterling Lord Literistic, Inc.

Gregory, Dick, with Robert Lipsyte. "Shame," from *Nigger: An Autobiography*. Copyright © 1964 by Dick Gregory Enterprises, Inc. Reprinted by permission of the publisher, E.P. Dutton, a division of NAL Penguin, Inc.

Grasha, Anthony F. "Nonverbal Communication," from *Practical Applications of Psychology,* 2nd ed., pp. 248–250. Copyright © 1983 by Anthony F. Grasha. Reprinted by permission of Scott, Foresman/Little, Brown College Division.

Hamill, Pete. "The Yellow Ribbon." Reprinted by permission.

Karr, Albert R. "Death on the Road." Copyright © 1982 by Dow Jones & Company, Inc. All rights reserved. Reprinted by permission of the *Wall Street Journal*.

Ostler, Scott. "A Little Voice Inside Me Just Kept Chanting, 'Stop, Bubba, Stop.'" Copyright © 1986 by the *Los Angeles Times*. Reprinted by permission.

Perl, Lila. "The Fast-Food Phenomenon," from *Junk Food, Fast Food, Health Food*. Copyright © 1980 by Lila Perl. Reprinted by permission of Clarion Books, a Houghton Mifflin Company.

Plutzer, Christina. "Getting My Act Together." Reprinted by permission.

Slack, Charles W. "If I'm So Smart, How Come I Flunk All the Time?" *Eye,* January, 1969.

Will, George. "On Her Own in the City" from *The Pursuit of Happiness and Other Sobering Thoughts*. Copyright © 1978 by The Washington Post Company. Reprinted by permission of Harper & Row, Publishers, Inc.

Wolkomir, Richard. "Shyness." Copyright © 1982 by The Conde Nast Publications. Reprinted by permission of the author and courtesy of *Glamour*.

Worthington, Denise. "Guarding Against Crime." Reprinted by permission.

Index